This book must be returned by the date specified at the time of issue as the DATE DUE FOR RETURN.
The loan may be extended (personally, by post, telephone or online) for a further period if the book is not required by another reader, by quoting the above number / author / title.

Enquiries: 01709 336774

www.rotherham.gov.uk/libraries

SIR WALTER WINTERBOTTOM

THE FATHER OF MODERN ENGLISH FOOTBALL

For Ann, Janet and Brenda
and in memory of Alan

SIR WALTER WINTERBOTTOM

THE FATHER OF MODERN ENGLISH FOOTBALL

GRAHAM MORSE

FOREWORD BY
SIR TREVOR BROOKING

JOHN BLAKE

Published by John Blake Publishing Ltd,
3 Bramber Court, 2 Bramber Road,
London W14 9PB, England

www.johnblakepublishing.co.uk

www.facebook.com/Johnblakepub facebook
twitter.com/johnblakepub twitter

First published in hardback in 2013

ISBN: 978-1-78219-138-4

British Library Cataloguing-in-Publication Data:

A catalogue record for this book is available from the British Library.

Design by www.envydesign.co.uk

Printed in Great Britain by CPI Group (UK) Ltd

1 3 5 7 9 10 8 6 4 2

Papers used by John Blake Publishing are natural, recyclable products made
from wood grown in sustainable forests. The manufacturing processes
conform to the environmental regulations of the country of origin.

Every attempt has been made to contact the relevant copyright-holders,
but some were unobtainable. We would be grateful if the appropriate
people could contact us.

CONTENTS

FOREWORD

First of all, may I please urge you to read this book about the life of Sir Walter Winterbottom and not stop here as you browse through this introduction. I guarantee you will find it a fascinating insight into how both football and sport in general has consistently struggled to overcome those 'internal politics' which often stifle the decision-making process.

There are some wonderful personal testimonies by numerous eminent individuals, and none more so than the address given by Sir Bobby Robson CBE at Walter's thanksgiving service. In fact, Walter probably had no idea quite how many people were inspired and influenced into following specific career paths by listening to his carefully chosen words of guidance.

He had two hugely important roles during his own career; firstly as Director of Coaching and England Senior Coach at the Football Association. Equally crucial was his next position as chief executive of the Sports Council. Both periods provided a constant flow of challenges and disagreements which would have defeated many, but his skilful persuasion impacted massively for the good of sport as we know it now.

I was part of the next generation that benefited from Walter's achievements, but only met him later on in his life when his gentlemanly manner and affable personality were still very evident. One person who greatly impacted on my own player development was Ron Greenwood, the West Ham manager, as I progressed through their acclaimed youth system. Ron was a wonderfully gifted coach, who unquestionably benefited all these players who came under his tuition. At different stages he would often refer back to his own learning curve and acknowledge Walter as his key mentor, who prompted him to start his coaching qualifications.

My own playing career ended in 1984 and looking back over my career since then it is fascinating to actually see a certain similarity of interest that I unknowingly shared with Walter. In 1985 while starting my broadcasting links to the BBC, I was also approached to become Chairman of the Eastern Region of the Sports Council. I readily agreed and that role later led me towards becoming a member of the National Sports Council structure before being appointed Vice-Chairman and then Chairman. I could definitely appreciate the problems Walter faced: getting decisions made, dealing with politicians, securing funding and the frustration of dealing with government departments. All these issues were still prominent when I left in 2001.

I then joined the Football Association at the start of 2004, and so again many of the frustrations he faced are still prominent today, with decision-making, committees and coaching resources forever debated.

One fact which is drastically different is, of course, the money and resource available in the game itself. Walter would be staggered at the sums now involved but would no doubt query whether all those huge amounts are being spent in the right areas. I believe the opening of our National Football Centre, St. George's Park in Burton, in autumn 2012 would definitely have brought a smile of satisfaction from

Walter. Improving the technical quality of our English coaches and players is an absolute priority from now onwards and hopefully someone in the next generation can look back and trace the success of St. George's Park on the early, innovative thoughts of Sir Walter Winterbottom, which finally can be set in stone.

Sir Trevor Brooking
Director of Football Development
The Football Association

PREFACE

Walter Winterbottom never wanted to write his own biography. I asked him many times, but he always politely refused. After he resigned from his job at the FA as Director of Coaching and England team manager he had many requests from publishers, but always turned them down.

I think that the reasons were two-fold. He had an unswerving loyalty to his employer, the Football Association, and he felt that publishers would only be interested in his story if he was 'digging the dirt'. He most certainly would not have done that, and in 50 years I have never known him speak ill of anyone. The second reason, I believe, is that he was essentially a modest person, despite his exceptional achievements. It was always his belief that credit should go to others. He never claimed any for himself.

I felt that this was a story that should be told, that his place in English sporting history should be documented. He was a pioneer. Not just the first, the youngest, and the longest serving England football team manager, but the person who created the FA national coaching scheme and the first Director of the Sports Council, a ground breaking organization that changed the face of British sport.

He had a profound influence on English football and it is no exaggeration to say that he was, of his generation, the leading technical thinker and exponent of football coaching in the world. Despite his high media profile as the manager of the England team, he believed that his most important work was as Director of Coaching, and tellingly, in his passport he listed his profession as 'FA Director of Coaching'. When he began there was strong resistance to the very idea of coaching from the amateur bastions within the FA, from the older players who believed 'you were born with it', and from club managers and directors. He developed strategies to overcome this resistance and built around him a group of young coaches who became his disciples: men like Ron Greenwood, Bill Nicholson and Jimmy Hill. By the time he left the FA after sixteen years, the national coaching scheme had become firmly established and internationally admired, and the foundations had been laid for the World Cup success that followed in 1966.

He had a much lower public profile in his role as the first Director of the Sports Council. The creation of this new organisation revolutionised sport: providing funding for the development of sports facilities and coaching, and working with sport's governing bodies and government at national and local level to provide facilities such as swimming pools and sports centres throughout the country.

Walter Winterbottom was one of a new meritocracy who had a profound effect on Britain in the second half of the twentieth century. He came from a working class home in Oldham, and paid for his education through scholarships and by playing professional football for Manchester United. In a sporting world still dominated by the Victorian creed of amateurism, he emerged as a new kind of public figure, a man who had seen sport from all sides: as a professional player, a teacher, a coach, a manager and a sports administrator.

As a person he touched the lives of many people. He was always full of praise and encouragement for those he worked with, whether it was players, coaches or chairman of sporting governing bodies. He was welcomed wherever he went by people who always wanted to know his views, especially if it was about a football match. His opinions, whether they were about football, sports administration or international affairs, were always totally his own and uninfluenced by the popular view. He was a man who could '…walk with kings, nor lose the common touch,' a person equally at home talking to players, managers, FA councillors, or leaders in business and government.

Although he had a very high public profile and great success in his life, those that knew him well would say that he was a man who was best known not for what he did, but how he made you feel.

GOTHENBURG, SWEDEN: 1958

Macdonald, the England goalkeeper made his only mistake of the game, throwing out a loose ball that was picked up by the Russian winger, Ilyin. His snap shot hit the post and agonisingly deflected into the goal to give Russia a 1-0 win and a place in the quarter finals. England had twice hit the post with shots that had the Russian goalkeeper beaten. But for the frown of fortune England might have won that match and could even have reasonably expected a place in the sharp sun of the final. Instead, at the end of a gruelling play off for a quarter final place, England were out of the 1958 World Cup and on their way home.

On the flight back many of the players were quiet, alone with their disappointment. Others passed the time with the banter and joking that is the trademark of professional footballers. Walter Winterbottom, the team manager, was left to silently reflect on the hand that fate deals and the barrage of criticism that would be waiting for him when they arrived at Heathrow airport.

Just six months earlier he felt that he had a team that stood on the verge of greatness. His commitment to youth had produced an outstanding team. In two years they had lost only once in 17 games. Then, only three months before they left for Sweden, the Manchester United team was left devastated by the Munich air disaster, in which eight Manchester United players were amongst 20 killed in a plane crash in the German city. Duncan Edwards, Roger Byrne and Tommy Taylor were dead: the spine of the England team was gone. Manchester and the whole nation grieved. There had been no time to rebuild and inexperienced players were brought in. Walter's young England team had fought well, drawing 0-0 with the eventual winners, Brazil, but were then dismissed by Russia in one break of the ball: one solitary goal. The media was less understanding and in no mood for forgiveness.

There had been criticism of the England manager's decision to base the team at the Park Royal, a luxury hotel in Stockholm. There was also criticism of his decision to arrive in Sweden after many other teams. But most of all there had been criticism of the team selection and Walter's insistence on not making changes to the team during the tournament. In the 12 previous years of his managerial reign there had been little personal antagonism shown towards Walter who had kept a low profile as England's first team manager; criticism was generally aimed at the players, the selectors and the FA. In 1958 that changed. Walter had previously been recognized for the impressive job he had done in reforming the structure of the national sides at every level whilst producing a highly successful senior side and was also getting his way with the selection of the team. If he was entitled to praise, the press felt, then he should expect the criticisms for failings.

The headlines which had gripped the country, reaching almost hysterical proportions, had centred on three players: Derek Kevan, Brian Clough and Bobby Charlton. Kevan was an obvious target for the press because he could be clumsy and sometimes fell over the ball; but he also was strong, forceful and drew defenders away from other players. Clough was the centre forward that the public wanted, a prolific goal scorer with second division Middlesbrough, but untried at international level and a player that Walter felt did not fit England's style of play.

But above all, the controversy focused on Bobby Charlton, a young player with outstanding potential. He had survived the Munich crash and quickly recovered to play with the phoenix of Manchester United, a team riding a national wave of emotion which propelled them to The FA Cup Final. He had scored three goals in three matches for England since the Munich tragedy, but Walter felt that Charlton was not ready and told Bobby that he needed to think more deeply about his overall contribution to the team.

A sense of rising tension had developed between Walter and the press corps, and as he flew home there was a mounting barrage of criticism. 'I say sack Winterbottom before we really reach rock bottom,' said one angry fan in the *Daily Herald,* following Walter's return from the ill-fated tournament. As he looked down on the clouds over the North Sea during the flight back, Walter reflected on the truism that newspaper critics have the advantage of writing after games have been played and that their selections are never exposed to the torture of having to play. But he accepted the criticism that went with the job of being the England team manager and his thoughts were focused on what he had learned in Sweden: the teams, the tactics and the skills shown by the best in the world. As he continued to ruminate on what might have been in Sweden he knew that the question that his critics would be asking was, 'Can England ever win the World Cup?'

The English domestic system, with clubs reluctant to release players for international training, conformity to a traditional British style of play and interference of selectors, did not help the building and development of international teams. But Walter believed it could be done. The thought uppermost in his mind was that he must continue to select young players and feed them on a diet of international experience at every level. The old ways of taking players in their twenties, throwing them into the team and asking them to do their best would not do. He was convinced that persistence with youth was the only way forward; he knew England's turn would come.

Air travel in the 1950s was a glamorous affair for the privileged, the rich and the famous and even visiting the newly opened Heathrow airport was an exciting event. When the England team's BEA flight touched down on a bright summer day in mid June there was an air of expectation among the crowd of family, friends and media that had gathered to meet the players. Billy Wright, the captain, spotted Joy Beverly – who he was due to marry on the 28th July – and her sisters Teddie and Babs. They were The Beverly Sisters, Britain's most famous female singers, and Joy and Billy were today's equivalent of 'Posh and Becks'. Standing back from the crowd was Walter's wife Ann with their three children Janet (15), Brenda (12) and Alan (9). Seeing his father, Alan broke away from the group of families, reporters and photographers and rushed up to him with tears in his eyes. 'Daddy, Daddy! Why didn't you pick Bobby Charlton?' he sobbed.

CHAPTER 1

RESISTANCE

1946 – 1949

The Spa Hotel in Buxton was a magnificent symbol of Victorian splendour. Set in five acres on the edge of the Derbyshire peak district it was a grand hotel where the ladies and gentlemen from the North of England came to enjoy the health giving properties of the town's spa water. It was not a place that professional footballers frequented. Billy Wright, winning his first cap for England, was somewhat overawed as he walked though the chandeliered entrance hall to the reception desk. The young lady smiled at him but with no hint of recognition. 'Ah, you're with the England football team,' she said after taking his registration form. 'They are over there in the lounge.' As he looked across, Walter Winterbottom, the new team manager, strolled over and shook his hand. 'It's Billy Wright isn't it? It's good to have you with us. Come over and meet some of the lads.'

'Though neither of us knew it then, that first handshake was the beginning of a long, close and rewarding friendship,' remembered Wright. 'My first impression of Walter was of a man standing well over six feet with a slight stoop, dark and well groomed appearance and the air of a schoolmaster. He spoke engagingly and without a trace, if ever he had one, of a Lancashire accent. His manner was unassuming and I, for one, liked him immediately.'

The date was 21 August, 1946 and the occasion was a get-together before a friendly match against Scotland in Manchester to raise funds for the Bolton Wanderers Disaster Fund. It was the first time that the England team had played under a manager, and the first time there been a meeting or training before an international match. Incredibly, Walter had never managed a football team before, let alone England. He was just 34-years-old, not much older than most of the players; only three years earlier he had been playing for Chelsea alongside players like George Hardwick, who was now the England captain.

Sitting in the lounge, Wright studied this man about whom he knew very little, but who he would get to know very well indeed over the course of his long England career. If Walter was nervous at his first meeting as the manager of football legends such as George Hardwick, Stanley Mathews, Wilf Mannion and Frank Swift, he didn't show it.

He asked the players to call him Walter, not Mr. Winterbottom and not Wally. Walter Hammond, the England cricketer, had been called Wally; Walter Barnes, the Arsenal and Wales full-back had been called Wally, but he felt that this was too familiar. Walter was a more informal greeting than Mr. Winterbottom but carried a mark of respect. The players always called him Walter and no one ever coined a nickname for him. Club managers, directors and FA councillors all called him Walter. Only his wife, Ann, called him Wally.

Later in a private room, Walter briefed the team on their Scottish opposition and encouraged the players to contribute their own ideas on how the team would play. George Hardwick thought 'his rather earnest prep school style of management and training methods were initially treated with deep suspicion by some of the senior players, who were uneasy with the new technical jargon.' But the relaxed atmosphere in the comfortable hotel and quiet grounds helped to ease their concerns about the new manager's coaching methods. Indeed, Frank Swift believed the stay at Buxton was a great success: 'I'm firmly convinced it had much to do with the foundation of the team spirit which gave England such a good run later in the season.'

But in the early years Walter faced resistance from the legendary stars of the golden years. In his biography, *Golden Boy*, Wilf Mannion recalls a pre-match training session at the Slieve Donald Hotel, Belfast, before Walter's next match, his first full international against Northern Ireland. 'It was a bitterly cold day and there we were practicing a flaming throw in, having to do it the way he wanted. Stan [Matthews] was saying "flippin this and flipping that. This is stupid. It's absolutely mad," but we had to do it. It was never even thought of until then. You just played... what a waste of time that practice was. We're still waiting to use it now!'

George Hardwick also recalled some of the difficulties Walter had with established players. 'Walter expected discipline. Once we were training at Southport before going over to play Ireland. Walter had us practicing the wall pass and Raich [Carter] was saying, "I was doing this when I was ten. What's the effing point?"'

Some players helped create the myth that Walter tried to teach ball skills to international players. It was nonsense, based on ignorance and fear of change, but the myth persisted. When Tommy Lawton went to his first training session Walter told the squad they would be meeting in half an hour to discuss tactics. 'We'll discuss what?' Lawton exploded. 'Are you trying to tell me you've got a blackboard and you want us to be there at one o'clock and you're going to tell Swifty how to play [in] goal? You're going to tell Laurie Scott and George Hardwick how to play full back? You're going to tell Neil Franklin how to play centre half, and God forbid, you're going to tell Stanley Mathews how to play outside right? And me, you're going to tell me how to score goals? You've got another thing coming. You've got as much chance of getting this lot down there as I have of flying. Good night.'

But other players like George Hardwick, Frank Swift and Tom Finney were altogether more perceptive, more thoughtful. 'I found that Walter Winterbottom was a very good tactician and a very good coach,' said Finney. 'In the early days, when I went into the England side, we had a great names like Tommy Lawton, Frank Swift in goal, George Hardwick, Wilf Mannion, Raich Carter, Neil Franklin and Billy Wright. I think Walter felt that – and he used to say so in the talks – it was no good him trying to tell us how to play the game. We had been selected for our country, and in his opinion we were good enough to go out and express ourselves on the field of play, and that was what we were allowed to do. He would generally go through the tactical side of opponents rather than talk about how we were going to play.'

Walter's job was made more difficult because of the perception that he had not played football at the top level. The dark curtain of war had come down on England and it had been ten years since Walter had played for Manchester United, and only then for one brief season before injury brought a promising professional career to an end. If it had slipped the mind of the older professionals it was not in Walter's nature to remind them. Lawton referred to him dismissively as 'That PT instructor.' There was also a perceived gap in social class. Walter had been a wing commander in the RAF. They were working class men who had known the cruel economic hardships of the 1920s and 30s. They were hard men who had served in the war. They knew what a wing commander was: you saluted and called him 'sir'. Walter may have come from Oldham and had the same working class background as them but by now he was, as Jimmy Armfield astutely remarked, 'more Stanmore than Oldham.'

Players from the pre-war period, like Lawton, Carter and Mannion, reacted the way they did because Walter was bringing about change. It was not the way managers did things back at their clubs. In a conversation with football writer David Miller, Walter reflected on the role of managers before the war:

The managers didn't manage, they signed the cheques. It was player power. The older players decided the tactics. Goalkeepers rarely came off their line, so Dixie Dean was able to head goals standing only two or three yards out. Full backs pivoted around the centre-half, so that the winger on the opposite side to where the play was had plenty of space in front of him, hence the value of a long cross-field ball by inside forwards. The game was nearly all long balls, and a loosely created midfield: final passes were laid on from the centre circle. Nobody had worked out even simple things, like the fact that the wing half, by moving towards the centre of the field, could pull the opposing inside forward with him and force the opposition to play the ball out to the wing.

The press was initially as skeptical as some of the players. During a training session before the first international against Northern Ireland, Swift and Lawton were seen fighting, wrestling and rolling over the grass. It was a typical wind-up, a joke that helped create a relaxed atmosphere and a break from the serious business of training. But some of the sports writers, who had the new manager under the microscope, were appalled. They were critical of Walter for exposing players to something out of the ordinary before a match. It was something that was simply 'not done in our day.'

To Walter's relief England won his first match as the international manager, beating Northern Ireland 7-2 in Belfast, a game also notable for Tom Finney's first cap and first England goal. The press was full of praise for the team. The more astute reporters recognized that things were changing. John Macadam of the *News Chronicle* wrote, 'When you have finished handing bouquets to this classic England side, reach down to the bottom of the basket and grasp one for Walter Winterbottom, team manager, OC tactics and one of the few intellectuals of the game of association football ... he is primarily a believer in the team principle and the coordination of 11 brilliant individuals into a cohesive machine.'

As well as pre-match training sessions and after-match meetings, Walter introduced an England team uniform: blue blazers bearing the FA badge and grey slacks. Again there were rumblings of discontent among some of the senior squad members who complained that they were being asked to dress up like public schoolboys. Hardwick was not one of them: 'I personally had no problem with the blazers because they identified you as an England footballer and I wanted everybody else to know it.'

Walter believed that international coaching was aimed at blending the skills that were already there. Practice games were a way of finding out how players could work best with each other, to know each other's style – a factor that was taken for granted at club level. For example, if Stanley Matthews wanted the ball rolled slowly to him, rather than played in front of him, a new wing half would practice providing the ball in exactly the way that Matthews wanted it. Later on, when Tom Finney played centre forward with Derek Kevan beside him, Kevan would want to go through at high-speed whenever a pass was made to Finney, expecting the return pass which he would get when he played with Ronnie Allen at West Bromwich Albion. But Finney played differently, he liked to check, hold and drift with the ball and Kevin didn't appreciate this. Walter showed them how to knit together as a team. The results streamed in and the fans rolled-up.

The immediate post war period was a boom time for football. Men came home from seven years of war and families were reunited. Football offered a return to normality. 'There was a great deal of fear which was inevitable in a war,' recalls George Hardwick. 'The people involved in the war, either in the forces, or making bombs or making aircraft, or making tanks, or whatever, had so little entertainment, and of course there was no lighting anywhere. Everything was pitch dark throughout the week, and it was a very dull life for everyone. Being able to get to a football stadium to see top class players was a great attraction. It was something we lived for and we could offer a degree of entertainment.'

But life was still tough in the years immediately following the Second World War. The economy was weak as the country reeled from the cost of two world wars. There were shortages and rationing of most things, leading to queues at the Post Office, local shops and the bank – people obediently accepted queues to get served everywhere. Working men lived close to their job and went to work on a bus, tram or bicycle, taking their lunch in a sandwich box with a thermos flask of tea. Sheds outside the factories were packed with parked bicycles. Most men enjoyed a smoke and Woodbines and Turf were the working man's pleasure. The heyday of cigarette cards – often works of art and many featuring footballers – had been before the war. Now they were rarely found because of the shortage of paper. But Turf cigarettes still ran a famous footballer series, ingeniously printing in one colour on the inside of the slide pack. Boys would run up to men to ask for the empty packets or pick them from the ground to complete a set of 52.

But despite the hardships people were optimistic about the future. The new Labour government was introducing nationalisation and a welfare state, promising a change in the social order and a fair deal for the working class. Britain was being rebuilt from the rubble of the war. New low cost housing, temporary and permanent, private and council, was a priority, offering the hope of a home to those living in old sub-standard accommodation or sharing with relatives (Walter himself was one of those able to move out of his mother-in-law's house to a large low-cost housing estate in the west London suburb of Hayes.

Some football grounds had to be rebuilt because of bomb damage. Manchester City shared their ground with Manchester United; Tottenham shared with Arsenal. It was still a time of hardship but watching football offered an escape from a drab life and the return to a friendly social routine at a cost of only 'one and three' (one shilling and three pence-roughly equivalent to 7.5p) for a place on the terraces.

Despite 1947 being one of the coldest winters on record, crowds packed grounds throughout the country. Fans dressed more formally than today – there was no money to spare on leisure clothes – usually wearing a jacket and tie, and a long heavy overcoat or raincoat depending on the weather. The ubiquitous flat caps of the pre-war period were less common and a team scarf was usually the only sign of allegiance. Attendances soared to a total of 35 million in season 1946/47, reaching an all-time high of 41 million in 1948/49. Such crowds would never be seen again. They declined to 27 million in 1964/65 and 20 million in 1980, recovering somewhat to 29 million in the 2009/10 season. The post war spectator bonanza extended to amateur football and the Amateur Cup Final attracted twice the pre-war record, leading to it being switched to Wembley for the 1949 final when 95,000 spectators saw Bromley play Romford.

It was not only football that benefitted from the post war euphoria – a chance at last to get out and enjoy life. Half a million Londoners flocked to the Epsom Downs to see 'Lovely Cottage' win the hundredth Derby. It was an excuse for a 'knees-up,' an unfettered day of fun and a flutter with Cockneys dressed in their pearly queen finery.

Billy Butlin saw the opportunity to offer a ration-weary public a new kind of holiday – a breakthrough from the dismal seaside bed and breakfast that locked you out all day. His first holiday camp opened at Filey in 1946, followed by Skegness and Clacton a year later. 'Butlins' offered a new holiday world, where customers had their own chalet. Evening entertainment, sport and recreation, were all provided at an inclusive low price.

Football also took its own first small steps to explore the post-war brave new world. In 1945 the FA agreed to a UK tour by the Moscow Dynamo – the first Russian club to visit Britain – which created much interest and curiosity. Before they came they demanded agreement to an extensive list of conditions: They must play Arsenal. Their own referee must be in charge for at least one of the games. They would eat all their meals in the Soviet Embassy. They would not number their players. Substitutes must be allowed ... the list was formidable but the Football Association agreed. The arrival of the Russians was cloaked in mystery and suspicion. Reactions to their visit typified Britain's conceited and patronizing attitudes. Journalists who watched the Dynamo players train at the White City reported, 'they are not nearly good enough to play our class of professional teams.' Nevertheless Chelsea bolstered their team with two players from Fulham as well as the recently signed Tommy Lawton, and a curious crowd of 85,000 packed into Stamford Bridge to watch the game.

When the Dynamo players came out the spectators noticed that the player's kit looked different, more stylish: blue shirts with a 'D' on the chest and shorts of a darker blue, considerably longer than most continental teams, with a white stripe around the hem and manufactured in what seemed like a lighter and better quality material than the Chelsea players. The spectators were even more surprised when this set of stylishly kitted, 'very earnest amateurs' held Chelsea to a 3-3 draw.

But the Russians didn't stop there: four days later Dynamo beat Cardiff 10-1. Although the next game against Arsenal – played at White Hart Lane – bordered on the farcical with thick fog and a partisan Russian referee, the Dynamos won 4-3, despite the fact that Arsenal were bolstered by Stanley Matthews, Stan Mortensen and Neil Franklin who were guest players. Bernard Joy, who was playing in the Arsenal team, commented on the way the Dynamos passed to open spaces, and his team mate Cliff Bastin astutely noticed that the Dynamo inside forwards passed the ball to their wing forwards "inside" the fullbacks.

In Glasgow, Dynamo drew 1-1 with Rangers, bringing an end to a relatively successful tour for the Russians. Not that the national press saw it that way: the majority of football writers found that we had nothing to learn from Dynamo, culminating in the *Daily Herald* declaring that even the best pre-1939 teams would have comfortably beaten Dynamo. Considerable ill-will had been engendered by the tour and plans for a return in 1946 were cancelled (indeed, it was not until 1954 that the Arsenal became the first British club to play in the Soviet Union).

Although the war had stunted the development of new players, England won six out of the eight games they played in the 1946/47 season, beating Northern Ireland 7-2, Republic of Ireland 0-1, Wales 3-0, Netherlands 8-2, France 3-0, and Portugal 10-0. They drew 1-1 against Scotland, and lost only one game, 0-1 away to Switzerland.

With such a fine run of results the press had little opportunity to find fault, but they were scathing after the 1-0 defeat by Switzerland and unfettered in their criticism of the new England manager. Hardwick leapt to his defence. 'Walter brought dignity to the game, to the players; he rose above all the horrible things that were said about him in the press. Before the Portugal game, I said to the players, "now we're gonna show these people what we can do; we're going to make them eat every word they've printed. We're going to go out there and crucify this lot." We were four up in ten minutes. We finished up 10-0 and I think we quieted the press and gave Walter back his hours of glory. We would play for Walter. He was a gentleman, one of the nicest men I have ever known.'

The press duly ate their words: 'Ten Goal Blitz Smash the Portuguese' was the jubilant headline in the *Daily Express*. It was one of the finest England performances of Walter's reign.

Ironically the success of Walter's early years in charge may have worked against him, reinforcing the mantra 'you've either got it or you haven't.' Resistance to his coaching ideas came from almost every quarter: from the press, from managers, from some players and even members of the FA Council. There was resistance to the very fact that there was an England team manager!

The old ways of training were deeply engrained. 'Years ago the ball never played a part as far as training was concerned,' recalled Nat Lofthouse. 'It was just lapping around the ground for about half an hour, three quarters. You'd do, I don't know, 30 or 40 laps, then you'd come and do bodywork with heavy medicine balls and weights, then limbering exercises.'

'Trainers discouraged players from having the ball during training' concurred Stanley Mathews. 'They used to say, "Well if you have too much ball you're gonna be tired on the Saturday. Managers had no influence on tactics: it was all left to the players,' confirmed Matthews. 'At Blackpool, Joe Smith used to say to us, "I can't tell you what happens when you go out on the field, it's entirely left with you lot."'

Tommy Lawton was just as scathing about managers. 'Oh team talks? They just said "Well you know what to do don't ya?...You've got the same shirt, you've got the same shorts and you've got the same stockings. Pass the ball to them. That's all you've got to do." That was the team talk. And off we went.'

'International matches were, let's face it, still a bit of a jolly in those days,' said Walter, 'a matter of "let's have a go lads." Hitherto trainers had been people who looked after baggage and saw you went to bed on time. My role was restricted by the fact that I was discouraged, both by the selectors and the managers of individual clubs, from playing people out of their normal position, even though it might have suited our team and in some instances the player himself.'

Football historians have recognized the 1940s and 1950s as an intricate mixture of continuity and change. Stanley Rous made a far sighted move when he convinced the FA Council to employ Walter as their first Director of Coaching. Walter was at the heart of everything – a bridge between the old world of the 1940s and the modern game of the 1960s, but he found that change came slowly. 'The lack of knowledge was abysmal really within the game,' recalls Walter, 'and the idea of coaching was to bring along players with more knowledge of how to keep fit, how to train, how to use tactics, the various skills, the variation of skill. You'd speak to famous players like David Jack, who was a great player with Alex James at Arsenal, and David would say 'The only way to pass the ball is hitting it with the inside of your foot.' And we used to say to him, "What about the outside of your foot?" and he'd say, "Oh no, no, no, that's not on." In other words they locked themselves into the process of playing that they'd been brought up to believe in, and one had to change this. When I said to him, "Look, the continentals are trapping the ball with a knee..." "That's rubbish," he would say. We were so insular that we wouldn't believe that other methods could be used for doing things, other ways of playing the game could be better than ours, and that had to change, of course.'

Walter began by persuading senior players to become qualified coaches. George Hardwick, Wilf Mannion, Neil Franklin, Tommy Walker, Jimmy Hagan, Tommy Jones, Joe Mercer, Ted Drake and even Tommy Lawton, all attended his coaching courses. Walter believed passionately that if the FA Coaching Scheme was to have credibility, the senior professional players must be involved. The second part of his strategy was to introduce coaching for schoolboys who would be more receptive to new ideas. So the professional players and schoolmasters who had qualified as coaches went into schools to coach schoolboys.

Walter understood that the Football Association, like all democratic institutions, relied on precedent and tradition, but it was a frustrating and inescapable fact that the FA was ruled by old men, and old men don't like new ideas. They feared that the old ideas they trusted would be seen as inferior and he had to find ways of overcoming this. He let FA councillors see his coaching ideas in operation and persuaded them to observe courses and take personal responsibility for encouraging the development of coaching in their own county associations. It was a Herculean task that required all his tact and patience, one that took all of his 16 years at the Football Association, before there was a general acceptance of coaching throughout the country.

Perhaps the most frustrating problem that Walter faced was the selection of international teams. It has always been widely acknowledged that throughout his time as manager, the England team was chosen by a selection committee. In fact there were three committees: one for the full international team, one for the amateur team and one for the youth team. It was a cross he had to bear.

Walter was never openly critical of the selection system. As an employee of the FA it would have been impossible for him to do so, but he later recalled:

I didn't have the full responsibility of picking my own teams, and I shall never forget the first meeting of a selection committee. We met in the Victoria Hotel, Sheffield, and we had eight selectors plus a chairman. The way things were done was, "Nominations for goalkeeper?" and we had five goalkeepers nominated and then, through a process of reducing that number, we gradually got it down two, and it was a vote then amongst nine people, and if it was four [votes] and four [votes] the chairman would decide which goalkeeper it was. Remember in those days, selecting a national team was really a means of giving recognition for high skill. It wasn't really looking at building a team to play on and win anything. It wasn't that at all. We were selecting players for that match, a friendly match against a country, and there was a reward in this: "So and so has been a great player, it's time we recognized his great ability and let him be in the next England team." There was a different slant on it. It's only when we got into World Cup football that people began to realize that we had to produce a team that might have a chance of winning the World Cup, and that meant playing the same players together as much as you possibly could.

Stanley Rous was openly critical of the selectors in his autobiography: 'They say of the camel that it looks so weird that it could only have been designed by a committee, and some of our

13

international teams were just as ill balanced as a result of the system.'
He gave an example of how a selection meeting might go:

*A typical exchange might start with Major Keys saying "But you
cannot include Ronnie Clayton. The last time I saw him play, our
own half back looked much more impressive." Then another
would add "Yes. When we played Blackburn he wasn't in the same
class as ours." Walter would point out that they were judging
Clayton on one away game, and in away games there is a
disadvantage for individuals as well as teams. Walter would say:
"The real reason I want Clayton is that he and Brian Douglas
understand each other so well that we are much better off when
those two play together, even if two others may be as good or
better as individuals." But within a few minutes the committee
might have ruled out Clayton and be considering other players of
their own nomination. By the time the process was repeated with
four or five other positions it was a hybrid side that was finally
announced to the press.*

It was ludicrous, of course, but the FA was the pillar of the football
establishment and the councillors were powerful men, many of them
club directors and chairmen. Walter knew that the system could not
be changed but he was determined to improve it.

At subsequent selection meetings he explained the problems with
the current system and made suggestions. His technical knowledge,
analysis, and skill at communicating ideas were such that he was
soon able to persuade the selectors to support him. Most of the
directors only watched their club's home games. Walter pointed out
the effect that the support of the home crowd had on their own
players and reminded them that they often played less well in away
matches, and that all internationals were in effect away games for a
club player. Conversely visiting teams played quite differently and the
centre forward they were observing from the visiting team was far

less likely to shine when he was playing away from home. But old habits die hard.

Walter asked the selectors to go to more games. He told them who to watch. He taught them to watch games more objectively, to be analytical, and to watch matches that didn't include their own team. He showed them how to look for particular qualities in a player and illustrated the importance of balance in a side. He explained that if a selector has a preference for attacking wing halves, his natural inclination was to select an attacking wing half, when in fact a defensive wing half may be required to balance the team.

He cautioned them from making snap judgments. He stressed the need to watch a player in action, watch him again, and then recommend a second opinion. Walter got groups of three selectors to watch players for borderline positions, trying to get consensus and eliminate the maverick selector. What he desperately wanted was continuity and to eliminate a player's fear of being dropped after one bad game. He would have to wait a long time.

Of course the few great club managers – Herbert Chapman at the Arsenal, Matt Busby at Manchester United or Stanley Cullis of Wolverhampton Wanderers – were strong personalities who resisted interference in the selection of their team. At international level coaching giants like Hugo Meisl of Austria, Vittorio Pozzo of Italy and Gustav Sebes of Hungary had total control – Meisl by the power of his personality at a time when international football was expanding in Europe, and Pozzo and Sebes because they lived in a one-party political system. In these regimes success in sport was an important way of building national prestige and a totalitarian management was seen as the only way to deliver this. Walter had to accept that this could not happen within the structure of English football.

Other European countries did not have the same bureaucratic constraints that shackled Walter. The Austrian FA overwhelmingly believed in the principle of giving full responsibility for selection to the man they chose as their team manager. In their view the man chosen should have strong strategic and educational qualities and his authority was recognised without question by the directors of the association.

The Swedish FA did use a committee, but it consisted of only a chairman and two members. The French also had a selection board composed of three members who selected the full international, as well as the 'B', amateur and the youth teams. At the beginning of the season they selected two teams – 'A' and B (which were kept secret). The team was then revised a week before each international match following consultation with the clubs to check on a player's health and condition. Although this was still a committee process it provided continuity.

Spain had tried various methods of selecting the national team. As a result they concluded that the committee decision is always reached by compromise: that the final result is a team selected by all and not really the choice of any. Thus they decided on one selector, the manager of the team, an experienced professional.

It was interesting that these views should be published in the *FA Year Book* and with the rider that they were 'not necessarily those of the Football Association.' It is likely that the article, ostensibly aimed at the wider football world but indirectly at FA councillors, was an attempt to open their minds to the pitfalls of the existing selection process. In that respect it failed. England continued with a ten man selection committee until 1958 and it was to be 16 years before there was acceptance that the team manager alone should be responsible for choosing his team.

In practice the selection of the England team in the early years of 1946-48 was not a major issue: such was dominance of the legends during the 'golden years' that the side, to a large extent, picked itself. Success on the field continued in 1948 with wins against Scotland 2-0, Italy 4-0, Northern Ireland 6-2, Wales 1-0, Switzerland 6-0 and Belgium. 5-2. Only a 0-0 draw against Denmark blemished the record. Indeed Walter remembered the win against Belgium for what he believed was Stanley Mathew's greatest ever performance:

In the second half of the game, we were struggling with the score at 2-2, when within the space of two minutes Stanley had twice dribbled his way down the wing and centred the ball for us to score two more goals. By this time the Belgian players were desperate to stop him at all costs. Suddenly he started to dribble from the halfway line again, beating one player after another until he reached the edge of the penalty area where the Belgian centre half was lurking. He made a desperate low tackling dive to grasp Stanley's shorts but succeeded only in pulling his shorts below his knees. And yet still Stanley continued on. Somehow he reached the goal line, centred, and we scored the final goal. It was an amazing piece of wizardry and as Stanley walked slowly and modestly back to the halfway line the packed stadium crowd, including the VIPs, stood and began a slow hand-clap in time with Stanley's walk and the players of both teams joined in this salute to his genius.

The brilliant 4-0 win against Italy in Turin was considered by many to be the swan song of this highly talented side. There was tremendous interest in the game both in Italy and in England. Italy had been World Cup winners in 1938 and England was still revered in many countries as the best team in the world. The press coverage was intense. By today's standards the media intrusion was mild, but even then Walter found that it could create problems for the players.

'We took the team to a quiet hotel away from Turin to escape the attentions of the press,' he recalled, 'but even so we fell for a newspaper stunt when a group of attractive Italian girls were photographed walking arm in arm in line with the players. The trouble about such photos is that it gives the impression back home that the players are having high jinks when abroad rather than doing serious training in preparation for the match.'

There was a tremendous buildup and expectation. From John Macadam's account in the *Daily Express* we can sense something of the supercharged atmosphere. The match came at the end of a 48-

hour period in which crowds, who had come literally from all over Europe, took part in incessant singing and dancing. Among them were British troops serving with the army in Trieste. An expectant crowd of 80,000 packed into the Stadio Comunale, many taking their place up to six hours before the start. Macadam described the scene in lyrical style: 'They came prepared for summer, suffered another thunderous downpour and then dried out in the brilliant afternoon sunshine, so that the umbrellas they brought for the mornings rain had to serve as protection from the heat, and the effect of the massed colour under the thousands of black umbrellas was as if an army of Renoirs had painted the living scene.'

Sports journalist Brian Glanville painted a slightly more daunting picture: 'When the team arrived in Turin, the temperature was high. The omens were unfavourable. The penalty-areas of the international pitch had been re-laid only the previous day. Walter Winterbottom lost his fountain-pen and when the teams stood in line before the kick-off, there it was on either side of a huge white pedestal on which the match ball rested, as though at some strange pagan ceremony.'

The arrogance of the Italians, who were supremely confident about their superiority, irked the England players. 'To say that they were cocky about beating us is putting it mildly,' Stan Mortensen remembered. Walter used the jibes of the Italians to England's advantage and roused his players to greater efforts despite the oppressive heat at their training camp at Stressa.

Walter often found luck against him but this was a day when everything went right. He counted it as one of England's greatest victories:

The game was billed as the match of the decade with the Italians predicting a resounding win by four goals to nil. In the event we won by that score, which thrilled us and surprised everyone. The British ambassador in Rome wrote to the Football Association saying that the English victory had done more for British prestige and trade in Italy than anything else in the last 20 years. After the game the two teams and their officials gathered in an exclusive restaurant to share a meal and exchange gifts, as was the custom. As we were going up the steps we were handed copies of the Turin sports newspaper, the front page of which revealed a photograph of their manager Vittorio Pozzo surrounded by a thick black margin, and printed over the picture were the words 'Mourir de Pozzo' [Death of Pozzo]. We thought that the poor fellow had died of a heart attack, but it was not so, for there he was at the top of the steps waiting to greet us! According to the paper, after this one defeat, he had been given the sack!'

In one of the big shops in the centre of Turin, on the Monday morning, there was a 10ft by 8ft picture of the England side. 'That was some sight I tell you,' said Billy Wright, 'that was some sight!'

'The greatest England side I played in was probably the one that beat Italy 4-0 in Turin,' said Tom Finney. 'Italy were then the World Cup holders. That was probably the greatest win away from home that England had, against an extremely good Italian side and a very partisan crowd as well.'

However in the 1948/49 season the stars of the 'golden years' began to fade. England lost to Scotland and Sweden, and only drew with Denmark although there were wins against Norway, France, Wales, Northern Ireland and Italy. England turned into a team in transition with frequent changes in the team as the selectors sought replacements. Hardwick and Scott had never properly recovered from leg injuries. Frank Swift, the giant goalkeeper who had been such a talisman had retired. Tommy Lawton, one of England's greatest centre forwards had joined a Third Division club as player-manager. Stanley Mortensen had suffered from injuries which seemed to affect his acceleration, and Mannion, who had been in dispute with his club, had been unable to play for long periods. But perhaps worst of all, Neil Franklin, who had arguably been England's greatest centre half, left England in a cloud of controversy to join the Independiente Club, in Bogota, Colombia. In doing so he was banned from English football. It was the beginning of the end of a golden era in English football: an uncomfortable truth that would be brought home when England went to Brazil in 1950 to take part in their first World Cup.

CHAPTER 2

IN THE
BEGINNING

1863 – 1946

The resistance that Walter faced when he joined the FA in 1946 was rooted in the origins and history of English football. 'In many ways we suffer because we started the whole thing. Its origins were physical and violent,' he explained in Bob Ferrier's book *Soccer Partnership*.

Football was controlled by the Football Association, the Football League, and the English Schools Football Association, organisations that were antediluvian and resistant to change. They had conflicting interests and the amateur versus professional antagonism still prevailed. In 1946 football in England was set in a time warp of the years between the two world wars.

English football was isolated from world football. The British had taught the world to play football but in the 1920s and 30s football in Europe and South America had developed rapidly and with a very different style to the traditional English way of playing. The 'masters' were being left behind. Unlike many European countries, England had no team manager, and the team was selected by a committee.

There was no support for coaching which had been enthusiastically embraced in Europe.

But although the FA could be rightly criticised at that time for being a moribund organisation it had served the game faithfully since its foundation in 1863. It had been formed to provide a common set of laws which would allow the emerging amateur football clubs in the south of England to play each other.

A formal structure and laws had been a long time coming. From the 13th century onwards football was nothing less than a violent maul, with a ball but no laws, played between rival towns and villages, sometimes with hundreds of players on each side, and hundreds more cheering their team. The 'goals' could be several miles apart and a running battle was carried on through the market place, streets and streams. Broken limbs and heads were commonplace, but the game remained popular in a peculiarly British way. Indeed it is kept alive today in the market town of Ashbourne, in Derbyshire where it is played on Shrove Tuesday and Ash Wednesday with no referee and no laws. The teams are known as the 'Up'ards' and 'Down'ards' and the aim is to 'goal' the ball at the opposite end of the town.

But in the mid-19th century the game took an extraordinary turn and was taken over by the rising middle and professional classes, who took a reforming interest in education, fuelling the growth of public schools and modernising their curriculum. A popular philosophy of the time was known as 'muscular christianity' – a belief that the purpose of games is to inculcate moral values. Football fitted this doctrine and prospered in the public schools. The ruling classes applied their aptitude for organisation and so the game evolved. Each public school developed its own way of playing: at Rugby school, in 1823, William Webb Ellis famously picked up the ball and ran with it; on the playing fields of Eton they developed their own code, outlawing handling; at Westminster and Charterhouse, where football was played in the cloisters, a dribbling game was preferred. This divergence of laws meant that schools could not play each other, and there was chaos when the boys wanted to play at university. The first move towards unification came in 1846 when Cambridge University produced the 'Cambridge Rules'. Its graduates spread the football gospel, and they helped to form clubs in the south-east of England, playing against each other. The rules evolved again in 1862 when J.C. Thring of Uppingham School devised a set of ten rules called 'the simplest game' – only the ball could be kicked, no tripping was allowed and hands could only be used to stop the ball and place it on the ground before the feet. In the north, Sheffield FC, the oldest recorded football club, produced their own set of rules in 1857 which were adopted by other clubs in the Sheffield area so that they could play against each other. The original document setting out the rules was sold by the club for £881,250 at Sotheby's in July 2011.

There was little coverage of football in the newspapers of the day which were dominated by more popular sports including cricket, racing, angling, wrestling, hunting, and boxing, but *The Field* – the country gentleman's newspaper – carried the announcement of the formation of the Football Association at a historic meeting in the Freemasons Tavern in Lincoln's Inn Fields on Monday, 26 October, 1863. The group that met there were players representing a dozen London and suburban clubs, but they were all professional gentlemen. Mostly they were the team captain or club secretary. The purpose of the meeting was to establish a definitive code of rules for the regulation of the game. Mr. Arthur Pember, a London solicitor, was elected Chairman and Mr E.C. Morley was made secretary. But it took six meetings and 44 days before agreement could be reached on the laws of the game!

There had for a long time been bitter arguments between two factions: those who believed that handling and hacking were essential elements of the game and those who advocated dribbling, and outlawed hacking and handling. Finally the hackers lost the day, and Blackheath, the club who represented them withdrew, and in 1871 became one of the founder members of the Rugby Union. Football had finally divided itself into two codes, Association and Rugby. The move also signified another transfer of power, with football having first belonged to the masses, then to the public schools. Now it was shifting to a small number of London clubs. The Football Association had established itself as the governing body – the 'parliament of football.'

Eight years later two important milestones were reached which would have a profound and lasting effect on the development of English football. Charles Allcock, the new FA secretary (1870–1895), proposed a knockout cup competition – the FA Cup – for clubs belonging to the Association. Its beginnings were modest, with only 12 clubs entering, but in 1872, on 16 March, a crowd of 2,000 turned up at the Oval to watch the Wanderers beat the Royal Engineers 1-0 in the final.

Then, in November 1872, England played the first international match, against Scotland. A member of the England team that day was Charles Clegg, a Sheffield solicitor who played for Sheffield FC (the same Charles Clegg presided over Stanley Rous' interview for the position of FA Secretary in 1935). The match took place in Glasgow before a crowd of 4,000, the largest gathering seen at any football match in Scotland, and although it was a goalless draw, it was considered a resounding success.

Football had been the bastion of the ruling classes, dominated by the public schools, universities and amateur clubs, where the players were gentlemen. But in 1885 that began to change when professional players first appeared. The FA Cup had captured the public imagination and clubs were developing in the north of England, nowhere more so than in Lancashire with famous clubs like Blackburn Rovers and Preston North End. They saw nothing wrong with paying players to achieve success and profit, and the clubs brought players down from Scotland, where they had a reputation for a clever passing game which was superior to the English dribbling style. This caused serious and continuing conflict between the clubs and the FA. Charles Allcock recognised professionalism as an inevitable development, but the guardians of amateurism at the FA could not accept it. The conflict was only resolved after six years of bitter quarrelling when the FA finally legalised professionalism in 1895.

The growth of professionalism fuelled a wish for clubs to have a more interesting fixture list than friendly matches and a few cup games, and in 1888 the seeds of the idea of a Football League were sown by William McGregor of Aston Villa. 12 clubs were invited to be members: Accrington, Blackburn, Bolton, Burnley, Everton and Preston from the north and Aston Villa, Derby County, Notts County, Stoke, West Bromwich Albion and Wolverhampton Wanderers from the midlands. The switch in power from the south to the north of England was emphatic and far reaching. It created a rival power base to the FA. It returned football to its working class origins and was a source of future conflict. 60 years later the financial imperatives of League clubs would severely restrict Walter's – and every England manager that followed him – access to international players and hamper the development of a world beating international team.

In the south of England the amateur tradition continued to flourish and was epitomised by the Corinthians. They were a supremely successful team that played attractive football and would almost certainly have won the FA Cup had they not excluded themselves by their own charmingly amateur rule: 'The club shall not compete for any challenge cup or prizes of any description.' By the time they changed this rule and entered the FA Cup in 1922, the halcyon days of the amateur at the top level of football were over, and they were unable to compete with the professional clubs.

The feud between the professional and the amateur sides of the game continued as the number of professional clubs grew and their influence increased. At the beginning of the 20th century there were 400 professional clubs and this increased the resentment of many at the FA. For them the last straw came when it was proposed that the county associations should affiliate the professional clubs within their areas. The FA was split apart, with Surrey and Middlesex (the homeland of the amateurs) breaking away to form a rebel organisation. The split lasted from 1906-1913, but was finally resolved by Frederick Wall (the FA secretary who preceded Stanley Rous) who imposed the authority of the FA to exclude the rebels from all competitions.

During the First World War, football, unlike many other sports, had continued but in a much truncated and regional form. This caused national controversy and deepened social divisions. In a letter to *The Times*, for instance, on 7 November 1914, A.F. Pollard, the historian and former Oxford rowing blue complained that 'every club that employs a professional football player is bribing a needed recruit to refrain from enlistment, and every spectator who pays his gate money is contributing so much towards German victory.'

Sir Douglas Haig, the most controversial of the war generals, bemoaned the tendency of his men '...to run around and play football when they ought to have been resting.'

Others saw such views as an attack by the upper classes on the working-class ethos of sport and explained it as 'pre-war snobbery decked in patriotic uniform.'

One of the consequences of this socially divisive issue was that many public schools – for so long the bastions of association football – and some grammar schools, switched from soccer to rugby union after the war. One headmaster praised rugby as 'unequalled by any other game as a school of true manhood and leadership.' This switch to rugby was a trend that continued in the 1920s and 30s and was of much concern to Walter during his time at the FA. He foresaw that it was these schools that produced the teachers who would coach football, but they were unlikely to do that if they had played rugby at school.

It was not until after the First World War that football matured into a game with a genuine mass following. The prevailing socio-economic conditions in the inter-war years had an important influence on the development of football as a working-class sport. Following a short post-war boom there was a severe slump between 1920 and 1922, followed by the Wall Street Crash and the worldwide depression which began in 1929 and lasted until the mid 1930s.

In such conditions grass roots football on streets and waste ground flourished. Street football, played by men and boys, abounded throughout the country, with coats thrown down on the ground to mark out goal posts and with a boy on the lookout for the local policeman. Raich Carter, the Sunderland and England legend, recalled the street games of the 1920s in Sunderland, 'when a lamp post served according to season as wickets or goal posts, and the ball was often home-made with rags and newspapers.' Boys played every day and at every opportunity, and informal matches were played on any scrap of waste ground, with no referee, no proper pitch, and no playing kit; but with bets waged on the outcome and spectators shouting on their team.

Although the boys did not realise it at the time, the hours they spent playing street football developed a high level of skill. When asked what Walter's legacy to football was, John Cartwright – a visionary football coach himself – thought for a while before replying. 'He could see that street football was disappearing and created a formal coaching structure that would replace it.'

In recommending the virtues of five-a-side football in an article in the FA *Book for Boys* in 1961, Walter recalled his own memories of street football in Oldham:

I can well remember the enjoyment and excitement I used to get as a boy, from our own brand of soccer played in alleyways and on the small pieces of open ground which, up north, we call 'crofts.' There would only be a few players on each side and we made tactical use of obstacles such as drainpipes, clothes line posts, buttresses and pot holes. The goals varied in size according to the shape and space of the playing area, and we made up rules on the spot about forbidden areas and methods of shooting so as to give the goalkeepers a reasonable chance. Often we started with two against two players but as others turned up the strength of the sides would increase to a five- or six-a-side. It was surprising how many different tactics of play we discovered: follow up dribbling; poaching and the long kick down field; changing direction round team mates; and all kinds of rebound play from walls.

Street football developed because of a chronic shortage of access to playing fields, and this was exacerbated in the 1930s when areas where football had been played were taken for house building and not replaced. The condition of pitches was poor and facilities were minimal, but local authorities were reluctant to spend ratepayers' money on public playing fields, even when they recognised the benefits in terms of health and social order.

Conditions for watching football were not much better either. The popular areas of many grounds were often no more than raised banks of earth, built upon refuse, clay, rubble or dust, which quickly turned into mud in wet weather. Concrete terracing was rare before the 1940s. There were no toilet facilities and overcrowding was commonplace; none more notorious than the 1923 FA Cup Final – commonly remembered as the 'white horse' final after one of the mounted policeman who held back the crowds – when an incredible 200,000 spectators tried to squeeze into Wembley Stadium (official capacity 126,047). Regardless of this debacle the football authorities refused to impose safety regulations and in 1946, in a disaster at Bolton Wanderers FC, 33 spectators were killed and hundreds injured due to massive overcrowding on the crude bank at one end.

Despite these privations, supporting your football club had become a passion. For many supporters it was much more than merely a game or a form of entertainment. The quintessential nature of this love affair with football was captured in fiction by JB Priestley in his 1929 novel *The Good Companions,* an interesting forerunner to Nick Hornby's *Fever Pitch* 70 years later.

For a shilling the Bruddesford United AFC offered you conflict and art; it turned you into a critic, happy in your judgment of the fine points, ready in a second to estimate the worth of a well judged pass, a run down the touchline, a lightning shot, a clearance kick by the back or goalkeeper; it turned you into a partisan, holding your breath when the ball came sailing into your goalmouth, ecstatic when your forwards raced towards the opposite goal, elated, downcast, bitter, triumphant by turns at the fortunes of your side, watching a ball shape Iliads and Odysseys for you …

And what is more, it turned you into a member of a new community, all brothers together for an hour and a half, for not only had you escaped from the clanking machinery of this lesser life, from work, wages, rent, dole, sick pay, insurance-cards, nagging wives, ailing children, bad bosses, idle workmen, but you had escaped with most of your mates and neighbours, with half the town, and there you were, cheering together, thumping one another on the shoulders, swapping judgements like lords of the earth, having pushed your way through a turnstile into another and altogether more splendid kind of life, hurtling with Conflict and yet passionate and beautiful in its Art.

Moreover it offered you more than your shillings worth of material for talk during the rest of the week. And the man who had missed the last home match of 't'United' had to enter social life on tiptoe in Bruddersford.

The development of technology allowed the media to become a key influence in the mass popularisation of football. The *Sheffield Telegraph* revealed in 1925 how a telephone, a special messenger and a shorthand typist made it possible for a journalist at the other end of the country to have a 1,500 word match report in print within an hour of the final whistle. The cinema, a mass entertainment medium then, introduced newsreel coverage of football in the 1920s and 30s. But perhaps the most significant influence was the growth of radio and the appeal of match commentaries. The BBC's first live outside broadcast of a professional match was Arsenal's home fixture with Sheffield United in January 1927. Although radios had been initially confined to the middle classes, wireless licenses rose from two million in 1927 to nine million in 1939 (71 per cent of all UK households). The weekly roundup of football results on Saturday afternoon became a national institution, probably driven by the need to check coupons from the fast growing and enormously popular football pools. Despite the BBC's enthusiasm for broadcasting live commentaries, the Football League was not impressed and in 1931 the League banned the broadcasting of all its matches, a ban that remained in force throughout the 1930s. The only exception to the ban on live broadcasting was the FA Cup Final. This was followed in the late 1930s by the FA approving the broadcast of the second half of some international matches and FA Cup ties. Radio was opening up the football experience to a wide and diverse audience, reaching some 50 per cent of all listeners according to a BBC survey in1939.

The British gave birth to football, nurtured it and passed it on to the rest of the world. It is generally considered that the export of football had followed the growth of the Empire. But that is untrue. The growth in football was in Western Europe and South America. It was the countries with which Britain had close commercial, educational and cultural links that adopted football first – Switzerland, Belgium and Denmark, followed by the Netherlands, Scandinavia, Germany and France and then in South America, Brazil, Argentina and Uruguay. The historian Bill Murray observed that the process was that first expatriate Britons, particularly bankers, entrepreneurs, engineers, managers and technicians, as well as teachers and students, began to play matches against one another in these countries. In time members of the local aristocracy were drawn in to make up the numbers or provide opposition. Finally these new indigenous groups assumed control of the game and the influence of the British declined.

One of the reasons that football developed differently on the continent and in South America was that in these countries it remained a largely middle-class and elite game well into the 20th century, in contrast with its predominantly working-class profile in Britain. An educated class was better able to think more deeply about the game, to teach it, and to organise and finance its structure (as they had done in England when the FA was first formed).

The role of the coach was evolving on the continent and Vittorio Pozzo in Italy and Hugo Meisl in Austria emerged as vastly influential figures who shaped the destiny of their national teams. Meisl, was influenced by visits from British teams from 1900 to 1911, initially amateur sides from the south of England such as the Middlesex Wanderers and the Corinthians. Pozzo, played football whilst at technical college in the Swiss town of Winterthur, but came to study English in Manchester and Bradford and developed his passion for the game there. English coaches were unable to find employment at home, and men like Jimmy Hogan, Jesse Carver and George Raynor became key figures in coaching abroad.

England's international experience was limited. To England internationals meant the regular and fiercely competitive fixtures against Scotland, Wales and Ireland – the British Home Championship. The continentals offered no opposition. In 1906 the English centre forward, Vivian Woodward, was able to plunder the French, scoring seven of England's 15 goals. Three years later he scored six in a 9-1 thrashing of Holland. England were still amateurs but they ruled supreme. They encountered no serious opposition in 1908 when they toured Europe and beat Austria 6-1 and 11-1, Hungary 2-0 and Bohemia 4-0. But that supremacy was soon being challenged. By 1920 the English amateurs were no longer good enough and were knocked out in the first round of the Olympics by Norway, losing 3-0.

This period saw the emergence of South America on the world stage. Uruguay came to Europe for the 1924 Olympics, sweeping all the European teams away and beating Switzerland 3-0 in the final. Terence Delaney, author of *A Century of Soccer* described the South American style of football as 'florid and passionate, an emotional game of swiftness and delicacy, where skills with the ball flourished, and robust shocks of bodily contact so necessary and "manly" to the English Victorians seemed crude and irrelevant.'

By 1929 England were no longer invincible. A tour of Europe took them to Spain. In the heat of Madrid in May England were rocked by the sophisticated way the Spaniards mixed up their game with orchestrated link up play and virtuoso bursts of dribbling. The fast and fit Spaniards triumphed by 4-3. England had been beaten by foreign opposition for the first time.

Austria came to London in 1932, coached by Hugo Meisl and his assistant, Englishman Jimmy Hogan. England won 4-3 but were often left chasing shadows as Austria showed their technical superiority. England were beaten by Hungary and Czechoslovakia in 1934 but these away defeats went largely unnoticed. England remained stubbornly isolated and inward-looking during this period of rapid development on the continent, staunch in the belief that it had nothing to learn and confident of the fundamental superiority of English football and the primary importance of its Football League. The England team were given a brief pep talk by an FA official and sent out to get on with it.

Meanwhile association football was developing rapidly away from its birthplace in England. Belgium, Denmark, France, the Netherlands, Spain, Sweden and Switzerland had met in Paris in 1904 to become founder members of FIFA. England stood aloof. One year later the FA reluctantly joined but then left again after World War One, unwilling to have anything to do with former enemies and after bitter arguments about broken time – payments to amateur players in lieu of time taken off – which the FA was adamantly opposed to. It was a period of change and development but the FA councillors withdrew hermit-like into their isolationist shell and declined to enter the subsequent Olympics in 1924 (Paris) and 1928 (Amsterdam) and remained outside FIFA, missing three World Cup tournaments: 1930 (Uruguay), 1934 (Italy) and 1938 (France).

But England still remained unbeaten at home by a continental team and the partisan and unshakable belief that England were the best team in the world was reinforced when England beat the Rest of Europe 3-0 at Highbury in 1938. England still had truly great players; Matthews, Carter, Bastin, Hapgood, Cullis, Mercer and Lawton. They faced political intimidation and huge jingoistic crowds in Berlin as the dark storm clouds of war gathered over Europe. But the English style of robust, fast, direct play overcame the Germans by 6-3 in Berlin and held the Italians to a 2-2 draw in Milan. Although England did not carry the title world champions, everyone in England steadfastly believed that they were still the masters.

One man could see the folly of such an insular and blinkered attitude: Stanley Rous secured the FA's agreement to rejoin FIFA in 1946. He was critical of England's lost years of learning from playing in foreign competitions and the missed opportunity to lead the world in football development. 'Our isolation was in no sense splendid. It was a matter for regret and a constant cause of difficulty,' he said.

In the same year Rous felt that the time had at last come when he might get acceptance from the FA Council for his idea of a national coaching scheme. His vision for the development of coaching was almost thwarted at the outset. At his interview Walter raised concerns about the proposed salary, which was £970 a year, and politely but firmly said that his family commitments meant that he would be unable to accept the position at that salary. Stanley Rous, who had to fight tooth and nail to get approval for the new position of FA Director of Coaching, saw his carefully laid plans heading for the rocks. He asked Walter to leave the room and addressed the FA councillors on the appointments committee.

'What you don't realise,' Rous said 'is that you are getting two men here for the price of one. We should ask Winterbottom to take charge of the England international team and include this in his overall responsibilities [The appointment of an England team manager had first been mooted in the minutes of the international selection committee on October 20, 1945]. Of course if we do that his basic salary level will have to be increased, but not by much and certainly not what it would be if we employed another person at a later date.' It was a typical piece of quick thinking, garnered perhaps from Rous' refereeing experience, and the deal appealed to the parsimonious councillors. Walter, at the age of 34 and with no experience as a football manager, accepted the huge challenge of the dual role, confident in his own ability.

Walter's appointment was not big news in the firmament of English football. It was approved but not even mentioned in the FA Council minutes. There was no press conference to herald the appointment of England's first team manager. There were no TV interviews to introduce the new man to the public. But it was the beginning of a football revolution and although the FA has made a number of mistakes they deserve credit for the wisdom behind the appointments of Stanley Rous and Walter Winterbottom.

Stanley Rous became a hugely significantly figure in the post war modernisation of English football. Walter Winterbottom founded the FA National Coaching Scheme and used his knowledge, ability, patience and persistence to gain acceptance of coaching and bring about change to a country hidebound by football traditions rooted in the past 100 years.

CHAPTER 3

THE EARLY
YEARS

1913 – 1930

Oldham was a boomtown of the industrial revolution throughout the 19th century and at its zenith, in 1909, produced more cotton than France and Germany combined. At its peak there were 360 cotton mills operating night and day. A local coal industry had grown up to support the cotton mills and every mill had a tall chimney belching smoke into the grey cloud permanently covering the Lancashire sky. The area was characterised by Victorian redbrick terraced houses, irregularly constructed on the hilly uplands. Buildings were covered with the black grime of a century of industrial pollution. Oldham was not a pretty town, but it was a tight-knit community that worked and played together. The work in the mills was hard, with twenty four hour shifts, and money was always short. But it was a happy neighbourhood.

It was here that Walter Winterbottom was born on 31 March 1913. His parents, James and Fanny, née Holt, had five children – Ethel, Hilda, Fanny, Molly, and finally Walter, the boy they always longed for. Fanny was in her 40s when she had Walter and much of the burden for bringing up the children fell to the eldest daughter Hilda. When Fanny was pregnant with Walter she was very worried about the risks of childbirth at such a late age, but the doctor reassured her: 'Don't worry my dear; you've done the right thing bringing this child into the world.'

Walter was the tiniest of all her children and when she saw how small her long awaited boy was, she cried.

'It's all right my dear,' the doctor once again reassured her, 'this one is going to make two of those girls.'

'Aye'she replied and I can tell from the way he kicked that he is going to be a footballer.'

The Winterbottom family lived in a small red brick terraced house at 31 Stafford Street, in the Werneth district of Oldham. James Winterbottom had taken on the responsibility of bringing up his two brothers following the deaths of his own mother and father, and Fanny helped him to raise his two brothers before they began their own family. Fanny was a homely wife and mother: she was short and dumpy and her round face always had a cheerful smile. James was kind and fun loving, a strong, gutsy character. His children were bright. They probably got their intelligence from him, but he worked all his life in the mills, mostly as a ring frame fitter in a textile machine works. He retired in his 60s due to ill health and later took a job as a caretaker at the local school. Fanny used to take in washing to help make ends meet and his sisters all went to work in the local mill at the age of 14 to keep the home fires burning.

The 1920s and 1930s, the period in which Walter grew up in Oldham, was a time of great hardship for the industrial heartland of Britain. The economic prosperity brought about by the industrial revolution and the might of the British Empire was declining, and the financial cost of World War One had crippled the country. Unemployment was over 20 percent and this led to great social unrest and precipitated violent strikes, including the General Strike of 1926 and the Jarrow March a decade or so later.

World War One helped to break down some of the social barriers of the previous century, but England remained a country divided by social class. Two thirds of the wealth of the country was in the hands of just one per cent of the population, but changes in the aristocracy were beginning to happen. They were still rich but now they became less idle! They began to move from being just landowners to working in finance and industry. The lounge suit was replacing the top hat and tails. There was a decline in the number of servants, and a middle-class family that used to have one servant started to employ a daily woman instead.

After the war working women had an alternative to domestic service and went to work on the land, in factories and on buses. Montague Burton brought mass production tailoring to the high street making suits affordable to the growing lower middle classes who were increasingly working in offices.

Much of this social background is reflected in Walter's own recollections of his early days in Oldham as a picture of the man unfolds; how the background shaped the person and why he had such respect for the establishment that ruled all aspects of society, business and sport.

But as a child young Walter was not concerned with such worldly matters and his life was confined by much narrower boundaries. All the terraced streets around Stafford Street were named after towns, and the junction where Derby Street crossed Stafford Street was the hub where the children played their street games. On warm summer evenings parents from the houses in Derby Street would come out to join in a game of rounders. It was an open and friendly community and doors of houses were left wide open without the slightest fear of robbery. The four streets, Stafford, Chester, Cambridge, and Derby, formed a rectangle enclosing a croft of rough land with an alley entrance from Chester Street and Derby Street. This plot was where Walter learned the basic skills of football and cricket.

Within 400 yards of their home were four public beer houses (as opposed to public houses which had a full licence). Any householder who paid rates could apply, with a one-off payment of two guineas, to sell beer or cider in his home – usually the front parlour – and even brew his own beer on the premises. Oldham had a reputation for having more public houses and public beer houses per thousand head of population than anywhere else in the country. Toiling in cotton mills must have been thirsty work! Every Friday evening Walter watched his father join the weekly jolly, a beer drinking sing-along that poured from the open windows and drifted down the street. This was their main source of entertainment – there was no radio, television, or even a local picture palace cinema. Of course, in the centre of Oldham there were the grand variety theatres but they were unaffordable to the working folk of Oldham's Werneth district.

Walter enjoyed visiting Granny Holt, his maternal grandmother. He would cycle up to see her and was intrigued because she had shiny brass fenders round her fireplace which were always covered up with newspaper. One day he plucked up the courage to ask her why she kept them wrapped up, to which she tartly replied, 'I take the paper off on Sundays.'

It was the tradition, like the whiting of the stone. Most of the houses had a small flight of five or six broad steps leading to the front door. Every week the daughters of each household would go on their knees, using a 'donkey' stone wrapped in rag, and dipped in a bucket of water, to give each step a bright yellowish layer of colour. Thereafter family members had to use the rear entrance to the house. The whole street took part in this ritual of competitive pride.

One of Walter's earliest childhood memories was the coming of silent films when he was seven years old. His excitement knew no bounds when a cinema, the Gem, was built at the bottom of Stafford Street. His mother took him as a special treat: the children sat on wooden benches at the front of the cinema, straining their necks to look up at the screen, deafened by the piano just in front of them. The pianist cleverly played music appropriate to the scenes from the film, creating emotions of fear and love, moods of sadness and anger, and sensations of speed or tranquility. When the cinema was packed out, children were obliged to give up their seats and sit or kneel on the floor in the aisle. Matinees for children were held on Saturday mornings: the cheapest entrance price of two pence also entitled them to a choice of an ice cream cornet or a comic. The poshest seats were at the back of the cinema in the balcony. Walter recalled fondly: 'Such were the limitations of my ambitions in those early days that I dreamt of the day when I might be able to pay to have a balcony seat, and I aspired to be the well-dressed manager of the cinema!' (Despite, or perhaps because of, his humble background, being well-dressed was important to Walter from childhood to old age. He was always appropriately dressed for every occasion).

The cinema was a treat and street games were the way children entertained themselves. As well as cricket and football there were individual games such as 'whip-and-top', marbles or riding your 'bogey' – a small plank with wooden wheels that could be steered by a piece of rope attached to the front wheels. When his father, an engineer, made one for him at his place of work, no boy could have been more proud.

Street games continued during the dark winter evenings. One that Walter vividly remembered, perhaps because it was so frightening for a small boy, was called 'Rallyo-two tens-Jack Robin.' It was a team game of hide and seek. Two teams of ten boys were chosen to balance each other in age and ability. The den was a lighted street lamp at the junction of Stafford and Derby Street, and the boundary of the hiding area was prescribed. The boys wore plimsolls [training shoes] for stealth. Walter recalled: 'my right plimsoll had a small hole in the sole which I covered each night with a new piece of cardboard.' One team went out to hide and after a given time the other team set out to search. Anyone caught by being touched had to stand near the den as prisoners, whilst those on the loose would attempt to creep close and then make a dash to touch the lamp post shouting *Relievo!* to free the prisoners. Among the older boys was one daredevil who would climb up on the roofs of the terraced houses and, hiding behind the chimneys, make his way to the den. It seemed very frightening to Walter then. 'I'm sure that the fear and excitement of the chase in those impressionable years is the reason why I still often have dreams where I'm escaping from people who are chasing me.'

Walter's father and mother left school at the age of 11. The school leaving age was raised and his sisters, Ethel, Hilda, Fanny and Molly, left school at 14, and like all the other children in the area went to work in a cotton mill. Later in life this was an ongoing source of regret for Walter, who felt that Ethel and Hilda, the two eldest, were bright and intelligent enough to go into higher education and even on to university, but this was unthought-of then for working class children and girls in particular. His regret was tinged with guilt in the knowledge that it was their contribution to the family budget that allowed him to continue with his own education.

Walter's first school in Oldham was the local elementary school but at the age of 12 an event occurred that changed his life. The headmaster, recognizing that he was a clever boy, recommended that he should apply for the Mary Clegg scholarship, which would pay the fees to enable him to attend the Oldham High School. He passed the exam and was duly awarded the scholarship which allowed him to continue his education to at least the age of 16. There was a lengthy family discussion on whether or not he should go. At first Walter was reluctant to give up his responsibility of becoming a breadwinner who would contribute to the family income – they had already discussed the work that he might do on leaving school at fourteen – but his parents unselfishly insisted that he should grasp this opportunity to better himself.

He was lucky. Few people in Oldham escaped the drudgery of working in the mills. 'Knocker uppers' went along the streets in the early hours with their long poles which had a flexible piece of metal attached to the top. They would use these to rap on the bedroom window, calling out the time and waiting for a shouted response. About the same time in the early dawn, the lamplighters would walk down the streets using their poles to turn off the gas lamps. All the workers in Oldham wore clogs. As they hurried to get 't't mill before 'ooter,' the clamour of wooden shoes clacking on the cobbled streets was a sound so common that it was hardly noticed. The tedium and the long hours of work were relieved only by the highlight of Oldham 'Wakes Week' when the whole town would take its annual holiday. Those who could afford it went to Blackpool or if you had pretensions, Southport or Morecombe. If you were employed in a better position than mill worker, and therefore earned more, you might even go further afield to somewhere exotic like Scarborough or Skegness. But for most working class families Blackpool was the favourite – it was bold, brassy and totally unpretentious. Throughout the year Walter looked forward to their summer holiday in Blackpool with the excitement and anticipation that only a child can understand.

'I first recall visiting Blackpool for a holiday when I was about five years old,' he later recalled. 'The family – my mother and father, my four older sisters and I – travelled by train, though the journey was only about 40 miles. As we got close we looked out of the carriage windows, trying to be the first to spot the famous tower and the big wheel. It was very exciting. We hired a horse and trap to take mother, the girls and the luggage to our digs, while dad and I walked. In those days people wore ordinary clothes to play on the beach or sit in deck chairs. There were a few cabins on wheels close to the edge of the sea where daring grown-ups would change into bathing costumes to have a dip. But most people just took off their shoes and stockings and rolled up their trousers and skirts to paddle in the shallow waves.'

The small bed and breakfast house they stayed in was opposite the rear exit of the Palace ballroom and sometimes in the warm evenings the door would be opened for ventilation. Walter would stand outside and listen to the dance music from the big band that drifted out onto the street. He peeked in to watch the graceful dancers; stirring an ambition that one day he would be able to afford to dance there himself. Several years later his sister Fanny and her husband Jack went to live in Blackpool and he achieved his ambition. Jack had played the banjo in a dance band in Oldham and Fanny loved to dance, so when he went to see them Fanny suggested that they go to the afternoon tea dance at the Palace. Walter jumped at the chance and they danced to the music of Reginald Dixon, the world famous organist. By then Walter had taken ballroom dancing lessons and was a proficient dancer. As they swirled around the ballroom floor amongst dozens of couples he must have thought back to those impressionable years when, as a small boy, he was enchanted by gazing at the dancers through the rear exit door of the Palace ballroom.

The central promenade at Blackpool had booths selling the sheet music of Feldman and Wright. Each booth had a pianist and a male singer, who also urged the audience to buy sheets of music at sixpence a copy. To popularise the music the soloist would encourage the group of onlookers to join in a sing-along of the chorus of each song. The haunting melody of popular romantic songs like 'Lily of Laguna,' written by Leslie Stuart in 1898, would echo down the promenade, and the crowd would pick up the refrain. Fond memories of Blackpool come flooding back, evoking the sound of the sea lapping over the golden sands, as Walter softly sings the chorus:

I know she likes me
Because she says so
She is my Lily of Laguna
She is the darling of my heart

Sheet music was popular because so many working class people were able to play the piano. It was how they enjoyed music: no pub in Blackpool would be without its pianist and everyone joined in the songs. It was the only way to listen to popular music because there was no radio and few people could afford a gramophone. Radio came along when Walter was fourteen years old and like many boys of his age he was excited when he was able to make a crystal set for the family to listen to music through head phones.

Walter sadly recalled his family returning home by train from Blackpool and being greeted at Werneth Street station by some 50 unemployed young men offering to carry their luggage for a 'tanner' (sixpence, or roughly two and a half pence at today's value). The family had to walk more than a mile through the streets from the station to their home; the young man they had hired bravely carrying their two heaviest cases. He staggered the last few yards totally exhausted, but his face broke into a broad grin when Walter's dad gave him another 'tanner'.

Mahatma Gandhi visited Oldham during this period of decline and unemployment in the cotton industry. Walter was reminded of the visit many years later when he was on a flight back from a football match in Holland. He sat next to Richard Attenborough, who was a director of Chelsea, and Attenborough told him that he had been in Holland to raise money to finance his latest film, *Gandhi*. Sometime later, when Walter saw the film, Gandhi was portrayed as being rapturously received in the streets of Oldham as a working class hero. In reality he recalled watching Gandhi, clad only in loin cloth and sandals, being resoundingly booed by Oldham's cotton workers because he had stopped the import of British cotton goods to India, causing unemployment in Oldham.

They were difficult times and families were often short of coal when the miners were on strike. George Orwell reflected the despair in his book *The Road to Wigan Pier*: 'Several hundred men risked their lives as they scrambled with women in the mud for hours ... searching eagerly for tiny chips of coal in slag heaps so they could heat their homes.' There was a disused pit about a mile from Walter's home where men and boys went digging each evening for near-surface coal. All through the summer after school Walter would go with a canvas bag and a small pick-shovel to dig. Some of the men dug tunnels to reach richer seams and tragically two tunnels collapsed, burying the men at their workings. The police then put a stop to it.

In 1925, at the age of 12, Walter entered a new world. The Municipal Secondary School (which Walter always referred to as Oldham High School) provided a very different environment from the one he had grown up in. It was a selective fee paying school with high academic standards which had recently been subject to examination by members of His Majesty's Inspectorate of Schools. Their report expressed their approval of the standards achieved by the headmaster, Mr. G.M. Handley, and his staff. Perhaps fortunately for Walter, the teaching of PE and science, his best subjects, gained the highest and most consistent praise from the Inspectors and the school was equipped with a fine science building and extensive playing fields.

Admission was by entrance examination and the payment of tuition fees (which in 1930 were two guineas a term), except for those lucky enough to win a scholarship. Uniform, textbooks and exercise books had to be bought from the school and a contribution of sixpence a week was required towards the upkeep of sports clubs and class libraries. Thanks to the generosity of the Mary Clegg scholarship, Walter's parents did not have to meet any of these expenses, which otherwise would have made it impossible for him to attend.

Even at the age of 12, Walter had an instinctive understanding that education was the only way out of the grinding poverty and drudgery of working in the mills, and he was determined to make the most of his opportunity. He was a late entry into the secondary school, because his headmaster at the elementary school had delayed putting him forward for a scholarship until the age of 12, and so he was placed in a mixed class, whereas the brighter pupils were in separate boys and girls classes.

At the elementary school level he had not been given homework; now he got down to serious extra study at home and this soon pushed him to the top of his class (even at that age he was competitive). It didn't make him popular with is former friends at the elementary school, who teased him about his school uniform as he walked down the street with his school cap hidden. But nothing distracted him from his work and at the end of the school year he was promoted to the boys only class in his age group. He was determined to work even harder to justify his family's encouragement for him to continue his studies.

On his way to and from school he would learn French and German vocabulary. Then he would settle down in the evening to do homework and read ahead, often staying up until midnight. His sister Fanny did shift work at the Ferranti factory. When she worked the 4am until noon shift, concerned about her safety, Walter would get up early in the morning to escort her to the tram. When he got back home he would continue his studies before going to school. His hard work paid off and at the end of his first year in the boys class he had taken first place overall, and was top in arithmetic, algebra, geometry, chemistry and physics.

But life at school was not all work. It was here that his love of sport developed and he was one of a team of boys selected for their prowess in cricket and soccer to travel to London to play a series of matches over a fortnight. The local Oldham M.P. who arranged the trip was a friend of a very rich London financier, Mr. Villiers, who had developed the Hackney Wick Boys Club, and it was he that sponsored the visit.

In London the boys slept on palliasses on the floor of a gymnasium, and a charming buxom lady called Mrs. Rainbow catered for them. Each morning, Mr. Villiers came to invite them to join him in a swim before breakfast in a cold open-air pool. They all thought he was a great sport. Jardine, the English cricket captain, helped at the club and he taught a few of the boys to play squash. Walter showed a natural aptitude for the game, which he enjoyed into his 70s. But the greatest excitement of his first trip to London was a coach tour at night around the West End. As the coach made its way up Park Lane the boys witnessed the opening night of the new Dorchester Hotel. The magnificent building was floodlit and a large crowd had gathered to watch the arrival of dignitaries, men dressed in white tie and tails and ladies wearing coronets and tiaras. The young lads from the deprived industrial landscape of Oldham were left gasping in awe at the sheer opulence of the scene.

Walter worked diligently throughout his years at the high school and at the age of 16 the time had come for him to take the matriculation examination which would decide his future. On speech day the school hall was packed with students, parents, staff and dignitaries who were gathered for the exam results and prize giving. The young Walter sat amongst an assembly of boys, a sea of eager upturned faces, nervously awaiting their results. He felt a wave of relief as his name was called out – distinction in arithmetic, algebra, geometry, chemistry and physics; good in French and German and credits in history, geography, English grammar and literature. Walter remembered the occasion with pride: 'The Mayor gave out certificates to those boys and girls who had gained a distinction in any subject. When it came to my turn he held up my five certificates in the shape of a fan, smiled, and wafted them over his face in a humorous gesture, which caused a ripple of applause from the assembly.' He was sad that his mother and father were not there, although it is not known why. How could he have possibly dreamed then that in many years to come he would be the person standing on the stage making the address and giving out the prizes as the school's most famous old boy?

CHAPTER 4

THE TEACHER

1931 – 1939

At the age of 17, Walter passed the Intermediate High School Examination and decided to become a teacher. His headmaster was disappointed that he did not want to apply to a university, but he had rejected the idea because his father was unemployed due to a long-term illness. He felt that his future should be focused on a job where he could live at home and produce income for the family. In later life he sometimes wondered what might have been if he had gone to university. He was certainly clever enough. The thought that he might have become a mathematics professor at a university like Cambridge intrigued him. Mind you, teaching was a well paid and well-respected career then. The High School records show that Mr Handley was paid £400 a year in 1910, which was increased by £55 a year in 1919 when all teachers enjoyed an increase in salary. Mr. Joslin, as principal assistant master, received an increase that took his salary to £325 a year. An interesting example of what such an increase meant at that time is provided by a Mrs. Beeton (not the cook book author!) in a history of the school. According to her calculations, Mr. Handley's increase would have financed a cook and a housemaid, while Mr. Joslin should have been able to afford a general servant at least!

As a result of his excellent High School exam results, Walter was awarded a bursary for a preliminary teacher training course. This required him to teach part time for one year at Werneth elementary school, prior to going to teacher training college. The High School had, since it's foundation in 1909, included in its curriculum a pupil teacher centre for 16 to 18-year-olds, so it was very convenient for Walter to slip into this period of practical work. Teaching took place from Monday to Thursday – the first three months as an auxiliary teacher, the rest of the year as a closely-supervised class teacher. Fridays and Saturday mornings were spent back at his own school following an academic course. When he successfully completed the preliminary year in 1931 he took up his place at Chester Diocesan Teacher Training College.

He had indeed been fortunate in attending a school which had such high academic standards. Many went on to higher degrees – 34 masters degrees and eighteen doctorates. Furthermore, the school had a tradition of producing teachers; providing over 1,000 teachers for the education system during its lifetime (1902-78), many of whom became headmasters and headmistresses in the Manchester area. Three of its former pupils were knighted. The late Sir Percy Lord took up one of the country's most influential educational posts as chief education officer of the old Lancashire Education Authority. Lord attended the school from 1914 to 1921 and returned to teach chemistry from 1927 to 1932. This was at the time when Walter was attending the school. They formed a long standing friendship and Walter used him as a referee when he applied for the position of Secretary of the Football Association.

The school had changed Walter's life and it was appropriate that he was, in some small way, able to repay the school by returning as the guest of honour on 26 July 1978, two days before the school closed its doors for the last time. It was then known as the Greenhill School, (having become the Municipal High School in 1930 and Greenhill Grammar School in 1951). The headmaster, Mr. Graham Stanley said, 'a school which set such high standards yet generated such affection, loyalty and friendship, was bound to produce people who were to reach the top of their chosen career. Amidst such success, one former pupil rose to become possibly the school's most famous "old boy"...' He then introduced Sir Walter Winterbottom to present the prizes at the final Speech Day.

At Chester Teacher Training College (now the University of Chester) a chance event occurred which was to have a major influence on Walter's life. In his short unpublished memoir written for his grandchildren, Walter recalled:

It was at Chester College that I met Eddie Lever, a mature student. He was a professional footballer at Portsmouth but he had got an injury which had affected his running, and so the club had generously agreed to finance his teacher training to start a new career. As you would expect Eddie was elected to be the captain of the college soccer team, and I became the secretary of the club which ran three teams. In retrospect this was another important turning point in my life because Eddie Lever influenced the development of my skill and knowledge in football. As a team we quickly learned the professional techniques of playing soccer from Eddie, and our reputation spread around, so we began to be invited to play friendly matches against top class amateur sides in the region. We had a few outstanding players, notably a centre forward, who, after leaving college, was selected to play for the England amateur team.

The only information about Walter's football prowess at Chester comes from a report of a match between Chester College and Bangor Normal College in a press cutting from an unknown Bangor newspaper: 'The Normal College first team lost to Chester 4-2 in a very exciting game. The defences were about equal, but Chester had the advantage at halfback, where Winterbottom, their centre half, played a very good game. The forwards on both sides played fast football but whereas the visitors attempted to dally with the ball, the home side tried shots from all angles.' Alongside the cutting Walter had inscribed in his neat handwriting, *'Memories of J Lever of Portsmouth who taught me much of my football.'* John Lever, who later became known as Eddie, became a teacher in Alton, but then went back to Portsmouth FC in 1946. Initially in charge of youth development, he was credited with the discovery of Jimmy Dickenson who became a Portsmouth and England legend. He became the manager from 1952-58 and in that capacity had regular contact with Walter as the England team manager and they remained close friends.

One of Walter's enduring qualities was the ability to win support from any group of people in almost any circumstances. He recalled an incident during his teaching practice at Chester College:

Our teaching practice for the final examination took place in Liverpool. For the next fortnight we left Chester at seven each morning to journey by coach to Birkenhead, and then crossed the Mersey by ferry, before taking a tram to our chosen school. We would return to college each day to prepare our lessons for the next day. The school to which I was allocated was Walton Lane, off Scotland Road, a very tough area with much unemployment. Some rioting mobs actually turned over a tramcar and I witnessed posses of police running to stop the rioting. Indeed I was advised by the school to go by a different route to avoid meeting up with any mob. The school used a piece of wasteland for games, and gangs of unemployed men played marbles there for small bets. I had to take my class there for the games session and to my astonishment I learned that the schoolboy teams had already been chosen by the men and bets placed on which side was going to win. After a few minutes the ball was hit high in the air and it fell through a pane of

glass in the nearby conservatory of Sheil Park. I had to spend the rest
of the games period settling the details of the damage whilst the boys
carried on playing to get a result. I think the boys took a shine to me
after this and gave me support when the examiner came to see me
teach, because I received a distinction in practical teaching!

It was a typically modest response.

In the decades before the Second World War, England was a class-ridden society and accents were a primary indicator of class. All BBC announcers and newsreaders spoke the so-called Standard English, meaning the soft tones of the alien south: harmonious Oxbridge voices of long vowels, distinct p's and t's. This was a foreign world to Walter: everyone he knew spoke with a Lancashire accent. This was brought to his attention when the external teaching inspector said curtly, 'You've got to do something about that accent – it's broad Lancashire.' Walter realised that to get on in the world he would indeed have to do something about it, so he began his own elocution lessons by reading out loud to himself, ironing out the long vowels, ('books' for 'bukes'), ('buses' for 'booses'), and catching the dreaded dropped 'aitch's.' Nevertheless, some of the accent must have remained because when he came to London in 1941 his wife, Ann, recalled: 'My mother said that she had a phone call from an RAF gentleman who wanted to come to lodge with us in Stanmore. She said "I think it was a foreign person!" I also remember that when he was playing football for Chelsea during the war he had to catch a bus to Putney. He asked the bus conductor for a ticket to 'Pootney'. The conductor replied, "Where the hell is that, mate?"'

On completion of the course at Chester Teacher Training College Walter graduated at the age of 21 with the Certificate of Education and the distinction of being placed first amongst a year of 53 students. The Vice Principal and Master of Method wrote about him: 'The fact that he secured distinction in Principles and Practices of Teaching is in itself a valuable testimonial. He teaches from a thoroughly sound background of information and he is at all times able to attract the interest and attention of his boys without any effort. His quiet but firm manner secures excellent class control at all times.' It was these qualities that gave him the foundations to coach football with such success in the years to come.

The college was so impressed that they encouraged him to apply for teaching positions in prestigious schools. He was adamant that he didn't want that and preferred to go back to teach in Oldham where he could support his family. In the four years since he matriculated he had been unable to help them financially and his mother sent him pocket money whenever she could. He obtained a teaching position at the Alexandra Road Junior School, Oldham, and began work there in July 1934, a fortnight before the summer holidays. He could hardly believe his eyes when he opened his first pay packet. At the end of the fortnight's work he received a cheque for £20 – six weeks pay – because it included holiday pay. It seemed like a windfall, as his father's weekly wage as a qualified engineer was only two pounds ten shillings (£2.50) a week. With a typically generous gesture he took the family on holiday to Morecambe – a step up from Blackpool!

Settled at home with his parents again and teaching locally, he applied himself to sport. Not far from the Alexandra Road School was the Royton Amateur Football and Cricket Club and it was here that he played regular first team cricket and football (he loved cricket and privately confided that he thought he was good enough to play for Lancashire). But it was on the football pitch where he excelled and it was not long before the name 'Winterbottom' was appearing in the *Oldham Chronicle*. 'Winterbottom paved the way to victory by clever intercepting and well judged passes to the forwards,' read one match report, and on another occasion, 'Their [Royton's] strength is in the middle, for Winterbottom is one of the best centre-halves in the league.'

Soon he was being selected to represent the Lancashire and Cheshire Amateur League. At the end of his second season with

Royton he came to the notice of Mossley AFC, a semi-professional club who played in the Cheshire League, and was signed by their manager Clifford Tarr. Mossley, nicknamed the *Lilywhites*, was a 'professional crossroads club,' where older players coming down from the Football League met young players on their way up. The club has the unique distinction of having spawned two FA Directors of Coaching: Walter Winterbottom of course and Howard Wilkinson, who began his distinguished managerial career as the player manager at Mossley in the 70s before becoming the FA Technical Director (1997-2002). Many of the players at Mossley were semi-professional, having jobs as well as being paid to play football, but Walter signed as an amateur. He immediately made his mark as a strong and skilful centre half and attracted headlines in the *Mossley and Saddleworth Reporter*.

MOSSLEY TURN THE CORNER. NEW CENTRE HALF'S FINE DISPLAY

The outstanding feature of a poor game at Seel Park on Saturday was the display of Walter Winterbottom at centre half for Mossley. Winterbottom, who created a very favourable impression in the trial games, showed considerable ability at Altrincham on New Year's Day, and on Saturday he enhanced this ... North End made several attempts to reduce the lead but Winterbottom repeatedly foiled Broadhurst and won rounds of applause for his timely interceptions.

The report included a photograph of an earnest looking young Walter, smartly dressed in a dark suit, white shirt and neck tie with a clip.

Furthermore, in a game against Wigan it was noted that 'Winterbottom again confirmed the good impression he has created since his appearance with the team at Altrincham. Mossley will be fortunate if they retain his services.' But, ironically, favourable reviews like this, and in particular the game against Altrincham, were to deal him a great disappointment. Walter remembered:

My first game was against Altrincham and I was to mark the centre forward Littlewood, who, in his heyday, I had watched playing for Oldham Athletic when I was a schoolboy. We drew the game 0-0 and I had stopped Littlewood from scoring. The local newspapers made a song and dance about this, and in consequence, and to my surprise, I was removed from the North v South amateur trial match prior to the selection of the England amateur side. Bernard Joy, who went on to play for the Arsenal, was instead chosen to play in my position of centre half. Later I learned that the reason I was withdrawn was because the FA officials assumed, wrongly of course, that as I had played for Mossley, a professional club, I had forfeited my amateur status.

The chance to win an England international amateur cap had gone but he continued to play some outstanding games for Mossley, a total of 22 games in the 1935/36 season and it was not surprising that he was being watched by Manchester United. Their legendary scout, Louis Rocca, spoke to Walter towards the end of the 1936 season and asked if he would like to play for United. He wasn't sure. He had had two experiences with Football League clubs already, which had not been happy ones. When he was training with Oldham Athletic he had been told that he had been picked for the first team that Saturday. He was excited to have his first chance in League football but arriving at Boundary Park an hour before the kick-off the manager bluntly told him, 'you're not playing.' When he asked why, the manager replied, 'I've changed my mind.' Walter turned angrily and walked out of the ground. Although the *Latics* were his local club, the team that he had watched as a schoolboy, he felt that it was wrong for players to be treated in this way, and vowed that he would never play for Oldham. He had also played some games for

Manchester City's 'A' side some two years earlier, which had come to nothing. Now Manchester United wanted him. It probably wouldn't lead to anything but, he thought, he had nothing to lose.

After the pre-season trial match in August, 1936, the United manager, Scott Duncan, called Walter into his office and told him that he would like to sign him as an amateur. To Duncan's surprise Walter refused. He was probably still irked that the FA's mistaken assumption that he was a professional had robbed him of his chance to win an amateur international cap, but now there was an opportunity to turn the situation to his advantage. He told Scott Duncan that if United wanted to sign him it would have to be as a professional player and insisted that he should be able to continue in his teaching job (there would be no clash with his teaching duties because there were no floodlights in those days, so matches were only played on Saturday afternoons except for cup tie replays). Scott Duncan smiled at the young man's confidence and offered him professional terms of £8-a-week during the football season, plus a bonus of £2 if the team won, and £1 for a draw. The summer wages were £6 a week.

Suddenly he was earning two good salaries and was well off for the first time in his life. Flushed with his good fortune, he celebrated not by buying anything for himself, but by purchasing the freehold to a terraced house for his parents in Oxford Street which was next to their rented house in Stafford Street. They were in their 60s now: James was in ill health and only able to work as a caretaker and Walter was concerned about their ability to provide for their old age. Buying the house gave them security and released them from the weekly burden of rent. It was his way of repaying them for the sacrifice that they had made by allowing him to continue with his studies instead of going out to work at the age of 14.

He continued to live at home while he was playing for Manchester United and teaching at the Alexandra Road elementary school. For two years he enjoyed teaching the children and coaching the school football team. (Some years after he retired, he received a letter from Ms. Joan Brown, a previous teacher at the school who was now a governor, telling him that the governors had placed a plaque in the building to mark his association with the school and encourage their Asian pupils to try harder at football.)

Walter was acutely aware of the dismal prospects for the children he taught. Most left school at 14 and less than ten per cent went from elementary schools to secondary schools and even then they mostly left at 16. Wages were low, apprenticeships were rare, hours were long, and most school leavers were funneled into dead-end jobs. Large-scale unemployment and unrest was a continuing blight on the social fabric of the nation. There was widespread concern amongst leaders in the country that this had led to physical and moral deterioration of the nation's young people and a belief that physical fitness was a way of addressing this.

So it was not surprising that an advertisement for a diploma course in physical education attracted his interest. Carnegie College of Physical Training, which had opened three years earlier, was the first of its kind, and had attracted considerable attention in the educational press. The advertisement specified that applicants should have the teachers Certificate of Education as a minimum, along with two years teaching experience. Walter thus qualified, but on top of that he had experience of playing football for Manchester United. It seemed to be an exciting opportunity which would take him further in the teaching profession and he immediately decided to make an application for one of the 60 places being offered.

Carnegie had come into existence through a belief in the value of physical educational and dissatisfaction with the kind of training then being offered – a variety of military drill that was common in boy's schools. Throughout the 1920s, Sir George Newman, the first Chief Medical Officer of the Board of Education, had expressed his concerns over the lack of training for male PE teachers. There was a groundswell of demand from education authorities and headmasters of public and grammar schools for masters who were competent to develop the physical activities of boys in conjunction with the general life and work of the schools. As a result, a government committee was set up with the Carnegie UK Trust, to explore the possibility of establishing a college of physical education for male teachers. In 1930 the Carnegie Trust offered a grant of £30,000 to finance the project in conjunction with Leeds Local Education Authority, which provided a site for the college within the grounds of the City of Leeds Training College at Beckett Park.

A condition was that the college should be self-supporting, with its only income derived from student fees and government grants provided to the students. The annual cost of training a student, including residence, was estimated at £150 a year. In its inaugural year, the Carnegie College of Physical Training received 115 applications, and 25 graduates and 33 certified teachers were accepted. Three years later, when Walter applied, demand for places far exceeded supply, with typically one person being selected from every six applicants, ensuring a high standard of students. At his interview Walter made it quite clear that he did not want a grant and would pay his own fees as he was being paid a good wage by Manchester United. His application was accepted and he commenced the course in September 1937.

The curriculum stimulated his thirst for knowledge and opened up a new world. Ernest Major, the first warden, believed that physical education involved the true interaction of the body, mind, and spirit – a philosophy first expounded by the Greeks. Walter, meanwhile, was soaking up knowledge: he found that lectures included the theory, history, and organization of physical education, the theory and practice of remedial gymnastics, and teaching practice for practical gymnastics. The City of Leeds Training College gave lectures on education and helped in teachers' practice supervision. Leeds University Medical School provided lectures in anatomy, physiology, hygiene and first aid.

Carnegie had been very successful in its first four years and attracted visits from HRH the Prince of Wales, directors of education, school inspectors, heads of schools and other educationalists. It was clear that the facilities needed to be expanded to provide a lecture room, a gymnasium for remedial gymnastics, boxing, fencing and indoor athletics training, a staff room and even an athletics stadium. The Carnegie Trust generously agreed to meet the whole cost of the project and the extensions were completed and opened towards the end of Walter's first student year.

These were exciting times for Walter who was busy opening his mind to new frontiers of teaching. He worked long and hard as he always had done and was proud when he received his diploma, but he hardly expected what followed. On graduating he was astonished to be offered an appointment as a lecturer at Carnegie with a salary of £360-a-year! This was a lot higher than a teacher's annual salary of £186-a-year and, combined with his wages of £8-a-week playing for Manchester United, gave him an annual income of more than £600-a-year. By comparison, the Chief Constable of Oldham was paid £312-a-year and his father was earning £130-a-year. He had no hesitation in accepting the position!

The appointment of a young student as a lecturer, and his celebrity as a footballer, gave Carnegie the opportunity to use Walter in their publicity for the college. In the years before the war the press carried more than fifty reports of the college's activities, ranging from the formal opening of the extensions, to the appointment of Walter Winterbottom – the Manchester United centre half – as a lecturer. This helped Carnegie, a small college of sixty students, to become and remain better known than its parent, the City of Leeds Training College, which was one of the biggest training colleges in the country with nearly 500 students.

Carnegie was already beginning to influence how physical education was perceived and taught. In the time that Walter was there former students had gained influential positions in newly created posts as Director of Physical Recreation at the Universities of

Liverpool, Leeds and Birmingham. Others took up positions as His Majesty's school inspectors, directors of education, university and college lecturers, and headmasters. While the disciples from Carnegie led the way, Loughborough College was not far behind and other PE colleges soon followed.

It was while Walter was a lecturer there that he had his first experience of international competition. He led a representative men's team from Carnegie to the Lingiad in Stockholm – the gymnastics festival held in honour of P.H. Ling, the world renowned founder of Swedish gymnastics.

'When our Carnegie team arrived at Liverpool Street station, carrying our luggage and wearing our raincoats, the press lined up to photograph us,' recalled Walter. But at that moment one of the photographers shouted, "Look behind you!" and they all turned to see the arrival of the ladies team. The larger-than-life Prunella Stack and her beautiful ladies from the League of Health and Beauty posed wearing smart all-white outfits, carrying, not battered suit cases, as we were, but bunches of flowers. We felt like the poor relations who had been upstaged, and the ladies team continued to get all the attention during our first two days in Sweden. Finally, we had had enough and all the men stood up and sang a rousing chorus of the ditty, "Why were they born so beautiful ..."'

In the summer vacations Carnegie opened its doors to external courses, and in 1938 Stanley Rous, who had been appointed the new Secretary of the Football Association in 1934, came to organise a residential football coaching course. As Walter was on the staff, and was a well known footballer, he was invited to help run the course. Although he had no way of knowing it at the time, he made a good impression because Stanley Rous was to become his mentor and have a life changing influence on his career – and sooner than he could have imagined.

CHAPTER 5

MANCHESTER UNITED

1936 − 1939

Moving from Mossley in the Cheshire League to Manchester United in the First Division of the Football League (now known as the 'Premier league') was a daunting step up. A crowd of 8,000 turned out on a sunny Saturday afternoon on 22 August 1936 to watch United's traditional pre-season trial and cast their critical eyes over the new players. An apprehensive young Winterbottom took his place alongside the rest of the squad of 31 players in the 'probables v possibles' game which would help the manger decide on his first team for the coming campaign. The probables ran out onto a perfect green pitch in the first team strip of red shirts with red sleeves and a white collar. The possibles wore the United change strip of red and white striped hoop shirts. At half-time the reds were beating the stripes 4-2 but as usual in a trial match a number of changes were made in the second half, one of which was bringing Walter on at centre half, and moving Vose, the regular first-team centre half, to right half. Walter made the most of his chance and the reds ran out the winners 6-2.

In his 45-minute appearance he had not only caught the eye of the United management but also that of the press. The match report in the *Manchester Evening Chronicle* noted Walter's arrival on the Old Trafford scene: 'In the second half four new players were introduced in addition to John. Winterbottom, a young centre half from Mossley, took the place of Vose who went to wing half in place of Brown. Winterbottom gave a magnificent display and is a star of the future.'

'Casual', the pen name of Alf Clarke, the renowned *Manchester Evening Chronicle* columnist, was also impressed: 'Another player who took my eye in the trial match was Winterbottom, a young centre half-back from Mossley. He is, I understand, a school teacher and United is his first professional club. Ideally built for the position (six foot and 12 stone), he showed himself to be a fearless tackler.' It was a promising beginning to Walter's career with United and he soon established himself in the reserve team. During term time he caught the tram after school to go to Old Trafford for training. During the school holidays he trained full time. In those days training was primarily concerned with physical fitness, running endless laps round the pitch, sprinting, exercises and working with a medicine ball. Almost no time was spent on improving ball skills. Then it was generally considered that you either 'had it' or you didn't. There were practice games but not even many of these. The players rarely saw the manager, Scott Duncan, and training was left to the trainers, Tom Curry and his assistant Bill Inglis.

In his first week Walter watched the experienced professionals training at Old Trafford. He felt confident that he could match them in all departments except one – heading. There was no time given to coaching skills during training sessions so he developed his own practice routine – heading a ball against a wall, and from constant practice he learned how to time his jump and strike the ball to get maximum power, to direct the ball accurately, to head high or low or to glance the ball until he was finally satisfied that he could head the ball as well as any of his teammates.

In the 1920s and 30s Manchester United were not the force that they have been in modern times. They were relegated from the old First Division in the 1930/31 season, conceding 115 goals. The situation on the playing field continued to deteriorate, crowds dwindled, and by December 1931 bankruptcy became a real threat. A new chairman, James Gibson, came in and invested money; he got the club back on track and appointed a new manager, Scott Duncan. They still flirted with relegation to the third division in 1933/34, but at last things began to improve: they finished in fifth place in Division 2 in 1934/35, and the following season (the season before Walter signed) they were promoted back into the first division.

Walter played his first five matches for the reserves in September, but was injured in a cup tie against Burnley. He returned to the reserve team in November. Then, early one Thursday morning in late November, schoolmaster Winterbottom arrived at the Alexandra Road School to be met by the caretaker, who rushed up to him.

'Mr. Winterbottom, sir, congratulations! You've been picked to play in United's first team on Saturday.'

Walter didn't believe it, but when he entered his classroom the boys were bursting to tell him the news.

'Sir, sir, you are playing against Leeds on Saturday. It's in the *Daily Dispatch*.'

He could still hardly believe it, even after they showed him the newspaper. Perhaps he was still conscious of the snub from Oldham Athletic. He had looked for the team sheet on the club notice-board at training the night before, but it had not been posted, and it was only when he reported for training later that day that he was officially informed that he had been picked to play. The experienced centre half, Vose, was injured and Brown was moved to centre half to replace him with Walter coming in at right half. It was not his regular position but in those days the centre half was considered such a key position that a chance could not be taken with an inexperienced youngster.

When he arrived at the Leeds ground with the team on Saturday he was handed a Post Office Greetings Telegram. It read: *'Winterbottom. Manchester United Football Club. c/o Leeds United Football Club, Elland Road, Leeds. Hearty congratulations. Best wishes for success today and others to follow. Royton Amateurs.'* It was a gesture of friendship from his former amateur team mates that touched him deeply, and he kept the telegram amongst his mementos.

Walter Winterbottom made his Manchester United debut on 28 November 1936 at the age of 22. As he ran out onto the pitch at Elland Road he was very nervous (as indeed he was before every game, particularly when playing against international players such as Matthews, Carter, Steele, Drake, Bastin and Glover), but this sharpened his wits and added urgency to his play. The fact that United were bottom of the League with only ten points created more pressure. Also making his United debut that day was Tommy Breen, a young Scottish international goalkeeper, who was to play brilliantly that season. The game kicked off before a crowd of 15,000 in bright sunshine. Those arriving late missed the sensational start with Leeds scoring in the very first minute of the game through Stephenson. United fought back but continued to miss chances in front of goal as they had in previous games. With both teams desperate for points it was a physical match which was unlikely to produce classic football. United pressed hard in the second half, but just as they looked like opening their account, Leeds went further ahead in the 80th minute with a goal from Thompson. United reduced the arrears in the 86th minute with a goal from Bryant but it was not enough. Walter trudged off the pitch feeling disappointed. Every player hopes to be on the winning side on his debut, but although the team had lost 2-1, the feeling was that they had played well enough to earn a point.

The match report in the *Manchester Evening News* noted that 'even at this early stage of the game one gained a good impression of the play of Winterbottom. He tackled and distributed coolly.' The article concluded, however, with the observation that 'Winterbottom seemed to tire in the second half after opening quite promisingly.' For a part-time professional playing his first game in the First Division that was to be expected – at least he'd made his mark.

Walter kept his place in the team, and a home defeat to Birmingham City was followed by a visit to Middlesbrough. It was a bitterly cold December afternoon in the north east and the snow was falling when United ran out onto the bone-hard pitch. Fenton scored a hat-trick for Middlesbrough, but United had their chances, two of which fell to Walter – once when he cleverly went past Stuart but pulled his shot wide of the far post and again going up for a corner when his powerful header was only inches too high. A hotly disputed penalty claim by United was refused by the referee and although Manley got one goal back to make it 3-2 it was too little too late. It was to be the story of United's season, missed chances by the forwards and perhaps more than their share of bad luck.

The following Saturday, at home to West Bromwich Albion, the team halted a sequence of defeats with a hard fought 2-2 draw that gave the crowd something to cheer about. This was only Walter's second match at Old Trafford, still playing at right half, but he was already receiving accolades. Writing In the *Manchester Evening Chronicle* the columnist 'Casual' proclaimed Walter's arrival as a United player, headlining his match report with the rather complimentary 'WINTERBOTTOM STAR': 'Winterbottom was doing great work for United and once forced his way through the defence, but his shot struck a defender to be cleared... Winterbottom was playing a fine game and particularly as an attacking half back... the free kick dropped to the far side of the goal. Winterbottom headed it back for Mutch to scoop it into the net for United's equalizer.'

With Vose still injured Walter was moved to centre half for the next three games. United had a splendid 4-0 away win at Bolton Wanderers. For once the forwards were on song with McKay, who was moved from left half to inside left, scoring two, and two more coming from Bryant. Bert Whalley, a local lad like Walter who had just been promoted from the reserves, came in at left half (Whalley later became assistant coach to Matt Busby when the war ended and tragically died in the Munich air disaster). Walter came in for praise in the *Manchester Evening Chronicle* which once again lauded his discipline at the back: 'Manchester's chief strength lay at half-back, where they appear to have found an excellent player in schoolmaster Winterbottom. He practically blotted out Milsom, as he had done on Christmas Day, and he was nearly always on the spot to save his full-backs when required.'

Walter's success at centre half was creating a selection dilemma. 'VOSE SETS A NEW PROBLEM' was the headline by 'Casual' in a *Manchester Evening Chronicle* article.

The success of Winterbottom has placed the club in a bit of a quandary. Few of us would have predicted that Vose would experience any difficulty in getting his place back again when fit and well. But Winterbottom has been so good that it would be unfair to the player to remove him. Up to last Monday's game at Bolton he has played seven times this season in the senior team, the last three at centre half-back. Although opposed twice to Milsom (Bolton) and Clayton (Wolverhampton), he kept them from scoring. His record while at right half-back also reads well. In four games in that position only one inside left (Stephenson of Leeds United) had scored against United. Even so, I consider him to be a better centre half-back than wing half. Now United's trouble seems to be where to play Vose.

On the back of the good away win against Bolton, morale was high for the visit from Sunderland and United were rewarded with a splendid 2-1 win. The match report in the *Daily Dispatch* stressed the influence of Whalley and Winterbottom: 'Perhaps more than anything else however, the dominance of United's half-backs was the principal feature. Winterbottom blotted Gurney out of the game, as a scorer at any event, and Carter held no terrors, for Whalley improves with every match.' (Carter was, of course, the brilliant inside forward Raich Carter, whose England career was cut short by the war).

The last game of the successful Christmas revival was at home to Derby County on 2 January, when Derby forced a 2-2 draw. Jack Rowley, who had replaced Bamford at centre forward, and who was to become a United star of the future, scored both goals, and McKay excelled again. The crowd was mesmerized by the brilliance of Duncan, Derby's Scottish international forward but it was Walter who impressed the United supporters – the crowd applauded him several times for his smart work in defence, pulling United out of dangerous situations. Archie Ledbrooke of the *Daily Dispatch* (then the north's leading morning newspaper) went as far as to headline his report with a glowing accolade:

WINTERBOTTOM THE FIND OF A LIFETIME
The whole style of United has been changed by Winterbottom, an intelligent player, who on Saturday stood on the field to be compared to the great Barker (Derby). In defence Winterbottom was the sounder but most remarkable was that the youngster beat Barker at his own game of flashing the ball out to the wings. Football is a notoriously deceptive game and swans often turn out to be geese, but this Winterbottom appears to me to be the find of a lifetime.

There was tremendous interest throughout Manchester for the next game, the local derby clash against Manchester City at Maine Road, which was expected to draw a crowd of 60,000. United had already beaten City 3-2 at home earlier in the season and were eager to continue their revival and complete the double. Prior to the game, there was inevitable press speculation on the team selection, particularly as three key players, Breen, Bamford and Bryant were injured and doubtful for this crucial match. Vose was fit again and the question was where to play him? 'Casual's' view was that Winterbottom, regarded as the season's best discovery, could not be moved from centre half. Although many felt Vose was equally good at right half, Brown was in his best form in this position. The *Manchester Evening News* columnist, 'The Captain' agreed and concluded that Vose's return to fitness was a problem, but that Winterbottom had been playing so well that it might have an unsettling effect on the half-back line if he were dropped.

In the event the Manchester United line-up was: Breen, Redwood, Roughton, Brown Winterbottom, Whalley, Mutch, Vose, Rowley, McKay, Lang. To everyone's surprise Vose came into the team at inside right. A huge crowd of 62,895 (just below the record for a United match at Maine Road, which was 63,000 in 1930) packed the terraces to see City win 1-0 with a goal from Herd. Playing in goal for City was 'big' Frank Swift who, after the war, was an England player when Walter became the England team manager. A local derby in front of such a large crowd produced an electric cup tie atmosphere. It wasn't classic football but it was a hard fought game, which City edged because they had better forwards and the genius of Doherty in midfield. The experiment of playing Vose in the forwards was widely criticised by the press and during the game he was moved to the right wing but was even more ineffective there.

Despite the big occasion, United's young players showed fewer nerves than their more experienced colleagues. The Manchester football writer Don Whitson reported: 'Curiously enough it was the youngsters of the losing side who claimed the lion's share of the individual honours. Winterbottom, United's clever young centre half, again justified his choice, even with Vose available, and there was no more effectively busy man in the field than young Whalley, who helped in checking the adroit moves of Toseland and Herd.' He continued, 'Except for a few typical Tilson flashes after the interval, schoolmaster Winterbottom ruled the City leader with a rod of iron. Had he faltered I think City would have won by a greater margin, but

Winterbottom's tackling and anticipation made him the outstanding man of his side.'

The 'Captain' in his 'Sporting Gossip' column in the *Manchester Evening News* returned to the issue of what to do with Vose following the disastrous experiment of playing him in attack and underlined the impact which Walter had made in his first season. 'Vose was good enough to play in an international trial last season as a defensive centre half-back, but he cannot now hope to displace Winterbottom, who, in a few matches, has made himself one of the most talked about centre half-backs in the game. I expect to see Vose tried out as a right half in the near future. Winterbottom, playing a firm, sound, and scrupulously clean game, was the star of United's defence against City... United's defence is re-established on sound lines. It should be good enough as it is reorganised to carry the club to safety but the attacks sadly needs attention.'

Scott Duncan, the United manager, interviewed in the *Manchester Evening News* (and photographed with his bowler hat and stiff wing collar and tie), reassured supporters after the defeat at Manchester City. 'There's no panic at Old Trafford!' he said, before going on to explain that the long spell of disappointment had been due to injuries, bad luck with too many shots hitting the woodwork, and forwards who were lacking confidence and becoming shot shy. On the credit side he pointed out the success of the young players he had brought in at no cost this season, in particular Walter Winterbottom and Bert Whalley.

The FA Cup failed to provide immediate good cheer for supporters. An unconvincing 1-0 home win against third division Reading in the third round was followed by an away draw to Arsenal. Highbury was covered with a thin layer of hard snow and a white mantle of fog descended over London, making it impossible to see the stands on the other side of the field. But the goalposts were visible from the centre of the field and the referee decreed that the game could be played. Arsenal managed the conditions far better than United and waltzed to a 5-0 victory. Their line-up included such famous names as Male, Compton, Bastin, Copping, the great Alex James and Ted Drake. The only satisfaction that Walter could take from the game was that he had marked the formidable Ted Drake and could at least say that he had stopped him from scoring.

But then United showed true fighting spirit by going back to Arsenal for a league match and surprising the 40,000 crowd at Highbury with a display of speed, skill and endurance, which brought them a 1-1 draw. It made a mockery of their 5-0 defeat in the FA Cup two weeks before. Because of injury to Roughton, Walter went to full-back and Vose came back into the side at centre half. The national press commented that Winterbottom, moved to left full-back in an emergency, strengthened the impression that he was not only consistent but extremely versatile.

Stanley Matthews was in the Stoke side when they visited Old Trafford. He played at inside left and Walter, who had been playing at right half was moved back to centre half. 'Freddie Steele strained a thigh muscle and went on the wing, Westland leading the attack, with Matthews taking his place,' reported Don Whitson. 'The scheming of Matthews was the highlight of the second half: no other forward could match him in ball control and ability to draw an opponent. But, try as he would, he could not get Westland past the heroic Winterbottom.' Walter himself later recalled how terrified he was: 'I stood off so as not to make the mistake of committing myself, and fortunately we managed to control him.' United won 2-1 but the final whistle must have come as a welcome relief to the Manchester United supporters. Continues Don Whitson: 'In the closing minutes it was a case of desperate defense against some thrilling swerving dashes by Matthews and the wing sparkle of Johnson. These two cast a spell over Griffiths, and only magnificent work by Winterbottom and Roughton robbed Stoke of a point that their superior football technique so thoroughly deserved.'

United picked up both points in a 2-1 win at home to Everton and

Walter, who was marking the legendary Dixie Dean, kept him from scoring. At last United were off the bottom and now only one point from safety. The following day (during the Easter fixture schedule) United were away to Liverpool. They were also desperate for points to avoid relegation and had been beaten 5-0 at home by Manchester City the previous day. On the way to Anfield from the station, the United coach passed six weddings and the players hoped this was a good omen – six goals perhaps? It wasn't to be. United gave away a silly goal after 23 minutes and with almost the last kick of the game, Liverpool scored in a goalmouth scramble giving them a priceless 2-0 victory. It was bitterly disappointing for the team and on top of that Walter was taken off injured in the second half. He played no further part in the remaining five games of the season.

United were relegated and he, like all the players, felt a deep sense of disappointment. But playing for Manchester United had been an incredibly exciting experience. He had displaced George Vose, the regular first team centre half who was in line for international honours. The impact he had made in his first season playing professional football was far greater than he could have reasonably expected. He had held down his first-team place in 21 consecutive first division games and two FA Cup ties. His versatility had been acknowledged by fine performances as an attacking right half and as a left back, as well as his natural position as centre half. He had received widespread acclaim from the press and from his manager. Indeed, the national press were already suggesting Stan Cullis and Walter Winterbottom as possible choices as centre half for England.

But playing for Manchester United then did not mean what it does today. Players were often local and part of the community in a way that is impossible in today's era of multi-million pound celebrities earning £200,000 a week. The car park was not full of luxury cars; players came to Old Trafford by bus or tram or bicycle; the dressing room had benches and pegs for their clothes and a large communal bath; and at half time they drank tea from a large enamel jug. After a home game Walter would catch the tram from Old Trafford to his parents terraced home in Oldham. It was not an unusual experience for the public to meet players in the street or on a tram. It gave them a personal connection with the team they supported. There were no television celebrities and fans followed football from newspapers. A mark of fame was to be included on the cigarette cards which were so popular before the war. Walter never appeared on cigarette cards and his full page photograph in *Topical Times*, a football magazine, is one of the few pictorial records of his playing days with Manchester United.

He had been nervous and exhilarated by the experience of playing in front of large crowds – 48,000 at Old Trafford, 62,000 at Maine Road – in grounds which were predominantly open terracing (at Old Trafford just one side of the ground had a covered stand with seats). Football was almost entirely a working man's sport and spectators stood packed together, shoulder to shoulder, meeting the same group of friends each week, creating a unique male affinity. They were exposed to the elements: rain, snow and fog, and came dressed in long drab raincoats, scarves and flat caps. In a decade of depression and hardship in the north of England, and the grind of hard labour in mills and factories, football was often their only escape, and they were passionate and knowledgeable about it.

The pitches were as rudimentary as the stadia. There was no drainage or under-soil heating, and the pitch was used for training every day. The grass soon disappeared from most of the pitch except the wings, and the mud created a heavy playing surface. In the harsh winters, frost and ice combined to break up the ground. The lace up leather ball, with an inflatable bladder, soon became saturated with water, making it heavy to kick and to head. These conditions were far from ideal for good football and often dictated the style of play. Football boots were made of hard leather which had to be softened with a cream called Dubbin and broken in before they were comfortable enough to wear. They laced-up above the ankle and had a hard toe-cap with a leather strap across the instep. Studs were leather and banged in to the sole with nails which sometimes came through to pierce the foot; they also wore down quickly making them sharp and dangerous. Shirts (or jerseys) were made of heavy cotton which became sodden in the rain.

During his first season at Manchester United Walter got to know many famous players. Some like Frank Swift, Stanley Matthews and George Hardwick were England players when he became the first England manager. Others like Matt Busby, Bill Shankly and Stan Cullis became club managers with whom, as the England manager, he had regular contact.

Some things he saw had surprised him. The players rarely saw the manager except on Saturdays and always in his formal suit, collar, tie and bowler hat. 'In my playing days' said Walter, 'it was all player power. Little was done by the manager. He used to sit in his office when we were practicing on the field. The older players would say, "Come on, we've got to do this, and that, and the other. Don't you go wandering up there, Winterbottom, leaving a big gap down here." You know, this sort of thing.'

Scott Duncan's title was 'manager/secretary'. In addition to his main duties of finding players, selecting the team and motivating them, he was involved in the business aspects of managing the club. Work with the players was left to the club trainer, Tom Curry, and this meant building fitness and stamina by running endless laps of the pitch and exercises which had usually been learnt in a military environment. The players trained in thick roll-neck woollen sweaters and shorts (which were called knickers).

Looking back on his playing days at Manchester United Walter recalled, 'There was no tactical awareness, you just played football, and people didn't have much knowledge about how to help each other, how to build a system. I used to ask Billy McKay, a Scottish international wing-half, how it was he could pass through to the wing man, as he used to do, always get it there, and he told me his little trick, but he said , "Keep it to yourself." And people used to hide from passing on information. They felt it wasn't the thing to do. There was a horror about letting other people know things instead of accumulating information, using it for the benefit of the whole team.' Walter saw all these things and he questioned them. His skills as a teacher, the sports science based knowledge he was learning at Carnegie and his experience of playing for Manchester United, led him to believe that there were better ways of doing things.

But there was a cloud on the horizon: a very black cloud. He began to find that he was having pains in his back, which affected him in strange ways. One week he could scarcely walk and the next he would be bouncing with energy. When he played the pain was often worse. The Manchester United club doctor sent him to see a specialist in Leeds, but the manipulation of his hip joints under anaesthetic did not improve the situation. Much later, during the war, this serious disease of the spine was diagnosed as *ankylosing spondylitis*, but at that time no one had any idea what the problem was or how to cure it.

Because of this, his appearances in the first-team became extremely restricted in the following season, 1937/38. He did not play in the first-team until September when he played four first-team games in succession. All seemed fine at first but then the back problem returned and he was confined to a total of seventeen central league games for the reserves. It was frustrating. He battled throughout the 1938/39 season and appeared in 25 central league games, but never felt fit enough for first team football. Like many other professional footballers, before and since, a career with huge potential was snuffed-out by injury almost before it began.

In a newspaper report in the *Daily Mirror* on 10 July, 1939, Walter spoke about his future in football, under the headline 'Honesty is the best policy'. He had been put on the transfer list by Manchester United because his injury was keeping him out of the first-team, but he told the *Mirror* that he was considering taking a season's rest because he felt it was unfair to go to a new club when he was not entirely fit. As far as he was concerned, if he was approached by another club he would refuse to go. He explained that he was physically fit and often felt on top of the world, but at other times he felt the 'rheumatic' attacks pretty badly. 'Next month,' he confided, 'I'm to have a trial at Old Trafford, and if I'm fit, I'll take up football again. But to me it doesn't seem fair that a club should sign me if I cannot give proper service. I'd sooner give up football entirely than not give of my best to the club.' His attitude was typical of the sense of integrity and fair play which characterised the code of conduct by which he led his life.

Walter never talked about his time playing with Manchester United, not because he wasn't proud of it, but because he was by nature modest, and did not feel that talking about his achievements would serve any purpose. He never kept a scrapbook, but press cuttings of the games he had played in were found folded in a brown envelope. It is not known whether it was Walter or his father who had collected them. Perhaps the main reason he never talked about his time as a United player was that as the England manager he remained entirely neutral, whichever club he was watching. Nevertheless, although he said nothing, he was privately hurt when Bobby Charlton once remarked, 'You didn't use to play for United did you Walter?' His natural reticence to talk about his playing career also explains why so many journalists and writers were unaware of it, and those that did had only the sketchiest idea of his outstanding potential in one brief season.

The only time he talked publicly about playing for Manchester United was much later in his life when he was interviewed by Ivan Ponting for an article in the United match day programme (30 November 1996, United v Leicester City). In one of a series titled 'Whatever happened to...' Ponting asked Walter what sort of player he was. Walter recalled modestly 'Oh, I could tackle and I wasn't bad in the air and I liked to get forward...' Ponting pointed out that

Winterbottom was renowned for his positional astuteness, and there was a time, after he had excelled for only a few months, when he was mentioned as a possible future international. When pressed on this Walter admitted with typical modesty, 'yes, there was some talk about myself and Stan Cullis being looked at. Stan went on and I didn't.' Pontin expanded on Walter's career and concluded, 'it is well nigh impossible to exaggerate the contribution of Sir Walter Winterbottom to the post-war development of English football.'

CHAPTER 6

LOVE AND WAR

1939 – 1945

Football was the last thing on Walter's mind at 11:15 am on 3 September 1939, as he gathered round the radio with friends and heard Neville Chamberlain's fateful words: '... I have to tell you now that no such undertaking has been received and that consequently this country is at war with Germany.' Carnegie College closed. The Football League programme was cancelled. Walter immediately volunteered to serve in the Royal Air Force and was selected for officers training in the Physical Training (PT) branch.

Football suddenly seemed an irrelevance and throughout the country professional footballers joined the war effort with the encouragement and support of their clubs. The entire Bolton Wanderers team signed up for the army, while many of the Arsenal players joined the RAF, including Ted Drake, Eddie Hapgood, Lesley Jones, Bernard Joy, Andy Kerchin, Laurie Scott and George Swindin. Leslie Jack was later killed returning to base in his Spitfire. The Arsenal trainer, Tom Whittaker, who later became the manager, became a squadron leader and was awarded the MBE on D-Day.

Tom Finney joined the army and became one of Lord Montgomery of Alamein's favourite players. Finney had driven a lightly armoured Honey tank through Italy and when enquiring about Finney after the war, 'Monty,' – who had a keen interest in football and was the honorary Chairman of Portsmouth FC – would often ask Walter, 'how is my soldier boy Finney doing?'

Although many players wanted to join fighting units they were often seen as more valuable in other capacities. Stanley Rous was asked to recommend coaches and players for training at Aldershot prior to being passed out as Sergeant Instructors (Army Physical Training Core). These included such famous players as Joe Mercer, Cliff Britton, Tommy Lawton, Matt Busby and Stan Cullis. Stanley Rous, who had seen action in the First World War, had immediately re-joined the army himself and been given the rank of lieutenant in the Royal Artillery but was persuaded by Lord Wigram that he would be of far greater use to the country if he was to stay to help raise funds and organize the many sporting activities which would be essential to maintaining civilian morale. He arranged for Rous to see General Auchinleck who readily agreed for Rous to be released and become a member of Lord Wigrams committee, where he made an enormous contribution to fund raising, particularly for the Red Cross, by arranging special events in every imaginable sport, even darts!

From the outset of war, physical training and fitness were seen as an important part of the war effort. The government also began to appreciate the need for recreation to continue as normally as possible. The initial total ban on all football lasted only a few days and friendly matches were soon aranged. For the first six months the number of spectators was limited to 15,000 but was later extended. In a country reeling from the Dunkirk evacuation and the blitz, football matches became an important way of seeking some normality of life. By September 1940 even playing football on Sunday was sanctioned for industrial workers. Churchill himself encouraged watching and playing football as a boost for the nation's morale.

Walter had made a strong impression on Stanley Rous when he visited Carnegie, and it was probably Rous, already a man of wide ranging influence, who had suggested to the RAF that Walter would be an asset to them in organizing physical training courses. Within days he was kitted out in an officer's uniform and becoming used to the strange experience of walking down the street saluting service men and women on his way to RAF station Uxbridge. After a month's training he was posted to RAF station Sealand, near Chester, a flight training station and maintenance unit.

But when he arrived at Sealand he was curtly told that he would not be organising any fitness training. Instead he was to assist the adjutant in helping with station administration. It soon became clear that this was the decision of Wing Commander Crampton, who as second in command of the station, had consulted with group command, pleading that the station was in desperate need of office administration staff.

Wartime experience in the RAF pitched Walter into a different world, but one which he would learn much from – a world where men of all ranks worked together with a common purpose. And for a young man mixing with trainee fighter pilots during war-time, there was a strange but exhilarating sense of danger and excitement. Exposure to military discipline was new and sometimes bewildering. Men's reactions to what seemed ridiculous disciplinary measures were often hilarious. It taught him much about the misuse of discipline, as his memories of his early days at RAF Sealand, and in particular the dreaded Crampton, revealed.

'Wing Commander Crampton was detested by everyone,' he recalled, 'especially by aircrew undergoing flying training, some of whom were young high-spirited recruits from Australia. Petrol was rationed and in very short supply, and Crampton suggested that some of these young daredevils had been filling up their cars with aircraft fuel. He instigated an inspection of all cars on the station and to his astonishment the only cars found to contain aircraft fuel were his own and that of the much disliked protestant chaplain.'

The whole station was in uproar at this news, but Crampton took his revenge on the motor-vehicle section sergeant by blocking his promotion. Soon afterwards, when Walter was moved to the Air Ministry, the sergeant concerned telephoned Walter to appeal for help. He told the full story to the air commodore in charge of postings, who was sympathetic and had the sergeant posted away from Sealand, and even better, with a promotion to flight sergeant. Walter quickly learned that knowing the right people was how things got done!

The Irish group captain in command of the station believed in the maxim that the punishment should fit the crime, but this was often taken to spiteful extremes. On one occasion a young pilot officer under training burst one of the tyres on his aircraft when landing. He taxied along the tarmac and back to the hangar but consequently the aluminium rim of the wheel was ground down. The poor fellow was punished by being made to return to the hangar each night to file down the rest of the wheel to the same level.

The same station commander also cruelly punished a warrant officer responsible for gas mask drill. When a siren went off, everyone had to put on their gas mask and continue to go about their duties. The warrant officer was responsible for seeing that everyone fulfilled this drill. Unfortunately he assumed that he was not required to put on his own mask as he walked about the station checking that everyone had theirs on. When the group captain heard of this he ordered the warrant officer to be stripped and doused with disinfectant!

One of the duties which Walter had been assigned to was station defense officer – RAF stations were issued with weapons and hand grenades in the event of German parachute attacks. Walter had to supervise the weapons training of all personnel. Each day for months he took squads of ordinary aircraftsman to the Chester army barracks to learn how to shoot guns and throw hand grenades. The shooting range for long-distance firing looked across a valley where sheep grazed. It did not take long before some 'erk' (accidentally or deliberately) shot one of the ewes. By an amazing coincidence, two days later lamb was served for lunch in the officers' mess!

He remembered one occasion when a real alert was sounded and he ran to take up his position on top of the control tower. From this vantage point he was horrified to see a large group of men with fixed bayonets charging around the corner of a hangar: charging in the opposite direction was another group similarly armed. They met at the corner and fortunately only minor injuries were sustained. This was not Walter's forte and he was relieved to be released from these duties when RAF defence personnel were attached to the station.

The station commander, realising that Walter excelled at mathematics, put him in charge of a team of officers responsible for decoding messages received from group command. The team operated on a 24-hour rota system, and one night when Walter was in charge, he received a phone call from an angry admiral in Liverpool telling him that the port of Liverpool was being bombed by the Huns, and demanding that RAF Sealand pilots should scramble and attack the German bombers. Walter politely explained that Sealand was a training station, but the admiral was far from satisfied. Walter reported the incident and the following night a brave young wing commander in charge of fighter pilot training took off with a select group of trainee pilots and successfully shot down two raiding German bombers. Although this exploit was against orders, it created such a swell of popular approval that the wing commander received a commendation from Fighter Command.

Understanding that young pilots needed to relax during their leisure time, Walter suggested to the group captain that he be given permission to organise a coach party to go to the Grand National at Aintree. This was well-received in the officers' mess and so Walter also ran a sweepstake. Unfortunately he was compelled to work on the day of the race so he was unable to go and had no idea of the result. Later that afternoon he received a phone call from the officers' mess.

'You lucky beggar! You had the winner.'

By the time he had finished his duty and gone to the mess the officers were already having free drinks on his winnings, but there was plenty of money left for him to take three of his friends to a dinner dance at the Grosvenor Hotel in Chester. They enjoyed a rare carefree evening of dinner, drinking and dancing and in the early hours of the morning drove back to Sealand in an open sports car singing bawdy songs. Back at Sealand they bribed the sentry guard to let them in without putting them on report. 'It was' Walter fondly remembered, 'such a memorable day!'

Walter wondered if someone behind the scenes was pulling strings for him again, because after six months at Sealand he was posted to the Physical Training and Drill School at RAF Cosford, a large unit of Technical Training Command. Here at last he could do the work he had been trained for. Wing Commander Crampton did his utmost to stop this move but was unable to block it. The new posting came with a promotion from pilot officer to flight lieutenant and two stripes on each sleeve.

Society in England began to change between the two world wars. The middle classes had grown from 20 to 30 per cent of the population. One in ten now owned a car! With the advent of the Second World War, the breaking down of social and class divisions accelerated. RAF Cosford, a very large station, reflected this, with officers from a wide range of social backgrounds who worked and played together. It was an environment that helped Walter to move comfortably among all levels of society later in life, although in the early years, assimilation was not always easy for a working class lad from Oldham.

On his first evening in the lounge of the officers' mess, a fellow flight lieutenant introduced himself and asked Walter if he would like a game of billiards. Although his experience was limited to a few games at the Manchester United ground after training, he was pleased to accept the invitation. He discovered that his friend's name was Charles Turberville-Smith and that he was a member of the aristocracy whose parents had a large country estate nearby.

Some weeks later Walter and several other eligible bachelor officers were invited to attend a hunt ball at Charles' parents stately home. They filed into the ballroom to face a line of young debutantes, all of whom were chaperoned by their mothers. The young officers made an unseemly dash to dance with the most attractive girls, so when Walter crossed the floor there was only one debutante left. She was a charming girl called Louise, only 18-years-old and watched over keenly by her mother, who had the appearance of the duchess in Alice in Wonderland. Louise turned out to be a very good dancer, as was Walter, and they enjoyed each other's company, spending the entire evening together. Later he realised that this was not the correct code of conduct for a debutante. The following day he received a phone call from Louise's mother. At first he was rather encouraged when she invited him to lunch with the family and play squash against an army captain billeted with them. He had already seen the ballroom so he was hardly surprised that the mansion had its own squash court and felt confident because he was a good squash player.

Stepping out of the RAF car that had delivered him outside the ornate iron entry gates he was overawed by the country estate which he had previously only seen at night. Entering through a small side gate he gazed up a steep slope covered in pine trees. In the distance he could see smoke winding up from the tall chimneys of the mansion. The snow lay a foot deep, crisp and untouched, and as he trudged through the snow the silence was abruptly broken by the barking of dogs as two large mastiff hounds appeared over a crest, bounding towards him. A commanding male voice called them off and a man appeared, introducing himself as Lord Turberville-Smith.

He explained that he was Louise's father and escorted Walter to his magnificent stately home.

Once inside Walter was introduced to a gathering of waiting relatives and offered sherry by the footman. He was disappointed to find that Louise was not there and her mother explained that her daughter had gone back to finishing school in Scotland. Slowly it dawned on Walter that he was being examined to see if he had a suitable background to be cultivated as a suitor. They went through to lunch in the chandeliered dining room and the growing realisation of why he was there made the lunch ever more humiliating as he fielded questions about his family and education. Only Lady Turberville-Smith herself seemed somewhat sympathetic to his predicament. To complete his misery, and symbolically enforce the superiority of the upper classes, the captain thrashed him at squash after lunch. He was only somewhat comforted the next day when Lady Turberville-Smith telephoned to say that she would like to apologise if the family had caused him embarrassment, but explained as tactfully as she could in her plummy upper-class accent that 'this is how the aristocracy do things!'

He was on more familiar ground back at RAF Cosford where he was now the chief PT instructor with a heavy work load. The unit was training 600 selected recruits every six weeks. On completing the course they were given the rank of corporal and sent to train personnel in drill and PT at RAF stations throughout the world. Walter found it frustrating that despite their qualification, many were wrongfully employed, although they were at least able to arrange team games and individual recreation activities for aircrew at fighter and bomber stations.

Some long-term friendships were made but not everyone enjoyed the Winterbottom fitness regime. It was at Cosford that he met Wing Commander Kenneth Robson who was in charge of the medical division of the hospital. Ken Robson subsequently became a very close friend and godfather to Walter's son, Alan. After the war Dr.

Robson became an eminent Harley Street specialist and was elected as president of the Royal College of Physicians. Years later, speaking at a conference (attended by Walter) he recalled: 'From time to time to in the war years, PT for officers reared its head, with bursts of strict application as a new commanding officer took over. While he was with us [at Cosford] it fell to Winterbottom to have us all in the car park at 7 o'clock in the morning doing press ups and jumping about - sometimes somebody fainted – and several times he called me up to be the team leader at tunnel ball.'

Dr. Robson may not have appreciated Walter's attempts to convince him of the benefits of physical fitness but he was an enthusiastic supporter of Wolverhampton Wanderers, and after the war Walter was able to introduce him to the club's directors and their manager Stan Cullis, with whom he became good friends.

In February 1941 Walter was promoted to the rank of squadron leader and posted to the Air Ministry in London where he could play a far more significant role in ensuring the fitness of the RAF fighting machine. Initially he worked under Wing Commander Daly, with responsibility for the development and organisation of physical fitness throughout the Royal Air Force. Fitness and training programmes were developed, an organization to train hundreds of PT instructors was created and training courses were designed for specialist techniques like parachute landings. Some of the officers in the PT branch were well-known sporting personalities. One of these was Squadron Leader Dan Maskell, the tennis coach, who was responsible for the rehabilitation of wounded RAF aircrew at Loughborough College. They remained friends and swapped coaching experiences in later years.

One of the most unusual assignments which Walter was asked to undertake was to advise the surgeon, Archibald McIndoe on physical rehabilitation. McIndoe achieved international fame during World War Two for his pioneering work with plastic surgery on Battle of Britain fighter pilots. The young men who survived the inevitable fire after a crash came to him with horrific burns. He developed experimental and pioneering techniques for dealing with very deep burns and serious facial disfigurement like the loss of eyelids. His patients became known as the 'Guinea Pigs.' McIndoe was a brilliant surgeon, but he also recognised the importance of the rehabilitation of casualties, and particularly for their social integration into normal life.

The surgeon asked Walter to provide a physical training rehabilitation programme as part of the treatment. Walter found McIndoe's theories fascinating (he was always interested in new ideas, and was an admirer of Dr. Edward De Bono, the originator of lateral thinking). On one occasion McIndoe told him that he encouraged women from the local community to come into the hospital to meet the patients (his 'boys' as he called them) and when they were well enough, to invite them into their homes. This much is a matter of record, but he went on to tell Walter that he sometimes asked women, some of whom were married, to sleep with the patients to help to restore their self-esteem. Walter later said that he was deeply moved that these women would do whatever McIndoe asked if it would help the boys who had offered their lives in fighting to save their country.

Walter had to find accommodation in London and The Air Ministry suggested that he consult Balloon Command in Stanmore, Middlesex. They gave him the addresses of several private homes which could provide lodgings for RAF personnel, and one of these was at 14 Holland Walk, Stanmore, the home of Mrs. Hilda Morris and her family. Walter was impressed by the homeliness of the house and the friendliness of the family, and readily agreed terms for the lodging.

Stanmore was a pleasant residential area on the outskirts of London. It had avoided the worst of the blitz in 1940/41 which devastated parts of central London, but its proximity to the headquarters of Fighter Command and Balloon Command meant that the area was regularly bombed by the Luftwaffe, mostly by a scattering of small firebombs which created panic in residential areas. One large bomb fell on Stanmore Common, close behind Holland Walk, and carved out a massive crater. Each neighbourhood formed a fire watching party and every household that could took turns to keep watch all night and be ready to alert others should a firebomb fall. A bucket of water and a stirrup pump were kept in readiness at the front gate. When the air raid sirens sounded everyone was called into action. There was even fear of gas attacks and everyone was issued with gas masks, including babies. The masks were kept in a canvas bag slung over the shoulder and carried throughout the day.

Walter fitted into his new lodgings easily enough and got on well with his landlady. Her second husband, Flight Lieutenant Reginald Morris, had been posted overseas in Israel, and she was working as a secretary. Her daughter, Ann, had left school and began work as a junior administrator in the local council offices. From the beginning Ann was attracted to this good-looking and worldly-wise officer, ten years her senior, who had come to live in her mother's house. Being young and inexperienced she had not imagined that her feelings could be reciprocated, but they were. There was little chance of a conventional courtship during wartime; he would come home from work late and sometimes they would play cards or have friends around. Occasionally they went to the cinema, often walking back because there was no late bus. Although they lived in the same house, there were few opportunities to be alone and she saw very little of their handsome lodger. The couple did not even go dancing until after they were engaged, when they went to Blackpool to meet Walter's sister Fanny and dance in the Tower Ballroom – that magical place that so entranced the young boy who had gazed longingly at the dancers as a child.

Walter's work was all consuming. He had been promoted to wing commander and was now Head of Physical Training for the Royal Air Force. He worked seven days a week at the Air Ministry and there were no holidays. Sometimes he worked throughout the night as part of a roster requiring staff to keep a watch over their building, looking out for German bombers and later on the V1 and V2 ballistic missiles (commonly known as 'doodlebugs'). Walter usually chose the Saturday night duty. Early the following morning he was in the habit of going to his club, the RAC in Pall Mall, to swim and then have breakfast. There was usually no one else about at such an early hour and he enjoyed the rare moment of calm and relaxation whilst swimming. One Sunday morning he saw a man with a large white beard swimming leisurely lengths of breaststroke. Because of his distinctive beard he recognised the man as George Bernard Shaw, the Irish playwright. Later, in the Roman style changing area, Shaw asked him for help in operating the weighing machine, and they got to know each other. Shaw, who lived in private rooms in a hotel in Whitehall, walked to the club regularly on Sunday mornings and they came to enjoy swimming and chatting together when there was no one else around. They talked at length about the war but never discussed Shaw's writing, or indeed football. Walter found him to be a most genial man, quite belying his stern and scholarly appearance.

With Walter so preoccupied, Ann, believing that a budding romance was going nowhere, volunteered for the Women's Auxiliary Air Force (WAAF), where many women were playing a vital role in key jobs normally done by men, and after initial training she was posted to RAF Ruislip. Also posted there were Eddie Hapgood and George Male, the Arsenal full backs who were now military policeman. Walter was playing as a guest for Chelsea at the time and when they checked Ann in and out of the camp they used to tease her that they would give Walter 'a good kicking' on the forthcoming Chelsea v Arsenal Boxing Day fixture, which was known as 'the battle of the roses.'

Walter was rather taken aback by Ann's decision to join the WAAF and confided in his long-standing friend, Bill Pawley, who he had met at Chester College. Bill told Walter that this was a 'special girl', not one of his 'love 'em and leave 'em girls' and urged his friend to make a move. 'Faint heart never won fair lady' Bill chided, and encouraged Walter to propose marriage before Ann was posted further away.

Ann's grandfather, Alfred Cousins, came from a seafaring family. He was a seaman who worked on the CS Faraday, a large iron steamship, custom designed and built for cable laying for the Siemens Company. The vessel, which was built in Newcastle in 1874, laid the first telephone cables across the Atlantic. When Alfred retired from the sea he bought a pub in Peckham. He was a widower when he met Ann's grandmother, and 25 years older than her, but they brought up his own children and then they had four of their own.

The youngest was Hilda and she became a secretary to a wealthy industrialist, Mr Nelson Richards, a chemist who had a substantial interest in the US Colgate Company and investments on Wall Street. He fell in love with his young secretary and when Hilda became pregnant with Ann at the age of 23, Nelson divorced his wife and married Hilda. For a while Hilda enjoyed the life of a lady in London, with a townhouse, a carriage and a governess for Ann and her two brothers. But Nelson lost his fortune in the Wall Street crash and the great depression of the 1930s and died soon after. With three children to bring up and little money, Hilda had to work to support her family. Her late husband had influential contacts with Ladbrokes and so she turned to the bookmaker for help and was offered a position as secretary to one of the directors. Although she later married again she was never able to regain the social position or prestige she had once enjoyed. But she was fortunate in that her husband had provided for their children's education and Ann was privately educated, growing up to be a refined, well-educated and well spoken young lady, but from a family that was down on their luck.

Walter realised that if he was intending to marry Ann he should take her to Oldham to meet his parents. Oldham came as something of a shock to her after the leafy suburbs of Stanmore but she liked

James and Fanny and they took to her. Outwardly James appeared full of fun but Ann could see that he was the backbone of the family; he talked with a broad Lancashire accent which she thought that he probably exaggerated to tease her, asking why 'a posh lass like 'er was courtin our Walter'. Later he asked her, 'as he taken y'oop t'th'ights yet?'

She of course had no idea what *'oop t'th'ights'* meant but when she asked Walter he explained that James meant 'up to the heights,' a local landmark. They climbed up the hill to the top of 'the heights,' sat eating an apple and counted the eighty mill chimneys spread out below them. And it was there that Walter asked her to marry him.

Seeking to impress his new fiancée, Walter decided that the time had come to celebrate in style. He had attended two or three dinner functions with Air Ministry officers at the Cafe Royal in Piccadilly, and was on first name terms with the head waiter. Things began to go wrong during their meal when the diners on the next table argued with the waiter about a wartime restriction limiting them to one bread roll each. The waiter became infuriated and later, serving roast beef from a trolley, he was enraged by an elderly lady who was offensive about the meat. Finally he completely lost his temper, put two hands beneath the silver salver and heaved the dish into the air. Guests everywhere were splattered with meat juice and a big slice of meat landed in the elderly lady's lap, while her high-pitched scream rang through the dining room. Walter's attempt to wow his young fiancée with the luxury of the Cafe Royal ended on a low note.

Ann Richards and Squadron Leader Walter Winterbottom were duly married at St John's Church, Stanmore, on Saturday, 5 December 1942. It was an austere occasion reflecting the hardships of war-time Britain. Petrol had been rationed from the outset, and butter, sugar, bacon, ham and tea soon followed. By 1941 cheese, eggs, milk and then clothing also needed coupons from the closely guarded ration book. Vicars must have been in short supply too because the clergyman was an elderly gentleman who seemed to have a speech impediment. Perhaps it was an early sign of dementia because he gave them the impression that they were being baptized, not married! Because of the clothing rationing there was no bridal gown, but the bride wore a coral coloured angora dress with a black fur jacket, a hat and a spray of peach roses. The bridegroom was wearing his RAF uniform. Bill Pawley was serving with the army overseas and unable to be Walter's best man but another good friend, Bobby Spiers, their next door neighbour, stepped in.

The reception was held at Ann's home, but they allowed themselves the luxury of a chauffeur driven car to take them to their first night together in the Cumberland Hotel, Hyde Park. They had booked a theatre show but when they returned they found that the hotel restaurant was closed so dinner was sandwiches in their bedroom! The next morning they took a train to Bournemouth to spend a short honeymoon in a cottage belonging to Stan Ashton, an officer in the same branch of the RAF as Walter who had taken two weeks leave to travel to his home in Rotherham.

Despite his back pain Walter was a playing as a guest for Chelsea at the time, and as the team had a friendly match against Portsmouth on the following Saturday, and Portsmouth was not far from Bournemouth, he saw no reason not to fit this in with his honeymoon. During the week he trained by running around the area. One night in the blackout he crossed a road bridge and ran alongside the railway line expecting, but failing, to find another bridge to return. He was gone for a long time and when he finally arrived home Ann was in tears – half in fear that she lost had her new husband and half because she had overcooked the precious steak ration which was the first dinner of their married life!

Ann went with him to Portsmouth to watch the match and was invited to sit in the directors' box. The game had no sooner started when the opposing centre forward jumped with Walter for a high ball and their heads collided, resulting in the two players being carried off the field. Walter's poor wife was holding back the tears, but to her relief he soon returned with his head swathed in bandages. This was the first and only time that Ann watched her husband play football. Following their honeymoon, the married couple returned to live with Ann's mother in 'Shelleys,' her home in Holland Walk, Stanmore, and their first child, Janet, was born there in December 1943. It was not an ideal arrangement but during the war housing was almost impossible to find. Three years later, and much to Ann's relief they were finally able to move into their own home, a small new house on an estate in Hayes, Middlesex, where their second daughter, Brenda, was born.

Ann was taken aback when out of the blue one day Walter asked her, 'How would you like to move back to Shelley's?' She was flabbergasted but he went on to explain that the owner was anxious to sell, and as he was the sitting tenant he would be able to purchase the house at a substantial discount to the market price. (Walter had always paid the rent as Hilda had limited means.) It was a pleasant four bedroom detached house in a quiet cul-de-sac and as Walter said to Ann 'it was an opportunity that was too good to miss.' She was still against the idea of moving back in with her mother but in an amicable family discussion Hilda said that she would like to move to a small flat in Battersea. It was a happy stroke of luck and their son, Alan, was born there two years later.

Walter's back pain continued to bother him and was sometimes acute, but it didn't stop him from playing occasional wartime football. He made 22 appearances as a guest player for Chelsea between 1941 and 1943. On 6 June 1942 he played for an FA-eleven against the RAF (which was rather odd as he was in the RAF) and he was disappointed to only be an unused reserve for England in a war time international against Scotland at the Empire Stadium, Wembley, on 10 October 1942.

Walter was in luck when an RAF doctor examined him prior to being discharged in 1945; the doctor took a blood test and diagnosed ankylosing spondylitis – a chronic inflammatory arthritis and autoimmune disease which affects joints of the spine. The disease has a strong genetic association and usually attacks young white males between the age of 20 and 40-years old, and in extreme cases can result in eventual fusion of the spine resulting in complete rigidity. The doctor referred Walter to Professor J.P. Raban at the Middlesex Hospital – a brilliant young radio-therapist who entered the Middlesex in 1922, qualified in 1929 and was attached to the Meyerstein Institute of Radio-Therapy before returning to the Middlesex Hospital in 1945. As a keen sportsman himself he took a particular interest in Walter's condition.

Raban's treatment was made up of three separate months of radio-therapy which treated different section of his spine and made Walter feel very ill. He was continually weak and drank a pint of milk each day to counter the effects of the radio-therapy and the risk of sterility. The treatment was new; there was no guarantee of success and there was danger of toxic damage to bone marrow and subsequent development of cancers. Nowadays physical therapy, exercise, and medicine are at the heart of modern treatment and it's likely that playing a high-impact sport such as football exacerbated Walter's condition.

But some months after the completion of the treatment Walter was running to catch a train and felt a new sensation in his back and instinctively felt an improvement. He was so happy that he just carried on running, then ran around the block again for the joy of it, missed his train, but was sure that the problem had disappeared. When he arrived home he rushed to Ann and exclaimed, 'I am cured!' before breaking down in tears in his wife's arms. Professor Raban, meanwhile, was most excited that his experimental treatment had been successful and frequently asked Walter to come back so that he could demonstrate his 'star patient' to others. Professor John Raban sadly died in 1949 at the young age of 44. Walter owed him a great debt of gratitude; he was completely cured with only the legacy of a slight stoop remaining. at last he was fit to take on the biggest challenge of his life.

CHAPTER 7

THE
MENTOR

After the war ended Carnegie College reopened its doors, but Ernest Major, who had been the warden from its inception, was unable to continue as he had accepted an appointment as HM Inspector of Schools when he was released from the army in August 1945. Walter applied for the position, which seemed to be a natural development of his previous work as a lecturer at Carnegie, and with his experience as Head of Physical Training in the RAF, he felt he was well qualified. He was shortlisted with two other candidates but the position was given to Mr. E. Bouffler, who had been Organiser of Physical Training to the North Riding Education Authority and a former Carnegie student (1935-6). When he heard that Bouffler had been appointed, in June 1946, Walter was disappointed, but as one door closed another one opened.

Stanley Rous had been kept informed of Walter's progress in the RAF and was clearly impressed with his rapid promotions and proven ability as an organiser. He had seen his aptitude for coaching and as Walter was living in London and playing football for Chelsea, he asked him to begin running coaching courses in a few grammar schools in Chelsea and Dagenham. The arrangement simply confirmed what Rous had always thought: that Walter had a natural gift for coaching and teaching men how to coach. When Rous heard about Walter's application to Carnegie he invited him to lunch and told him about a new position he wanted to create at the Football Association, that of 'Director of Coaching'. Walter duly accepted the role and Stanley Rous – ever a man of vision and authority – became Walter's mentor, beginning a friendship and partnership that changed not just The Football Association but English football for good.

Stanley Rous came from the village of Mutford in Suffolk, where his father was a grocer and provision merchant, who also dealt in coal and glass. As a boy he was an enthusiastic if not highly skilled footballer playing in goal for his school team, arguably chosen for that position because he was over six feet tall at the age of 14. Having been introduced to football at school he decided to organise a village football team: 'I was 15 at the time,' he recalled, 'and now marvel at my temerity in calling a meeting in the village school and addressing the assembled farmhands and off-duty fishermen.' A new team was formed, with Rous in goal which played in a league in the Norwich area. He also liked to go to the Norwich City ground (then called the 'Nest') and it was there that he watched his first Football League match and some of the great players of the day, including Charles Fry who played football for Southampton and cricket for England, and England football international Harold Fleming of Swindon. It was watching games at Norwich that drew his attention to the influence that the referee could have in controlling the game, and it was in this direction that his active football career more profitably took him.

As Stanley Rous had decided that he had no interest in his father's business, and his two sisters Hilda and Ruth were teachers, his father suggested that teaching would be a suitable career for his son, and so he attended the teacher training centre in Beccles. In the lunch hours after doing practical teacher training in a local school, he organised football practices. Always one with a good sense of humour he liked to tell the story of a boy he taught there, Arthur Oldham, who became a fish merchant in Lowestoft. 'Mr. Oldham later wrote to me when I became the FA Secretary 'offering to send me a "good fry" fresh from his boat and asking for a Cup Final ticket, adding "I hope you remember me well since you was the best English master what ever taught me."'

World War One interrupted Rous' teacher training. He joined the Army and for the next four years saw service in France and then Egypt, Palestine and Lebanon. He reflected that he was fortunate to escape the privations and the holocaust of the major fronts, and even had the opportunity to try his hand at refereeing football matches in Egypt. When he returned to England after the war he attended St Luke's College Exeter, and it was there that he completed his teaching qualifications and took his first serious steps towards becoming a referee. He quickly progressed through the pyramid of referee exams and leagues.

Whilst Rous was a master at Watford Grammar School, his career as a football referee blossomed and in eight years he became one of English football's most celebrated referees, officiating in 34 international matches and the 1934 Cup Final. One incident in a match between Millwall and Charlton Athletic, an intense local derby, exemplified his sense of humour and quick thinking:

At a crucial point in the game I saw a defender's hand fist the ball away in a goalmouth melee. As I blew the whistle for a penalty the players untangled themselves and looked at me in surprise. It was then I realised it was the goalkeeper, not a full-back, who had punched the ball. I walked on past the penalty spot, past the goal posts, to the edge of the crowd and called at the top of my voice 'If the man with the whistle blows it again I will have him removed.'

Then I restarted the game by dropping the ball and the mistake was retrieved without disaster.

Rous was firm and authoritative. There was a tradition that no one was sent off in an FA Cup Final: referees were loathe to spoil this show case match and players dreaded a lifelong blemish on their record. When Rous refereed the 1934 final between Portsmouth and Manchester City, the Portsmouth right back Mackie was using threatening language to Eric Brook, the Manchester City winger. Rous warned Mackie that he would be sent off if he carried out his threats.

'Sure you'll never send me off at Wembley Mr. Rous,' said the player.

'Try it once more and you will find I will,' Rous replied in a firm and convincing tone. He had no more trouble with the player after that.

The qualities needed to be a top referee like Rous were invaluable in his role as Secretary of the Football Association. A referee has to make instant decisions and make them decisively; to maintain dignity at all times, to face up to abuse, to be reasonable, impartial and above all to be respected for his integrity. Rous had all these qualities.

As a referee Rous had developed many football contacts throughout the county Football Associations, and was himself the Hertfordshire representative at the Football Association. So when he saw an advertisement for the position of Secretary of the Football Association in 1934 (commencing salary £800 and with residence), he decided to apply for the job. On 22 May, a week after refereeing the FA Cup Final, he found himself at 22 Lancaster Gate being interviewed along with five other candidates.

With his limited experience he felt he had little hope of getting the job and so he was relaxed and determined not to be overawed by the elderly and stuffy interviewing board members. Nevertheless he was taken aback when the chairman, Mr. William Pickford, told him 'the

President [Sir Charles Clegg] is deaf and unlikely to hear your answers, but may ask you questions. Direct your replies to me, but don't shout as I have a heart condition and must not be upset.'

Instead of being frustrated he turned the tables by using his ability to lip read – a skill he had learned when teaching games to a deaf and dumb school near Watford – framing his words carefully so that they were intelligible to Sir Charles. (His opportunism may have been a turning point in the interview, because two years later Charles Clegg's sister told Rous that her father had said 'we've appointed a new Secretary today, a nice young fellow who was the only one of the candidates who could converse with me.')

When two months had gone by and he had heard nothing further Rous had written off his chances and had not informed his headmaster of his application. He was therefore distraught to find the headmaster engulfed by a horde of press photographers who were telling him that the school's games master, Stanley Rous, had just been appointed as the FA Secretary. When he recovered his composure the headmaster shook hands with Rous in front of the posse of photographers. Rous was able to explain the unfortunate circumstances, apologised, and they parted the best of friends.

After he left Watford Grammar School, the *Fullerian*, the school magazine, published a tribute to Stanley Rous which provided an insight into his character that is rather different from the autocratic image which the press has sometimes attributed to him. 'Men may come and men may go, and even schoolmasters must go when the fates decree. Mr. Rous became a master at Watford in September 1921 and his position amongst us was so peculiarly his own that it is difficult to think of living our ordinary lives in the school without him.' The article went on to praise Rous as a good schoolmaster, a wise and thoughtful teacher and remembered him for his skilful training of boys in the gymnasium and indefatigable work as 'games master.' But most touchingly they remembered him for his deep and unfailing kindness, his love of his neighbour and his untiring energy to do a good turn for somebody, no matter what the cost in time and trouble to himself.

Stanley Rous's first day at the FA was something of a shock. The outgoing secretary of the last 39 years, Sir Frederick Wall, was asked by the photographers outside FA headquarters at Lancaster Gate to shake hands with Rous. 'Why should I?' he said testily, and walked off, leaving Rous with his hand half held forward and his mouth wide open.

Nothing could have highlighted the heralding of a new era more than their contrasting dress as they stood together on the pavement. Sir Frederick Wall, in his 80s with a bushy white moustache and wearing a double breasted blue pin striped suit with a carnation in his button hole, a white wing collar and silk bow tie, bowler hat, gloves and umbrella: Stanley Rous, aged 39 in a two button single breasted lounge suit, white shirt and long silver tie. Sir Frederick Wall had held the job for 39 years, but despite his lengthy tenure was inexplicably unprepared to pass his experience on to his successor. When they met for a handover meeting Wall simply said, 'the job's straightforward. You can read up on the files. There's nothing much more I can tell you.'

The Football Association that Stanley Rous took over in 1934 was an archaic and moribund organisation. At his first meeting with the FA Council, item number five on the agenda had been submitted by the Surrey representative. Sadly he had died a few days before the meeting which began with a minute's silence in his memory. The President, Sir Charles Clegg, had asked to speak to this item on a legal point. When item five was reached he stood up and delivered a pre-prepared 15-minute speech, then called on the Surrey representative to reply.

'He can't. He is not here' everyone chorused.

'He must be here,' thundered Sir Charles, 'the item must be adjourned until he is present.'

'He is dead!' one member shouted.

Rous pushed a note in front of Sir Charles which said: 'We had a minute's silence already for the Surrey man who died last week.'

'Why didn't someone tell me?' snapped a furious Clegg.

A further indication of the archaic traditions Stanley Rous inherited was apparent after he attended his first football match as the new FA Secretary. He had been wearing a pair of plus-fours, and received a letter of reprimand from the chairman, Sir Charles Clegg, saying that he'd seen a photograph of Rous in a newspaper, inappropriately attired.

'I would remind you,' read the letter, 'that Sir Frederick Wall would go to matches in a top hat and frock coat'. Rous compromised with a sober lounge suit and bowler hat. Times were changing, but not quickly!

He was under no illusions about the high profile and importance of the job, or the size of the task confronting him. He inherited a staff of only five. Work began at 10 am and was carried out at a leisurely pace. Rous began by getting to know the organisation, establishing his position, modernising the office administration processes and creating a friendlier outward face for the FA. He made himself accessible and became directly involved in all the main activities. Some of the old traditions were swept away.

In his memoir *Football Worlds* he recounted 'before council meetings the tradition had been for £20 to be given to Sir Frederick Wall so that he and his wife could do the catering. They cut sandwiches the night before, provided the coffee, saved what they could and sent out to a nearby cafe for more cakes if the food ran out. That did not appeal to me as part of the Secretary's job, and I arranged instead for members to eat in the Merchant Navy Club restaurant which adjoined the FA office. A full meal there cost only 7s 6d a head, so they ate better for less money and trouble.'

Drawing on his extensive refereeing experience he was soon able to contribute to the modernisation of the game by clarifying and rewriting the laws in a modern idiom, but again there was opposition from the old guard. Mr. William Pickford, the president, who had been on the laws committee for more than 40 years warned him not to tinker with the laws. But Rous prevailed and his simplification of the 17 laws of football was accepted by the International Board in 1938.

He had already made a major contribution to refereeing by conceiving and getting international approval for the diagonal system of refereeing – the referee covering midfield and moving from corner to corner, with each linesman taking one half of the field on the touchline farthest from the referee.

It wasn't long before he set about proving his belief that both playing football and refereeing were eminently teachable, and that standards could be improved through coaching. Between the two world wars coaching in England was almost unknown and dismissed contemptuously. Englishmen who wanted to work as coaches had been forced to go to the continent to find employment. It was Jimmy Hogan that Stanley Rous first turned to when he ran a trial coaching session. Because of the cynicism surrounding coaching he was anxious that the event was seen to be a success.

The course was held in 1935 over a three-day period at the Duke of York's headquarters in London, but it was a disappointment. Jimmy Hogan had built a reputation for himself as an outstanding coach, particularly with the Austrian National 'wunder team' where he worked with the famous Austrian manager Hugo Meisl. But Rous found that Hogan's sessions were badly organized, and although he was able to skilfully demonstrate the many different ways to control the ball, he did not give the students time to assimilate the skills that they'd been shown or explain how to practice them. Rous concluded that Hogan on his own lacked many of the organisational skills a coach required: 'I came to realise that [Hogan's] great reputation abroad was in part fortuitous. Because he could not speak Austrian to the players he had to content himself with endless demonstrations of his own high skills. He would for instance have a board put up with a hole in the middle barely large than a football. From 15 yards range he would slot eight shots out of ten through that hole. Hogan himself was content with the demonstration. It would at first interest the players too, who tried it themselves, but they soon became disillusioned and bored when hardly a ball went through the hole. It was then that Hugo Meisl would take over and show the players how to go on practising that skill until they were as proficient as Hogan. They were an effective team.'

Having been a teacher and games master for 13 years, Rous understood the principles of good teaching and believed that they could be applied to football coaching. He was aware of the reputation that Carnegie College was developing for itself and so for his second course in 1938 he enlisted their help. He obtained the cooperation of the warden, Ernest Major, who suggested that Winterbottom, his senior lecturer, would be able to help him to organise the one week residential course. A number of managers, trainers and senior players attended, along with some club directors who had come along to give their verdict. Although Hogan was again present, this time he was supported by Wilson another Carnegie lecturer. 'Those who came to scoff left to praise,' reported the press. Walter's organisation had impressed Stanley Rous. The success of the course augured well for coaching but the war intervened.

Rous was 51 when Walter joined the FA in 1946. By then he was a man with authority and influence. As Secretary of the Football Association he had high level relations with the War Office, the Board of Trade, The Red Cross and St. John's Ambulance. He was also chairman of the Central Council of Physical Recreation and on the board of the National Playing Fields Association. He was at ease with royalty, leaders in politics, the services, sport and business. He had learned the art of politics and could sway a meeting with his logic. The time had come for him to realise his vision of a national coaching scheme and persuade the FA councillors to appoint Walter as the FA's first Director of Coaching. It was an inspired partnership which was to have a profound effect on the future of English football.

Rous' relationship with Walter was one of mutual respect founded on what they had in common. Both had been to teachers training college, been active as teachers, and shown an appetite for learning and hard work. They both had a deep love for football, but where Stanley's passion had taken him to the top as a referee, Walter's had taken him to the highest level as a coach. Perhaps that was the defining difference in their personalities. As a referee Stanley was used to exercising firm control, making judgments and sticking by them. As a coach Walter was concerned with assessing potential, getting the best out of individuals and improving their performance. Both put service before self, and most importantly shared a vision of a national coaching scheme. Both had enduring personal qualities of integrity, loyalty and fair play that formed the foundation for a longstanding professional relationship.

It was their complimentary skills which made them such an effective team. Without Sir Stanley Rous' ability to manage endless bureaucratic committee meetings and get approval from FA councillors, Walter would not have been able to put his ideas into practice.

Walter appreciated Stanley's qualities more than most and in 1972 he wrote the foreword to Sir Stanley Rous' memoir:

Stanley Rous – the great man of football – who is held in high esteem the world over for his immense contribution to the organisation and development of the game he so dearly loves... When I first met him on an FA course just before the last war, he revealed his keen interest in teaching method and his inspirational leadership. Throughout his life he has been encouraging others to busy themselves in improving and developing the game of Association Football, and his sympathetic understanding of people, and supporting interest in what they are keen to do, is the source of much of his charm. It is remarkable how much Stanley Rous has fitted into his life... as with all his work; he has fulfilled this task with style, dignity and human understanding.

'Walter might well have been writing about himself,' commented Brian Scovell when he quoted this extract in his own book *The England Managers*.

CHAPTER 8

A RUDE AWAKENING

1946 – 1950

In his first three years as England manager Walter had a low media profile and there was little public understanding of what he did. England's impending departure for Brazil, and the 1950 World Cup attempt, brought him more into the public eye. In January the *Sporting Chronicle* published an interview and portrait of the England manager: 'See a tall slim scholarly looking fellow, his crinkly hair blowing about as he talks to a bunch of fellows who listen attentively in tracksuits, and you would think that a young professor is giving a lecture on the effect of nuclear energy and sport... yet as England team manager and chief FA coach, [Walter Winterbottom] has not only been in the thick of it on the field, but is in the thick of it off the pitch – as one of the world's greatest soccer strategists.' The interview concluded: 'His biggest test is yet to come in the World Cup. But with his usual diligence and love of finding a solution to tactical soccer puzzles it can be taken for granted that he will make England's contribution no small one. He leaves nothing to chance.'

In February Bernard McElwaine, in *The Leader* magazine, probed deeply into Walter's background in an article titled 'Soccer Bandmaster': 'Training footballers from different teams to play in a harmony is an expert's job. It's Walter Winterbottom who waves the baton. We shall see the results when England visit Brazil.' McElwaine went on to explain Walter's diligence in watching opponents so that he could brief players on weakness and opportunities. He told readers how Winterbottom introduced new players to the international scene, concentrating on getting past their nervousness and welding them with the established stars. Perhaps most significantly the interview revealed Walter's philosophy on managing international players: 'He has two rules for himself. Never criticise after a match. If players have played badly they know it already. Never criticise at half time. Criticism on failure is fatal. He avoids looking directly at a player, or calling one by name in a critical mid-game period when tired players flop on the benches for their rest. The stars – if they are losing – are hypersensitive then and easily depressed. Quietly, almost off-handedly, the team manager may address a few suggestions at random and make more specific ones when the conversation becomes general.'

In May 1950, the month before the team left for Brazil, Archie Ledbrooke of the *Daily Dispatch* wrote, 'The FA's chief coach is producing a new type of footballer; ones who behave like ambassadors.' He went on to say that some professional club officials were apt to look down their noses at the work Walter Winterbottom did. There was a story circulating, he reported, that only well-behaved players were chosen for England nowadays. 'The intelligent chaps who know how to behave when put on show are the same men who, by their general outlook, will prove to be most receptive to the football ideas which Winterbottom wishes to exploit.'

Ledbrooke was convinced of the impact that Walter was having: 'Not a single player who has turned out for England in the last four years has failed to go back to club games as an improved footballer.

The style of the English team has had a profound effect on club methods, especially in constructive defence.'

He went on to bring attention to the wonderful spirit and greater sense of pride that had been instilled into players pulling on the England shirt. 'Before the war it was often said that many players did not care much about wearing an England shirt: they played without enthusiasm. Now every man of the 2,500 professionals in the Football League is bursting to win recognition and on the field our international team shows wonderful spirit.'

The *Oldham Chronicle* previewed the 1950 World Cup with the headline, 'Oldhamer will guide England through the World Cup' and announced that Walter Winterbottom, the most important man in English football today, will have the eyes of all soccer fans and sports writers on him as he supervises the training, diet and leisure of the England players. The newspaper reported that Mrs Fanny Winterbottom, Walter's 75-year-old mother, who lived at 142a Oxford Street, Werneth, Oldham, had met a *Chronicle* representative this week and said she was excited and proud. 'Proud because, although my boy has achieved much success in life, he has not let it go to his head, and is the same shy, modest chap, with a smile and a "How do" for all the neighbours, friends and his old pals. Walter's dad died three years ago' she added; 'he would have been so proud of Walter today.'

Walter phoned his mother before the departure to Rio and told her 'There is a lot expected of a grand lot of players and myself. Don't be too hopeful of us bringing that cup back, but we are all very optimistic and we will do our best.'

England and Italy, along with the hosts, Brazil, were touted by the British press as favourites to win – an optimistic and partisan view that ignored developments in world football. England had no experience of playing in a World Cup tournament, let alone winning it. Furthermore, although results had been very good in the 29 international matches that England had played under Walter (23 wins), not a single game had been against South American opponents. The media conveniently failed to notice that the swan song of the legendary team of the 'golden years' had been in Turin two years earlier.

England's preparation for their first World Cup fell far behind those of other countries. This was largely because of resistance from the Football League to releasing players for more international matches and training. The World Cup in Brazil began in June, but the English squad did not get together until mid May and then only for a short European tour, with away games against Portugal (won 5-3) on 14 May, and Belgium (won 4-1) four days later. Early in June the squad met at Dulwich Hamlet's ground for three days' light training 11 days before their first World Cup game, and even then they didn't have the use of the first-team pitch.

Walter was only too well aware how inferior his preparations were. 'All the South American teams would give up their best players for six months before the competition, so they could train together and go on days out so they built up an understanding and team spirit. We met in London and had one kick about at an amateur clubs ground because all the League clubs reseeded their pitch in the summer. We played a couple of seven-a-side games and that was it. Off we went.'

In their book *World Cup*, Brian Glanville and Jerry Weinstein contrasted the different approaches by comparing the managers of England and Brazil: 'By contrast, the Brazilians approached the tournament with a monastic devotion which recalled Pozzo's Italian teams of the 1930s. The contrast between the two team managers was indicative enough. Walter Winterbottom, England's manager, was cogent, polished, and urbane, giving the suitably English and fittingly balanced impression that victory would be a very pleasant thing, but defeat would not bring about the immediate collapse of the British Empire. Costa on the other hand, was dedicated and intense, a brooding man, moustached and hugely salaried; at this period he was earning more than £1000 a month. Winterbottom, while earning considerably less (a little over £1000 a year) was also expected to do considerably more, since he combined his job with that of Director of Coaching at the Football Association.'

A number of changes had been made to the organisation of the tournament since 1938. In a well intentioned attempt to find a fairer way to decide the best team in the world, FIFA dropped the knockout competition and arranged the tournament as a league. Sixteen teams qualified (England by winning the Home Championship) and were divided into four pools of four teams. The winners from each pool would play each other in the final league, with the team finishing top being declared the winners. Unfortunately for FIFA the tournament was dogged by late withdrawals from three countries, with the result that two pools consisted of four teams, one of three, and one of only two, creating an unfair competition at the outset. The tournament had already been weakened by the absence of powerful football countries like Austria, Hungary, Czechoslovakia and Argentina; and Germany was still banned from international competition. England were in a pool of four with Spain, Chile and the United States. The results, furthermore, of the three previous tournaments had shown that the home nation had a huge advantage and that South American teams did well in South America whilst European teams triumphed in Europe; in 1930 Uruguay won as host nation, in 1934 Italy won at home and in 1938 Italy were the victors in France.

The England team flew out in a Brazilian Panair Lockheed Constellation. They arrived in Brazil on 20 June (five days before their first game), after a long and draining flight lasting thirty one hours, with refueling stops in Paris, Lisbon, Dakar and Recife, before finally arriving in Rio de Janeiro. The FA party consisted of just 17 players, four referees, two trainers, eight sports writers and the team manager.

A measure of the lack of importance attached to England's first World Cup can be judged by the FA's instruction that Stanley Matthews should go on a goodwill FA tour of Canada and

Manchester United's decision to tour the USA at the time as the World Cup. (Stanley Mathews, Jack Aston and Harry Cockburn were subsequently recalled to join the England squad in Brazil midway through the tournament.)

The accommodation Walter had chosen was the Luxor hotel on the Copacabana beach and most players were happy enough with their surroundings, although Walter restricted their use of the beach to avoid sunstroke and fatigue. Training at the nearby Botofogo club ground took place in the morning and early evening. England certainly did not have the resources that the Brazilian team had, with two doctors, two masseurs and three chefs. There is a popular and much repeated myth that Walter assumed the chefs responsibility when the players found the South American food not to their liking. However, where Brian Glanville made this comment in his book *The Sunday Times History of the World Cup*, Walter had handwritten in his own copy, 'NO'. The truth is probably that he gave instructions to the hotel chef on the meals he wanted the team to have.

England's first game was against Chile in the mighty Maracana stadium in Rio. Although it was to become one of the largest and most famous stadiums in the world, designed to hold 200,000 people, it had hardly been completed when the tournament began. Parts of the stadium still resembled a building site. A moat surrounded the pitch with grass that was very different from that experienced in Europe.

England won 2-0. In the first half they had to defend for long periods against a lively Chilean attack and Bert Williams did well to keep the ball out of his net. In the second half Mortensen headed a fine goal following a cross from Mullen. Later good work by Mortensen and Finney led to Wilf Mannion smashing the ball past the Chilean goalkeeper for England's second goal. A bonus for Walter was the creditable performance of Hughes at centre half, replacing the incomparable Neil Franklin – who had been banned from football.

Although England had won they were not impressive. The players seemed tired two months after the end of their long football season, and seemed affected by the Brazilian climate. In his autobiography, *Captain of England*, Billy Wright recalled how he began to find it difficult to breathe after playing 45 minutes on the Rio pitch: 'After running about in a match at home I take a deep breath and fill my lungs. In Rio when I did this nothing seemed to happen and although oxygen was available for us to take at half-time – we gave it a test but found it of little use – I appreciated that these were the kind of conditions we had to expect and overcome if the World Cup was to be won. Perhaps it was the difficulty to breathe which was directly responsible for my feeling leg-weary early in the second half.'

England's next game was against the United States in Belo Horizonte, 280 miles inland. They stayed at Morro Velho as the guests of a British gold mining company that employed 2,000 British workers. A comfortable and homely facility, Billy Wright described the camp as 'a piece of England in the heart of Brazil.' It was isolated but provided an ideal facility for training and relaxing and the players were made to feel at home by the British workers.

England were of course expected to win easily, but the USA were not quite the pushover that the British public had been led to believe. They had reached the semi-finals of the World Cup in 1930 and in their first game of the 1950 tournament they took lead against Spain and held it until the last ten minutes before the Europeans recovered to win 3-1. Tom Whittaker (the Arsenal manager, who had toured South America with the Arsenal, and whose advice Walter had sought when planning the trip), cabled home warning, 'United States, reckoned as 500-1 outsiders for the trophy, should give England much needed match competition.'

Although the American team was a multi-racial melting pot, the nationality of some players was dubious. Eddie McIlvenny, the captain, was a Glaswegian who left Britain less than 18 months before; Gaetjens, the centre forward was a Haitian; Maca, the left back was a Belgian. Despite their multi-racial background the team was generally recognised as experienced professionals.

Concerns about a potential giant killing upset grew when the England party saw the stadium at Belo Horizonte. It was small, primitive and closed in, with ten foot walls on three sides like a squash court. The pitch itself was cramped and bumpy. When Walter inspected the changing rooms he found them unsuitable and instructed the team to change at the nearby Minas Athletic club and come to the stadium in a bus. The same team that had beaten Chile was selected by Mr. Arthur Drewry, the sole selector. The team selection for this match has been a matter of ongoing controversy ever since. In his autobiography, *Football Worlds*, Stanley Rous was unequivocal on the subject.

Stanley Matthews seemed to me the ideal man to undermine a team like theirs, which was clearly long on spirit and short on skill. Special arrangements had to be made for him to join the party and it seemed sense to put him in for this game. That I thought also to be the view of team manager Walter Winterbottom, so I went to see Drewry to urge some changes, and especially Matthews inclusion. Drewry was adamant, however, that we should not change the team that had beaten Chile 2-0.

No one will ever know whether it would have made a difference. The score that remains in the record books, and that the media never let Walter forget, was that the United States won 1-0. If anything the game was even more one sided than expected. England were always on top, hitting the post early on and with shots raining in from all directions. They seemed likely to score at any time. And then, after 37 minutes, the unbelievable happened – the United States took the lead. Bahr, the left half back produced a shot which Williams had covered, but suddenly Gaeetjens, the Haitian centre forward, dashed across the goal. The ball hit his head and took a deflection, skidding into the net with Williams going the wrong way.

The United States packed their defence for the remainder of the game and England attacked continuously, hitting the woodwork on several occasions, but failing to score. The Americans resorted to kicking the ball into the crowd, and when they did the spectators, who were enthusiastically supporting the underdogs, passed the ball amongst themselves before returning it to the pitch. Then, at last England appeared to have broken the deadlock. A well placed free kick by Alf Ramsey was met by Mortensen who rose perfectly to head the ball into the net. The ball beat Borghi, the goalkeeper, and crossed the line, but it was then scrambled away. To the player's anger, the referee waved away the England players claim of a goal and awarded a corner kick.

When the final whistle blew hundreds of delirious spectators ran onto the pitch to carry off the jubilant American team. It was their greatest triumph and Bill Jeffrey, their manager, thought that the result had given them a golden opportunity to popularise football in the United States. For Walter and the England players it was a bitter disappointment that would linger in their memory for ever. Although Walter conceded that his team didn't take their multiple chances he was untypically angry with the referee: 'We scored a perfectly good equaliser but it wasn't allowed. The crowd was jeering that decision – the man handled the ball in his own net. But after that the Americans thought they could get away with anything – shirt tugging, fouls and everything. The refereeing was a farce. If FIFA had wanted to, they could have suspended the referee for a lifetime.'

The British press were predictably merciless. The headline on the front page of the *Daily Express* blazed 'British Sport Meets Its Worst Day' (to make matters worse the England cricket team had lost at home to the West Indies for the first time on the same day) and continued, 'United States footballers – whoever heard of them – beat England 1-0 in the World Cup series today. It marks the lowest-ever point for British sport.' *The Times* reported: 'Probably never before has an English team played so badly. The chances missed were legion. With the American goal at their mercy, the forwards blasted over the bar or hesitated near the goal to allow the defense to rob them of the ball.'

Many years later Walter took a more phlegmatic view:

Football wouldn't be the same without these results, but that does not make them any more palatable when you are the victim. At Belo Horizonte, the grass was the South American type, with tufts every six inches or so, like individual plants, and spaces in between, so that the ball tended to sit up, and our forwards repeatedly hit the ball on the rise. We so dominated the game it was impossible to believe that we could lose, and it was said that in all we hit the bar and posts 11 times. Jimmy Mullen had the most chances and, of course, there was the occasion towards the end when a header by Mortensen was almost certainly over the line before it was scooped out, but the referee would not allow it. This is not to make excuses. We missed our chances and paid the penalty. We had no proper preparation the way teams have today, and our players were not used to foreign, unfamiliar conditions, the way league players are nowadays, with regular overseas competitions.

But all was not lost. If England could beat Spain in their final pool game they would remain in the competition. They returned to the Luxor hotel in Rio and Arthur Drewry had a discussion with Walter about the team selection. The next morning four changes were announced: Eddie Baily in place of Wilf Mannion, Bill Eckersley for Jack Aston, Jackie Milburn instead of Roy Bentley and Stanley Matthews in place of Jimmy Mullen. The players were in good spirits and determined to redeem themselves from the defeat at Belo Horizonte. Walter had received reports on the Spanish team from Tom Whittaker and two British referees, and it was felt that the square-playing Spanish backs would be exposed by passes through the middle.

England played well and it was a match they should have won but once again luck deserted them. Jackie Milburn scored with a header from a Finney cross, but to their dismay the Italian referee, Galeati, gave the goal offside. Photographs later proved that he had ignored a Spanish player who put Milburn onside. A goal would have given England heart and demoralised Spain. From then on a combination of great goalkeeping by Ramallets and extreme leniency by the referee prevented England from scoring. At half time the Brazilian radio commentators agreed that England's football was the best seen during the World Cup tournament. But in the 47th minute Spain took the lead with a goal from Zarra. They then defended in numbers, upsetting the crowd with their tactics of body checking, shirt pulling, tripping, digging with their elbows and wasting time by kicking the ball out of touch at every opportunity. Billy Wright recalled: 'Once Eddie Baily, who played well, got the Spanish defense going the wrong way, and then pushed the ball into what would have been an open space for Mortensen. A defender, though, caught the ball like a cricketer and smiled – and Spain were probably saved from conceding a goal. Several passes intended for Matthews were also cut off in this manner, and these shady tactics did not make this a match to remember.'

The England players kept their composure and continued to press, but to no avail and at the end 80,000 Brazilians rose to their feet waving 'Adios' with their white handkerchiefs in a friendly gesture of farewell. England were on their way home. The press was scathing. The *Daily Herald* summed up the nation's despair with a black border around the page which read: 'In affectionate remembrance of English football which died in Rio on July 2, 1950, duly lamented by a large circle of sorrowing friends and acquaintances. RIP. NB. The body will be cremated and the ashes taken to Spain.'

Inexcusably the FA left none of the England party behind to watch the final stages of the tournament. It would have given them invaluable experience. It seems extraordinary that even the English journalists left with the team, having no further interest in the tournament.

But not everyone had their heads in the sand. Tom Finney could see that times had changed. 'It was new for England. It gave us an insight into how good the South American countries were. They were very skilful players and it was obvious you had little or no chance of playing against those sides then. We were by no means the best in the world. That was not true at all. The only reason you were probably thinking that was because you never played these sides; never saw anything about them because they were so far away.'

In later years it begged the question, what if the World Cup had been held in 1946 – the zenith of the golden years – when it would have been held but for the war. Could England have won then? Walter thought so. 'I think we would have had a good chance. We had young players such as Finney, Mannion and Wright, who were so good they were keeping out the likes of Horatio Carter, mixed with older ones such as Matthews and Swift.'

In the final pool the South American teams emphatically demonstrated their world dominance. Uruguay drew 2-2 with Spain and then beat Sweden 3-2. Brazil thrashed Sweden 7-1 and then demolished Spain by 6-1. But surprisingly in the final match Brazil, the hosts and favourites, were beaten 2-1 by Uruguay, who regained the World Cup which they had won in 1930.

'Thus ended the most spectacular World Cup yet,' concluded Brain Glanville, 'a World Cup organised on a doubtful basis, which nevertheless provided excitement and brilliant football... above all it represented the triumph of South American over European football. The South Americans had plainly reached a level of conception and execution by comparison with which European football was mundane and banal.'

Walter had learned many lessons: the need to have the team together for much longer beforehand; more time to adjust to local conditions, weather, grounds and diet; a better understanding of referees from different continents; experience in dealing with physical provocations unknown in British football; learning how to counter teams with entirely different styles of play.

He still had to deal with resistance from some of the players. Matthews wrote, 'I blame this [World Cup failure in 1950] on the pre-match talks on playing tactics that had been introduced by our team manager [Walter Winterbottom]. You just cannot tell star players how they must play and what they must do on the field in an international match.'

Jonathan Wilson wrote in *Anatomy of England*, 'It's easy with hindsight to mock his blinkeredness, but Matthews was only reflecting what many players thought. The hatred of theory, of anything that required mental effort, particularly if it was abstract in nature, was endemic, not merely in football but also in British society.'

Walter pondered the overriding question: how could he get England to embrace coaching in the way that it had been in Europe and South America? His problem would be getting anyone to listen. The World Cup was a relatively small tournament at the time and had taken place thousands of miles away; there was a sense of remoteness about it all, with no television coverage and no media frenzy when the team returned home. Did anyone really care? Jonathan Wilson perceptively summed up Walter's dilemma. 'Like Cassandra, his tragedy was that he could see the future, but he couldn't do anything about it.'

Looking back years later Walter hinted at England's isolation: 'The 1950 World Cup put our position in the world in sharp perspective. Before the war, most of the South Americans and best European sides were quite unknown. So we went to Rio pretty well unprepared. Arsenal had been to South America... and gave some indication of what we were going to face. We began to realise what needed to be done... but it was to be a very long time before we could do it.'

Stanley Rous, writing in his autobiography, was scathingly frank about the restrictions which Walter had to endure in Brazil. 'The World Cup defeat underlined the stupidity of divorcing the team manager from team selection or giving him such limited powers that the side he fielded was rarely one of his own choosing. At least [at the 1950 World Cup] there was one man, Arthur Drewry, who took responsibility in this instance, and had the opportunity to pick a team as a team. At home the established system was too deep rooted for early change and was even more chaotic in concept, with the whole committee responsible for the choice.' When Walter returned home from Brazil he lost no time in putting forward his suggestions on what should be done at a meeting of the International Committee on 5 June 1950. It was decided that a technical subcommittee should be appointed, consisting of the chairmen of the senior, intermediate, amateur, and youth team selection committees. This committee met on November 8, 1950 and it was decided to seek the opinions of managers, ex-international players, club chairman and directors.

The topics for the meetings were: (i) the time available for training before international matches, (ii) ways to bridge the gap between the goals of 'club and country,' (iii) the standard of hospitality offered to foreign teams, (iv) methods of gaining wider support for important matches and (v) an investigation into the current rules with a view to establishing a better system for the development of young players.

Four meetings were held within 12 months. There was no shortage of opinions but there was a depressing fragmentation of views. Amongst the managers, Arthur Rowe felt that preparation for foreign tours should be done at home with a minimum time spent in a foreign country. Although the principle of team get-togethers and match practice before an international was becoming accepted, Raich Carter thought that the heavy pressures of the English season meant that extra ball practice would be detrimental, and that young players would learn more from match experience. Joe Mercer felt that the League system, by its own nature, would produce players of outstanding ability and that coaching should be integrated into match practice; he also believed the teaching of individual skills to international players was worthless.

At subsequent meetings Tommy Lawton and Laurie Scott argued that pre-match training for internationals should be as long as possible. Jimmy Hagan insisted that match practice must always be included, but Stanley Cullis was afraid that players might be kept from important tactical work with their clubs. Playing men out of position was generally thought to be unwise. The divergence of views underlined the breadth of the resistance Walter faced. Consultations with clubs continued. Although there was a little agreement on a positive plan of action at least a bridge was being built between the professional clubs and the Football Association.

Walter's patient approach brought some small victories. Club chairman conceded that clubs benefited from having international players and they were conscious of the importance of England's performance. They approved a programme of 'B' matches each season along the lines of the senior programme. This meant that Walter was able to give international experience to promising players before blooding them in the full international team.

But the task of leading English football into a modern era in which it could compete with the best of South America or the continent was a daunting one. Walter was under no illusions: he was in it for the long term. It would take hard work, patience, persistence and every ounce of his intellectual ability and organisational skills to realize the vision he had for the future of English football. But he was determined to see it through.

CHAPTER 9

COACHING
THE COACHES

1946 – 1955

Allen Wade, who followed Walter Winterbottom as FA Director of Coaching and wrote *The FA Guide to Training and Coaching* in 1967, said in the introduction to his book:

There are, reputedly, two stages through which worthwhile ideas must pass before they are accepted. In the first stage they are ignored, in the second, ridiculed. Coaching has passed through these stages and is now accepted as a necessary process in the education and development of more skilful players at all levels. Indeed, if this were not so, the whole process of education from early school years to university level could be viewed with doubts and reservations.

In the past, coaching was ignored because the reservoirs of so-called natural talent seemed limitless. It was subsequently ridiculed, probably because some players, eminent in their time, had not been taught, so it was assumed that no one could be taught. Had this belief prevailed in the musical field, the development of great instrumentalists would surely have been under a handicap.

Wade's introduction acknowledges the stubborn resistance to coaching that Walter had faced and the success he achieved in changing attitudes to coaching during his 16 years as Director of Coaching (in the fly-leaf of the copy he gave to Walter, Wade wrote, 'Please accept this effort in recognition of the tremendous part which you played in dragging football out of the doldrums. I hope you do not disagree with too much of it!')

Walter understood that the reason for player's resistance to coaching was based deep in the genesis of the game. In the book, *Soccer Partnership* he explained to Bob Ferrier, 'in many ways we suffer because we started the whole thing. Its origins were physical and violent. From the start a premium had been put on the man who was a strong runner and an adventurous individual dribbler, and defenders were needed who were equally strong and could make uncompromising tackles.'

These early players believed that only by playing, did they learn the game and indeed train for it – along with casual advice from older, more experienced players. The business of being taught the game, sitting down and thinking about its problems, was simply not considered. 'Everything passing through the game of football was by word of mouth' said George Hardwick. 'The written word wasn't readily accepted, because football had existed for so many years without it.'

This attitude persisted through the first half of the 20th century. Walter had experienced it himself as a player at Manchester United before the war and not much had changed by 1950 when Bobby Robson was a young player. 'When I came to Fulham as a 17-year-old in 1950 coaching was very limited. A lot of our training was without the ball. Stamina and endurance for ninety minutes on heavy pitches with the old leather footballs was what it was all about. Nowadays you can count 40 footballs on the pitch at training. Back then you were lucky if there were two anywhere in sight. Having no footballs around for training was standard practice. Even for shooting practice there might be eight of you with one or two footballs at the most, so once you had taken your shot you had to wait around until it came to your turn again. We'd run five laps, walk one, then run three, walk one, run two, walk one, and that was it. There were no tactics.'

The English attitude to coaching was in stark contrast to continental Europe. As late developers European countries embraced learning and coaching, and employed English coaches who were unable to find work in their own country because clubs simply did not believe in coaching.

At one of the first coaching courses he held at Carnegie College Walter asked the 58 trainers who were present if they had read the laws of the game. Only three had! Perhaps it wasn't surprising to find that when he questioned them they didn't know the answers either! The smug attitude he initially encountered ran along the lines of 'We know it, we know it all, we don't need new ideas, this is the way to play this game, we have always played it this way, and it's a good way.'

The Football Association ran coaching the way they ran international team selection – with a committee. There were eight council members on the Instructional Committee. In addition Stanley Rous, Walter Winterbottom and a staff member, JR Witty, were invited to attend. Walter lost no time in putting forward detailed proposals for a national coaching scheme. Both he and Rous had an extensive teaching background and so it was not surprising that the cornerstone of the FA coaching policy was education in its widest sense. It naturally followed that the primary target for coaching should be boys between the ages of 11 and 18 who would be most receptive to new ideas and provide a broad based pyramid for higher playing standards. An early priority was to establish football coaching visits and courses in teacher training colleges so that schoolmasters and games organisers would understand modern coaching methods. A network of coaches had to be trained to do this.

In considering how to structure a national coaching scheme Walter considered two options: either using a small group of centrally controlled experts to travel around the country or a series of decentralised regional schemes making use of part-time coaches working through the county football associations. He chose the latter. It was clear to him that this way would encourage more senior players to take up coaching and give them opportunities for coaching practice – there was little point in persuading players to qualify as coaches if they had nowhere to coach. His proposals were accepted by the Instructional Committee in August 1946.

Although it might seem that a committee hampered the executive function of a coaching department, that was how the Football Association was structured then and Walter dealt with it in the same way that he had with the International Selection Committee: with well reasoned arguments on how coaching should be organised. He recommended that committee members actively participate by visiting courses and encouraging the coaching scheme within their own geographical area. In many ways it must have been easier than dealing with the International Selection Committee, where everyone was an expert on team selection. At least no one on the Instructional Committee claimed to be an expert on coaching!

Walter's ability to motivate people helped him to gain support from the Instructional Committee. He made people he worked with feel important; that their views and contribution mattered. 'If you treat a person as he is, he will remain as he is,' he told the London Referees Society. 'If you treat him as though he were what he could be, and should be, he will become what he could and should be.' The maxim applied to everyone he dealt with.

The county Football Associations were asked to accept responsibility for organising regional coaching schemes and visits to schools and youth clubs as well as funding courses for the preliminary coaching certificate. Walter suggested that they set up their own coaching committees with a secretary and a chief coach who would be responsible for selecting and employing a panel of part time coaches – supervising their work and planning their courses. They were helped by additional resources from local education authorities and the Central Council of Physical Recreation (CCPR). In London, the Secretary of the London county FA, Bert Fuller, along with Harry Littlewood of the CCPR (who was at Carnegie College when Walter was a lecturer) ran extensive coaching programmes.

Coaches who were professional footballers made regular visits to schools and youth clubs. They were paid £2 for a two hour coaching session, a useful supplement to the £20 maximum wage they earned from playing football. Limitations of budget and time meant that each coach was only able to make three visits to a group each season. Nevertheless they were able to stimulate interest in coaching and give advice to games masters, who were, after all, the people regularly in contact with boys. One of the early problems they faced was the lack of footballs in schools and youth clubs which meant that they were unable to practice skills and had to confine themselves to coaching 'in the game.' Walter was furious. 'This is a nonsense' he said, 'we must provided county associations with supplies of footballs so that each visiting coach can take along a net of balls.'

A fourteen year-old schoolboy gazed out of the window waiting for the coach to arrive. Like most boys of that age he was in thrall to the romance of football and thrilled when it was announced that Jack Mansell, a Portsmouth and England B player, was coming to his school to run a coaching session. There was much chatter and excitement amongst all the boys as they crowded round the window when the track-suited football star arrived; they examined his Volkswagen car; they gathered round him as he asked the school games master how many balls he was bringing to the pitch. When the games master replied 'just one', Mansell raised his eyebrows with surprise and urged him to find as many balls as he could. Mansell also brought his own net bag with eight footballs.

The boy vividly remembered the demonstration of how to make an accurate pass. Jack Mansell stood with his legs astride and casually asked the captain of the first X1 to step forward and pass the ball through his legs from a distance of about five yards. Incredibly, this rather tall, strong boy, who played at right back, ran up and blasted the ball above the coach's head. 50 young faces turned to the sky, watching the ball sail over trees into the adjoining farmer's field. There was a long embarrassed silence. Perhaps it suited the coach's purpose, because he was then able to demonstrate how to do it properly, by making the pass with the inside of the foot. It was a lesson the boy would never forget. Sadly there were no more coaching visits to his school. The episode demonstrated that many schools simply had no idea how to coach the game, and that boys, although enthusiastic players, were generally ignorant of basic skills and thirsty for knowledge. But without teachers who were willing to learn how to coach no progress would be made.

Walter introduced coaching qualifications at two levels: the FA Preliminary Certificate and the FA Certificate and Badge (the advanced coaching level). The Preliminary Certificate qualified the coach to teach the fundamentals of the game to boys and youths. The examination consisted of practical tests in coaching a class of boys, demonstrating the separate skills of the game, and passing written papers on the laws of football and coaching technique. This preliminary certificate was taken at courses run by the county FA's or at one of the FA's central courses for schoolmasters and youth leaders.

The full qualification was the Football Association Certificate and Badge, which could only be taken at one of the FA's central courses. Candidates from within both teaching and football attended courses at Lilleshall, Loughborough College, Carnegie College, Bisham Abbey and Birmingham University during the summer close season. These courses were always run under Walter's personal supervision. It wasn't easy to persuade famous experienced players to attend a coaching course. Perhaps understandably it felt like going back to school: they had a fear of failing examinations. Such was their apprehension about the questions on laws of the game that a list of 100 questions and answers was produced and issued in advance to all candidates taking the preliminary examination. Walter's close personal contact with England players, and his persuasive manner, helped overcome their reluctance to come to a coaching course and provided the foundations for a body of players who became experienced coaches.

'We had 300 in 1947 taking our full coaching award which was a big number,' said Walter, 'and there was a change in the attitude because they went back to the clubs, and stereotyped methods of training were being pushed on one side and new methods coming in. And this ultimately meant that these players, instead of becoming trainers running around with a sponge, were now becoming coaches who knew how to coach the game.'

An advanced course was held at Lilleshall each summer for professional players and qualified FA coaches. (Lilleshall was a stately home and estate in rural Shropshire which had been purchased by the Central Council of Physical Recreation after the war and substantially renovated to provide a National Recreation Centre where governing sports bodies could hold residential coaching courses.) It proved to be an ideal environment for coaching and considerable experience was gained from the courses, with much interchange of ideas and suggestions coming from the students themselves. Walter made sure that the courses always had a social element which created a relaxed environment and built friendships. There was a tradition that on Thursday evenings an impromptu concert was staged when everyone was encouraged to perform a party piece. When Jimmy Hill was an instructor there he recalled that George Curtis, a coach who was a Southampton player, jumped up each year to recite Kipling's poem 'If.'

'I suggested that while he was reciting, perhaps two or three of us could hum 'Land of Hope and Glory' gently in the background. The only problem was to make the music fit the poem, but after a few rehearsals we had it precisely timed. On the night though, George left out two lines of the verse which meant he was getting to the end of words before the hummers were able to catch up with him. As on the pitch, George was ahead of the game. So with the realisation that he was going to reach the goalline first, the slow double *piano* of the hummed voices in the background suddenly acquired a touch of panicky *accelerando*. By dint of exceptional fortune we reached the final chords almost together to tumultuous applause.'

Walter encouraged young professional players to think of coaching as a career and a cadre of around 20 were appointed as FA staff coaches. They became known as his disciples and spread the message of coaching at local, national, and eventually international level. In this way a new breed of managers emerged which began to change attitudes to coaching in League clubs. Over the years many of this elite group became famous as managers and coaches, including Bill Nicholson, Don Howe, Alan Brown, Ron Greenwood, Dave Sexton, Malcolm Allison, Joe Mercer, Vic Buckingham, Jimmy Hill, Bobby Robson, Jimmy Frew, George Ainsley, and Allen Wade.

They coached and mentored hundreds of players, many who then themselves became managers and coaches. And so the gospel of Walter's teaching spread far and wide. Bobby Robson was one of those that benefited. 'I got lucky when I went to West Bromwich Albion because Vic Buckingham was the manager, and Vic was a manager/coach. He was one of Walter's disciples, so I came under the influence of a man who had the right ideas about training and teaching the game.' Buckingham moved to Holland where he found that his belief in pure skill was more welcome. As manager of Ajax he won the Dutch league in 1960, and perhaps more memorably, discovered and nurtured a young man called Johan Cruyff, who became one of the greatest footballers Europe has ever produced.

Another of Walter's disciples from the Lilleshall courses was Alan

Brown. Alan became a mentor to managers and coaches like Billy Bingham, Lawrie McMenemy, Don Revie, Jimmy Adamson, Brian Clough, and Howard Wilkinson. Indeed he was such a believer in coaching that at one time when he was the manager of Burnley he was able to field a whole team of qualified coaches! Under Alan Brown Burnley started its own scheme of coaching schoolboys and youths at their practice ground. He wrote in Walter's copy of his book *Team Coach*: 'To Walter with sincere thanks – the greatest man in football – you had that quality of inspiration for all men.'

Although he still faced resistance to coaching Walter had the unique advantage of being the Director of Coaching and manager of the England Team at the same time. In the early years this was a great benefit – he was able to work with the best players in England – see them in close action against the best players in the world. This experience gave him a clear insight into what to coach, and through his work with international players, he learned how best to coach certain aspects of technique and team play.

Despite the urgent need for more coaches Walter insisted that high standards had to be maintained, recognising that in football, as in any sport, being taught by a bad coach is counterproductive. From the early courses it was clear that many enthusiastic candidates did not reach the required standard and the failure rate was high, so he introduced the entry stages of demonstrator and probationary coach and assessments were arranged with the county FA's to check coaches' progress.

Walter was very clear about the qualities he wanted in a coach. The coach must know the game well and be able to analyse it and break it down into the elements to be taught. They should have detailed knowledge of how skills are performed, methods of coordinating team play, the function of team positions and general tactics in attack and defence. Walter wanted men who were willing to learn; men who would not fall into the trap of simply 'pouring out their knowledge.' Teaching the right knowledge at the right time was a technique that had to be acquired through learning. Coaches were needed who would take an active part in the coaching session, but not show off their own skill in demonstrations. Above all he was looking for men who understood that the right kind of practice was of primary importance in intelligent coaching.

Coaches came from all walks of life and were not paid a retainer or salary when they were invited to join the panels run by the county FA's. They were part time and were paid for each session they took. Voluntary helpers at a junior level were encouraged and paid expenses. Every coaching session had to be organised for at least 30 boys and schools had to make proper facilities and equipment available.

Although coaching was generally welcomed in schools, its wider acceptance was more difficult. Football was now firmly established as a working class game, enjoyed by a demographic inherently suspicious of intellectuals. This problem was not confined to the fans of the game, nor the players, coaches and managers. Many chairmen of clubs were self-made men with limited education. Thus Walter's brand of intellectual coaching was met with widespread scepticism. Walter's intellect was a two edged sword: a very considerable asset in the vision needed to plot the way ahead, but a disadvantage in persuading players, coaches and managers to think more deeply about technical and tactical developments. In essence the problem was that players, coaches and managers thought they knew it all: the chairmen of clubs knew they knew it all!

Inevitably progress was slow but Walter was in it for the long haul. In the words of Winston Churchill: 'To build is the laborious task of years; to destroy can be the foolish act of a single day.'

Initiatives were taken to counter the trend for public and grammar schools to switch from soccer to rugby, which concerned Walter because it affected the supply of teachers who wanted to coach football.

A joint committee was set up between the Incorporated

Association of Headmasters (IAHM) and the FA to propose new ideas for the development of football in schools. Personal relationships were established by inviting headmasters to the Amateur Cup Final each year as guests of the FA.

One of the ideas to come out of this was 'Schools Week.' The FA invited the most promising footballers from public and grammar schools to a one-week coaching course at Oxford University (and later at Cambridge). One of the first pupils to take part in the course remembered: 'Eighty boys attended the "Schools Week" for a combination of coaching and match play. I was one of those boys. Can you imagine that: as a schoolboy being coached by the England team manager?' The course was supervised by Walter himself, assisted by four qualified coaches and six university students. The boys were chosen from some of the best soccer playing Grammar and Public Schools in the country. It was an example of the vision and long term planning that was the essence of Walter's professional life.'

The number of qualified coaches grew slowly but steadily. By 1953 there were 215 coaches with full certificates and badges, and 1,012 with preliminary certificates. Even this small number of coaches made an impact, making over 15,000 visits to schools and clubs. The FA was then spending around £10,000 a year on courses, a significant part of its budget.

Because Walter insisted on maintaining high standards the pass rate averaged only 42 per cent. At the courses held at Lilleshall and Loughborough College in 1953, of the 203 candidates attempting the examination, 21 gained the full coaching certificate and badge, and 65 were awarded the preliminary certificate. From these small beginnings hundreds of courses were run in the years to follow and thousands of ex-players and teachers, and some from other walks of life, qualified as coaches of association football operating at local, national and international level.

Despite the growing interest in coaching Walter was far from satisfied. He felt that the time had come when schools and youth clubs should be encouraged to develop their own coaches. 'Where there is inspiring leadership and good coaching the general standard of play in schools and clubs is high,' he remarked. The county football associations were key to providing this training but not all were supportive. By 1952, nineteen of the 43 had not run a single course.

But there were encouraging signs. New courses were being introduced, including courses for schoolboys which were held at Highgate School and Lilleshall, each attended by a 100 boys from 69 schools. To advance links with education, the FA fielded representative teams to play matches against universities such as Oxford, Cambridge and London. Colts games were arranged with the FA sending teams to play against leading public schools.

Professional players were responding to courses designed for them in greater numbers. In the 1952/53 season 151 players applied to attend courses at Lilleshall and St Luke's College, Exeter and 107 were accepted. One of the players accepted for the course at Lilleshall was Ron Greenwood who was playing for Brentford at the time. During the long train journeys to away matches Greenwood had heard some of the other Brentford players talking with tremendous enthusiasm about the coaching courses they had attended. They said that coaches like Walter Winterbottom, George Smith, Alan Brown, Sid Cann and George Ainsley had opened their eyes. He was intrigued, so along with Jimmy Hill and Jackie Goodwin, who were also playing at Brentford, applied to attend the course.

In his biography *Sincerely Yours,* Greenwood relates what a life changing experience his first meeting with Walter was:

Walter and his coaches – Walter above all – gripped us with their ideas. They taught us how to teach but, more than that, they seemed to take us right inside the game. There were new subtleties to think about, new dimensions to work on, new experiments to be tried. Theory and practice was always nicely balanced and everything was geared to getting the best out of individuals and teams... Our enthusiasm was endless, the touch-paper had been well and truly lit, and at the end of the week I remember wishing the course could go on forever. My wife Lucy spotted something different in me the moment I got home. 'You've changed,' she said, 'You've come alight!'

Jimmy Hill was another thinking player who was inspired by his exposure to Walter's coaching. He was a young player who thought it made sense to do everything he could to learn about his profession and make prudent provision for the future when he could no longer play. 'Come the summer, off we went to Lilleshall to meet Walter Winterbottom, the man who, single-handed, was to revolutionise England's attitude to coaching,' Jimmy said. 'He succeeded in turning England from a relatively heathen football country in which footballers were supposedly born multi-talented into one in which it was accepted that it was possible to improve individual and collective skills, technical knowledge and performance and achieve better results.'

What Jimmy Hill learned from Walter was that acquiring knowledge was one thing but being able to pass it on as a teacher was another, and he embraced the new teaching philosophy wholeheartedly.

An advanced course at Lilleshall was introduced for senior coaches and trainers who already held the full qualification. Here they were given a higher level of training in coaching methods, examination procedure, and the assessment of candidate's ability. They were able to exchange ideas and discuss new developments. Walter always had an open mind; he always wanted to hear new ideas that could improve playing standards. Discussions would range from evaluating different tactics to the ideal pressure to inflate a football, the design of football boots, kit, treatment of feet or the shape of studs. 'Analysis and synthesis were at the heart of his work in coaching,' reflected one coach. 'Walter was a student of the game – once a student always a student.'

The courses soon attracted international interest and coaches came from Mexico, Iceland, Switzerland, Sweden, France, China, Holland, Belgium, and Italy. Many of the foreign countries were taking on the development of Walter's ideas faster than their English counterparts. There were those who felt that Walter was held in higher esteem abroad than he was in England.' To paraphrase a well known saying he was 'A prophet not recognised in his own country.'

Initially many of the coaches Walter trained were unable to find work in England, and took appointments abroad. In 1947, twenty four ex-professional English players were appointed as trainer or coaches overseas: 13 in Holland, others in Belgium, Sweden, Denmark and France. Only two were able to find employment in England. Over the years this changed as Walter was able to spread his influence to the boardrooms of professional clubs and gain the respect of club chairman and in this way he was able to encourage them to appoint coaches to their staff.

Although progress was being made in training coaches the lack of facilities was a cause for concern. The reason some clubs and schools did not have a really effective coaching scheme was often due to poor or inadequate facilities, particularly on dark winter evenings when rain had soaked the pitches. This usually meant that a boy would go for weeks without any ball practice (the need for regular ball practice was a repeated theme throughout Walter's years in football). He stressed the need for floodlight facilities with semi-permanent surfaces, or indoor halls, which could provide all-weather practice areas. Regular training was essential to raise standards of performance. 'We must provide our young players with opportunities equal to those often found abroad,' asserted Walter, 'where young footballers frequently train and practice three times a week nearly all the year round.'

Walter found that the standard being reached by the professional and ex-professional players who were visiting schools and clubs was sometimes disappointing and should be improved. This led to the introduction of refresher courses of a more intensive nature to provide players who were coaching with a more specialised knowledge of their subject.

Trainers at professional clubs needed courses of far greater depth. Walter considered that courses of as much as three to five weeks duration were necessary if these men were to be given the opportunity for deeper study into the principles and methods of training and rehabilitating injured players (his view was endorsed by the National Association of Trainers and Coaches.)

No stone was left unturned in his quest to improve the influence of coaching. In 1953 Walter made representations to the Army and Royal Air Force, asking them to introduce extensive football coaching schemes. Here, at least, he knew there were excellent facilities and natural leaders who would make successful coaches. He argued that this would benefit the services by adding to the attractions of service life and helping the recruitment of regular servicemen. Matches were arranged between FA representative teams and the Army and the RAF to stimulate the development of football in those institutions.

Up until 1954 Walter had no staff at the FA, only secretarial and clerical support (staff coaches were part time and paid by the hour for assignments). Norman Creek was then appointed as Assistant Director of Coaching and given the responsibility for managing the FA amateur teams and the Great Britain team at the 1956 and 1960 Olympics. Creek, who had been a master at Dauntsey's public school, had played for the famous Corinthians and represented England five times as an amateur player. Creek was appointed, not by Walter, but by Graham Doggart, a senior FA councillor. They had been friends at Cambridge, were both Cambridge blues, and both played together for the Corinthians. Creek initially refused the position because he could not afford to move to London, but Doggart bought him a house. It represented a strengthening of the old school, Oxbridge, and amateur ties within the FA.

Walter encouraged coaches to form their own regional coaching associations – where coaches could meet for lectures and have a forum for an exchange of views. Bert Fuller and Harry Littlewood were instrumental in setting up the London Football Coaches Association (LFCA) and Arthur Rowe (who introduced 'the push and run' style at Tottenham) became chairman. A coaching committee was formed which included Jackie Goodwin, Dexter Adams and Bertie Mee.

The LFCA met at the Clarendon Court Hotel, Maida Vale, and ran coaching classes during the winter months in a gymnasium off Baker Street. Afterwards a group of staff coaches would meet in a nearby café and drink coffee for hours – like plotters in a soccer revolution – whilst ideas were thrashed out. Baker Street was a hothouse for coaching, achieving almost a cult status in football folklore. Walter had fond memories of the lively nature of those discussions, with characters like Ron Greenwood, Jimmy Hill, Frank Blunstone, Tommy Harmer, Jim Clarkson, Gordon Jago, George Curtis and later John Lyall and John Cartwright. Jackie Goodwin, the vice chairman, was an ever present (the idea of inviting members of the press to a central coaching course came out of one of these sessions and soon afterwards Brian Scovell and Ken Jones were amongst twenty or so sports writers who attended a Lilleshall course).

Walter was invited to be the President of the LFCA and continued in this role until he died. It was a mark of the affection and esteem in which he was held by the LFCA that six years after his death the committee introduced an annual award for the top football coach in England which they named 'The Sir Walter Winterbottom Coaching Award.'

Attending coaching courses and gaining badges was only the beginning of the development of coaches. It was an evolving process. Walter worked behind the scenes as the puppet master, advancing the careers of his brightest protégés and helping to put them into influential positions. Ron Greenwood's career in coaching provides a perfect example.

When Ron Greenwood first met Walter at Lilleshall it entirely changed the way he thought about football. Walter convinced him that coaching had a big future at a time when the majority of professionals scorned it. 'Walter, though, was a visionary' Greenwood said. 'He explained that new methods of training were being investigated and new ways of teaching were coming to the fore. Training was being related to technique as well as stamina; all over Europe the game was evolving fast. Walter told me "We might have given the game to the world but now we're in danger of being overtaken." This was revolutionary stuff and many were not only wary but downright hostile.' But Greenwood was convinced and decided that this was his future and that when he retired from playing he would try to make a career as a coach.

Greenwood's first coaching engagement was with Ealing Grammar School. Each session was supposed to last an hour and a half but the first lasted nearly three hours simply because it was so enjoyable. Soon afterwards, when Oxford University had a vacancy for a coach, Walter put Greenwood's name forward to the university on a shortlist of three. Greenwood got the job and had three years experience coaching the Varsity soccer team. As he was still a Chelsea player he was unable to see Oxford play as often as he would have liked, although he did watch the Varsity match at Wembley when he was injured (his opposite number that day, coaching Cambridge, was Bill Nicholson). Greenwood felt that Oxford University gave him a perfect introduction to the art of coaching, in particular because he was dealing with intelligent and responsive students who were eager to learn.

The position was rotated after three years. Jimmy Hill took over at Oxford, and Ron Greenwood became the coach at Walthamstow Avenue, one of the country's leading amateur clubs where he stayed for two years. This was an FA coaching appointment and he was paid three pounds a session which had to cover his expenses for the long journey from South Harrow by tube and trolleybus. But he was still playing for Chelsea, so money was not an issue and the reward for him was experience. He learned from Walter that 'this was the way the Hungarians brought on their coaches, giving them jobs with schools and smaller clubs and then gradually raising the standard.'

In the late spring of 1956 Eastbourne United offered Greenwood the job of coach, and this time it was a paying position which matched the money he was getting as a player at Fulham. He took the plunge and hung up his boots to become a professional coach. At the same time the Sussex county FA appointed him as their chief coach and in this capacity he spent a great deal of time at teacher training colleges and schools throughout the county 'generally spreading the gospel.' In addition to his other responsibilities he was picked by Walter to coach England's youth team, taking over from George Smith who had become the first paid manager of the England youth squad in 1953. Greenwood had already been involved with England's youth side at Lilleshall while attending courses as a staff coach, and found it exciting to be working with the best young players in England. He recalled saying to Walter on one of these occasions 'Just look at them... the future of English football is no problem.' (The players they were working with then included Jimmy Greaves and Bobby Charlton).

Greenwood's reputation was growing and in 1957 Bob Wall asked him to be the club coach at the Arsenal. He discovered later that Arsenal had asked the FA to help them find a coach. Greenwood's name was put forward with two others and Walter's hand was clearly behind this appointment as well. In his autobiography Greenwood said 'I was the first full-time coach Arsenal appointed but, more than that, the first FA staff coach to be given such a job by any League club. I was not a manager; I was a coach pure and simple. The whole concept of coaching was on trial because the FA (Walter) felt that if I made a success of it then other clubs would follow. If I failed, the traditional resistance to coaching would harden. The bridge between the new and the old would widen.'

George Swindin was the Arsenal manager, and he was happy to leave the coaching to Greenwood, although initially there was resistance from some of the players who resented the whole idea of a coach. But Greenwood's methods were successful and he stayed as a coach with Arsenal for three years. During this time he again came under Walter's wing; this time as the manager of the England Under-23 team in succession to Bill Nicholson, who had become the manager of Tottenham Hotspur. Finally Greenwood moved to West Ham where he became one of the new young breed of managers schooled by Walter. Once again he was influential in guiding his protégé's career, as he explained in his foreword to Ron Greenwood's autobiography, *Sincerely Yours*: 'It also fell upon me to play a part in Ron's appointment as manager/coach at West Ham. My opinion was sought and Ron, as one of a new type of managers coming through, seemed admirably equipped for the post. He found full opportunity to apply his ideas about positive football at Upton Park.'

Greenwood himself of course became the England team manager in 1977; the ultimate accolade for Walter's protégé.

Coaching the coaches was only part of the story and Walter organised courses in related areas. Training a first-class team was becoming more scientific and required expert understanding and ability. Having studied sports medicine at Carnegie College, Walter was able to develop courses for trainers covering the workings of the body, muscles and nerves, massage, and treatment of injury. He encouraged discussions on the training methods that could get the best out of a top-class player.

Referee courses were organised in conjunction with the Referees Association on the same basis and with the same purpose as the coaching courses, and they continued to grow in number and scope. They helped to develop a better understanding of the laws by players and greater consistency of control and higher standards by referees.

Courses for groundsmen were held at the Board of Green Keeping Research Station at Bingley. There they were given instruction on the general care of turf, use of fertilisers in controlling pests, and of course the endless problem of maintaining pitches in good condition – no easy task in an English winter of rain, snow and frost, with the pitch being continually used for training as well as matches.

Club secretaries were not forgotten either. For them the emphasis was on courses aimed at increasing business efficiency and eliminating bureaucracy at the professional clubs. At all of these courses everyone enjoyed the opportunity for experienced and like-minded people to come together and exchange ideas.

With education as the cornerstone of the FA coaching scheme it was not surprising that books and films became an important part of the campaign to reach a much wider audience, and at the outset Walter was given the responsibility for the publications department.

The film company, Gaumont-British Instructional Limited, produced a series of coaching films, sponsored by Gillette industries. Under Walter's direction, ten films were made by 1950. They featured famous players showing how to coach during a game; demonstrating ball control, trapping, kicking, goalkeeping, throwing in, and attack and defense tactics. These films were very popular and distributed free to colleges, schools, clubs and libraries. Players gave their time and help for nothing. 'Walter called once to ask me to demonstrate some skills in a coaching film; trapping and passing and things like that,' recalled Jimmy Armfield. 'I went down to his house, in Stanmore, and stayed the night with him. Can you imagine that happening now? There was no talk of fees or anything like that. We liked him so much we knew he wouldn't even be thinking about money – which he probably wouldn't anyway.'

Walter had been introduced to Jack Bramley who owned 'Educational Productions Limited.' a publishing company in Wakefield, Yorkshire. They became friendly and he encouraged Jack and his wife Jo to publish a simple technical book explaining the basic skills and laws of football. It was called *Know the Game* – a soft cover booklet which sold at two shillings and six pence (25p)

Walter the young scholar – always smartly dressed! (c. 1925)

Above left and right: Walter, proud to be a Manchester United player (1936/37).

Below: Congratulations from ex teammates at Royton Amateurs on Walter's first appearance for Manchester United. (Away to Leeds United, 28.11.1936)

Above: Walter instructing a class of student PE teachers at Carnegie College, Leeds, 1939.

Below left: Squadron Leader Winterbottom, Air Ministry, c.1941.

Below right: Walter and Ann on their wedding day, St. John's church, Stanmore, 1942.

Above: An early FA experiment in 1945 – Wing Commander Winterbottom coaching schoolboys at Stamford Bridge.

Below: Walter (back row, third from the right) with the England team that beat Sweden 4-2 in 1947. Players left to right. Back row: Scott, Langton, Swift, Franklin. Middle row: Mortenson, Lawton, Hardwick, Wright, Taylor. Front two: Finney, Mannion.

bove: Walter with Peter Harris, Jimmy Dickinson, Tom Finney and FA chairman of
ectors, Arthur Drewry. 1949. (Drewry became President of Fifa in 1955.)

low: Walter the coach with his mentor Sir Stanley Rous, c.1952.

Above: The manager with his captain, c.1954. Billy Wright went on to win 105 England caps under Walter.

Below: The England team that lost 6-3 to Hungary at Wembley in 1953 in the 'the matc[h] of the century.' Left to right. Back row: Ramsey, Wright, Merrick, Johnston, Dickinson, Eckersley. Front row: Matthews, Taylor, Mortenson, Sewel, Robb.

Above: In a relaxed mood in the Wembley dressing room with Jimmy Greaves and Bobby Tambling before Walter's final game in charge (v Wales, 21.11.1962).

Below: With a happy England squad at Lilleshall shortly before the 1958 Munich air disaster. Tommy Taylor, Roger Byrne (middle row left) and Duncan Edwards (middle far right) were amongst those tragically killed when Manchester United's aircraft crashed.

Above: Walter (front row, sixth from left) at a coaches' group youth course at Lilleshall in 1960.

Below: Walter and Harold Shepherdson with the England team in 1960. Back row: Armfield, Flowers, Springett, Swan, Haynes, Wilson. Front row: Douglas, Viollet, Clayton, Baker, Charlton.

and was widely distributed through bookshops. It was an introduction for those who wanted to take football seriously and proved to be so popular that the series was eventually expanded to cover almost every sport.

The first publisher the FA chose to work with was the Naldrett Press Limited and then later Heinemann. One of the most popular books which they published was the FA *Book for Boys* – a football annual which contained articles by experts and famous players and cleverly blended entertainment and education. Walter directed the content and invited contributors from all sides of the game. The first volume, published in 1948, included such articles as 'How are you keeping?' by Frank Swift, 'The Referee' by George Clark, 'Schools Football' by WR Ward, 'Football Fit 'by Tom Whittaker, and 'The Centre Half - Attack or Defence?' by Norman Creek. Well known sports writers also contributed. Walter himself wrote 'Plan your Attack' and perhaps predictably, 'Coaching the Coaches'. The dust jacket featured an original painting capturing the drama of football and the book was produced to a high standard with black and white photographs and beautiful illustrations. It was priced at ten shillings (50p) and came out in time to meet the Christmas gift market. The series continued, becoming bigger and better throughout Walter's 16 years at the FA and became an important part of football literature. He was involved in the production of other more specialised books published by the Naldrett Press for the FA, including, *How to Become a Referee, The Professional Footballer,* and *The Soccer Club Secretary.*

The first coaching *Bulletin* was issued in September 1946 which became the new and improved *FA Bulletin* in 1948 and evolved as the *FA News* in August 1956.

The *FA Year Book*, which was introduced in the 1948-49 season, was a football almanac, similar to Wisden's long established cricket almanac. It contained a review of all the main events in professional and amateur football and was an influential vehicle for Stanley Rous to comment on major developments and for Walter to suggest and explain new aspects of coaching.

Although he was away from home a great deal, running courses or travelling with England teams, when he was in his office at 22 Lancaster Gate he spent much of his time designing courses and working on FA publications. Tom Prentiss was a member of the administration staff working for Walter in the coaching department and when asked what Walter did, he replied, 'Writing. He seemed to be endlessly sat at his desk writing.'

An important landmark during this period was the publishing of Walter's first book, *Soccer Coaching* – the first modern soccer coaching manual. The book evolved from the coaching courses at Lilleshall and from the exchange of ideas with colleagues like Dave Munrow, players, managers and coaches. Published by William Heinemann Ltd. in 1952, it was a hard cover book with 247 pages and was simply but effectively illustrated with line drawings and charts showing players' movements on the pitch.

The book begins with instruction on the individual skills: kicking, passing, trapping, heading, tackling, dribbling and throwing in. Each one is explained in detail – for example 12 different ways to kick a ball to achieve different objectives – and suggest ways to practice. It goes on to explain tactics for attack and defence and concludes with methods of coaching.

In his review of the book John Arlott wrote: 'By the comparative standard of a football library… this is probably the most important book ever written on the game, from the point of view of its potential effect on play it is certainly so.' He went on to say that the outstanding quality of the book was that it would appeal to a 12-year-old boy, a club player, a professional player or an international.

Because it was the first book of its kind, it dealt with the basics; it did not try to be sophisticated. Jimmy Armfield, who still has a signed copy, refers to it as the bible of football coaching, even consulting it now for the new coaching book he is writing.

'Everything in it still stands up today,' he said, 'it's simple and easy to understand. It was a skeleton of football coaching and over the years that followed, others put the meat on it. Of course a book written 60 years ago looks dated but it's still relevant today.'

The first paragraph of Walter's introduction captures the essence of his philosophy of coaching:

Things have a way of going wrong in football. Attacks break down, clearances are blocked, open goals are missed, throw ins go straight to the feet of opponents, perfectly placed centres are scrambled away. The football field is anything but a chessboard... nevertheless, it is obviously unsatisfactory to rely on haphazard chances to achieve results. A planned approach can bring perfection nearer to realisation... the task of a coach is to direct practice so as to improve and blend the various skills, and minimise the chance factor by sheer efficiency.

Because he had been a schoolmaster, sports writers found it easy to label him as a bespectacled academic and dismiss coaching with the cliché of blackboard teaching. The blackboard teaching label owed much to a strand of working class anti-intellectualism which had little time for 'book learners, chalkers on blackboards and purveyors of theoretical knowledge.' Even the intellectual but acerbic Brian Glanville dismissed him as 'that tall pedagogic Walter Winterbottom.' It was typical of comments by some sports writers – though not always as erudite – and in this way the media made the task of coaching and educating more difficult.

It was true that in the early years his appearance gave the impression of an academic. Glanville described him as looking like a public school games master, of the type idolised by junior forms. 'He has that typical combination of athleticism and scholarship, a tall and agile figure, inevitably smoking a pipe and wearing horn rimmed spectacles; the classic Corinthian, whose bookshelves contain Homer and Xenothon, side-by-side with the Badminton Library. In conversation he is brisk, incisive and practical, with an aptitude for the generalisation which seems obvious only when it is made. "Football is a game where superiority in match play can't always be indicated by goals because of the difficulty of scoring."'

The press unfairly latched on to 'blackboard' epithet for years, a claim that annoyed Walter because it was untrue and because it did a disservice to the image of coaching. His advice to coaches always stressed the need to be practical: 'Tactics need to be well rehearsed on the field before they can be expected to bring results in an actual match.'

One newspaper, the *Evening Standard*, put the other side of the story in 1954, reflecting Walter's frustrations:

The Football Association fights a battle for public faith and common sense. They are trying to combat years of neglect which have left Britain's footballers the most uncoached but glamourised players in the world – and now they must combat criticisms of 'hush-hush' stupidity. In the middle of the battle is Walter Winterbottom, popularly imagined, as a result of distorting cameos, to be the Schoolmaster of Soccer. He is seen capped and gowned, blackboarding his theories and formulae with academic disdain for their application on a cold winter's day. This illusion has grown more attractive the harder he has worked as Director of Coaching for the FA and as England's team manager... Walter does not like blackboards.

The article went on to quote Walter: 'People, especially the critics, talk of coaching as if it meant getting in a huddle over a secret plan. But they haven't seen much of it, for the simple reason there is hardly any real coaching in this country. We are only just beginning. And it has very little to do with secret team tactics.' Asked what he would most wish for as England prepared in earnest to improve her soccer he snapped with frustration, 'accept coaching as organised and concentrated practice; and trust our coaching schemes which have been widely used and praised by the very countries which are beating us at our own game.'

Although he was a patient man Walter was irritated by the ignorant and mistaken myths that swirled around the training field – the belief that laps around the pitch were required to achieve fitness. He advocated that ball practice, when properly devised, can do the entire job of getting a player into shape for his game. 'This is directly opposed to the popular idea that the players should train without the ball to prevent staleness. Clearly the greatest need in any ball-game is the perfection of ball-play.' And in an untypical touch of sarcasm he added 'a billiards player does not train by walking round the table; nor will a footballer better his football skill by running around the field.'

The demand on Walter's time was relentless. In addition to the week-long central coaching courses in the summer, which he supervised personally, he visited county FA Courses and coaching demonstrations at schools and teacher training colleges. He examined students at 'Schools Week' at Oxford and Cambridge and often made trips abroad to advise on coaching courses; particularly to Magglingen, Switzerland's 'University of Sport,' where he ran players and referees coaching courses for FIFA. He travelled with England teams at all levels and every Saturday in the season was spent attending a football match somewhere in England. His writing – books, articles and course design – spilled over from the office to his study at home. He worked every evening. His long suffering wife Ann kept a diary, and in response to his denial, was able to prove to him that he spent more than six months away from home each year. It is difficult to overstate the contribution Walter made in creating a national coaching structure and gaining acceptance of coaching at all levels of the game. Its significance has generally gone unrecognised except by those coaches he inspired, in England and abroad.

Amongst them he was considered to be of his generation, the leading technical thinker and exponent of coaching association football in the world.

CHAPTER 10

A MOUNTAIN
TO CLIMB

1950 – 1953

Despite the humiliating set back of elimination from the World Cup in Brazil in 1950, England's record in the following three seasons was good, winning 13 of the next 22 games and losing only two. Nine of these games were home internationals, and this was frustrating. It was not that Scotland, Wales and Northern Ireland were weak teams. Scotland in particular was always strong opposition. One of the only two games lost in the last three years was against Scotland at Wembley. The problem was that all the British teams played with the same style and Walter knew that the real test of England's calibre lay in how they tackled the best teams abroad. He found the Home International Championship parochial and unsatisfactory. 'The games obviously have less importance than the bigger picture' he said.

He was also handicapped by the number of Scottish and Welsh and Irish players in the English First Division. In a 1982 interview in the *Guardian* he complained 'I could go to a league match and have only five English players to look at out of 22. That never happens in other countries and it's worse now because of the imports. The best national teams have always been built around club sides. Before the war Arsenal had nine England players but it never happened in my day. The clubs needed to get players after the war and the cheapest players you could get hold of easily were the Scots. The logical answer would be a British team. I could see no problems but the Scots would never agree. Getting rid of the home internationals would help. I got tired of them. I tried to get Wales and Northern Ireland to give them up but they wouldn't listen. They unbalance the [England] fixture list.' (It was a long time before this obstacle was removed. The British Home Championship ended after the 1983/84 season, due to a decline in its popularity and fixture congestion with the more important European Championship, which England first entered in 1964).

There were growing signs of the vulnerability of England's unbeaten home record against foreign teams. In 1950 Yugoslavia drew 2-2 at Wembley, a match notable for the exciting debut of Nat Lofthouse who scored both goals. England remained unbeaten against foreign teams at home, but it had much to do with the unfamiliar conditions they faced and the moral advantage of England's long history of soccer supremacy.

In 1951 Argentina came to Wembley and although England won 2-1 they struggled to break down a funnel defence. A year later, in November 1951, Austria came to London. Although perhaps not as accomplished as Hugo Meisl's 'Wunderteam' of the early thirties, they were one of Europe's leading teams and they had the brilliant Ernst Ocwirk, the best attacking centre half in the world. The result was a 2-2 draw, with England deploying the funnel defence tactic which Walter had experienced against the visiting Argentineans six months before; England though, unlike their South American counterparts, frequently looked technically inferior to their opponents. Nevertheless in the return match, England's brand of fast direct physical football triumphed in a game which England won

3-2. Lofthouse was outstanding, scoring two goals and earning himself the sobriquet 'The Lion of Vienna.'

Walter continued to suffer at the hands of a nine man selection committee of which he was not a member – a situation that resulted in chopping and changing and some whimsical decisions that must have been hard for him to accept. In the game against Wales, which England won 4-2, Les Compton, an Arsenal stalwart, was called up for his first cap at the age of 38. In the following match against Northern Ireland, Billy Wright, who had been injured, was now fit to play, but the selectors stuck with Compton and an unchanged team. Against Scotland in 1951, Jack Froggatt, who had previously been capped twice at outside left, was selected at centre half; the game ended in England's only defeat of the season. He was one of four players tried in that position in seven matches that season. Against Argentina the inside forward creator, Wilf Mannion, was unavailable due to injury. The selectors moved the centre forward Mortensen, to inside right and brought in another centre forward, Milburn of Newcastle. The team was left unbalanced with no one to scheme the openings, when Eddie Baily of Spurs would have been an obvious choice.

Yugoslavia, Argentina and Austria had presented styles of play that were quite different from those in England, presenting new challenges. Walter had boldly confronted the critics who accused him of being too theoretical with an article in the *FA News* titled 'Are we theoretical enough?' He pointed out that England had lost its supremacy and argued that changes were needed: 'The pupils have caught up with the teacher, and it is time for him to refresh his thinking... the challenge from abroad now expresses itself in methods and styles which are highly unorthodox and intriguingly different.'

In England in the 1950's teams all used the WM system which had revolutionised the game when it was introduced by Herbert Chapman at the Arsenal in 1926. Chapman changed the traditional line-up of two full backs, three half backs and five forwards by making the centre half a third central full back (stopper) with the two full backs pivoting round him. With the M below the W they formed the bottom 3 points of the M and the top 2 points were the two wing halves. The 2 bottom points of the W were the inside forwards and the top 3 points were the two wingers and the centre forward. They didn't use numbers to describe the formation in those days but if they did the literal transposition of WM might have been 3-4-3.

The midfield 4 usually had one inside forward in an attacking role and one in midfield in tandem with an attacking wing half. The other wing half played a defensive midfield role and so in modern terms it could have been called 3-3-4. There could be variations on who played which role in midfield but it was universally known as the WM system

The WM formation had been unchanged in England for 30 years but teams from abroad had new ideas. In an *FA Year Book* article Walter explained the Austrian 'bolt' formation, which England had come up against when playing Austria home and away. In the bolt formation one full-back marks the centre forward and the other plays behind him to check any breakthrough (making a bolt). The two wing halves mark the wingers so that these four players become the last defensive line. The centre half takes up a roaming mission in midfield and is often joined in midfield by the centre forward, leaving the two inside forwards and wingmen as the attackers, making the bolt formation 1-3-2-4.

Walter explained the difficulties of marking when an English team with the WM formation clashed with the Austrian team's bolt formation, and how each tried to counter the other. He showed how new ideas were being used to counter the problem of overcoming a team whose players retreated into a solid defensive wall – one idea being that the attacking team would pass the ball backwards in a wide semicircle well behind the halfway line and then come forward again, in order to draw the defenders out of position. This might be seen as a crazy extreme to those used to English football, but Walter pointed out Alex James had sometimes made a long pass back to his own goalkeeper for a similar purpose.

A misguided criticism that continually annoyed Walter was that coaching destroyed individual ability. 'Many overseas teams are living demonstrations that thorough coaching leads to the fullest expression of individual qualities' he said, and put the counter argument that 'a common system of play [the English WM system] is a strong deterrent to freedom and freshness.' It was because every team played with the same system there was no incentive to try something new and naturally when they came up against new systems in international matches it was very hard to adapt.

In May 1953 Walter took the England team on tour to South America. It was England's first summer (close season) tour, which, like most new ideas, was criticised before the team left. Critics considered that it meant too much football at the end of a hard season. It was certainly a tough tour with long flights, bad weather and illness, but it was a valuable international football learning curve. Fortunately, although the selectors (there were still nine of them) picked the squad, only the chairman of the selection committee, Howard Shentall, travelled. It is probable that Winterbottom had Mr. Shentall's ear because the team was largely unchanged for the four matches.

It was not unusual for the England team to be feted as honoured guests when visiting foreign countries and Argentina was no exception. General Juan Perón invited the England party to a special audience. Perón had been re-elected as president in 1951 but his charismatic wife, Eva, the darling of the people, had died of cancer a year earlier at the age of only 33. As a mark of respect Walter, Billy Wright and FA officials visited her tomb and laid a wreath. Perón was a charming but controversial character who championed the working classes but was hated by the military and the upper classes. He was ousted and exiled in a military coup in 1955, but when Walter, Billy and the FA party met him he was one of the most powerful men in South America. They sat round a long oblong table in the Cabinet room drinking coffee and chatting amiably. 'I remember you first sending a team here in 1905' said Perón, 'Nottingham Forest were the visitors and they beat us, but by 1912 we learned a lot from you and gained our first victory over Swindon Town.' The president smiled disarmingly and continued: 'You taught us football but we hope you will win. Why, I've even got my money on England. We like our guests to go home happy and we know you will go home happier still if you win.' Everyone laughed politely but Walter and Billy were not fooled into believing him. Indeed, he promised his team that if they won he would give them a large Mercedes-Benz which they could then raffle and share the proceeds.

But there was bad feeling and Latin trickery to follow. A warm up friendly match had been arranged which was designated as an FA XI against Buenos Aires, but it turned out to be the full Argentine international team. England lost 3-1, much to the delight of General Peron. They were determined to have their revenge in the next match, a recognised international. Having come up against a deep lying centre forward, Lacasia, in the last game Walter had a rare chance to make a tactical change to counter it in the rematch. He had a discussion with the players: 'We decided that Johnston, the centre half would go with him [Lacasia] in the early part of the match with Billy [Wright] and Jimmy Dickenson covering the gap in the middle, then Johnston would fall back in favour of someone else so that the Argentinean team would not quite know if we were going to persist in man to man marking.' It was a pity that the game was abandoned due to a torrential rainstorm after 21 minutes with the score at 0-0, because no conclusions could be drawn.

A 2-1 victory over Chile in Santiago followed, but they then lost 2-1 in Uruguay – not a bad result considering that Uruguay had won the World Cup in Brazil three years earlier. Billy Wright thought that 'for all round football skill I have yet to see anything superior to that produced by the Uruguayans.' England were on top for long periods of the game, and were unlucky not to score on several occasions. A 6-3 win over the USA in the Yankee Stadium in New York gave England revenge for their humiliating World Cup defeat in Brazil but Walter was unconvinced with his team's showing on the tour: 'Some good players are coming through but in team play we are way behind.'

As the England team manager Walter inevitably met many celebrities from all walks of life who followed football. One that surprised him was Yehudi Menuhin who came to watch the game in New York in 1953, and later in Los Angeles in 1959. Walter had met the world-famous violinist several times in the director's box at the Arsenal and had often been invited to his concerts but had never been able to attend because of prior commitments.

The tour had not brought glory but much had been learned about South American opposition. They had experienced different pitches, a different kind of physical intimidation, different refereeing standards and a different style of play. 'We noted artistic touches and technical moves by our opponents that I am sure the players will go back and discuss with their club colleagues,' said Billy Wright.

One of the most beneficial aspects of the tour from Walter's point of view was that he had the team together for four weeks. This was quite different from the usual international format: games were played on a Wednesday with the manager only having access to his players two days before the game. To make matters worse, with a full league programme on the preceding Saturday, it was quite normal for Walter to field phone calls at home from club managers on Sunday to say that players had been injured and would be unable to join the England squad on Monday. Some of these claims were dubious and inevitably led to a last minute rejigging of the side.

Walter's problem was that for changes in style to happen in the England team it was necessary for them first to be embedded in the way the top English clubs played. The English game was rooted in the traditional third back game introduced by Herbert Chapman. In the 1950s Wolverhampton Wanderers, under their manager Stan Cullis, were the greatest exponents of this style with wing halves by-passing midfield with long balls played to fast raiding wingers. All the other teams in the League played this way so there was little tactical challenge. Walter worked behind the scenes, talking to managers about new ideas, but in the early 1950s most were, like Cullis, of the 'old school' and unreceptive.

The *FA News* gave Walter the chance to explain his views about playing styles to a wider audience: 'Sometimes a style stems from the special talents of one or more key players... others are deeply rooted in the traditions and temperament of a club or nation. But they are nearly always subject to change. Sometimes this is gradual,' he said, citing Frank Swift's technique of throwing the ball to midfield players to maintain possession and begin an attack instead of a long upfield kick which would invariably come straight back. He used a diagram to illustrate how Matthews and Finney had developed a pattern of moving deep into their own half to collect the ball instead of being isolated on the wings.

He drew attention to the fluid interchanging of forwards which had become a marked feature of football on the continent. Challenging the traditional English style he questioned the value of each defender marking a given opponent closely throughout the match, irrespective of how the attack shapes. 'The new style,' he said, is to maintain the block defensive structure and for the whole defence to retreat and entice the opposing attack into its meshes. He gave the example of the South American tactic of the retreating defence and the all-out attack strategy in which half backs and full backs joined the attack to press home an advantage –a vision of the 'total football' that was to come in the 1970s. He was a man ahead of his time: but for the most part managers remained rooted in the past.

The belief that England were still the best team in the world persisted and was bolstered by a match between England and a FIFA team in October 1953 which had been arranged to celebrate the 90th anniversary of the Football Association. Although all the players came from Western Europe – Austria, Spain, Yugoslavia, Germany, Italy and Sweden – the press and the public billed the team as the 'Rest of the World.' In reality it was a scratch team, with no Hungarians and a team that had never played or trained together before, but they came within minutes of taking away England's unbeaten home record. The result was a 4-4 draw, which on the face of it appeared to be a credible result against the 'Rest of the World.' The uncomfortable truth was that it highlighted the growing superiority of European football, and England's record was only salvaged by the award of a penalty in the dying minutes of the game, from which the ice cool Alf Ramsey equalised. The game demonstrated the contrast in style between English and continental football, with England fighting back doggedly against swift, artistic attacks by the FIFA team. The match report in the *FA Year Book* confessed 'the English defence seemed mesmerised at times by the lightning footwork and close passing of the continentals.

The failure of English League teams to experiment with new playing styles was not because there were no managers or players who had new ideas – especially the few who had taken their club sides to the continent or South America – but because of the fierce competition and commercial demands that discouraged clubs from trying new ideas. There were notable exceptions like Arthur Rowe, Matt Busby and Vic Buckingham. Arthur Rowe at Tottenham had developed the 'push and run' style; he had been a player with Spurs, coached in Hungary before the war and then managed Chelmsord City before coming to Tottenham who were then in the Second Division. When the players came back from the summer break he asked them if they would practice with a new style of football based on a quick, short, passing game. They did and it proved to be devastatingly successful. Spurs won the Second Division and the League Championship in successive years. The main value of 'push and run' was the rapid change of position by players, making marking much more difficult. It depended on players working closely together to develop an understanding. 'That was Arthur's contribution,' said Walter, 'welding a team who could play this style of football which was so attractive to watch. It was silky stuff, and everybody seemed to have plenty of time with the ball and yet they were running into space. This work off the ball is essential if you are going to play a good game of football.' Rowe was a staunch believer in coaching and as the first chairman of the LFCA was influential in passing on his ideas.

Matt Busby was a believer in youth. He coached a crop of promising youngsters and was not afraid to put them in the first team at 17 or 18. United played not so much with tactical innovation, but with great attacking flair. Busby had a belief that good football would produce winning results and developed a style that mixed short passing with accurate passes of up to 40 yards which frequently led to goals being scored.

Vic Buckingham was one of Walter's disciples who became the manager at West Bromwich Albion in 1952. In the 1953/54 season they won the FA Cup and were runners-up in the League, playing an attractive style of possession football which he developed further when he went to Ajax.

But for the most part managers were discouraged from trying different tactics because of the imperative of winning and the fear of failure. Club chairmen were generally dominant characters of the old school who wanted nothing to do with new thinking. This had a knock-on effect when Walter asked England players to try out new ideas – 'My manager doesn't like me to play that way,' came the reply, and when they did, managers would complain to Walter that their player 'had come back and now he wants to play a different way.'

In preparation for the game against Austria in 1951 Walter wanted to counter the threat of their famous attacking centre half, Ocwirk, who was tremendous at coming through and shooting from distance.

'I happened to speak to Billy Wright some time before the game,' recalled Walter, 'and asked him if he'd mind playing inside forward instead of wing half to counter him – he'd played there for Wolves so there was no problem and he was keen to do it, being able to mark this fellow and play a more attacking role. We played him at inside forward and there was an unholy row from the chairman of Wolverhampton; he made statements to the press saying players ought to play in their club positions; it would mean that the club manager would have problems with the player when he got back and so on.'

Walter continued to use the success of continental teams to try to convince the doubters. The main difference between the continental and South American style of play, compared to the British, he contended, was in the emphasis given to accurate passing and patterned approach play. The problem was that if English teams were to adopt this style, accurate passing and close ball control had to be of a far higher standard. It was something that had to be nurtured from an early age.

World Sports magazine introduced the topic of teaching ball skills to children. It highlighted the complacency that existed. In the article Dr William Meisl (the brother of Hugo Meisl, the great Austrian coach) introduced readers to a series of Swedish soccer tests which aimed at teaching ball control to youngsters. He wondered if such a scheme could work in Britain and asked four leading football personalities, Matt Busby, Stan Cullis, Bernard Joy and Walter Winterbottom for their comments. Their answers were revealing.

Matt Busby, the Manchester United manager, was supportive: 'I do find that British players generally have lost the art of first-class ball control; invariably one finds the ball breaking away from players as they try to control it.' He went on to say that the sooner we try to develop young boys along these natural lines, with the necessary facilities and coaches to encourage them, the sooner we will develop natural ball-players again.

Stan Cullis, the manager of Wolverhampton Wanderers, was curt and dismissive: 'The tests would add interest to the training of schoolboys. It is an idea to commend all schoolteachers.'

Bernard Joy, then a columnist with London evening newspaper *The Star*, found that he could not agree more with Dr Meisl's practical tests. He said they were a target for youngsters 'but I would like to see a League club introduce these tests to their teams and I guarantee that the number of players who would fail to reach even the silver badge standard would shock the management.'

Walter was clearly frustrated by the ignorance of practical testing and the unwillingness of clubs to provide facilities for youngsters to be coached and tested in practical skills. He pointed out that these tests had in fact been used in FA coaching courses since the war and many forms of test activities had been devised and introduced in British schools. 'The idea of practical testing has been written about in *Soccer Coaching* [his coaching manual] where methods of relating the test activities to the needs of the game are also discussed.' He continued, 'in Sweden boys are coached and tested by professional clubs, where they play most of their football for the junior teams of the senior clubs; whereas in England there is no facility for schoolboys to have training or coaching with senior clubs.'

1953 was a year in which the nation experienced both pride and humiliation. It was the year of the coronation of Queen Elizabeth II and as if by divine intervention the news that Edmund Hillary and Sherpa Noray Tenzing had successfully conquered Mount Everest reached the Queen on the morning of her coronation. It was a day of great celebration of British tradition and optimism about the future.

It was also the year of the most famous FA Cup Final – remembered by everyone that saw it as the Matthews final – famous because with Bolton leading 3-1 with only 20 minutes to go, Matthews turned on a magic spell of wizardry to lay on three goals for Blackpool and win his first Cup Final medal at the age of 37. Stan

Mortenson had scored a hat trick but it was Matthews who was carried shoulder high from the pitch by his team mates.

It was the first FA Cup Final to be seen by a mass television audience: 19.5 per cent of homes now owned a television. Sales of the 9 inch black-and-white models, stowed in polished wooden cabinets, had been substantially boosted by the coronation of Queen Elizabeth II. When Stanley Matthews received his winner's medal from the new Queen he was acclaimed, not just by 100,000 fans at Wembley, but by 10 million viewers at home and the whole nation now saw him as a sporting icon.

The 1953 Cup Final and the feel good factor that it generated throughout the country focused on Stanley Matthews and the English WM formation that gave wingers space to dazzle and an a old fashioned centre forward like Mortenson a stream of crosses to convert. It relied on the individual ability that Matthews typified and that writers like Geoffrey Green of the *Times* eulogised: 'Each swerve each flick, each pass, was a delicate brush stroke and his work had all the bloom of water colours.' Jonathan Wilson in the *Anatomy of England* maintains that the 1953 final stands as the apogee of the old winger-oriented style of English football.

Some saw wider significance. 'This was the moment at which football was able to finally shed its working-class skin and be embraced as the equal of cricket as part of the English national culture,' wrote Richard Holt and Tony Mason in their book *Sport in Britain 1945-2000*. The historian Matthew Taylor thought that it encapsulated the notion of a 'new Elizabethan Age' in which... Britain would still retain a glorious place in the world.'

But renewed belief in English supremacy and optimism for the future, were to be severely challenged six months later when the Mighty Magyars – the all conquering Hungarian team – came to Wembley determined to steal England's record of never being beaten at home by a foreign team.

England would field four members of the victorious Blackpool team: Stanley Matthews, Stan Mortenson, Ernie Taylor and Harry Johnston in a match that would focus a spotlight on the differences in style between an England team that was characterised by individuals and a Hungarian team that had been coached and trained as a cohesive unit.

The game was billed as 'the match of the century' and it was to be a watershed in English football history.

CHAPTER 11

A DAY OF RECKONING

1953

'To think of football as merely twenty-two hirelings kicking a ball is merely to say that a violin is wood and gut, Hamlet is so much ink and paper. It is Conflict and Art.'

J.B. Priestley

The 25th of November 1953 was a day of reckoning in English football. The Hungarian team which came to play at Wembley was one of the finest teams of all time. They were the reigning champions from the 1952 Olympics, undefeated in their own country since 1945, and unbeaten anywhere in 25 internationals played throughout Europe in the previous four seasons.

The press built the game up and their pre-match bravado typified the arrogant and insular attitude which continued to prevail throughout England. 'England can beat Hungary inside ten minutes in this colourful match of the year at Wembley this afternoon,' declared a bullish Desmond Hackett in the *Daily Express*. 'They have only to play the old England style of football, the game of the bold attack, the long pass, the hard tackle, to break down the gay pattern of the Hungarians.' His prediction was that England would win 3-2. Frank Cole of the *Daily Telegraph* welcomed the first visit of a team from behind the Iron Curtain and warned of the quality of the Hungarian team. Nevertheless he felt that the team which England had selected would be more effective than the team which had drawn against the FIFA 'Rest of the World' team in the previous month and headlined his piece 'Matthews and Robb may be match winners: firm tackling will check Hungary.'

Privately Walter did not share the media's blinkered optimism. He was familiar with the Hungarian team. He had watched them win the 1952 Olympics and he had flown to Budapest earlier that year when they were surprisingly held to a 2-2 draw by Sweden. Typically the press took this result as a harbinger of an English win. Walter saw a Swedish team that came only to defend and a Hungarian team using the match as a practice game for the match that really mattered, against England at Wembley. He chose his words carefully on his return. 'The Hungarians are good enough to beat any side in the world.'

Not many people thought that England would actually be beaten. Ron Greenwood recalled that Dave Sexton, Malcolm Allison and Jimmy Andrews (all players who were going to become outstanding coaches) had gone to watch the Hungarians warming up before the match in the old greyhound area outside the stadium. The visitors had been told they could not use the pitch so they found this bit of grass at the back, and Jimmy Andrews happily told the story of how he pointed at one of the Hungarian players and said to Malcolm Allison: 'Look at that fat little chap there... we will murder this lot.' The fat chap was Ferenc Puskas, widely regarded as one of the greatest players of all time!

Billy Wright, England's captain, was under no illusions about the size of the task. 'We had to counter the wiles of the deep lying centre forward, Hidegkuti; we – or to be more specific, I – had to try to dampen the genius of Puskas; we had, somehow, to stop their tear away wingers Budai and Czibor, and we had to find an answer to the cultured aggression of Kocsis and Bozsik. Oh yes, we had problems.' He went on to talk about the tactics which they had agreed with Walter. 'We decided to place our faith in the retreating defence, which simply meant that we held off the man in possession until exactly the right moment to challenge, covered tightly, and kept a tight rein on opponents who were searching for space.'

The England team on that historic day was: Merrick (Birmingham City); Ramsey (Tottenham Hotspur); Eckersley (Blackburn); Wright (Wolverhampton Wanderers) capt.; Johnston (Blackpool); Dickinson (Portsmouth); Matthews (Blackpool); Taylor (Blackpool); Mortensen (Blackpool); Sewell (Sheffield Wednesday); Robb (Tottenham Hotspur).

The Hungarian team was: Grosics; Buzansky; Lantos; Bozsik; Lorant; Zakarias; Budai; Kocsis; Hidegkuti; Puskas (capt.); Czibor. The game was one of the most talked about and most analysed in England's history. In the warm sunshine of a November afternoon stolen from late summer, a crowd of 100,000 packed into Wembley to watch an enthralling game that they would remember for the rest of their lives. Although England were beaten 6-3, the crowd was stunned by a level of football that they had previously thought impossible.

The start could not have been more electric. In a moment of high drama Hidegkuti scored in the first minute, which knocked the stuffing out of the English players. He got two more, Puskas scored two and Bozsik one. Puskas's first goal is perhaps the most remembered: Billy Wright, normally the surest of tacklers, moved in to dispossess Puskas. The Hungarian dragged the ball back with the studs of his boot as Wright launched himself into the tackle. His striking leg met thin air and in the same sublime movement the incomparable Puskas pivoted, his left foot flashed and the ball was in the back of the net. Three of the Hungarian goals came in one devastating 15-minute spell in the first half, putting them in an unassailable position. England stuck bravely to their task with goals from Sewell and Mortensen and a penalty from Ramsey. But England's proud unbeaten home record had been emphatically smashed.

The press was fulsome in their praise for the Hungarians. Frank Coles of the *Daily Telegraph* reported: 'It was indeed, a famous victory, achieved by the most brilliant display of football ever seen in this country. The Hungarians flashed before our eyes as fit and as fast as a track team. The mantle of masters rest gracefully on their shoulders. In scientific ball control of the highest degree, in speed, and above all in shooting ability, they outmatched England. From goalkeeper to outside left they held the whip hand.' Although Hidegkuti had scored three goals, Cole reserved his greatest praise for Puskas. 'The most complete forward however, was Puskas, inside left and captain. He scored a fantastic goal and was the architect of Hungary's most dangerous attacks which flowed with the sweet rhythm of a team fashioned in all the arts and crafts of the game.'

Desmond Hackett of the *Daily Express*, so confident the day before, was humble in his admiration for the Hungarians: 'It it is easy to howl down the defeated England side and jeer "What a team!" But those who appreciate football will rejoice that there are such players in the world as the Hungarians and will exclaim "What a team!"' Hackett, however, declined to place the blame at England's door: 'Fault this England 11; condemn them as inexpert strolling players: and then look around and find a better team. We must admit that the Hungarians are the best we have ever seen. While England moved stiffly, and had to bring the ball under control, the Hungarians were able to shoot accurately and powerfully from any angle and ended the myth that Continentals are goal shy.'

In the second half a typical autumn mist had crept into Wembley stadium replacing the warm sunshine and giving the pitch an ethereal setting that prompted Geoffrey Green to write in *The Times*: 'England were strangers in a strange world, a world of flitting red spirits.' 'England' he proclaimed 'was no longer a major world power in the game.'

Bernard Joy, a formal Arsenal player and then the *Evening Standard* football correspondent, pointed to the successful combination of tactical awareness, fitness, and mastery of the ball, but in fairness to England pointed out that Hungary brought a new conception of the game, whereby the football interests of the country were devoted entirely to the cause of the national team.

One of the spectators that day was Ron Greenwood. The contrast between his morning and afternoon exposed the different attitudes to football in England and on the continent. At 9:30 that morning he was training with the other players at Chelsea – which consisted only of the obligatory laps round the pitch. The club had provided the players with tickets for the match, but only half of them bothered to go. At 3pm Greenwood was in the stand opposite the Royal Box, feeling a flutter of expectation. His first intimation that this game would be something different came when he watched Puskas waiting for the coin toss, flicking the ball up a couple of times, catching it with his instep, and returning it to the centre spot – commonplace now perhaps, but nobody had seen it done in the centre circle at Wembley before. For Ron Greenwood that afternoon was his own road to Damascus. It proved to him beyond all doubt that football can be a game of beauty and intelligence, a lovely art as well as a muscular science. He describes his impressions of the match in his own biography, *Yours Sincerely*:

The Hungarians simply played football differently. They used another language in more senses than one. Their game was based on the short pass although they were always ready with a long one when the moment was right; they were never predictable. They kept the ball on the ground and they fizzed it about. Their pace was tremendous but it was the ball that did the hardest work. The players moved with cunning and intelligence. They understood the value of space, how to make it and how to use it, and they had that special kind of understanding which only comes with familiarity. They were outstanding individuals with the sort of relationship with each other that is normally found only in the best club sides; and, of course this was not just a happy accident... they were all on the same wavelength... their players were free agents. They ran all over the place and it was this above all which confused England.

English football was very much concerned with numbers in those days. A player was given one to wear, and a particular job went with it: five marked nine, two marked eleven, three marked seven. England's defenders were so used to playing this way they found it impossible to change for even one game. They were simply caught out. Harry Johnston, for example, found he had no one to mark because Nandor Hidegkuti, the Hungarian number nine, played all over the park. One moment he would be picking the ball up just in front of his own penalty area, the next drifting wide, the next coming into a movement for a second or even third time – but always, lethally, he was ready to become the extra man in the opposition's box. He did not go near Johnston and he did not let Johnston approach him. Harry wanted someone to latch onto, but all he saw was space.

The Hungarian way was different: they used moving triangles – much more difficult, of course, but infinitely more effective. Their players were always on the move so the size, angles and direction of their triangles were constantly changing. Their style was all about understanding, rhythm and intuition; and linked together by the lovely skills of the Hungarian players, the effect was devastating.

Little was known about football in Hungary and the fact that they were so-called 'amateurs' strengthened the misconceptions that existed in England. How had Hungary become such a great team? What lessons could England learn?

In deciding on a new playing system Hungary manager Gustav Sebes and his assistants considered the systems being used in England, Austria, Italy and Russia. They concluded that if they wanted to be the best, none of these were ideal. The most important thing was that players did not have fixed duties. They believed that attack should start at the same time as the team was defending. Attack and defence should work harmoniously as one, with the whole team actively engaged all the time. Sebes considered that his plan was the most revolutionary change in systems since 1926, when Arsenal introduced the WM formation. Success soon followed and in 1952 the team triumphed at the Olympic Games in Finland.

Preparation for the 1954 World Cup under a Soviet system was something that Walter knew all about, but could only dream about for his England team. The Hungarian training programme was organised for a year in advance. A systematic, day by day activity plan was drawn up for each individual player according to his capabilities and particular responsibilities. This would include other sports such as track and field athletics, swimming and winter sports. The players trained with their own clubs, but as they all came from Honved or Red Banner they still played together and their club coach was guided by Sebes who frequently called the national team together. Training was geared to peak for three key events: the fixtures against England and Soviet Russia and the World Cup in Switzerland.

Ferenc Puskas believed the team of the 1953/54 season was the most inspiring in the history of Hungarian football (and they were never to reach these heights again). Winning the match against England in London was a burning ambition for Sebes and Puskas. Only once, in Budapest in1934, had Hungary beaten England, by 2-1. On all other occasions Hungary had been soundly thrashed. The last game had been in London in 1936 when England won 6-2. Puskas knew the result of every England home game from 1923 to 1953. This was the team they wanted to beat: the unbeaten home record they wanted to end.

Although they were the Olympic Champions, and despite having been unbeaten for three years, the Hungarian players were nervous before the start of the match. In his book, *Captain of Hungary*, Puskas recalled, 'I saw nothing but preoccupied players trying to disguise their nervousness but I felt a bit happier when I glanced into the English players' dressing room and saw the same tension.' But scoring in the first 60 seconds gave Hungary a tremendous psychological advantage, boosting their self-confidence and undermining England's. 'That goal was a tonic' said Puskas, 'I could feel a steadiness come over our game and our players settled down whilst England, in particular their captain, Wright, was still very nervous.'

'England just could not cope with the situations we developed,' he added, 'and what seemed to puzzle their defence particularly was the fact that the attacks were often led from behind... Johnston had no idea how to keep Hidegkuti marked... later in the match Hidegkuti was shadowed by Wright and Dickinson, but by doing this they left Kocsis and myself unguarded.'

Later, reflecting on the game, Puskas compared the England players of 1953 with the England team that beat Hungary 6-2 in 1936. Perhaps surprisingly, he judged that the England team of 1953 had the better players. His analysis suggests that what had been witnessed at Wembley was not so much the decline of English football but the ascendancy and ultimate supremacy of the Hungarian style of football: the triumph of teamwork over individuals.

In victory Puskas was generous to Walter. 'He is truly a nice man with a profound knowledge of the game. When we beat England [in 1953] I wondered how he must have felt. I should not like to have been in his shoes... I could then sympathise with him entirely. Such is the life of a footballer! One victory, one defeat; it is always difficult to face defeat, but we can always learn from it. And only in this spirit can we love football as a sport.' It was ironic that Puskas himself was to experience the bitter taste of defeat the following year when Hungary were unexpectedly beaten in the final of 1954 World Cup.

Although the press was generally fair and objective in their reports after the match, some football writers subsequently judged Walter critically. Brian Glanville said 'Winterbottom asked his centre half, Harry Johnston, whether he preferred to man mark Hidegkuti or stand off him. Johnston replied that he preferred to stand off him, the logical corollary of which was clearly to assign another player to shadow Hidegkuti. Amazingly it wasn't done.'

Billy Wright saw it differently: 'It was the system of playing Nandor [Hidegkuti] deep that pulled us about in that particular game. It was between Jim Dickinson or Harry Johnston who would pick up, it was always the closest to him would pick him up. Well, because of their great skill and because of that system, they created more space than we thought.'

Perhaps the last word on this epoch-making match should go to Walter himself. In an interview with Ken Goldman, the editor of *Soccer Coach*, the London Football Coaches Association magazine, Walter gave an insightful account of the game and the events leading up to it:

I saw the Hungarians win the Olympic Games title in Helsinki in 1952 and they were fortunate only in that they had so many world-class players in the same team, and at the same time, all playing so brilliantly. The authorities had a plan to produce a great national side and in consequence everything was moulded to that. Most of the players came from the two main Budapest teams which enabled them to assemble during the week for training as a group to play against local sides in order to hone their teamwork. It was a supreme effort of organisation and training, the like of which I had never heard of or seen before, although it has subsequently been copied in South America where they suspend their league and cup competitions in order to give their international players the chance of the fullest preparation. That is something we still cannot do in Europe, but Hungary, because of its own political system, was able to achieve it in the 1950s.

They had at least five or six magnificent players including Grosics, the goalkeeper, Bozsik, a wing half, Czibor, a winger, and Puskas. Kocsics and Hidegkuti were strikers, both particularly adept at playing the ball early and crossing it on the run. The players also had the ability to work out different themes amongst themselves, not always augmented by their manager Gustav Sebes, who was not really a coach in the modern mould. However, Sebes had one idea which the Dutch still utilise, which was to ensure that players were capable of playing in every position. This gave them the adaptability to rotate so that defenders could attack, and when they did, forward players dropped back to slot into their positions. It was not just a simple overlapping but a rehearsed set of moving tactics which I thought at the time was exceptional. England by contrast had no chance to be involved in that kind of thing. Our system was totally against any preparation and training at all. We could not have any get-togethers and typically against Hungary in 1953, the then selection committee chose the team seven days before the match, and over the weekend several of those players were injured. That meant that automatically a player who was selected as reserve for the position was called on to play, and when Tom Finney was injured the selectors introduced George Robb, an amateur player, who had to compete against a team of Hungary's ability in his first international.

Just before our match I had watched Sweden luckily draw in Hungary and whilst the press tended to think we would win easily I tried to point out that the Hungarians were actually a great side. I had noticed that Hidegkuti played a withdrawn role but that it was slightly different to what had been played against us by a FIFA select team earlier that season, and caused considerable problems. We therefore discussed the tactics to be adopted for the Hungarian game and Harry Johnston felt that he preferred to stay in his natural position rather than follow Hidegkuti around and close mark him. Therein was encapsulated the problem, because without rehearsing both our tactics and especially those of the opposition, the situation became hopeless. None of our team had had the experience of playing against a withdrawn centre forward and the first time they came up against it was in match play in this important international.

Looking back on films of the match you can see we had as much of the game territorially in attacking terms; the Hungarians are so good at scoring that we were three down before we knew where we were. That meant they could play defensively if they wished and the fact that we scored three goals against them was a fine achievement. They were not afraid to shoot from outside the penalty area and as a result scored a couple of marvellous goals.

The defeat by Hungary had a profound affect throughout the country. It wasn't the first time that England supporters had witnessed the skills and different styles of continental teams. They had seen the 2-2 draw with Austria in 1951 and the 4-4 draw with the FIFA team earlier that year. Those results could be explained away. But a defeat, and such a convincing home defeat, at last brought the football public down to earth to face reality – England were no longer the best team in the world. Walter patiently and realistically saw things for what they were and was at the heart of everything. He saw it not as a disaster, but as an opportunity to shake English football out of its complacency and accept the need for modern coaching methods.

In his book the *Association Game*, Matthew Taylor commented: 'Looked at from a broader perspective, 1953 can be seen as a decisive moment in the relationship between football and English national identity. At a time when Britain was retreating from its empire and losing its political influence on the world stage, the England football team increasingly came to be regarded as an embodiment of the nation itself.'

The Times observed: 'The ordinary man finds the form of our professional footballers a more convenient indication of the state of the nation than all the economists soundings.'

Holt and Mason in their book *Sport in Britain* argued that 'in the wake of the combined shock defeat by Hungary and the Suez crisis of 1956, there was a change in the way in which the England team was perceived by press and public alike. Matches against foreign opposition were taken more seriously and 'winning' became more important.'

There was debate, analysis and earnest soul searching throughout the football world. Newspapers made daily demands for something to be done. Everyone was casting round for scapegoats. Some sensible questions were asked by the press. 'Do we really need a panel of nine to pick a team of eleven?' pointed out one newspaper article.

Walter called a meeting of club managers a few weeks after the game to discuss the lessons learned. Greenwood remembered the effect it had at Chelsea. 'Ted Drake [the Chelsea manager] came back to Stamford Bridge after the meeting, summoned all his players together and told us how the new future was going to be. Then we went out and did 20 laps straight off!'

Brian Glanville, in his book *Soccer Nemesis*, summed up the aftermath: 'Never was the inadequacy of most British managers and directors better illustrated than by the way they now reacted. It was at once decided that British footballers had been surpassed... because they did not do enough [fitness] training. Consequently a number of clubs immediately increased their hours of training, obliging players to report in the afternoon, as well as in the morning. Defeat had failed to bring a grain of wisdom.'

In the return match in Budapest the following May the selection committee made seven changes to the team that had lost at Wembley. It was an entirely inappropriate knee jerk reaction that included some strange selections. Peter Harris of Portsmouth was included, having last played five years before, as well as the Fulham centre forward Bedford Jezzard, who made his international debut. England were again overwhelmed, this time losing 7-1 – the country's worst defeat. Johnny Haynes (who had not yet won his first cap and was a substitute that day) remembered being amazed by Walter's calmness after the match. 'I never saw him go off his head completely after a match or at half-time,' he said. 'Even when we were hammered in Budapest he didn't lay into anyone. We were lucky not to lose by double figures, but he didn't blow his top. He was very down, you could tell, but as a football purist, I think in a funny kind of way he was almost excited to watch the brilliance of the Hungarians. He didn't see it as his fault. The team wasn't down to him – it was the selection committee's team and all the newspaper reporters knew it.'

Walter admitted to reporters on the gloomy flight out of Budapest that his England team were inexperienced and outclassed. 'None of our lads played below his club form, but it just wasn't good enough. We've no excuses. It has been obvious for some time that under our present system we cannot compete against nations who throw everything overboard for the national team.' There was not a reporter on the plane who disagreed with him. The inescapable fact was that the English club system offered woefully inadequate preparation and practice time to the national team.

The mood in the papers next day was one of embarrassment, sadness and awe. The *Daily Mail* featured a large front page headline: 'BIGGEST DEFEAT EVER FOR ENGLISH SOCCER – THE HUNGARIANS ARE FROM ANOTHER PLANET' There was not a whisper of criticism directed towards Walter, partly perhaps because at that time the media culture disapproved of personal attacks on individuals, but mostly because there was an understanding of the problem and a feeling that 'we were all in this together.'

Brian Glanville, with the benefit of hindsight, remained critical of Walter and continued to believe that he was tactically inept: 'The fact that the Hungarians would show themselves greatly superior to any team England might at that time have deployed was unquestionable. But knowing what Winterbottom did about their strengths and methods, surely it would have been possible at least to devise a plan to limit the damage?'

Walter had faced deep lying centre forwards before – in the 'friendly' against Argentina earlier that year when Jose Lacasia had dropped deep and against the 'Rest of the World' team when Gunnar Nordhal had operated as a withdrawn centre forward. But players never encountered these tactics playing for their clubs and Walter's problem was that he had no preparation time to practice a style of play that would counter these tactics, and even when he tried there was resistance from players who wanted to stick with what they knew. What he faced was a systemic failing of the English game.

The Hungarians came to England again in 1954, but this time in the form of Honved, Hungary's leading club. They met Wolverhampton Wanderers at Molineux under floodlights before a capacity crowd of 55,000 (although it was to be two years before floodlights would be permitted in a League game). The match attracted great national interest as Honved fielded six of the national team that had humiliated England, including Ferenc Puskas. Wolves were captained by Billy Wright who once again had the opportunity to face up to Puskas.

It was a cold December night but the atmosphere under the floodlights was electric. Wolves, urged on by a passionate crowd, fought back from a two goal deficit to achieve a famous 3-2 victory. When Bill Slater, the Wolves left half, was later asked if they had learned from the England defeats by Hungary and changed their tactics he replied, 'No, we just played our normal game. We couldn't have done anything else with the players we had, but unlike England, we did have the advantage of playing together all the time – I often used to think that in those days a top club side would do better in international matches than a selected team – and then the pitch was in poor condition, there had been heavy rain which favoured the Wolves style of play.'

Stan Cullis, the authoritarian Wolves manager said, 'our win convinced me that rather than bother about how continental teams played against us, we would use or own methods and be quite happy using them.' It was a great victory but it undermined Walter's case for change. It was not until 1960 that the advent of European Cup football finally brought home the uncomfortable truth to Cullis. Against Barcelona, Wolves spent the whole match within three yards of the ball and never touched it. Barcelona ran rings around them by using the ball and movement off the ball.

Whilst Walter campaigned for a change in attitudes to English football on the pitch, Stanley Rous joined the debate by raising awareness of how far the infrastructure of English clubs had fallen behind the rest of the world.

Writing a open letter in the *FA Year Book,* ostensibly written to the man in the street but indirectly aimed at the Football League, he empathised with the crescendo of public criticism surrounding the two Hungary defeats. Clubs in South America and many parts of Europe catered for a range of sports, he said, and ran many football teams at all age groups. New purpose-built stadia were being built throughout both continents.

He bemoaned the poor facilities for spectators. In England, most stadia had been built in Victorian times, with stands added piecemeal: grounds had become surrounded by houses and factories; supporters were packed onto concrete terraces, mostly open to rain, cold winds, snow and sleet; children had to be lifted onto Dad's shoulders. Toilet facilities were limited and very basic, while the refreshments were tea or Bovril and a meat pie. The conditions were hardly conducive to developing good players either. Pitches which were in constant use for training soon became a rutted quagmire bare of grass, making skilful play with the ball on the ground difficult. Clubs grew up around a single team and did not serve the full needs of the local community. Facilities for youth were sadly lacking, with less space for boys to play football in the streets let alone on proper pitches. It was a blunt and truthful analysis but it was to be 40 years before these ideals became a reality.

Walter saw the defeats by Hungary not as setbacks but as a unique opportunity. The positive outcome was that at last it would be difficult for the football establishment to say 'We are the best in the world.' As long as it was accepted that English football ruled supreme, change was never going to be accepted. Now FA councillors, the Football League, club directors, managers and players would, albeit reluctantly, have to begin to listen to his arguments for change and his vision for the future.

CHAPTER 12

EPIPHANY

1953 – 1954

The impact of the defeats to Hungary spread far and wide. After years of playing in a kit that had had hardly changed in the first half of the 20th century there was at last an enormous shift in attitudes. 'Shirts were made of heavy cloth with collars and long sleeves, which were often rolled up to the elbow,' recalled Ken Goldman, the editor of *Soccer Coach*. 'Now they had V-necks and short sleeves, and were made of much lighter material. Shorts were lighter and cut away. But the biggest change was in the style of boots. Foreseeing the trend, Stuart Surridge, a Surrey cricketer who had a sports shop in the London district of Borough, imported continental boots from Adidas. The sleek new boots, which were more like slippers, were low cut around the ankle and no longer had such a hard toe cap. They caught on like wild fire.'

But the most far reaching impact was the awareness of tactics. Arguments about tactics were now carried on at games, in buses and trains on the way to and from matches, in pubs after the game and at home. The debate was fueled by the popular press – the main source of opinions. (BBC TV's *Match of the Day*, with highlighted recordings of League matches, was still ten years away, and live football on TV even further in the future.)

Popular discussions deliberated tactical conundrums such as 'is the centre half a third full-back or an attacking midfielder?' 'Should the centre forward be the spearhead of the attack or withdrawn behind the rest of the forward line?' 'Is an all-out attack better than a three pronged attack with a retreating defence?' 'Was the quick, close, accurate passing game used in South America better than the long-range passing and cross field play favoured by Wolverhampton Wanderers?'

There was a widespread misconception that one style of play – the Hungarian way – was the only solution to winning matches. Walter argued that although there was of course a place for tactics, it was player's ability that produced winning teams.

Manchester City, who had watched the Hungary game and seen the impact of Hidegkuti, produced their own variation of the Hungarian style, using Don Revie as a deep-lying centre forward. Once the players adapted, it was very successful and Manchester City reached the FA Cup Final in 1955 and 1956. But, as City goalkeeper Bert Trautmann recalled, 'unfortunately, later on, when a lot of players had left us, City persevered with the so called Revie plan and we struggled, because we didn't have the players. That proved to me that you had to have good players, intelligent players, to play anything.'

Walter believed that too much importance was being attached to systems. 'It's only too simple to quote matches in which a team with one particular system of tactics has triumphed over opponents using another, only to discover later that the team favouring the latter has defeated one favouring the former!'

'Football history' he warned, 'is littered with clubs which rise to the top by perfecting their own very definite style of play, but after a year or two, and as changes occur in the membership of the team and in the form of individuals, the splendour nearly always wanes though the basic style remains the same.'

'The truth was' Walter insisted, 'that football is a test of skill by eleven men against eleven. If the players in team A are much better than those in team B, then A will be the better team, even though occasionally luck, injuries or a dip in form, may mean that they will not always win.' He continued, 'It is only when players have roughly the same degree of technical excellence and physical fitness that well rehearsed tactics bring results.' Jimmy Armfield clarified the point that Walter was making. 'Walter chose his team and then decided the tactics that best suited those players.'

The 1954 World Cup in Switzerland followed only one month after the 7-1 crushing in Hungary and a 1-0 defeat in Yugoslavia giving Walter the unenviable task of raising the spirits of a demoralised team. A major problem he faced was the constant string of team changes that failed to build any consistency and understanding. At centre half, nine players had been tried since the loss of the incomparable Neil Franklin in 1950 and none had been able to stake a claim to a regular place. Harry Clarke (Tottenham Hotspur) came in for one game against Scotland, but was replaced by Sid Owen (Luton Town) for the next three games. Stanley Matthews, initially neglected by the selectors, joined the World Cup squad, perhaps in response to clamour from the press and public. The goalkeeper, Gil Merrick, had held his place since 1952, but was not world class and his confidence must have been shaken after conceding 13 goals in two matches against Hungary. The selectors also brought in two new full backs before the World Cup, with Alf Ramsey and Bill Eckersley making way for Reg Staniforth (Huddersfield) and Roger Byrne (Manchester United). At halfback though there was consistency, with Billy Wright (Wolves) and Jimmy Dickinson (Portsmouth) continuing their long-standing partnership.

In the two seasons immediately before the 1954 World Cup no less than 40 players were selected for England's 15 international matches.

Selectors made frequent changes, some players had serious injuries and some had retired. In their book *World Cup*, Brian Glanville and Jerry Weinstein acknowledged that the coming and going was not entirely the fault of the selectors and that the FA was handicapped by the rigid outlook of the League clubs: 'It was absurd to suppose that rhythm, team spirit, and understanding could be built up in a few days training sessions, which was the only arrangement permitted England team manager, Walter Winterbottom, before the departure for the continent. Indeed, in the face of the importance attached to the World Cup by other countries and their preparations, England started off at a hopeless disadvantage. Even within the severe limitations imposed by their domestic football structure, England's national interest required, but did not receive, a minimum period of realistic preparation. England's predicament was profound.'

By contrast even the Scottish team was given a month's special training in Ayr before the competition began under their first ever team manager, Andrew Beattie, the former manager of Huddersfield Town.

The 1954 World Cup was the most representative competition since its inception in 1930, with countries from almost every quarter of the globe taking part: Hungary, Czechoslovakia, England, Scotland, South Korea, Uruguay, Brazil, all participated in the fifth staging of the tournament, and were joined for the first time since the end of the Second World War, by West Germany. Of the other major football nations only Argentina and Russia were absent: the former because of differences with Uruguay and Brazil, while Russia – in a tense Cold War with America – had a policy of only entering international competitions when they had the strongest possible chance of winning.

But once again FIFA was criticised for the way that the tournament was organised. The format included four pools, each with four teams, but instead of each team playing each other, two teams in each group were seeded, and kept apart. This made it likely that the two seeded teams would have the same number of points and so it was determined that teams level at full time would play extra time, and if at the end of the group matches two teams were still level on points, they would play-off. England and Italy were seeded in group four with Switzerland and Belgium.

Hungary was naturally the hot favourite to lift the Jules Rimet Trophy. When they arrived in Switzerland they were established as one of the most powerful and successful teams in history. They had not suffered a single defeat in four years and were universally acknowledged as one of the most attractive and artistic sides ever to be seen.

For the first time there was television coverage, provided by the Eurovision TV link up. The number of matches televised live was limited and the coverage was not without technical problems, but it was a treat for those homes that now had a television. England's first game against Belgium was one of the games that was shown live and in many homes in England neighbours gathered together around the television.

They were thrilled by a nail biting game. Belgium were no push over. They came to Switzerland having eliminated Sweden in qualification and with a 2-0 victory over Yugoslavia (where England had just lost 1-0). But despite having been a goal down in the first half-hour England played magnificently with an elegance not seen for several seasons. Their play was swift and incisive, with deep frontal passes splitting the Belgian defence down the middle, causing the Belgian goalkeeper to make a series of spectacular saves. With 15 minutes to go England were 3-1 up. But then the defence let England down with Owen proving he was not the answer at centre half and Merrick just as unreliable. What's more the team were desperately unlucky when Dickinson headed an own goal past Merrick to give Belgium their late equalizer to make it 4-4. It was a game England should have won easily but Walter had been encouraged by the overall performance. Stanley Matthews had one of his sensational matches which thrilled the crowd and Tommy Taylor, a 'Busby babe', made his England debut at inside left, making an excellent impression and laying on England's first two goals.

England's next game was against Switzerland in Berne in a temperature of over 100 degrees. Switzerland had pulled off a surprise by beating the fancied Italians 2-0, but they were unable to produce the same form against England who beat them 2-0, the goals coming from the two Wolverhampton forwards, Mullen and Wilshaw. The game was described as unexciting and drab; perhaps both teams suffered from the temperature, but the three points were enough for England to top their group and go through to the quarter finals.

Not that the English football writers were particularly impressed: 'One thing was abundantly clear' said *The Times*, 'England, in a world sense, represents a Third Division side that has found its way into the last eight of the FA Cup.' The Switzerland game was notable for the first appearance of Billy Wright at centre half. When he arrived at the tournament he had 58 caps for England at wing half and thought that his international career might be nearing its end; in the latter stages of the game against Belgium, however, an injury to Sid Own forced Walter to move Wright to centre half and he kept him in that position for the game against Switzerland. It proved to be an inspired move and Wright was to hold that position to win another 46 England caps. Interestingly when Wright returned home to his club, his manager, Stan Cullis, told him he didn't want him playing at centre half and moved him back to wing half. Shortly after that, the regular Wolves centre half, Shorthouse, was injured and Cullis moved Wright back to centre half; he was so impressive that Cullis kept him there for the remainder of his career. Another positional change Walter made in the game against Switzerland was to move Tommy Taylor to centre forward, where he was outstandingly successful for England until his tragic death in the Munich air disaster.

In the quarter-finals England met Uruguay, the World Cup holders, on a beautiful, hot Sunday afternoon in Basle. Matthews and Lofthouse came back from injury with Finney playing on the left wing. The goal-snatching Wilshaw was preferred to the less experienced Tommy Taylor. The game provided a fascinating contrast of styles. England produced a stirring performance with a combination of short and long passes, hard first-time tackling and chasing which the Uruguayans could not match. Billy Wright was magnificent at the heart of the defence, as was Stanley Matthews, this time operating, not from his usual right-wing position but from deep inside left, and acting as a link between defence and attack.

Uruguay scored an early goal but England equalised through Lofthouse, seizing the initiative. The South Americans reacted by reinforcing their bolt system of defence and bringing eight men into the penalty area before England went very close with shots from Lofthouse and Wilshall. Then, tragically, just after a Wilshaw effort that was only inches wide of the goal, a Uruguay counter-attack saw Varela, their centre half, score with a long-range volley.

Uruguay once again came under the intense pressure, but after another breakaway a free kick against Byrne saw the brilliant inside forward Schiaffino score to give Uruguay a 3-1 lead. Schiaffino was then withdrawn into a central defensive position, where he gave an outstanding performance. Still England rallied and Finney scored to make it to 3-2.

With the crowd urging England on the Uruguayans were really in trouble. A shot from Matthews hit the post and another shot was punched over by the goalkeeper for a corner. Then disaster struck. Uruguay found a gap in the English defence and Ambrose easily pushed the ball past Merrick. England had lost 4-2 and were out of the World Cup.

Despite their exit, the team had made many friends and admirers for their spirited performance. 'Englishmen at least could be proud of their team that day,' admitted the oft-critical Brian Glanville in his book *World Cup*. 'Three times they were a goal behind, but they fought with matchless courage to save the game. Indeed, but for some unkind twists of fate, England might have won.' In his copy of Glanville's book,

Walter had underlined the names of the Uruguayans, Abbadie and Schiaffino, annotating the pages with the words 'bad [English] defense.'

Bob Ferrier, in his book *Soccer Partnership*, was probably directly reflecting Walter's views when he wrote: 'One could indict Gilbert Merrick for goalkeeping errors in that match, but the fact is that defensively England were still suspect, lacking players of true world class at a time when the forwards were doing a reasonable job.' Ironically it was generally felt that the team in Switzerland was probably the least talented but the most successful in England's first three World Cups.

Although England were out, the tournament produced some outstanding games, controversies and shock results. In the semi-finals Germany triumphed over Austria by 6-1, and Hungary overcame Uruguay by 4-1.

Hungary were involved in four controversial games. In an amazing pool match they beat West Germany 8-3 but Puskas received a vicious kick on the back of his ankle and was carried off the field. 'In retrospect it was the kick that won the World Cup,' remarked Brian Glanville dryly.

Puskas was unfit to play in the quarter final against Brazil. Hungary won 4-2 in a bad tempered game which became universally known as the 'Battle of Berne,' for which Brazil were largely blamed. In the semi-final, Hungary, without Puskas, were up against Uruguay, the world champions, in a game which Charlie Buchan, the veteran English journalist, described as 'one of the greatest games I've ever seen.' Billy Wright who stayed behind to watch the game with Walter said 'It was as near perfection as we will ever see.' It was considered to be one of the great games in football history for both its technical skill and its excitement, and although the Hungarians triumphed in the end, their 4-2 win only came in extra time. 'We beat the best team we have ever met' said their team manager Gyula Mandi.

Hungary were through to the final against West Germany, having scored an incredible 25 goals in four games. It seemed that nothing could stop the Hungarian goal machine, but in one of those upsets that makes football so fascinating, West Germany did. Puskas insisted on playing in the final, although many thought he was unfit, and his inclusion weakened the team. Finally this wonderful Hungarian team were defeated, losing 3-2 following a combination of bad luck, missed opportunities and a bad refereeing decision. And so it was that Fritz Walter, the veteran West German captain, and not the great Ferenc Puskas, who walked up the steps to collect the trophy from Jules Rimet himself.

When the Hungarian team arrived back in Budapest the once adoring public were unforgiving, with blame inevitably laid at the door of Gustav Sebes, the national coach. I had never suspected that the World Cup would be such a test of nerves.' said Sebes. It was the beginning of the end of an era for one of the greatest football teams the world has ever seen.

Brian Glanville, astutely observed: 'Yet when the smoke cleared, when Puskas and Kocsis decamped a couple of years later, it became perfectly clear that all we had been seeing was an illustration of Walter Winterbottom's dictum that every great team is built around a core of great players. When Kocsis and company were present, every man looked a giant; Sebes was a wizard, Mandi an inspired manager. When they went, the fabulous structure of Hungarian football proved to be nothing of the sort; the lean years began.'

Like Sebes, Walter was the subject of much criticism when he returned home, but he accepted it as part of the job and never allowed himself to become bitter about it. It was a quality that Graham Doggart, the Chairman of the Football Association, admired: 'In hardly any other walk of life is the success or failure of an individual judged so much on performance of others as that of a football manager. Mr. Winterbottom philosophically realised that if the team under his control was successful he was considered a hero; if unsuccessful he was considered a failure. Yet above all he was loyal to the players he managed and would always be ready to defend them against any kind of criticism.'

Walter's experience in Switzerland had shown that England still lagged behind the rest of the world in giving the international team the thorough preparation needed for a major championship. There could be no excuses about the host country, weather, food or accommodation. Hungary, Germany, Uruguay, Brazil, Austria and Yugoslavia had all put first class teams into the competition, but England had failed again and Walter believed he knew why, and what he had to do next.

He saw that without exception, the successful football nations were devoting much more attention to the development of young star players, both at club and international level, and that their international teams spent more time together in training and practice games which in turn built understanding and team spirit.

Walter believed that although a structure like Hungary's could only be achieved in a totalitarian political system, the principle of developing young star players could be established. He had introduced the concept of 'B' internationals in 1947 as a feeder for the senior team. Now he had to get support from clubs to release players for an Under-23 team. It would give maturing young players a progression of international experience through school, youth (under-18), Under-23 and England 'B' levels. Players could be tested in the Under-23 team, gaining experience and playing together, before being thrown into the cauldron of full international football.

From now on his team would be built from young players, developed through the Under-23 matches. *'The time for arbitrary selection of teams was over: the time for building teams had arrived.'* declared Walter.

CHAPTER 13

SHATTERED DREAMS

1954 – 1958

If you can dream-and not make dreams your master
If you can think-and not make thoughts your aim
If you can meet with Triumph and Disaster
And treat those two imposters just the same ...

Rudyard Kipling

Walter presented his recommendations soon after he returned from Switzerland in a detailed report submitted to the FA Technical Subcommittee on August 9, 1954. It said, 'Within the framework of the present league system, it is thought that a great deal more can be done towards bringing England players and teams to a higher standard of performance in the next four years.' It put forward proposals on key issues: team selection, training sessions, co-operation by league clubs, coaching at league clubs, special training for selected players and most significantly the introduction of an Under - 23 team. The idea was well received by FA officials and by clubs. Now he could put his faith in youth.

The ridiculous amateur selection committee process was still a handicap and he recommended changes: that the team should be selected by three people – the team manager, the chairman of the selection committee and one other member. It would then be put forward for approval by the full selection committee. It was still a compromise but it met with agreement and was a big step forward. His report also proposed that players should be brought together for two days prior to every international match. Training sessions were planned at Lilleshall, or at the grounds of clubs where the managers could brief their teams to play in the style of England's next opponents: perhaps Tottenham if they were playing a short passing continental team or Bolton if they wanted a robust test before playing Scotland. Of course this could only happen if the club manager and his training staff cooperated, but several had told Walter that they would.

Yet there were severe constraints on what he could achieve on his own in the short time he had with the players. Walter knew that the most important contribution to improving standards had to come from the clubs themselves. He had to persuade them that they should improve the quality of training and coaching provided to young players with international potential. There was a need for them to provide more training grounds – floodlit for evening training in the winter. They had to be encouraged to appoint qualified coaches as well as inspirational managers. First-class players with potential ability to become coaches were lost to the game because many clubs still had little use for real training and coaching schemes.

His recommendations were direct and forceful, building on the more loosely framed post mortem after the 1950 World Cup, and were generally accepted. He continued to develop his relationships with club managers, building a bridge between the amateur bastion of the FA and the all powerful professional clubs, and over the next three years his hard work and initiatives began to bear fruit.

Walter wanted to keep together the team that had lost to Uruguay in the last match of the World Cup, but six changes were forced on him for the first match of the 1954/55 season. Despite some good results in 1954 – including a 3-1 win over the world champions, West Germany, and a 7-2 humbling of Scotland – many changes were dictated by injury and loss of form. It was not until the autumn of 1955 that Walter was able to establish the process of team building that he was striving for, and his belief in the Under-23 team began to bear fruit.

The Under-23 side was now having its own summer tours, giving players time together to build teamwork and understanding, and a nucleus of young players graduated into the full international team. The incomparable Duncan Edwards of Manchester United, who had played in the first Under-23 match in Bologna 15 months earlier, came into the team against Scotland in April, 1955. On 2 November, against Northern Ireland, two more young players made the step up – Ron Clayton of Blackburn Rovers and Johnny Haynes of Fulham. In the next two years Clayton, Haynes and Edwards played in every match when fit. The full backs, Hall and Byrne, had also come up through the chain of Under-23 and 'B' matches, preparing them for their full caps, along with Tommy Taylor.

The summer tour of 1957 showed that others were ready, and Don Howe of West Bromwich Albion, Bryan Douglas of Blackburn and Derek Kevan from West Bromwich Albion joined the ranks of the senior team. Others like Jimmy Armfield and Alan A'Court were waiting in the wings.

One of the benefits of Walter's international development structure was not just that it provided a path from schoolboy to full international (as Johnny Haynes had taken) but it gave developing stars more international exposure. Even after they had been introduced to the senior team Walter continued to pick them to play in Under-23 and 'B' team sides, and in different team combinations, so they got used to playing with each other.

It was not long before the strategy began to prove itself with a run of good results. In the two seasons from 1955 to 1957 England played 17 games, winning twelve, drawing four and losing only one. There were splendid home wins against Spain (4-1), Brazil (4-2) and Yugoslavia (3-0), and away wins in Finland (5-1) and West Germany (3-1). Qualification for the 1958 World Cup in Sweden was achieved comfortably with wins over the Republic of Ireland and Denmark. The only doubt in the team was at inside right, where Kevan, Robson, Brooks and Atyeo had all been tried.

Despite an unexpected home defeat by Northern Ireland, 1957 ended on a high note with a 4-0 win over France (six of the team had graduated from the Under-23s), and Walter, along with most of the country, looked forward to the World Cup in Sweden the following summer. England, it seemed, stood on the verge of greatness: the core of the team – Byrne, Clayton, Wright, Edwards, Taylor, Haynes and Finney – were all world class and had developed a fine understanding of playing together. But fate had a cruel blow to deliver: they were destined never to play together again.

Walter was working in his office at 22 Lancaster Gate on the afternoon of 6 February, 1958, when he received a phone call that shook him to the core. British European Airways flight 609 carrying the Manchester United team had crashed on its third attempt at take off from a slush covered Munich airport. 23 people had been killed, including eight players, four of whom were England internationals; Roger Byrne, Duncan Edwards, David Pegg and Tommy Taylor. The whole country was in shock and disbelief that the heart had been torn from 'The Busby Babes' in such a devastating accident.

The Manchester United team were returning from playing Red Star Belgrade in Yugoslavia – a European Cup quarter final match which they had drawn 3-3, taking them through 5-4 on aggregate (Manchester United had been the first British team to enter the competition – against the wishes of the Football League secretary Alan Hardaker – in the previous year when they were beaten in the semi final by Real Madrid). In those days travelling to European mid-week matches and returning to meet Saturday league commitments was not easy, and due to the difficult journey endured in the previous round, the club decided to charter a plane from British European Airways to ensure minimal travel time and disruption.

On the way back the Airspeed Ambassador aircraft (registration G-ALZU) stopped in Munich to refuel. Weather conditions were poor, with slush on the runway. The Captain, James Thain, who had flown the aircraft out, had handed the controls to his co-pilot Captain Kenneth Rayment for the return flight. They made two abortive attempts to take off but each time it seemed that the engines were getting insufficient power. After the second attempt the passengers were asked to disembark and return to the terminal. It started to snow again and it seemed that their return would be delayed until the following day. Duncan Edwards sent a telegram to his landlady, 'All flights cancelled, flying tomorrow. Duncan.'

But just 15 minutes later they were asked to board the plane again. Many were nervous. Liam Whelan was heard to say 'this may be death, but I'm ready.'

The station engineer, Bill Black, suggested that as the two earlier attempts had not been successful they should hold the plane in Munich overnight and re-tune the engines. Captain Thain was anxious to stay on schedule and believed that if they opened the throttle more slowly it would overcome the problem, and as the runway was 1.2 miles long he believed it was a practical option. He made the decision to take off again.

As the plane rolled forward to begin its take off Captain Thain began reporting the speeds to control tower. At 117 knots they reached V1, the point of no return. The call of V2, 119 knots, the minimum speed for take-off, never came. Instead the air speed dropped from 117 knots to 105 knots. Rayment shouted 'Christ, we won't make it.' The aircraft skidded off the runway, through the perimeter fence and across a road, hitting a tree and a building. The wing and tail were torn off and the plane caught fire.

Seven players died immediately: Geoff Bent, Roger Byrne, Eddie

Colman, Mark Jones, David Pegg, Tommy Taylor and Liam Whelan. Duncan Edwards hung on bravely for 15 days before he died. Walter Crickmer (club secretary) Tom Curry (trainer) and Bert Whalley (coach) all died. Walter knew all three from the time that he was playing for Manchester United. Bert Whalley had played alongside him in the half back line. Big Frank Swift, England's first goalkeeper under Walter, then a journalist with the *News of the World,* died on the way to hospital. Archie Ledbrooke of the *Daily Mirror* – the Manchester journalist who had once described Walter as 'The Find of a Lifetime' – died along with seven other journalists.

Captain Rayment died but Thain survived although he never flew again. He was blamed for the disaster, but after a ten year fight to clear his name it was established that slush on the runway was the cause of the crash.

There were 21 survivors from the 38 passengers. Of the surviving players, Johnny Berry and Jackie Blanchflower never played again and Ray Wood's career effectively ended. Dennis Viollet and Kenny Morgans played but never fully recovered their best form. Bobby Charlton, Bill Foulkes, Albert Scanlon and Harry Gregg played on with Manchester United. Matt Busby was terribly injured, physically and mentally, but was persuaded by his wife Jean to come back to United 'for the boys who died.'

The whole nation mourned, whichever team they supported, whether or not they were football supporters. 50 years later Simon Barnes, chief sports writer for *The Times,* eloquently explained the phenomenon which had gripped the country:

Sport is life. It is the most vivid form of being alive, at any rate in public. Sports triumphs and disasters, joys and sorrows, shame and glory have intensity impossible to find elsewhere on a regular basis and it acquires an added meaning and importance from sport's essential triviality. Sport may be said to be the precise opposite of death. That is why deaths in sport are so profoundly shocking, so uniquely affecting. Death is not supposed to happen here.

Death is never fair, but deaths in sport have an unfairness that seems almost malicious... it seems impossible that they should die. But they do, and when it happens it is something that touches us more deeply than you would have thought possible from the death of a stranger.

We see our athletes not only as human beings who eat and breathe and bleed like the rest of us, but also as characters who enact undying mythologies for us. They are not Duncan (Edwards) and Ayrton (Senna) and Tommy (Simpson); they are also Hercules, Odysseus and Agamemnon.

The story of eight players who died in Munich 50 years ago is profoundly important to all of us who follow sport, even more so to anyone who has an association with Manchester United. It is right that it is so.

Walter had many associations with Manchester United and the England players who died. It was a day of personal grief in which his heart went out to their families and friends. It was a day when he feared for those still badly injured. It was a day he would never forget.

He had a deep personal affection and admiration for Duncan Edwards. He said at the time 'it was in the character and spirit of Duncan Edwards that I saw the revival of British Football.'

Many years later, when Walter was in his 80s, he recalled, in a filmed interview, his memories of the day Duncan Edwards died:

And then I heard the news, that Duncan Edwards, fortunately, hadn't been killed, and my heart leapt, because here was the player who counted a great deal more than anyone else probably, in the England side...the sadness of it was, a few days later my wife came to me, because she heard it on the news, that Duncan had died too...

and again the dejection you feel. In fact I was almost in tears... I have great sadness in realising, not only what a tremendous loss to Manchester United and to England ... the England team, but also a loss to football. He was a magnificent boy, always cheerful, always smiling, always ready for a laugh and a giggle; he was a lovely lad.

Duncan Edwards was only 21 when he died, and had played only 151 games for Manchester United and 18 for England. And yet no English player ever had greater accolades:

Sir Bobby Charlton: 'He was the best player I ever saw or am likely to see.'

Sir Bobby Robson: 'Surely he would have gone on to be one of the greatest players the world has ever seen.'

Sir Matt Busby: 'If ever there was a player who could be called a one man team, that man was Duncan Edwards.'

Terry Venables: 'He was my hero and my inspiration.'

Jimmy Armfield: 'Edwards was the best footballer in Britain at the time, a big powerful man, but more than that, he was technically gifted and had a great shot – we've not had a player like him in my lifetime.'

Just days after the Munich air disaster the FIFA committee met in Stockholm to make the draw for the 1958 World Cup. England felt they had drawn the short straw with a tough group containing Brazil, Russia and Austria. There were just five 'practice' matches remaining before the tournament began.

The hole left in the England team by the tragedy was enormous: Roger Byrne (aged 28), the Manchester United captain with 33 caps, a full back with a will of iron, an intelligent man who played to his limits; Tommy Taylor (26) with 19 caps was a centre forward in the classic mould of Lawton; Duncan Edwards (21) with 18 caps was an attacking left half who Matt Busby described as incomparable and David Pegg (22) a boy with great promise and one cap, were all dead.

Dennis Viollet, Bobby Charlton and Albert Scanlon, all potential England players for Sweden, were injured and in hospital. It is generally accepted by international coaches that to be in with a real chance of winning the World Cup they need four or five truly world class players; Walter probably had six but three died in Munich.

Walter remembered the way that Edwards and Byrne played together: 'Always in close touch with each other, one man constantly shielding the other. It was dominated by Byrne, the stronger individual personality, the more experienced, the more knowledgeable about tactics, the man with the greater football intellect. Edwards, on the other hand, massive, indomitable, supremely in love with football, was a boy who could respond to instruction and play any type of game to order.'

It was now that Walter's policy of building a team by keeping it together showed itself to be a two edged sword – keeping the team together with few changes meant that there had been limited opportunities for others to break into the team and show their worth. He hoped he could patch the team up and bridge the gap, but he failed.

Although there were comfortable wins with a new side against the Scottish League and Scotland, Walter warned 'no one can judge England on these two performances. We have to see them in hard matches on the continent before we can assess their true strength.'

Bobby Charlton made his first England appearance against Scotland and scored an outstanding goal. Against Portugal he scored both goals in a 2-1 home win but was otherwise ineffective. At the time he was considered immature in everything except his shooting, which was phenomenal, and for this reason he made the World Cup squad. His natural shyness developed into a post Munich melancholy which affected him for many years. It was hardly surprising after all he had been through. He explained his feelings in his autobiography *My England Years:* 'It is difficult after all to be jubilant when so often, any time of day or night, and especially night, your strongest urge is to cry, for what has been taken away, and, you fear, might never be replaced. The problem was that deep down I didn't think it was right to feel so good again, so quickly after the crash.'

The next match was away to Yugoslavia. The heat was oppressive. Harold Shepherdson, England's new permanent trainer, recalled that despite a six hour flight and an early evening arrival at their hotel Walter took everyone by surprise, telling him, 'we will have a training session right away.' But the attempt to acclimatise was to no avail; England lost 5-0 in a temperature of 90F in the shade. Bill Slater, not one given to exaggeration, said that after 15 minutes he felt absolutely exhausted, with rubbery legs and a swimming head. But even allowing for the heat, it seemed that there were players who did not accept their responsibilities and Walter was critical of Charlton, Haynes, Douglas and even Finney, but none more so than Clayton who had a 'shocker.' 'They had a player who was brilliant and he murdered Ronnie Clayton,' recalled Tommy Banks who sat on the bench next to Walter. 'I said to Walter, come on, they're buggered. Walter said "I know, you're in against Russia."'

Peter Lorenzo in the *Daily Herald* was unequivocal in his verdict: 'For 11 staggered, crushed Englishmen – and a handful of their stunned countrymen in the stands – it was the funeral pyre of their World Cup dreams… On today's form our chances in Sweden have gone up in the smoke of those flaming torches that still smoulder around me as I write this, the saddest soccer dispatch I have ever had to send from foreign soil.'

The visit to Russia, just one week later, was an intimidating experience. It was the first time that an England football team had played in Moscow. After the war Russia had annexed the countries that had been occupied by the Nazis – East Germany, Poland, Bulgaria, Hungary, Czechoslovakia, Romania and Albania – which now formed part of the mighty USSR. The ideologies of the USSR and the USA were diametrically and dangerously opposed and the communist regime posed a huge threat to the western world. Indeed from 1957 to 1961 Kruschev openly and repeatedly threatened the West with nuclear annihilation. He claimed that Soviet missile capabilities were far superior to those of the West.

Just two years before, in 1956, the Russian tanks had rolled into Budapest to crush the Hungarian revolution. Premier Imve Hagy and other ministers were summarily executed. Two hundred thousand escaped from Hungary. Ferenc Puskas was fortunate that he was away with the Honved team at the time. He never returned and the Mighty Magyars were no more. Sport had great political significance in Russia and the atmosphere that faced the England team on their arrival was politically charged.

The FA party had flown to Moscow in an Elizabethan aircraft. The Russians had not seen this type of plane before and were impressed. On take-off it would rise from the runway at a spectacular angle of seventy five degrees. They were so fascinated that they asked the pilot to give them several demonstrations. As it was not a military plane he obliged in a surprising spirit of *entente cordial*.

Before leaving England Walter had sought advice from the Foreign Office as well as Vic Buckingham who had toured Russia as the manager of West Bromwich Albion. He was told that there was a shortage of fruit, English boiled sweets and chewing gum, so the FA took two or three cases of fresh fruit to be included in the team's diet. The Russians seemed bemused by this at the airport and Walter was puzzled when the crates were delivered to his bedroom. But when he went down to the large private room where the team were to have dinner he understood why the Russians had been so surprised: running down the centre of the table were heaped baskets of apples, oranges, bananas and grapes. There was obviously no shortage of fruit in these circles and, accepting that life in Russia sometimes moved in mysterious ways, Walter arranged for their fruit to be donated to the British Embassy.

The day after the England team arrived in Moscow the Russians launched Sputnik 3, the third in a series of earth orbiting satellites that had given Russia the lead over the United States in what became known as the space race. Sputnik 3 was an automatic laboratory spacecraft which was designed to collect a wide range of scientific data about the earth's upper atmosphere. Its predecessor, Sputnik 2 had captured the public's imagination because it had carried a dog, 'Laika.' Although the Sputnik programme had no military pretensions, the Americans believed that if the Russians could successfully launch a satellite they could soon launch an intercontinental missile with a nuclear warhead. This galvanized them into mounting the incredible Apollo space programme that successfully put a man on the moon in 1969.

Naturally Sputnik 3 was of great political importance to the Russians and Sir Stanley Rous was invited to a presentation to celebrate their success. He was unable to attend and Walter was asked to take his place. He was collected and taken by car to a large gymnasium, where several notable visitors, including President Nasser of Egypt, were being filmed whilst being asked for their opinions on the success of Sputnik 3. When it came to Walter's turn he praised the Russian space programme, but then teased them by suggesting that they had timed the Sputnik 3 launch to offset the defeat of their national team by England the following day! There was no television in Russia then, but the film, with all its tributes, was shown in cinemas the next day.

The England team were welcomed throughout the world and Russia was no exception. Walter was always proud to take the England team to new countries, and was aware of their responsibilities as high profile ambassadors. Nowhere could this have been more true than in the USSR at this politically sensitive time. England trainer, Harold Shepherdson, remembered that after training the team was officially entertained by visits to the Kremlin and the Bolshoi Ballet. '*Swan Lake* was nice in small doses' he said, 'but not for four and a half hours. At the Opera House, *Prince Igor* – Russian verse and song – was heavy going after three and a half hours. We visited the mausoleum in Red Square where Lenin was lying in state but the Russian State Circus was more to the players' liking, as was the film *Bridge Over the River Kwai*, even though it was in Russian without sub titles!'

The British Ambassador, Sir Patrick Reilly, accompanied Walter and other FA officials to an evening hosted by a Russian minister. Naturally the supper began with vodka and caviar. One of the FA officials was Harry French, a director of Middlesbrough and a fruit merchant who was a down to earth self made man. Noticing that Mr French was puzzled by the caviar, and looking uncomfortable, Sir Patrick Reilly diplomatically covered a piece of warm toast with butter and a dollop of caviar and handed it to Harry for him to taste. Everyone stopped talking and turned to await Harry's verdict.

'Well, what do you think Harry?' enquired Sir Patrick.

'I don't rightly know but to me it tastes like the tail end of finny haddock,' replied Harry.

The Russian hospitality was impeccable and Walter recalled his surprise when their small private party was joined by Galina Ulanova, one of the 20th century's greatest ballerinas of whom Prokoviev said 'she is the genius of Russian ballet, its elusive soul, its inspired poetry.' Ulanova danced for them accompanied only by a pianist, and Walter, who admired excellence in any athletic field, was entranced by her performance.

Walter's family name was never an embarrassment to him, although his children, Janet, Brenda and Alan underwent a good deal of teasing and variations on the 'Winterbottom' name at school. Walter himself tells an amusing story from another function in Moscow organised by the British Embassy: 'Sir Patrick and Lady Reilly arranged a reception at the Embassy for the England team and officials. I arrived late and was creeping along the wall of a side reception room full of people when suddenly Lady Reilly spotted me and said to the general amusement of everyone, especially the players, "Oh, you must be Mr Winterbottom. I am usually good at putting names to faces but in your case I have put the face to the name"... everybody laughed and later she apologised to me.'

After the very poor team performance in the 5-0 defeat against Yugoslavia it was clear that changes had to be made for the match against Russia. For the first time Walter consulted the senior players: Wright, Finney and Haynes were asked to attend the selectors meeting and it was agreed that the defence had to be strengthened. Macdonald was handed the goalkeeping jersey, while Banks replaced Langley at full back, Clamp replaced Clayton at right half and Robson replaced Charlton at inside forward to better link with his team mate Kevan at centre forward. The Wolverhampton Wanderers half back line of Clamp, Wright and Slater was selected providing more continuity from club level. Kevan retained the centre forward position despite a clamour from the press to put Clough in. Walter had not wanted to include Clough in the party to go to Russia before he had played an England 'trial' match (an Under-23 game against Wales in which he subsequently played poorly in Walter's view), but the selectors had overruled him. Walter was not moved by the press argument that Clough might 'come off'. He thought Kevan was an obvious choice and the Russians feared and respected him. Clough did not make the World Cup squad and the media did not hold back in their criticism of Walter's decision.

This time England were a vastly a different team, and the result was a 1-1 draw against a strong Russian side. Walter was happy with the result, although a bumpy pitch prevented much top class football. He thought England probably had more chances with 20 shots to the Russians' nine, and the late Russian equalizer came after Ivanov had clearly handled the ball, but Walter admitted that the Russians finished much stronger and showed that they had superior fitness.

The results from 1955 to 1957 – only one defeat in 17 games – were so good that Walter had nurtured real hopes of going far in the 1958

World Cup in Sweden, perhaps even winning it. But the Munich air disaster had been a devastating blow to the team, both physically and psychologically, and there were ongoing issues within the squad: the Fulham and Blackburn players, Johnny Haynes, Bobby Robson, Bryan Douglas and Ronnie Clayton were tired following an exhausting battle to gain promotion from the Second Division; the squad was beginning to look more and more inexperienced with recent call-ups Colin McDonald, Tommy Banks, Eddie Clamp, Bobby Robson and Bill Slater totalling six international caps between them. Of the remaining first team players, Don Howe, Bryan Douglas and Derek Kevan had little more than 18-months international experience and only Johnny Haynes, Billy Wright and Tom Finney had significant international experience. To compound Walter's problems, the FA had inexplicably taken only 20 players to the World Cup instead of the permitted 22, and the press was critical of the decision to leave the aging Stanley Mathews and Nat Lofthouse out of the squad. The challenge was all the greater because of the strong group England were in: Russia, Brazil and Austria. England did not travel to Gothenburg with high hopes.

On arriving in Sweden Walter was roundly criticised by the press for his decision to stay in the Park Royal, a luxury hotel in Gothenburg instead of a training camp in the country and attacked for bringing his squad to Sweden only two days before the tournament began.

He defended his decisions in Ferrier's book, *Soccer Partnership*. His planned trip to inspect possible training camps in Sweden coincided with the Munich disaster, but on a visit soon after, seven possible bases were checked. The Brazilians had claimed the Hindas Hotel, a pleasant spot less than an hour from Gothenburg; the Russians had chosen a more Spartan camp also at Hindas. Lisekil was perfect but entailed a drive of more than three hours each way. Walter sought the advice of George Raynor, the English manager of the Swedish team. He was of the opinion that as the Hindas Hotel was not available, the Park Royal in Gothenburg would be the next best. The hotel proved to be excellent. It was quiet with good food and music. Gothenburg was not riotous and had the feel of an English provincial city. There was no criticism amongst the players, who in the main came from large industrial cities and were prone to boredom and introspection when taken deep into the country.

The decision about when to arrive in Sweden was taken after Walter had consulted those players who were experienced in travelling and playing abroad. The general opinion was that when the team had a comfortable and short journey to make, it was best that the team practice should take place in England because the players, especially the married ones, preferred to stay at home as long as possible.

But above all the headlines which had gripped the country, reaching almost hysterical proportions, had focused on the retention of Derek Kevan, the spurning of Brian Clough and the dropping of Bobby Charlton.

The centre forward position had been a problem since the tragic death of Tommy Taylor in Munich. The truth was that there was not an obvious replacement in the country. Nat Lofthouse, still going strong, had been considered, but he had had a shoulder injury (and had not inexplicably been left behind as some football writers had suggested). The selection of Derek Kevan of West Bromwich Albion, ahead of Brian Clough of Middlesbrough, dominated the press headlines.

Derek Kevan had been a target for the press from his first appearance for England against Scotland the year before. He was criticised because of his obvious lack of ball skill. It was true that he occasionally fell over the ball but, Walter argued, critics failed to set his weaknesses against his strengths. He was forceful and powerful; his goal scoring ability drew defenders to him and away from other players.

Brian Clough, through his extrovert personality, had won the public's support. He had made himself a national figure scoring 42 goals for Second Division side Middlesbrough in the Cup and League. He was a young player with a lot of potential but Walter thought that his style of play did not fit into the England forward line. He felt that Clough's success as a centre forward with his club was based on playing deep, with flying wingers cutting passes back into the middle, which Clough would run onto. Either the forward line would have to be rejigged to fit his style or he needed matches to fit himself into the team's pattern, and it was too late for either.

But above all the controversy centred on Bobby Charlton. Charlton was a young player of outstanding potential. His fast recovery from the Munich disaster and performances for Manchester United, as they fought their way to the Cup Final, had grabbed the attention and sympathy of the British public. He was the hero of the hour. But he was also inexperienced: he had not played for United's first team until the previous year and had not had the opportunity to gain international experience in the England Under-23 side. He came straight into the England team after the Munich disaster and scored three goals in his first two matches against Scotland and Portugal, but, in Walter's view made only a slight contribution to the overall team effort. He was seen at that time as a player loitering with intent, waiting for a scoring chance to turn up – a specialist player that England could not afford, as was shown when he played in the 5-0 defeat against Yugoslavia. He was dropped for the next game against Russia and did not feature in any of the World Cup games in Sweden.

In his autobiography, *My England Years*, Bobby Charlton recounted his side of the story. 'He [Walter] was a gentleman with a kindly manner but he did not soften his message when he took me to one side [in Moscow] to say that the England selectors, of which he was only one, had decided to drop me after my third game, which I had gone into with the encouraging record of three goals in two matches.'

Charlton, furthermore, reflected sombrely on Walter's words as the team toured Lenin's tomb in Red Square: 'The manager said I had to think more deeply about my contribution to the team. I had to study, particularly, the one made by Johnny Haynes, a great midfielder, who, he said, was willing to do things that apparently I wasn't.'

Walter told me, "Bobby, you have to do a lot more running. The next time you see Haynes, study every move he makes. He always wants the ball, and when he's passed it he's always looking to receive it again. It's not enough to do everything positive, you also have to think negative at times; you have to think of denying the other team the ball. It's always going to be a vital part of the game. If Haynes loses the ball, look at his anger as he fights to get it back."'

This verdict came as something of a jolt for Charlton. Naturally he was disappointed – he thought he could still score goals that made a difference. But when he reflected on what he had been told he accepted it. He respected Johnny Haynes, who had almost a cult following among up and coming midfielders; indeed, Charlton's teammate, Johnny Giles, had told him that Haynes had been his main inspiration. Nor was Charlton surprised that Walter wanted more from him. It was the same message that Jimmy Murphy, the United assistant manager, had been drilling into him – that one of the dividing lines between a true professional and a merely talented amateur was his willingness to work off the ball, to be constantly involved in both the rhythm and the reading of the game. 'In some respects the only oddity was in hearing those words in the cultured tones of my England manager,' added Bobby, 'because I had indeed heard many variations of them in the more basic language and the Rhondda Valley accent of Jimmy Murphy'

Bobby Charlton learned the lesson, and handled it in the way that made him such a dedicated and successful professional. 'I held no resentment towards Walter Winterbottom, not then or later, when my continued absence from the team became a major issue in the press.' Charlton's place, in Moscow and in Sweden, was taken by Bobby Robson.

There was no suggestion that the decision had come from anyone other than Walter, but Charlton later came to understand how the bureaucratic selection committee handicapped Walter's plans: 'There was no doubt Winterbottom had a minefield of a job, which, looking back, he ultimately could not win. I was certainly not going to give him any more grief than he was already experiencing on the back pages of the newspapers and no doubt, in the committee room.'

In England's opening World Cup game in Gothenburg they faced Russia once more, and again it was a draw: this time 2-2, with goals from Finney and Kevan. To add to England's misfortunes, Finney, arguably their only world-class forward, had been picked out for harsh treatment by the Russians and was injured in a late tackle which left him with a badly twisted knee. Although every effort was made to get him fit – he was taken to a top specialist in Gothenburg by Shepherdson – Finney was unable to take any further part in the tournament. It was a serious setback and it certainly didn't help that the next match, again in Gothenburg, was against the favourites, Brazil. Don Howe, who was the right back in that team, recalled Walter's tactical preparations:

Garrincha was probably in the best form of his life and Didi, and Zagalo the left-winger, were outstanding players. And Pelé turned out to be a star although he was only 17. Walter sat next to me and asked, 'What do you think about Zagalo?' I told him I'd heard about him but not much more. "Well," said, Walter, "Bill Nicholson [Walter's assistant manager] saw him and said Zagalo will play deep and I don't want you to go that deep. I want you to tuck in with Billy Wright in the centre and leave Zagalo to someone else." It worked. We stopped Zagalo and the game ended 0-0, the first time the Brazilians had failed to score. Walter was really chuffed, putting his arm round the players. He was as proud of that as any result he'd ever had.

Harold Shepherdson also remembered the careful planning for the Brazil game.

It was after midnight on the Sunday of our match with Russia that Bill Nicholson got back from watching Brazil play Austria. He sat with Walter and I into the very early hours of the morning and his summing up of the Brazilian team was one of the most brilliant I have heard... 24-hours before we were due to play Brazil, Walter staged a practice match with the reserves plus himself and Nicholson acting as 'Brazilians'. Nicholson took the part of the Brazilian right half, Didi, the man who was certain to shadow Haynes, while Walter played as their right back, De Sordi. I refereed this fascinating game.

The tactical preparation paid off, with Howe playing as a second centre half with Wright, Clamp as an attacking full back and Slater playing tight on Didi. England drew 0-0 and were the only team in the tournament to stop Brazil from scoring. The Brazilian team – with stars like Gilmar, Santos, Zito, Zagalo, Vavá, Garrincha and the introduction of the brilliant 17-year-old Pelé – was perhaps the greatest ever. They were a revelation, finally winning the tournament in style, but it might easily have been different. Although Brazil had the best of the first half in the game against England, the pattern changed in the second and Walter's team might even have won. They were certainly unfortunate to be denied a penalty when Kevan was brought down in the box.

The defence was magnificent with Tommy Banks, a tough Lancastrian miner – who Glanville described as having the appearance of a Great War private of the trenches – surpassing himself: 'Once,' wrote Glanville admiringly, 'when Don Howe skied the ball, he brought it down with a delicacy any Brazilian might have envied.'

Many years later Walter told an amusing anecdote about the Brazil game:

Bill [Slater] was late putting his boots on. I asked why he was messing around and it turned out he was borrowing boots from another player. They'd all been asked to bring two pairs of boots! I couldn't believe that a player like Bill Slater – he had been to Carnegie and was a lecturer at Birmingham University – was having to borrow a pair of boots just before we went on the pitch for a World Cup game. I think it was a superstition because he'd done the same thing at the Wolves and played the game of his life.'

Bill Slater laughed when questioned about this. 'Oh no, not the boots story! Actually it's partly true,' he admitted. 'I did borrow Peter Sillett's boots. Peter was a full back at Chelsea. He was in the party but he didn't play and his boots fitted me just perfectly. I took two or three pairs of boots but they didn't feel right. I don't know why. Peter wasn't playing and his boots were really comfortable so I asked if I could borrow them. But I wasn't superstitious. I know some players are. You know putting on the right boot before the left and that sort of thing.'

The two draws meant that England needed a win in the final group against Austria. It should have been easy; Austria were a team with problems and England were expected to win. Austria, however, went two goals up, forcing England to fight back to a 2-2 draw, with goals from Haynes and Kevan, and once again a controversial goal was disallowed for an alleged foul on the keeper by Derek Kevan. But it was a disappointing result. The draw meant that they then had to go into a play-off with Russia to determine who would go through to the quarter finals with the group winners Brazil.

So England faced Russia again for the third time in four weeks and Brabrook and Broadbent came into the team. Twice Brabrook hit the post with the Russian goalkeeper beaten, and each time the ball rebounded clear; one Russian shot hit the post but this time the ball rebounded into the net. On such fine margins are World Cups decided and England were out. Even the usually critical Brian

Glanville considered they were unlucky to lose 1-0. Walter could only wonder how far his team might have gone but for a frown from fortune.

The play off had to be fitted into the qualifying group schedule as an extra game. It meant playing four games in ten days. Bill Slater felt that this was the key factor: 'We were tired. I know I was.' Afterwards in the dressing room Harold Shepherdson surveyed a room full of despondent, desperately tired players and thought, 'well, you don't deserve it. Kevan nearly had to be carried off the field and I had to cut Johnny Haynes socks off his feet because of the many blisters.'

Napoleon said he preferred his generals to be lucky. Walter could have been excused for looking back and concluding that he had not been lucky in World Cup matches; against the USA in Brazil, against Uruguay in Switzerland and against Russia and Brazil in Sweden. He brought the subject up with Bob Ferrier. 'Luck,' he said 'was a factor that had to be considered, no matter how reluctantly.' He pointed out that, 'in a low point scoring game like association football, luck plays a tremendous part, not in the play but in the result.' Referees decisions, penalties given or not given, goals disallowed, balls hitting the inside of a post and not the outside were all sometimes deciding factors. Of course in a long league season luck tends to even itself out, but in the few crucial matches of a World Cup competition it can determine the result. He cited the Hungarians who were so very unlucky to be beaten by Germany in the 1954 World Cup final, although Hungary were by far the superior team. Brazil were lucky in Sweden to have no serious injury problems. Sweden were lucky in 1958 to play all their matches bar one in their home stadium. England managers that followed Walter, especially Bobby Robson, had their own reasons for rueing the role luck plays in World Cup football.

On the way home the England party ran into Gustav Sebes. Hungary too were out, beaten 2-1 in a group play off against Wales.

Recalling that famous win at Wembley in 1953 he confided to Billy Wright: 'You only get a great team once in a lifetime'. Shepherdson could not help wondering if it might have been Walter saying that if the Munich disaster had not robbed him of so many great players; there were many who would have agreed.

The World Cup tournament in Sweden was the first World Cup that had full television coverage and it marked the beginning of a change in the way the media reported football. Public awareness of international teams and players was much higher and this led to a different style of writing by the press. Instead of solely reporting on the match, sports writers began to become interested in personalities and controversy.

Of course team changes – or the lack of them in Walter's case – were the main topic for criticism. Walter firmly believed that playing what he believed to be his best team unchanged was the right strategy, and pointed out, somewhat aggrieved, that if England made a mistake by not changing players so did Brazil and Russia. He defended his policy, saying that there was no precedent or logic for changing the team in a world championship, especially when it was inexperienced. 'It is almost an axiom in football that the successful teams gain their experience because they are allowed to play unchanged, save for injuries,' he said. 'The only reason for changing a team is if it has lost confidence, which only an injection of fresh blood would rectify. This England team had never lost confidence.'

In his book *The Second Most Important Job in the Country* Niall Edworthy saw 1958 as the year that the press attitude to England managers changed. 'Winterbottom had manifestly done an impressive job in reforming the structure of the national sides at every level whilst producing a highly successful senior side. During that period it became increasingly clear that the selectors would, more often than not, defer to the wishes of Winterbottom. If Winterbottom was entitled to praise for England's achievements then it was only fair that he should receive criticism for his failings; thus, in a clear departure from the earlier policy of sparing Winterbottom when the search for scapegoats began, the press now seemed eager to develop a sense of confrontation.'

The *Daily Herald* ran a photograph of a sombre-looking Bobby Charlton above angry letters from readers calling for the manager's removal. 'I say sack Winterbottom before we really reach rock bottom,' wrote A. Grinstead from Birmingham. (At that time readers' letters were a way for newspapers to avoid the diplomatic inconvenience of attacking a target directly.)

Niall Edworthy explained: 'For post-imperial England, still coming to terms with its falling status in the new world order, the failure of its national team was interpreted as just one more example of the country's decline. The gentlemanly tone that characterised coverage of England in the immediate post-war years had given way to something altogether more vicious and vitriolic. Over the four years that followed Sweden in 1958, the relationship between the press and the England management deteriorated sharply.'

Walter accepted that media criticism went with the job of being the England manager – although it did upset him when it affected his family, as he had seen when his son Alan greeted him at Heathrow with the admonishment, 'Daddy: why didn't you pick Bobby Charlton?' Even in the late 50's, when the media spotlight was nowhere near as bright as it is today, he was under pressure, accepting that whenever an England team loses – not necessarily because of a bad performance – there is a witch-hunt, a hue and cry which takes precisely the opposite view of the manager, whatever that might be.

CHAPTER 14

HOME
AND AWAY

1946 – 1960

Although Walter was dedicated to giving service to football, and was a loyal servant of the FA he continually had worries about his personal finances, and was disappointed that the FA failed to properly recognise the value of his services.

When he joined the FA in 1946, his salary had been an issue, but he accepted the improved offer of £983-a-year to manage the England team in addition to his job as Director of Coaching. By 1952 this had been increased to £1,400, but by 1955 he felt that the time had come to write to Sir Stanley Rous to ask for a re-appraisal of his salary.

In his reply Rous politely rejected his request and rebuffed Walter's suggestion that he would by now be financially better off if he had remained in the RAF. He pointed out that Walter was still a young man (then 42 and in the prime of his career) and that he was, in addition to his salary, receiving additional benefits such as a bonus of £250 for a foreign tour, £15 for acting as manager of the Football League team and £100 from broadcasting and TV fees. In response to Walter's suggestion that the hardship of his time away from home should be taken into account (six months a year), Rous had the temerity to suggest that this was a benefit, as he was no cost to his household when he was away. It was not, of course, within Rous' authority to make decisions on salary – these were made by the Staff Committee, based on recommendations he put to them – but he advised Walter it would be inopportune to make definite proposals to the committee now. Perhaps because Sir Stanley – although on a modest salary himself – had no children and was given free accommodation in a penthouse flat above the FA office at 22 Lancaster Gate, he was unable to fully appreciate Walter's situation.

In January 1956 Walter received a small increase in his salary to £1,750, which he considered unsatisfactory. In September he again wrote to Rous, politely but firmly drawing to his attention to the sharp rise in the cost of living which was affecting salaries at the FA. Walter used his own situation as an example, basing his case on in-depth research, and asked Rous to raise the issue with the staff committee. In his letter Walter quoted a Ministry of Labour report which stated that from April 1947 to April 1955 the average weekly earnings in British Industry had increased by 76 per cent. Another recently published report showed that wages and salaries had increased by 66 per cent from 1948 to 1955.

Walter gave examples of the increased costs of everyday items that affected him: tube fares up by 122 per cent; bus fares up 100 per cent; coal up by 100 per cent; electricity up by 100 per cent; rates up by 40 per cent and school fees by 75 per cent in the period from 1948-1955.

In the same period his salary had increased from £1,077 to £1,727, an increase of 65 per cent which was not even keeping up with the cost of inflation. He reminded Sir Stanley that when he was appointed to the FA post he was 'encouraged to understand' that his salary would be raised from £1,000 to £1,500 in real terms in approximately five years by increases of £100-a-year. In effect, he told Sir Stanley, the rapid increase in the cost of living meant that his present salary after ten years of service represented almost the same value to him as it did when he was first appointed.

When Walter joined the FA he had one three-year-old daughter. Now he had three children: Janet was 13, Brenda was nine and his son, Alan, was seven. A growing family was expensive to clothe and feed, and he wanted to give his children the best chance in life by educating them at private schools. No one would ever have accused Walter of being selfish, avaricious or concerned about material wealth but it was understandable that he wanted a standard of living that was appropriate to his position.

His plea fell on deaf ears. Three months later he received a modest increase of £250, an increase of 11 per cent 'to compensate for increased cost of living' and his holiday entitlement was increased to three weeks – hardly compensation for months spent away from home.

Planning Alan's education was a particular worry. He had raised this subject in a discussion with Sir Stanley, and wrote to confirm their meeting: 'I am anxious that he should be educated at a well known soccer playing public school such as Highgate. You know the background of this situation which prompts me to think in terms of such schooling for my son [It is not clear what his meaning was, but as the FA were very keen to promote association football in public schools it is likely that he was referring to the public relations value of the England football manager's son attending a football playing public school] and you know also of the concessions I am willing to make.' He knew that the Football Association was considering the possibility of helping in the education of footballer's children and he went on to ask if it would be possible to apply such a scheme to assist in the fees for Alan's schooling.

There is no record of Rous' reply and nothing came of the suggestion, but as often happened in Walter's life, good fortune smiled from another direction. Ken Robson, Walter's friend from

RAF Cosford, now a Harley Street surgeon and Alan's godfather, heard about Walter's dilemma and generously agreed to pay for Alan's education at Highgate School.

There was still no resolution to the salary question, however. In January 1958 Walter again received only a modest increase taking his salary to £2,250, with the addition of a weekly allowance of five Luncheon Vouchers, each worth three shillings! Three years later he felt forced to raise the subject with Sir Stanley again, this time in even stronger terms. He pointed out that although he appreciated that it was difficult to evaluate his job, because it was unique, the FA should at least value his services in line with managers of First Division clubs.

In his letter he reminded Sir Stanley that in 1948 (thirteen years earlier) Mr Rutherford, the Chairman of Newcastle United, had spoken to them both about Walter becoming their manager at a salary of £2,500. He went on to say that many of the coaches he had developed were now with senior clubs or working overseas at salaries much greater than his own. He declined to mention other lucrative offers he had received from clubs – offers he had always dismissed out of hand in his unquestionable loyalty to the Football Association and England. He went on to raise the question of whether the FA would provide him with a company car and gave examples of how this worked for business executives. Most club managers were given a company car, and with the amount of travelling Walter did to coaching courses and matches, it was not an unreasonable request: one which some might have considered essential. He had never felt able to afford a car himself.

In response he received a letter from Sir Stanley to say that the Staff Committee had agreed to an increase taking his salary to £2,600. In addition The FA would provide an interest free loan, repayable in two or three years, to assist in the purchase of a car, for which business mileage would be paid at 10 pence a mile. It was a mealy-mouthed and totally inadequate response.

He declined to take up the offer of a loan for car purchase, feeling unable to meet the repayments and the salary matter was never resolved. The final postscript to the inequity of the Football Association's refusal to re-evaluate Walter's salary was revealed after he resigned in 1962. It was unhesitatingly agreed that two men were required to do his job. Allen Wade as Director of Coaching and Alf Ramsey as England team manager were appointed with a combined salary of around £7,000 per annum, nearly three times Walter's final salary (Ramsey's biographer, David Bowler, said that Ramsey was reportedly given an annual salary of £4,500, not dissimilar from that he had been receiving at Ipswich. It is unlikely that Allen Wade would have been offered less than £2,500 as Director of Coaching).

The FA's unwillingness to pay a fair market rate for the job created a financial strain and worry, but Walter was fortunate in that fate had again smiled on him. Ann had made good friends with her neighbour, Mrs Massey Smith, who lived next door but two. Her house at 16 Holland Walk was an imposing detached, double fronted, four bedroomed property, standing at the top of a cul-de-sac overlooking Holland Walk. It was a large, well-appointed family house, with two sitting rooms and a dining room down stairs. Mrs Smith, who was an elderly widow of comfortable means, confided in Ann that she was going to move to a flat and said she would like Ann and Walter to have Shockleigh House. Ann was flabbergasted; it was a wonderful house, but she knew Walter's circumstances and that they could not possibly afford it. When she reluctantly explained the situation, Mrs Massey Smith told her not to worry, 'you can just pay me what I paid for it.' It was a substantial discount to the market price – an offer which they could afford and gratefully accepted.

Shockleigh House was not just an ideal family home. It was a place where Walter enjoyed entertaining his many friends from the world of football. Officials and coaches from overseas football associations were frequent visitors and often their children were invited to stay to improve their English, so Janet, Brenda and Alan were exposed to international friendships from an early age. Walter was an attentive and generous host, always interested in new ideas and lively debate, and in this way he and Ann made friends who lasted a lifetime.

Christmas was a special time. Ann and Walter always had a large party for friends and neighbours. Although they rarely saw him, he took an interest in his neighbours and they enjoyed his company but the talk was never of football. Walter always found time to care about others. One Christmas he invited the telephone switchboard operator at the FA to spend the day with them 'because she was a spinster and would be on her own.' Christmas was a time for games. He had a store of them, often brain-teasing games that adults, children and eventually grandchildren alike enjoyed.

The week-long residential courses at Lilleshall continued to keep Walter away from home for most of the summer. 'I didn't know him as well as I would have liked to' lamented Walter's eldest daughter Janet, 'he was away so much.' But they loved it when he was there. He read books to the children and was diligent in helping them with their homework.

Ann found her own ways of coping with her husband's long absences. She had a support network of friends she met at the school gate and when Janet was 12 and Alan started school she immersed herself in charitable work. She became involved in church and community affairs and was an active member of Stanmore Young Wives, the Mothers Union, the Women's Institute, the Darby and Joan club and St. Saviours orphanage in Harrow. Walter supported her whenever he could and every Christmas they would go together to spend time with the children at St. Saviours.

Football was a very small part of her life: twice a year she would go the FA Cup Final and the FA Amateur Cup Final as an official guest. When there were home internationals Ann and her friend sat in the car park with their sandwiches, took their seat in the stand for the game and then went home for tea.

'My father always put his work first, but in that respect was no different from other leaders in business, the professions or politics' said Janet. 'When he came home from the office he would have dinner with the family and then go upstairs to his study and work,' Although he was not able to spend as much time as he would have liked with his children he was usually there when he was needed. Janet recalled a difficult time when she was taking her GCE 'O level' exams: 'I was very nervous and lacked confidence but he would take me out for walks in the evening and just talk to me. It was very reassuring.' Later, after leaving school, she was working in a hotel in Evian Les Bain on the French side of Lake Geneva. 'My father would come to Switzerland for meetings with FIFA and always made a point of coming to see me. I would catch the train to Geneva and we would have dinner and stay in a hotel there. I will always remember the first time we went to the hotel reception to check in. He said, "This is my daughter Janet," and they looked at him knowingly and smiled, "Yes, of course sir."'

Brenda concurred: 'We were used to him being away but he was a wonderful father and we were a very happy family. When we were young he somehow found time to make toys for us. Our family lunches every Sunday were important for us all and we loved the parties he organised.' When Brenda completed her GCE 'A levels' she wanted to go to art college, but Walter, feeling that this might not provide a sound career, advised her to become a teacher, as he had done himself. She took his advice, attended East Hampstead Park teachers training college, and was proud when her father was invited to the college as a guest speaker.

Janet and Brenda, who had little interest in football, were less affected by the media spotlight on their father than Alan. Alan, who was mad about football, suffered, not just because he had a famous father, but because his father was the manager of the England football team. At Highgate School, he was endlessly teased by the other boys and sometimes even masters when England lost a match or his father was criticised in the press (there were compensations though: he was very proud when Walter took the England team to play the Highgate School First X1). Alan did well in the school football team and desperately wanted to be a professional footballer but Walter did not think he was good enough to make the grade at the top. It put him in a difficult position. If he was honest the boy would be deeply hurt and angry; if he encouraged him it would lead to eventual disappointment. His solution was typical of the way he went about solving problems: He telephoned Ron Greenwood, then the manager of West Ham, and asked if he would take Alan into the West Ham squad for pre-season training. He explained to Ron that he believed that when Alan was training with top professionals he would realise for himself that he was not going to be good enough to make the grade as a professional footballer. The plan worked, and through his friendship with Sir Charles Forte, Walter was able to introduce Alan to a business career and he continued to enjoy playing football for the Old Cholmeleians (Highgate School Old Boys) for many years.

Walter spent most of his summer each year at Lilleshall overseeing courses: courses for trainers and coaches, an advanced coaches course, courses for youth players, for school masters, for schoolboys and for referees. The international development of coaching was becoming more important: Walter invited famous coaches to lecture at Lilleshall, including Gustav Sebes, the mastermind of the glorious Hungarian team which had beaten England in 1953. Sebes gave a talk to a fascinated audience on the development of coaching in Hungary and credited the immense success of Hungarian football to the concentration of the best talent in a few clubs and the player's willingness to accept rigorous coaching routines. Walter took part in the first international course for trainers and coaches organised by UEFA in 1961 – a significant step forward in the development of football coaching.

The FA coaching strategy continued to focus on schools. In addition the FA provided grants to help university teams to arrange fixtures against schools. 'Schools Week' at Oxford and Cambridge remained an important annual event, and was now being concluded with a match against representative teams – in 1957 they played against a Scotland Boys X1 in Glasgow.

Walter reached out to the media to help spread the coaching message to children. The BBC filmed at national coaching courses. Recordings were shown on BBC Children's TV programmes and Walter also appeared on the BBC's *Blue Peter* TV show. Coaching sessions at Lilleshall, Chelsea and Arsenal were broadcast by ITV on children's shows.

Sports journalists were encouraged to attend courses to see for themselves what coaching was achieving. One such journalist was John Davies of the *Daily Mail*, who was called into his editor's office in June 1957 to be told: 'The Football Association is holding a qualifying course for coaches all next week. I want you to go. I don't mean to go and watch – but actually do the course.' A stunned Davies reluctantly packed his kit.

Davies was impressed with the glorious setting at Lilleshall with its lush playing fields and modern facilities. He reported that the course was run by a team of seven coaches headed by Winterbottom, with Ron Greenwood, the ex Fulham and Chelsea star running his group. The journalist wondered why 90 professional footballers would give up a week of their close season holiday to undergo a rigorous coaching routine. He found some, like his roommate Trevor Lawless, the Oldham centre half, were aiming to become full-time coaches after retiring, and expected to take three or four years to reach the standard required for the full coaching badge. Others came simply because they wanted to improve their skills and learn more about coaching: Jack Crompton, the ex-Manchester United goalkeeper and FA Cup medal winner, then with Luton Town as a trainer, was working to progress from the preliminary badge to the full coaching certificate.

'But,' said Davies, 'the dominant figure in this glorious setting... is

Winterbottom himself. Even I have come under the spell of this man who, quite justly I think, is considered to be one of the best football coaches in the world. Wherever a coaching group is gathered Winterbottom can be seen going round, encouraging, advising, cautioning... this is where the foundations of England's soccer future are being laid. If sincerity of purpose is anything to judge by that future looks mighty bright.' The number of qualified coaches was growing every year and Walter and his staff encouraged them to join their regional football coaches associations to keep in touch with developments and the latest techniques.

Through the late 1950s the lack of facilities for youth was a major concern. Walter's cause was strengthened in 1960 by the publication of the far reaching Wolfendon Committee's report, *Sport & the Community* – soon to have a major impact on his own career – which stressed the need for better facilities, coaching, and leadership to attract young people to sport.

Walter's annual coaching report in 1959/60 also highlighted the need to bridge the gap between schools and youth clubs, and between youth clubs and senior clubs. He was concerned there simply weren't enough pitches, changing rooms or canteen facilities for boys who had just left school and wanted to continue to play and practice football. He encouraged senior professional and amateur clubs to provide youth sections which could offer year round facilities for training and coaching.

With so many schoolmasters having taken courses and qualified as coaches, he saw less need for professional players to make regular visits to schools to coach, freeing them up to spend more time with promising groups of youth players.

The National Association of Boys' Clubs (NABC) ran a one week soccer coaching course twice a year, which was attended by 94 boys who were training to be leaders. Walter was very supportive of such initiatives and through this became friendly with Frankie Vaughan who was a generous contributor to, and supporter of, the NABC.

Frankie Vaughan was one of the pop idols of his day (called a 'crooner' back then), famous for his 1955 chart hit which ended with the (daring for the time) innuendo, 'Give me the moonlight, give me the girl, and leave the rest to me.' He finished his act by doffing his top hat, twirling his cane and a producing a high kick which had girls screaming wildly. Walter took the England team to the London Palladium before a midweek international one evening and Frankie Vaughan invited them all back stage before the performance. During his act he had the spotlights turned on the team and introduced them to the audience.

The Boys Brigade was another group Walter supported, providing six FA coaches for 750 boys at their National Camp held at Lilleshall. The business world was encouraged to help. The Central Council of Physical Recreation (CCPR) ran a soccer course at Bisham Abbey for selected young men from major companies and Walter hoped that this would lead to large commercial organizations making their playing facilities available for coaching courses. The Services were already giving much attention to the needs of youth and arranging competitive matches. An Army Youth Cup competition was started and the FA regularly sent a representative team to play service youth teams.

But there was no escaping the fact that if England were to improve at international level the foundations had to be laid in the First Division clubs. Chairmen and directors were all powerful and their acceptance and adoption of new ideas was fundamental to progress. To keep them up to date with coaching developments a report was published by the FA Technical Committee and sent to club directors.

The report – almost certainly written by Walter – defined the responsibilities and relationships of the manager, the coach and the trainer for the first time:

The manager should be responsible for the scouting system; signing players approved by the board; dealing with players salaries and conditions of employment; overall control of staff, the planning of tactics; and in conjunction with the coach, the overall planning of training and coaching and the selection of the team.

The coach, appointed by the manager, should be responsible for the day to day programme of fitness and coaching; development of tactics; reports on players and supervision of the apprentice professionals.

The trainer, appointed by the manager, should be responsible for the treatment and rehabilitation of injured players, treatment of minor injuries during match play, facilities and equipment and supervision of junior staff working at the ground.

It asked chairmen to consider a coach's career development, preparing him for a move into a manager's position or a more qualified trainer's role.

Clubs were urged to provide better coaching facilities: a large gymnasium or sports hall for year round practice, regardless of weather and daylight was essential. The report concluded with detailed recommendations on modern methods of fitness training, coaching, diet, health and treatment of injury.

It was a bold initiative but Walter could see that the long term solution to influencing chairmen and directors was to encourage leading players to make a career in coaching after their playing days. A new breed of managers, who were FA qualified coaches, would be in the best position to influence chairmen and get agreement to bring in new ideas.

After an England training session in 1959 Walter spoke to two of his players, Bobby Robson and Don Howe, as they walked off the training pitch. 'What are you going to do when you pack up playing, Bobby?'

'I don't know' replied Robson, 'I don't think cleaning windows is an option!'

'Why don't you both come on one of the senior professional players' coaching courses at Lilleshall?' said Walter. 'You might want to begin a new career as a coach: opportunities are opening up now for people like you.'

Walter had the gift of spotting talent, inspiring men to reach their potential and guiding their careers. Both Bobby Robson and Don Howe went on to become distinguished and successful coaches. Bobby Robson began his managerial career with Fulham when he retired as a player in 1967 and went on to manage at Ipswich, PSV Eindhoven, Sporting Club de Portugal, FC Porto, Barcelona and Newcastle. He followed Ron Greenwood as the England manager from 1982-90 and in the 1990 World Cup went one step further than his mentor, Walter, reaching the semi-finals where England were desperately unlucky to be beaten in a penalty shoot out against Germany.

Don Howe played with Bobby Robson at West Bromwich Albion and for England, and went on to manage West Bromwich Albion, Galatsaray SK, Arsenal and QPR. It was as a first team coach that he enjoyed most success, however, coaching the Arsenal team which won the double in 1971 and assisting managers Ron Greenwood, Bobby Robson and Terry Venables in the England team.

Many of the professional players who Walter encouraged to become coaches had a huge influence on the next generation of players. Malcolm Allison, for instance, was the captain of West Ham when he went on one of Walter's courses at Lilleshall. A flamboyant character, Allison was as well-known for his fedora and cigar as he was for his passion for football. He came back to West Ham inspired by what he had learned at Lilleshall and immediately began coaching sessions for the young players every Tuesday and Thursday evening. They took place on the car park and entrance to the Boleyn Stadium, a far cry from today's training facilities!

One of those young players was John Cartwright, a young West Ham professional who recounted Malcolm Allison's influence on his career: 'I was one of a group that included all the well-known players who graduated to the England World Cup team and we were captured by Mal's infectious enthusiasm. Mal saw the importance of coaching as an added extra that would improve the player's football intellect as well as their playing abilities and he urged us to go on the

FA coaching courses.' And so it was that a 17-year-old Cartwright went along to the Arsenal Stadium at Highbury to take part in the FA preliminary coaching course which was run by Walter:

It was on Thursday afternoons for six weeks. I remember that we were allowed to use the away team dressing room at Highbury and that it had a heated floor. Luxury we had never seen before! The course was in two sections. The first part was based on theoretical aspects of the game and the second on practical coaching. The theory lectures took place in the tea room which was situated along the tunnel that lead from the dressing room, down some steps and out onto the Arsenal pitch. We did our practical sessions on a red-ochre surface that was situated behind the terracing where the famous clock was. The sessions usually lasted for about three hours: one hour theory and a couple of hours on the practical. When we finished we were given a cup of tea before going home. On the final afternoon we were given a piece of coaching to do as an examination of practical ability and this was followed with the theory test on the game. I passed the test and proudly took home my preliminary coaching certificate.

Although Walter was in charge of the course he had a number of fully qualified coaches helping him. The work we did then was very basic but it was the beginning of our coaching education and both the theory and practical work addressed the basic requirements of game structure in the theory and organisation of technical practices.

What I noticed about Walter was that he was an organised man and this was evident from the way the whole course, from arrival to departure, was arranged. This ability to organise efficiently and effectively was extremely important and throughout my own coaching career I have stressed the need for preparation and systematic, progressive practice. He was a visionary who saw that street football was disappearing due to traffic and rebuilding, and began teaching football that was organised along academic lines.

When we got back to West Ham Mal was always asking how the course was going. He was a great help to us because he could take the work we had done on the course and enlarge on it: on the training ground, or in the large communal bath after training or in Cassetari's Italian restaurant across the road from the stadium. Cassetari's was the West Ham University of Football. There the sauce bottles and the salt-and-pepper pots were players we moved around the table as Mal explained the finer points of the game and we were all encouraged to join in. They were heady, happy days.

It was a time when there was a changing of the guard. Ted Fenton was the West Ham manager at the time and he was only too happy to let his captain, Mal, more or less 'run the show' and Ted mostly took a backseat at team talks and when we were training. He was definitely from the old school and he and Mal were not on the best of terms throughout this period. When Ted left Ron Greenwood took over and it was the beginning of a new era.

When he finished playing John Cartwright dedicated his life to coaching and was described by Terry Venables as one of the finest coaches of young players in England. Walter met Malcolm Allison again many years later in 1968 when Allison was enjoying great success as the co-manager of Manchester City with Joe Mercer. Manchester City were playing at West Ham and they had drinks together in the board room after the game. There was no mistaking the warmth of Allison's greeting or the sincerity of Walter's praise for Malcolm's team.

Walter continued to write more coaching books throughout the fifties. His classic, *Soccer Coaching*, first published in 1952 was revised and reprinted in 1957 and 1960. This was followed by *Modern Soccer*, published by Educational Productions in 1958 and *Training for Soccer*, published by Heinemann in 1960.

The FA *Book for Boys* had reached edition no 15 by 1962, and although sales were never as high as the peak of 60,000 copies in

1949/50, it remained popular, packed with articles by a range of football personalities, and continued until 1974. As well as directing the content Walter always contributed the lead coaching article, with titles such as 'The Twist (Screening)', 'Have You Tried Five-a-Side?', and 'Think ahead-and Run'.

The voice of the Football Association, the *FA Year Book*, also continued to sell well, although not again reaching its peak of 68,000 copies in 1952. It featured articles on a wide range of topics that helped both Rous and Winterbottom to communicate the changes happening in football throughout the fifties. It continued in a more modern format until the final issue was published in 2011.

Films of significant matches, such as the European Cup Final, were made available to coaches and film strips were widely available to schools and clubs and even featured in an illustrated form in a national newspaper.

Walter accepted every opportunity to write about coaching. In an article for the *Royal Marines* magazine he reiterated his views on modern training methods, stressing the need for year-round practice facilities, modern fitness training, better ball skills and positional versatility. The mantra of fitness training had always been based on long distance running to build stamina but, he pointed out, the Hungarians found that sprinters made better footballers than long distance runners. He expounded his own philosophy of using a ball to develop stamina with a sequence of activities related to the physical needs of the game. He found the space in a short article to describe six sets in a circuit that anyone could do: a sprint run of 20 yards and return; a running jump to head the ball; sitting and then sprinting; running with the ball, flicking it up to head it and then continuing the dribble; driving the ball against a wall and finally running with the ball and making turns. In this way, he maintained, a player's endurance could be built up.

He explained that when a player lacked a particular skill, such as ball control, it could be improved by subjecting him to the pressure of constant and varied service from a trainer, so that the player learned to control the ball in real conditions before making a pass. As an example he quoted a film he had just watched showing the great Alfredo Di Stéfano, the Real Madrid star, constantly striving to improve his skills while at the same time improving his fitness. He was served a ball which he would catch on his instep, then run forward bouncing the ball on his right foot and volley a shot at goal. He would repeat it, again and again.

Walter concluded by stressing the need for versatility – forwards who can defend and defenders who can attack. The idea of the complete player, he explained, 'is to be able to adapt his play according to the situation in the game. When a full back goes forward he can continue to press his advantage, knowing that team mates have rotated around him to cover his position.' He was a visionary who saw this before the Dutch National Team announced 'total football' to the world in the 1974 World Cup.

CHAPTER 16

WALTER'S BOYS

1958 – 1962

After the 1958 World Cup in Sweden Walter began rebuilding his team. Tom Finney and Billy Wright were coming to the end of their international careers and Walter was looking to his Under-23s for new talent. Tom Finney played his last game for England in October 1958, winning his 76th cap in a rousing 5-0 defeat of Russia (some compensation for defeat in Sweden); Stanley Matthews had played his last game for England against Denmark in 1957 at the remarkable age of 42.

Finney and Matthew's parallel retirements sparked one of the most enduring football debates of the 20th century: which of these two legends was the better international player? Walter's view was that 'based on the statistics you would have to say that Finney was the more efficient player.' (Finney: played 71; goals 29; assists 14. Matthews: played 34; goals 3; assists 23.) 'but to be fair,' he said, 'Matthews was the entertainer, his appearances were often restricted and the war took away the years when he was in his prime.' (He won his first England cap in 1934.)

After the war ended Matthews was 30 and Finney 22. They both played at outside right then and Matthews was the first choice; but in the away fixture to Portugal in 1947, instead of choosing between them, Walter picked them both. 'It was a master stroke' said Finney, 'as I was naturally left footed, I took the number 11 jersey, a position I had yet to play at top level, and the combination of the two totally different styles worked a treat.' England won 10-0!

'Finney throughout his career has been a tightly turning, close-dribbling player of darts and flashes, sudden stops and accelerations,' said Walter, recalling the magic of the two players, 'he has been a man of tremendously quick skill and perception in getting through an opening to score... he is ephemeral, wraithlike; here and gone.'

'Matthews is vastly different: he has been able to dominate a team and a game more than any other player... on unaccountable occasions Matthews has been ringed around by four or five defenders and by feinting, swerving, fluttering his feet, sometimes without even touching the ball, he has them running around and overbalancing until one laughs out loud with sheer wonder and delight, until the onlooker as much as the defender is exhausted with the ecstasy of it all. Ball skill for Finney has been the means to an end. For Matthews it has been the essence of his play.'

The Finney-Matthews debate has continued for decades but Walter's private views were unequivocal: 'Tom could play in all the forward positions – outside right, outside left, centre forward. He was the more complete footballer.' The feeling was mutual: 'People used to say he (Walter) had a soft spot for me,' said Finney, 'and I would not dispute it – I certainly had a high opinion of him, both as a man and a manager.'

Another player who was reaching the end of his career at this time was Billy Wright who played his final game for England against the USA on the summer tour of 1959. It was the end of a remarkable England career and partnership with Walter that began in Buxton in April 1946 and ended in Los Angles in May 1959. He won 105 caps and played 90 matches as captain (a record shared with Bobby Moore) including three World Cups. Because he was able to avoid injuries and maintain consistent form he played in 70 consecutive matches (still a record today). He was never spectacular; Walter found him solid and dependable: 'When reflecting on a match and assessing who had played well and who had played badly almost invariably I decided that Wright had played well.' As a captain, Walter found him, not flamboyant or verbose, but one who led quietly by example and enthusiasm.' 'Everybody looked up to Billy Wright – he always gave you confidence when you played with him,' agreed Johnny Haynes.

Walter's relationship with Billy Wright was based on mutual respect. 'At half time,' remarked Walter, 'when something can often be done, he has been able to give me more positive opinions on the way play has been trending and the reasons for it than any other player.' Billy Wright was an unashamed admirer of his England manager, describing Walter as 'a man of many parts: a practical man – yet a visionary; a man of action – yet an idealist; a teacher – yet a student.'

The 1958/59 season had began well enough with a five games unbeaten run which included the 5-0 win over Russia, but the summer tour to South America in May 1959 was disappointing with defeats in Brazil, Peru, and Mexico. An 8-1 win over the USA provided a consolation but it could have been a banana skin. There must have been some nervous moments when the USA went ahead but Warren Bradley equalized, Bobby Charlton scored a hat trick and England were comfortable winners. 'I have often wondered what would have happened to Walter if we lost that game,' recalled Jimmy Armfield. 'I was pleased for Walter. The FA people would have been under pressure from the press. They would have been.'

The tour was notable for the introduction of two more players who graduated from the Under-23s to become England legends: Jimmy Armfield and Jimmy Greaves. Both were playing for the

Under-23s in the San Siro stadium in Milan the night before the senior squad left for South America. Armfield was captain, and England won 3-0, putting on a performance which he considered was the best by an Under-23 team during his time. Jimmy Greaves scored twice. They knew they had made a good impression on Walter but could not have imagined the drama that was to follow. Back at the hotel after the match Walter told them he wanted them to join the senior squad leaving for Brazil the next day. They were astonished. Walter brought them back on a night train to Zurich where they boarded a private aircraft provided by Swissair. The only other passenger was the managing director of Swissair. It whisked them back to Heathrow in time to climb aboard the flight to Rio with the rest of the England team. They had never had such attention. 'Somehow, I couldn't really believe it was happening to me,' said Jimmy Armfield, 'in those days we didn't see ourselves as superstars.'

Armfield made his debut against Brazil and Greaves against Peru. 'Before the game against Peru I was very nervous' said Greaves, 'but Walter Winterbottom eased my nerves somewhat by stressing that I was under no pressure whatsoever and that my future England career would not depend on this one game alone. Walter told me to go out and play my normal game and to make sure I was always available to outside right Norman Deeley and right half Ronnie Clayton. He also stressed that I would play off Bobby Charlton and that the pair of us should stay relatively close together. It was a revelation to hear Walter talk to each and every player in the dressing room, informing them what he expected from them. At Chelsea, Ted Drake more or less confined himself to "All the best!"'

Jimmy Armfield noticed how Walter chose to handle players: 'He also had a steely side, Walter, that presented itself in Mexico. We had lost a couple of games and he was going to change the team – I know he was because he asked me about a couple of players. It was boiling hot, 100 degrees, and we had a noon kick off. We were on the training ground and I think he was going to rest one or two of the senior players. He shouted to a couple of the young players at the far end, "Come on over," you know, and I heard one of them say, "Oh bloody hell, what's this for?" I heard him say it. I saw his face change – I was looking at him, and when they came in he didn't put them in the team. He left the team as it was.'

The England party returned from South America to a barrage of press criticism aimed at Walter and many of the players. Greaves thought that it was far worse than contemporary players have to endure. The FA came in for particular criticism as being 'light years out of touch with what is happening in the modern game.' David Jack, writing in the *Empire News* scathingly declared, 'The England selectors have much to answer for and the abject failure of this tour brings into question their very worth as decision makers regarding the composition of our national team.'

Greaves thought that in many respects such criticism only served to strengthen Walter's hand: 'He wanted sole responsibility for the team so that he could build a side over a four year cycle that could win the World Cup. He was given a free hand for one match later that year, bringing in young players, including me, but when that team failed to impress it was back to square one.'

After another poor season in 1959/60, with defeats by Sweden (home), Spain and Hungary (away) and only one win at home to Northern Ireland, Jimmy Armfield recalled a turning point in England's fortunes:

Walter did a good thing. He got us all together at Lilleshall early in the 1960/61 season. It was winter and bitterly cold – oddly, I can clearly remember that he gave us all 'polar track suits' which were made out of what I can best describe as white candlewick material. He said there was going to be a new policy. There would be no more chopping and changing the team. We were the 18 players who would be the basis of the squad so that we would have a settled team in the build up to the 1962 World Cup.

He explained that we were going to play 4-2-4. I was thrilled to bits. I wanted to overlap and it suited me perfectly. He thought he had the players to do it. What he did, he picked the team and then the system. He put that in our minds early on. Then he went onto working on ball practice all the time, and told us, 'we've got to improve our ball skills if we are going to play like this – it's got to be touch and go and movement off the ball – movement off the ball, first touch, movement off the ball.' I can hear him saying it now. There was never any sort of, you know, the same sort of scenario you got at your club. It was totally different. But more than anything it was the camaraderie.

Somehow Walter insisted on getting his way with the selection committee and the new policy of consistency worked. Five of the first eight games Jimmy Armfield played for England had ended in defeat. Now with a settled team they won seven of the next eight games he played. The team was full of goals, scoring 44 and conceding only 11. Walter used just fourteen players in those eight matches. 'We had a good team then' mused Armfield and reeled off the names: 'Ron Springett (Sheffield Wednesday), myself at right back, Mike McNeill (Middlesborough), Bobby Robson (West Brom), Peter Swan (Sheffield Wednesday), Ron Flowers (Wolves), Bryan Douglas (Blackburn), Jimmy Greaves and Bobby Smith (Spurs), Johnny Haynes (Fulham) and Bobby Charlton (Manchester United).'

There was great spirit and confidence in the squad. Jimmy Greaves thought that Walter was creating an England team that was good enough to go on and win the 1962 World Cup in Chile: 'The old guard had gone and Walter had created a young England team that was finely balanced and in tune with one another as players: one which played well as a collective unit while at the same time allowing individuals to express themselves. We weren't just beating other teams we were steamrollering them.'

The first game in the successful 1960/61 season was a 5-2 win away to Northern Ireland in October. It was a satisfying result but much more significant was Walter's introduction of a new tactical plan. During the game there was a buzz of excitement and speculation in the press box when journalists realised England were playing with a 4-2-4 formation for the first time in place of the traditional WM formation. Brazil had used 4-2-4 in the 1958 World Cup in Sweden and it was duly copied by some continental teams, including West Ham. After the game Walter was surrounded by journalists questioning him about the tactical switch. One of them was Donald Saunders of the *Daily Telegraph* who reported 'as always he handled his interrogators deftly and all we really learned was that he was reasonably satisfied. Though there was some head shaking among more conservative members, the majority verdict of the press was that he had sound reason for this satisfaction.'

The new formation was successful because he had the players who could make it work. The system depended on two intelligent midfield players who could link defense and attack, and Johnny Haynes and Bobby Robson fitted this role perfectly. It also required a second centre back to partner Peter Swan, and Ron Flowers, an attacking wing half with Wolves, adapted to this new position with ease.

Walter had succeeded in persuading Joe Richards, the chairman of the selectors, to keep an unchanged team, despite dips in club form during the season. Another revolutionary step forward was his success in getting League clubs agreement to releasing the first team plus the reserves and replacements for 'get togethers' as Walter called them. They met up for two or three days at a time between internationals at Lilleshall where they took part in practice matches, explored tactics and watched films of games. Perhaps most importantly it was a chance for the players to get to know each other and build a relationship, with each other and with their manager. 'We were always classed as Walter's boys,' said Jimmy Armfield. 'Johnny Haynes, Ronnie Clayton, myself, Ray Wilson, Jimmy Greaves, Bobby Smith, Bobby Robson, Ron Springett, Brian Douglas; we were

Walter's boys as opposed to Carter, Mannion, Lawton and Matthews. They were players that he inherited.'

The changes quickly bore fruit and excited the press and the public. Spain were the next visitors to Wembley three weeks after the Northern Ireland win. The success of Real Madrid and Barcelona, and players like Di Stéfano, Santamaria, Suarez and Gento were known even to the parochial English fans, particularly since Walter's side had been beaten 3-0 by Spain in Madrid only the season before. The crowd sensed that England were on trial again and there was a ripple of expectation and excitement in the stadium which had not been felt since the 'Mighty Magyars' came in 1953. The game was a real test for England: Armfield was magnificent, and Haynes, in his first game as captain, linked smoothly with Robson in midfield, testing the once impregnable Spanish defense with intelligent thrusting football that gave them a well deserved 4-2 victory. To top it off, towards the end of the game Robson delighted the crowd by nut-megging a Spanish player at the beginning of a long passing sequence in which the Spaniards were unable to get a touch of the ball.

For once the usually reserved crowd was overjoyed, with many believing that England had turned the corner. Ignoring the rain, spectators threw hats, programmes and newspapers into the air and sang in delight.

And it wasn't just the crowd that relished the win; writers and journalists alike agreed that this was a platform upon which Walter could build a successful team. In his book, *World Cup 1962*, Donald Saunders concluded that this had been a vastly improved performance by England. 'The defense had held their own against some of the best ball players in the game; the forwards had won a stern midfield battle and grabbed four goals.' What's more, the game boosted the team's confidence and was a vindication of Walter's strategies. The press in the rest of Europe conceded that England now had a nucleus of world class players, much improved tactics and a coach of the highest order. Walter's name was being mentioned in Europe with such world renowned tacticians as Herrera (Italy), Herberger (Germany), and Feola (Brazil).

Wales were beaten 5-1 in November before the five month winter break from international football, but now Walter was getting his group together for several winter get-togethers at Lilleshall. In April, Scotland came to Wembley and suffered their heaviest ever defeat to England, losing 9-3. 'I am sure the memory [of that game] will remain with me even when I am old and grey and full of sleep and nodding by the fire,' recalled a nostalgic Jimmy Greaves some years later. It was the striker's first experience of a game between the 'auld enemies', and when the teams emerged from the Wembley tunnel he thought he was in Glasgow – over half the 100,000 crowd were Scots and the noise was deafening. The Scots were confident of success but England were on a great run of results; Greaves thought England would win but that it would be tight.

At half time England were winning 3-0 with goals from Bobby Robson and two from Greaves who was on the end of two perfect passes from Johnny Haynes. The players were cock-a-hoop in the dressing room but Walter was more cautious. 'Walter Winterbottom didn't say a great deal' said Greaves, 'like the supporters I think he was stunned. He just told us to keep playing football and make certain we kept it tight during the opening ten minutes of the second half because he was certain the Scots would come out all guns blazing and give it a go.'

And they did. They came at England with a vengeance. Within three minutes of the restart Dave Mackay pulled one back and then minutes later Wilson made it 3-2. Dennis Law hit the crossbar but then the game changed again. Greaves took a controversial free kick, passing to Bryan Douglas who made it 4-2. The Scots lost their composure and Johnny Haynes and Bobby Robson began to dominate the midfield. Goals followed from Bobby Smith (2), Johnny Haynes (2) and Jimmy Greaves completed his hat trick. The

London Evening News estimated that Haynes made a total of 51 passes, varying in length for six to 40 yards, and only five failed to find a colleague. It was probably the best game that he ever played for England and the players carried their captain shoulder high from the pitch.

It wasn't a poor Scotland team with players like Dennis Law, Dave Mackay, Ian St John, Billy McNeill, Eric Caldow, Pat Quinn and Davie Wilson but England were simply unstoppable. The Scots weren't helped by the fact that their goal keeper, Frank Haffey, was a late replacement and had a poor game. The Scottish fans were merciless in their ridicule of the poor fellow. With the cutting wit that football crowds seem to spontaneously create they came up with the chant 'What's the time: nearly ten past Haffey'!

The 9-3 triumph was one of six games that Walter picked out as his outstanding victories that were seldom mentioned by the media. The others were: 10-0 against Portugal in Lisbon (1947), 4-0 against Italy in Turin (1948), 7-2 against Scotland at Wembley (1955), 3-1 against West Germany in Berlin (1956), only two years after they had won the World Cup, and 3-1 against Italy in Rome (1961).

Three weeks later Mexico were brushed aside with an 8-0 win, despite the fact that Greaves was unable to play and the injured Smith was replaced by Gerry Hitchens. Bobby Smith, a strong, aggressive and bustling centre forward, and a key player in England's great run in 1961, never really recovered from an ankle injury which kept him out of the Spurs and England team for much of the 1961/62 season. Greaves, who had a fine partnership with Smith, recalled: 'For a man of his size his play possessed a lot of finesse and he was particularly delicate about laying the ball off. We dovetailed beautifully, though I never felt that Bobby has ever been given due credit for his part in my goal haul.'

Terry Venables remembers meeting Smith's replacement, Gerry Hitchens, and the rest of the England team when he was an England schoolboys player: 'It was amazing. Walter invited me and Alan

Harris to spend the day with the England team at the Hendon Hall Hotel before the Mexico game. I was very in awe of [Walter] because we were just young boys. He was very kind and was genuinely interested in me and Alan. We had a fantastic day watching training and then having dinner with the team and meeting players like Gerry Hitchens, Johnny Haynes and Bobby Charlton. Asked why he thought he was invited he replied, "I think Walter wanted us to know that we had been noticed and to encourage us."'

In May 1961 a squad of 19 players left London for the summer tour with matches in Portugal, Italy and Austria. The game against Portugal was the second of four World Cup qualifiers (the first had resulted in a 9-0 win in Luxembourg). Donald Saunders considered the Portugal game to be England's severest test which could decide whether or not England would go to the World Cup in Chile in the following year. Portugal were fortunate in that nine members of their team came from the successful Benfica team that had reached the final of the European Cup, giving their national team the huge advantage of always playing together. Greaves and Smith came back into the team and there was an air of expectation in the England camp. One concern was the blinding heat in Estoril on the outskirts of Lisbon. The match was due to start at 4pm when the temperature would be over 80°F, and Walter wanted to be better prepared for the kind of heat which sent England to defeat against Yugoslavia in Belgrade in 1958. Donald Saunders noted that 'Winterbottom, who, despite his scholarly manner, can be a hard task master, was obviously determined that there should be no repetition of that fiasco. He decided that his men should become acquainted with football beneath the blazing sun as soon as possible. Accordingly they went flat out for 40 minutes that afternoon at the National Stadium against Burnley FC, who were on tour in Portugal.' Despite the gruelling conditions England fought hard against Portugal to achieve a creditable 1-1 draw and a valuable World Cup qualifying point. At the final whistle an exhausted Haynes sank to the turf and threw first one boot and then the other across the pitch in a gesture of glorious relief.

Friendly matches in Italy and Austria followed within days, but Walter felt that it was important for the team to get used to playing three hard internationals in a week – it was the tough schedule they could expect in the World Cup.

England won 3-2 in Italy. It was a game that Walter remembered because of a story he liked to tell about the Italian player, Omar Sívori. Born in Argentina, the young forward had been transferred from the River Plate club in Buenos Aires to Juventus for a world record transfer fee of 10 million pesos (the equivalent of £91,000). He was of medium height but lightly built, a fast mover and very conceited about his skill. Latichev, the Russian referee, and a stickler for proper behaviour, blew his whistle to get the teams to assemble for the kick-off. But the Italian players swarmed around him to indicate that they were a player short. Then lo and behold Sívori made a special appearance, bowing as the crowd repeatedly chanted his name. Latichev ordered Sívori to pull up his socks, which he did, only to roll them down again as soon as the game started, much to the crowd's amusement. England were lucky to score the first goal and held on to the lead until half time.

It was well known that teams in South America would tease the opposition when they were in control by passing to each other in a way that retained possession. But Walter knew that Sívori had his personal showing off act known as the 'Sívori dance. 'He would signal to the crowd that he was about to do this whenever he scored a goal by raising his arm in salute to the spectators, then receive the ball from the kick off and dribble along the half way line to the touch line, defying opponents to dispossess him before he reached the huge terrace packed with fanatical supporters. The crowd loved it. Walter warned his players about this demoralising experience and asked them to stop Sivori at all costs.

Walter picked up the story: 'The Italians equalised late in the second half and soon afterwards Sívori went on a solo run to score a remarkable goal to put them 2-1 up. The stadium erupted with the chant of 'Sívori!' from his adoring fans. My heart sank, for I realised the little beggar would try to do his dance. Sure enough he stood in the centre circle, the ball was passed to him and he raised his arm as the signal for the start of his trick. Three English players rushed to tackle him, but collided with each other. He had almost reached the touchline and who should appear but little Jimmy Greaves who ran behind him, poked his foot behind Sivori's legs and managed to kick the ball away. England regained possession from this tackle and went down the field for Gerry Hitchens to equalise.'

With just four minutes left to play England snatched victory with Jimmy Greaves pouncing on a pass from Haynes and racing into the penalty box to drive home a hard low shot. A jubilant Johnny Haynes rolled down his stockings and proceeded around the back of the goal and along the touch line doing a hopping dance in imitation of Sívori. 'The crowd was furious, but it was a sight that warmed my heart,' said Walter, 'one that I would never forget.'

In the final end of season tour game three days later England failed to unlock an Austrian defence and lost 3-1. Although it was a disappointing end to the season there was much to cheer and real cause for optimism with the World Cup just one year away. But Donald Saunders found that 'Winterbottom was far from contented as we walked home from the "end of tour" banquet that night' and thought that the manager was unduly depressed by the failure to sweep aside the Austrian blanket defence. Events in the autumn – the beginning of the crucial 1961/62 season – revealed how right he was to be concerned. The team began to lose its marvellous momentum.

In the first place they lost Bobby Smith – who had such a good understanding with Jimmy Greaves – through injury. Then, soon after their return from Vienna, Jimmy Greaves was signed by AC Milan and Gerry Hitchens was transferred to Inter Milan. The repeated refusal of Italian clubs to release British players for internationals meant that Greaves and Hitchens would be not be able to play for England again before leaving for Chile. Walter had no choice but to search for replacements.

In the first warm up game of the 1961/62 season England played Tottenham, the League and Cup double winners, in the Charity Shield. Johnny Byrne (Crystal Palace) and Jimmy Robson (Burnley) were called-up in the absence of Hitchens and Greaves. Spurs won the game 3-1, proving what Walter already knew: that a very good club side that played together every week could beat a national team that met nine times a year. The match left Walter with the job of finding a solution to the problem of the forward positions. In the World Cup qualifier against Luxembourg at Highbury in September two more forwards were tried; Pointer and Fantham. Haynes was injured and replaced by Dennis Viollet. England were a shadow of the team that had won 9-0 against Luxembourg in the previous season and although they eventually won 4-1 they were jeered by an impatient crowd who had expected a goal feast. The players left the pitch to a storm of boos following them into the depths of the tunnel. Walter did not sleep well that night. In five weeks time he faced a sterner test: the final World Cup qualifier against Portugal. To his relief Luxembourg had incredibly beaten Portugal 4-2, but England still had to at least draw in order to qualify.

The Football League was cooperative in allowing Walter to pick and manage their representative team against other leagues and this gave Walter valuable practice games. The Football League comfortably beat the League of Ireland 5-2 in Bristol, boosting confidence, but in Cardiff Wales held England to a 1-1 draw. More changes to the forwards, moving Douglas to inside right, bringing in Connelly at outside right and with Pointer at centre forward, revealed only how much the sharp finishing of Greaves, Smith and Hitchens was missed.

The hurdle of the World Cup qualifier with Portugal was crossed with a 2-0 win, but despite goals from the Burnley pair, Pointer and

Connelly, England were far from convincing. The 4-2-4 system was still working well but it was no longer producing goals. Some thought that it had forced Haynes to play too defensively but Donald Saunders had no doubt that the problem lay with the failure of the other four forwards to see a gap and move swiftly through it.

In November, England, masquerading as the Football League, took on the Italian League at Old Trafford. Bobby Robson and Bryan Douglas were rested and Fantham and Kay were given another chance. Once again the England forwards were unable to unlock the thickest of blanket defences and lost 2-1 to goals from counter attacks, ironically the first coming from Gerry Hitchens who was representing the Italian League and was one of their leading scorers. It was deeply frustrating for Walter but he had no option but to carry on without Hitchens and Greaves. The next day he watched Johnny Bryne play in the Under-23s team that beat Israel. Against Northern Ireland 13 days later Byrne was restored at inside right to partner Douglas on the right wing. Another new player was tried at centre forward, this time Ray Crawford who had played a big part in Ipswich's successful team in the First Division. It was not a success and England stuttered to a 1-1 draw. Danny Blanchflower was able to declare it 'a moral victory for Ireland.'

There seemed to be no solution to the absence of Greaves, Smith and Hitchens but then, at the beginning of December, Walter had an early Christmas present: Tottenham brought Greaves back to England for a record transfer fee of £99,999 and in his first game for Spurs on 16 December he scored a hat trick against Blackpool. Then early in the New Year an injury to Les Allen allowed Bobby Smith, who had been in the Tottenham reserves since his injury, to get back in the Spurs team to play alongside Greaves. England's hopes were lifted.

There was a four month gap after the Ireland match until April, when England played three games in a four week period before leaving for Chile. This time England mastered the Austrian blanket defence to win 3-1, despite the absence of the Greaves and Smith partnership as they were needed for a European Cup semi final against Benfica the following night. The pair returned for the game against Scotland at Hampden Park but having beaten Scotland 9-3 a year before, England were surprisingly beaten 2-0. To make matters worse Bobby Smith, who had returned in this game, was injured again, putting him out of the World Cup squad. Three weeks later Switzerland came to Wembley and although England won 3-1 the press was critical, reporting that Hitchens was a disappointment, and that Greaves, Charlton and Connelly were indecisive. Walter sharply rebuked his press critics, reminding them that Switzerland also qualified for the World Cup in Chile. Of more concern to him was that both Bobby Robson and Peter Swan were injured. Would he once again, he wondered, be thwarted by unwanted team changes on the eve of a World Cup?

CHAPTER 15

REJECTION

1962

If you can make a heap of all your winnings
And risk it on one turn of pitch and toss
And lose, and start again at your beginnings
And never breathe a word about your loss

Rudyard Kipling

Walter Winterbottom walked out of the Football Association offices on Monday, 19 February, 1962, his shoulders heavy with the greatest disappointment of his life. He walked down the steps, past the brightly polished brass plate announcing that this was 22 Lancaster Gate, and past the press entourage. He answered their barrage of questions politely but bluntly with the words 'no comment'. In the growing darkness of the cold winter evening he pulled his overcoat around his neck and stepped out briskly into Bayswater Road to walk the short distance to Lancaster Gate tube station before disappearing into the anonymity of the London Underground. The crowded one hour journey on the Bakerloo line to Stanmore gave him time to collect his thoughts.

The FA Council had met to choose a successor to their secretary, Sir Stanley Rous. Walter had been groomed for the position by Rous and was widely expected to take football's top job. Instead by 50 votes to 20, they had voted for Denis Follows, the Honorary Treasurer at the Football Association. How could it have happened? What had gone on behind the scenes? What was he going to do now?

Despite the resounding support of the national press that morning, which urged FA councillors to look no further than Walter Winterbottom, there had been tell-tale signs that all was not well. The job had been advertised in the national press, a sign that they were looking for change, and perhaps most significantly Sir Stanley Rous had not been invited to give his views to the appointments committee or the chairman.

And yet Walter's credentials were immaculate: he had played professional football for Manchester United; graduated in physical education from Carnegie College and become a lecturer there; during the war he was responsible for physical education in the Royal Air Force. What's more, in his 16 years with the FA he had developed the national coaching scheme and become recognised as the world's leading technical thinker and exponent of coaching association football. He had proved his ability as a sound administrator and Sir Stanley Rous had groomed him as his successor.

Perhaps the Council's decision was best summed up by Donald Saunders of the *Daily Telegraph*: 'Although [Dennis] Follows has done much backroom work as honorary treasurer since 1956, and as the University Athletic Union's representative on the Council since 1948, his contribution to the game can scarcely be compared with that of Mr. Winterbottom… Mr. Follows' appointment must, I think, be interpreted as a victory for the amateur side of the game.'

With a heavy heart Walter made the 20-minute walk from Stanmore Station, down the hill and into the village, past Cullens', the grocers emporium, the record shop, the post office and the off-licence, and turned left into the Uxbridge Road, past the large but fading Victorian homes and the Elms tennis club and onto Holland Walk. He hadn't noticed these familiar landmarks on his journey, his mind focused on the events of the day. The inescapable conclusion was, he considered as he approached his house, that he had no alternative but to look elsewhere for his future.

When he turned the key to open the front door his wife, Ann, was there to put her arms around him. She didn't need him to tell her the news – it had repeatedly been announced in news bulletins on the radio. They kissed and she whispered 'there are people here to see you.' Waiting for him in the lounge was his friend Jimmy Hill and Roy Peskett from the *Daily Mail*. They were emotional and angry.

'We're going to blow this thing wide open.' Jimmy Hill said.

'You'll do no such thing' replied Walter. He had behaved like a gentleman throughout the election campaign and he was not going to behave any differently now.

When Jimmy and Roy had departed, Ann and Walter cried and hugged each other for a long time. 'What are you going to do now?' she asked.

'I don't know,' he replied. 'I can always go back to teaching you know.'

The death of Arthur Drewry in early 1961 (who by then was President of FIFA) set off a chain of events in world football that were to have a profound effect on Walter's career. Sir Stanley Rous was just past normal retirement age but had no reason to think that he would not continue in his position as Secretary of the FA. He certainly had no expectation of being nominated for the Presidency of FIFA, but he was.

Rous found himself in something of a dilemma. The FIFA Presidency was unpaid and since paid officials were not eligible for election to the Presidency he would have to give up his salary of £3000 a year and the flat at Lancaster Gate that went with the job. It was not an easy decision. The risk was that he would resign from his job at the FA but might then not be elected by FIFA. Graham Doggart, the new Chairman of the FA, encouraged him to accept the nomination and Rous formed the distinct impression that Doggart already had someone else in mind for his job.

Rous wondered about the possibility of continuing as FA Secretary in an honorary unpaid role, but Doggart scotched that idea, saying that he thought there could be a conflict of interests. Finally Rous allowed his name to go forward, and he was duly elected as President of FIFA on 28 September 1961.

In the run up to the ratification of his appointment at FIFA Congress in June 1962 Rous felt that there was pressure for him to leave the FA. The words 'urgency' and 'emergency' were being bandied about regarding appointing a successor and the chairman asked the FA Council to approve a motion that Rous would remain 'until the date, not later than 1 June 1962. Rous himself wanted to stay on until 1963 in some capacity to complete planning he had been doing with Walter for the 1963 FA centenary celebrations and the 1966 World Cup. Doggart did not agree to this but assured Sir Stanley that the Association would be glad, after his ceasing to hold secretarial office, to use his services in an advisory capacity in connection with the centenary celebrations in 1963. Rous was never consulted.

It had become clear to Rous that Doggart wanted him to leave and already knew who he wanted as his successor. In a letter to Lt. Col. Linnitt, a friend and influential council member, he wrote: 'the Council will have to watch most carefully the type of man they appoint to succeed me. The double first and triple blue may be all right for the rugby world but not for soccer. If people like you and I have met with any success in our football relations it is because we are able to appreciate the feelings of the man on the terrace as well as the "Gent" in the Royal Box.'

The letter would appear to express Rous' concern that his protégé, Walter Winterbottom, non-university educated, a professional and a man in touch with the grass roots of football, might not get the job and that that Graham Doggart, educated at Cambridge, and a pillar of the amateur football establishment, might be looking for a Secretary more in his own mould.

A Council meeting on 2 October 1961 recorded the resignation of Sir Stanley Rous following his election as President of FIFA on 28 September and the chairman, Graham Doggart proposed that the officers be authorised to take steps to appoint a successor.

This motion was opposed by Dr Harold Thompson, the member for Oxford University. Thompson proposed instead that an appointments committee be formed consisting of three officers and four members. This was approved and the committee members were: Mr A.G. Doggart (Chairman), Major J Stewart (Vice Chairman), Mr J Richards (President of the Football League), Mr J.W. Bowers, Mr N Hillier, Mr J.H.W. Mears and Dr. H.W. Thompson. Harold Thompson had now put himself in a position where he could influence the outcome, and that is exactly what he did.

The Appointments Committee met on the 17 October 1961 and an advertisement was placed in the *Times* on 23 and 24 October and in the *Daily Telegraph* on 24 and 25 October. The wording of the advertisement was elementary, making no reference to the experience or qualities needed for the job. Without the encumbrance of any formal frame of reference the Appointments Committee was free to make any recommendation they chose:

THE FOOTBALL ASSOCIATION

Applications are invited for the post of Secretary of the Football Association. The successful applicant would be required to take up his duties not later than 1 June, 1962. A substantial salary will be paid according to experience. Applications, to be submitted by 10 November 1961, should state age, whether married or single, present occupation, qualifications and experience, and should be sent, accompanied by the names of two persons to whom reference can be made if necessary, to the Chairman of the Football Association c/o Brinkworth & Co, Chartered accountants, 12 Clarges Street, London, W1. All applications will be treated in the strictest confidence.

Within the world of football and the media Walter was considered to be the ideal successor to Sir Stanley, and Rous himself had long thought Walter would be the ideal person to follow him: 'He had an international reputation, was acceptable at all levels of the game, was brilliant administratively, and was a forward thinker of sound, but original judgment.'

The tone of the letter Walter wrote in response to the advertisement indicated that he was somewhat irked to have to apply for the position in this formal manner:

'As members of the Council know me and are aware of my abilities and past career,' he wrote, 'I feel that I should confine my letter to a brief statement of the information requested in the advertisement.' He gave a factual resume of his education and career before joining the FA and continued: 'You will know that I have a wife, Ann, and three children, Janet (17), Brenda (14) and Alan (12).' Percy Lord, Director of Education for Lancashire, and Sir Stanley Rous provided Walter's references, the latter of whom he said 'can best report to you on my work during the last 15 years and help you to assess my abilities for the responsible duties of Secretary to the Association.'

Sir Stanley Rous must have suspected that all was not going to be plain sailing for Walter. In a hand written personal note, undated, he chides him for his participation in Bob Ferrier's book, *Soccer Partnership: Billy Wright and Walter Winterbottom*

Walter,

I've read lots of this book and of course it interested me immensely but as I read, I must admit that I wished it wasn't you who were saying the things you do. For Billy and Ferrier it is quite proper but for a member of the staff – even in personal capacity – (and the personal and official cannot really be separated) to be praised by a player while he is still in the office seems to me to be unfortunate.

I can't express what I feel but I am sure that you will find a lot of people even FA members who will take 'sides'. You won't make enemies, but I can imagine the press asking people named in the book whether it is fact such and such a thing happened.

It's defensive in parts. You are too strong and in too strong a position to have to defend yourself or your actions. If this were Billy's book and you wrote the tribute to him that would be quite alright. He could make his to you incidental and not so direct. You could still share in any receipts from the sale of the book.

You see, Walter, I don't want you to do anything which will make members of the FA – the Thompsons and Follows anti-you at this stage particularly.

If you could praise members of the FA for their leadership you'd be liked for it, but you can't.

This is all in haste – and sketchy and all my fears may be unfounded. I sincerely hope so?

Sir Stanley's cryptic letter is interesting for many reasons. It is a pity it is undated because the book was published at some time in 1960 and yet Arthur Drewry died on 25 March 1961, creating the beginning of the rumours and political manoeuvring around Sir Stanley's departure and the appointment of a new FA Secretary. Did Stanley not see the book until mid 1961? Was there plotting before then to resist Walter as Sir Stanley's eventual successor? It is significant that even then he identified Thompson and Follows as Walter's potential enemies in the fight for the Secretary's job. It is also interesting that Sir Stanley takes such strong exception to the book. It is hard to find the praise from Billy Wright that is mentioned. There is an appreciation of Billy Wright by Walter, but not the reverse. There is nothing that appears to be critical of the FA; indeed, the book even goes out of its way to point out the merits of the committee selection system. Nevertheless it is an unusual book which reads as if Ferrier, a respected football journalist, had simply provided an anonymous vehicle for Walter to express his views. The book is, as Ferrier said in his preface 'neither a biography nor chronicle. It is rather an authoritative survey of things seen and done, lessons learned and conclusions drawn.'

It would have been completely out of character for Walter to publicly say anything critical of the FA or any individual in it. But Rous was an astute politician, and he must have known that there were those who did not wish to see Walter succeed him, and that this book could, unwittingly, provide them with ammunition.

The press advertisements attracted 72 applications and on Monday 19 February 1962 the full FA Council met in the Devon Room at the Great Western Hotel, Paddington. It appeared that only three candidates had been put forward by the appointments committee, and that the advertisement had in fact been a red herring. It was surprising and yet revealing that Sir Stanley Rous, with his wealth of experience of what the job required, was not asked for his views on any of the candidates by the appointments committee before the Council met, and was excluded from the discussion at the meeting. Writing about the election of Sir Stanley's successor in his book, *The Official History of The Football Association* , Bryon Butler said: 'There was a body of opinion within the FA, however, which believed no Secretary should ever again be allowed to get himself into such a position of power and authority.' It is reasonable to suggest that this was part of the debate that went on between closed doors, and that Thompson and his camp would have portrayed Winterbottom as Rous' man – another strong individual who would take on himself more power than was right.

The Chairman asked Follows and Rous to withdraw from the meeting and after a discussion it was agreed that there should be a secret ballot to decide whether Follows or Winterbottom should be the new Secretary. The voting was 50-20 in favour of Follows and

ove: Walter with Bill Nicholson, the Tottenham first team coach, who was his assistant ∩nager for the 1958 World Cup in Sweden.

ow: Two heavyweights! Walter with boxing legend Henry Cooper at the World ∩rting Club in 1960.

Above: Discussing tactics at half time in an England trial match against Fulham in August 1961.

Below left: Getting stuck in on the training ground in 1962.

© *Getty Ima*

Below right: Walter leaves 22 Lancaster Square after the biggest disappointment of his life – not being elected as Secretary of the FA – in 1962.

Above: Walter with Johnny Haynes, England captain, before playing Scotland in 1962.

Below: Walter with Jimmy Hill at an England training session in 1962. © *Getty Images*

Above: Jimmy Armfield presents a set of crystal glasses from the players after Walter's final England game, against Wales on November 21st 1962.

Below left: Walter walking across the Wembley turf with trainer Harold Shepherdson as he makes his last appearance as England manager.

Below right: Walter arriving at the Central Council of Physical Recreation in January 1963, as he prepared to take over the post of General Secretary to the Council.

ove: An accomplished after dinner speaker, Walter was a frequent guest of honour who
*ormed and entertained. The Duchess of Bedford is on his right and Ann is on his left.

low: Walter, Director of the newly formed Sports Council, and Denis Howell, Minister
Sport, inspect the Council's first annual report.

Above: Walter with Prime Minister Edward Heath for the sailing events in Kiel during the 1972 Olympics.

Below: One of the many sports centres opened by Walter around the country.

alter, with Ann, at Buckingham Palace, receiving his knighthood for services to sport 1978.

Above: Two great sporting knights reunited: Walter presenting the 1987 PFA Merit Award to Sir Stanley Matthews.

Below left: Walter and Ann celebrating their golden wedding anniversary in 1994.

Below right: A great grandfather: contented, but still pondering the future. 1997.

the Chairman formally declared the appointment to take effect in May 1962.

It was a decision which shocked the entire football world. Managers, coaches and players were at one with the media in seeing the result as a setback for English football. 'The worst decision the Council has made in the history of the Football Association was to choose Denis Follows ahead of Walter Winterbottom to be the Secretary of the Association,' declared Jimmy Hill, 'I cried for the future of English football.'

Why was Winterbottom, so ideally qualified and experienced, and clearly the favourite in the eyes of all but the inner circle at the FA, so resoundingly defeated?

Ironically it was his close association with his mentor, Sir Stanley Rous that was at the root of the problem. Rous was known as a man who was used to getting his own way and councillors came to feel that they were excluded from decision making – that the power was with the Secretary.

There was no doubting Stanley Rous' skill in meetings. Walter admired the way he went about getting decisions he wanted through sharp thinking and political astuteness. It was something that Alan Hardaker, a shrewd and tough negotiator himself, had observed: 'If Stanley had been a politician he would very probably have become Prime Minister.' Too often some Council members had felt by-passed and they wanted a Secretary who they could control. One of these councillors was Harold Thompson, an ambitious man who was used to having his own way: a man who Brian Glanville described as 'the Machiavellian professor who undermined and outflanked Rous.'

Harold Warris Thompson had a distinguished academic career. He gained a first in chemistry at Oxford and a PhD at Humboldt University in Hamburg before returning to take up a fellowship at St John's College, Oxford. He was a brilliant scientist who became an expert in the field of infra-red spectroscopy and during the war worked for the government, helping to identify the origin of enemy aviation fuels. In 1946 he was elected a member of the Royal Society, became a Council Member in 1959 and their Foreign Secretary in 1965.

He was dedicated to the British amateur sporting traditions and was part of association football's amateur elite. He gained a soccer blue at Oxford and was the Treasurer of Oxford University Football Club for 22 years and the Oxford University representative on the FA Council from 1941. He was instrumental in the formation of the Pegasus Club in 1948, which combined the teams of Oxford and Cambridge universities and enjoyed considerable success, winning the FA Amateur Cup in 1951 and 1953. He was the club's honorary secretary until 1954, when he became chairman and even the de facto manger, running everything. His time there was not without controversy, however. Tony Pawson, a fine amateur player and football writer, recalls that he seemed to enjoy drawing attention to the failings and weakness of the team: 'We all believed he took a piece of paper to every match with a forecast of defeat. If we won it stayed in his pocket. If we lost he would flourish it around saying "I knew you would lose this one."'

His autocratic manner was often the cause of friction and led to Pegasus being disbanded in 1963. According to Dilwyn Porter, a football historian, Thompson's impact in the latter years of Pegasus was entirely negative. His compulsive interference led to the resignation of a number of the club's officials, including John Tanner (later the Chairman of the FA Instructional Committee), who on one occasion hit Thompson in sheer exasperation.

It was not surprising that such an arrogant and ambitious man should have constant clashes with Sir Stanley Rous and seek revenge for what Brian Glanville describes as 'the years in which Rous, time and again swatted him like a fly' (the tables were turned in 1976 when Thompson realised his ambition of becoming the Chairman of the FA and regularly sent lengthy memos to the then Secretary, Denis Follows, with a series of instructions that he expected to be carried out).

There were also personal reasons for the acrimonious relations between Thompson and Rous. Thompson was a man who would force his attentions on women at any opportunity – a man who Brian Glanville describes as 'notorious for lubricious attention to women' – and these indiscretions brought Rous, a man with strict moral values, into conflict with Thompson. For all of these reasons Thompson hated Rous, and when the chance came to exact retribution, he took it by ensuring the defeat of Walter Winterbottom, Sir Stanley Rous's protégé and favoured candidate, installing instead a man with less influence who he believed would be more compliant: Denis Follows.

How did Thompson achieve this in what was after all a democratic system requiring a majority vote from 80 Council members? We know that he was the prime mover in proposing an appointments committee and placing himself on it. He had a sharp intellect and was skilled in the manipulation of committees through his work at Oxford University, with government and the Royal Society. Having been a member of the FA council for 20 years and served on its committees, including the instructional committee, he was well versed in the ways of the FA. He would have known how, when and who to lobby. His strongest card to play was that Winterbottom was Rous's protégé and could become a powerful Secretary who would follow in Rous' footsteps.

But then, on the weekend before the Monday election, Thompson had a stroke of luck and was quick to take full advantage of it. The national press, so often a critic of Walter as the England team manager, universally came out backing him for the FA Secretary's job. The *Sunday Pictorial* on 18 February had the headline 'LEAD WALTER TO THE ALTER' and concluded with the words: 'So I say again to the FA Council, lead Walter right to the altar and offer him the Secretary's chair when you meet in the comfy calm of your London hotel.' But there was also a caveat: 'Perhaps the big unwieldy Council,' continued the piece, 'has had its nose put out just slightly in the past by the worldly success and power of Sir Stanley Rous. Two strong men in a row would inevitably offend the Council for it is a very mixed bunch.' It went on to criticise the age and background of Council members and their lack of football knowledge.

JL Manning, the crusading sports columnist of the *Daily Mail* headlined his piece in the Monday morning paper 'FA FACE HOBSON'S CHOICE' and made a strong and well argued case for appointing Winterbottom:

Stories of plotting in committee and arm twisting in the lobby to prevent Mr. Walter Winterbottom from becoming Secretary of the Football Association are exaggerated... The importance of the decision has been represented as only a little less than choosing the prime minister's successor... But Doggart's procedure will be judged by what sort of man it produces not by what kind of men it convinces. English football needs something more than an Oxbridge type or a redbrick tip-off. It needs a man whose practical experience and worldwide reputation promise to mature into the kind of philosopher and father figure that Sir Stanley has made so acceptable and necessary. The training he has given Winterbottom cannot be ignored.

The tipping point, according to Brian Glanville in his book *England Managers – The Toughest Job in Football* was an article in the *Observer* on the day before the election. In a piece carrying the headline 'WHY FA HESITATED TO NAME NEW BOSS', the *Observer* set out the background to the election. The well-reasoned article suggested that many councillors would be fighting their own instincts if they voted for Winterbottom because there had been a tradition of amateurism in the FA and Winterbottom was a professional; but it also maintained that Winterbottom was the best man for the job. Most significantly, it profiled the three candidates, describing Walter Winterbottom as Lancaster Gate's 'greatest signing,' George Clarke as 'modest with a sense of humour' and Denis Follows as 'cool, pedantic, plain, prim.'

'Thompson's strategy for frustrating Winterbottom was simple but deviously effective,' writes Brian Glanville. 'On the morning of the vote by the sere and yellow ranks of FA Councillors, he approached them one by one with a copy of the *Observer* newspaper... and asked them if they were prepared to be corralled into voting by a mere newspaper article?'

'Absurdly, his campaign succeeded. The old gentlemen seemingly bridled, and decided against all logic and good sense to do Winterbottom down, voting instead for the FA treasurer, Denis Follows, whose chief appointment had been with the British Airline Pilots Association.'

Glanville's version of events was corroborated by *The Observer* on the following Sunday. In the *Daily Mail*, J.L. Manning reported that a member of the Council had told him that the large majority against Winterbottom was due to the wholehearted support of his qualifications by *The Observer* and the *Daily Mail*. Fleet Street sports writers were astonished that Winterbottom 'may have lost through spite against the press.'

It is generally accepted that Thompson was the architect of Walter's failure to be elected and yet there had to be more to the affair than that. The Chairman of the FA is a powerful position and it seems inconceivable that anyone could be appointed as Secretary of the FA without the full support of the chairman.

Graham Doggart had only been elected as chairman in 1961 but he had already become frustrated by the power that the FA Secretary had assumed. Rous himself was aware of the difficulty that existed in their relationship and wrote, 'In any organisation like the FA or FIFA, there is always a difficult relationship between a working chairman or president and a full-time paid secretary. The Chairman's is the senior appointment, but the day to day matters go through the secretary and inevitably he is the man with the most contacts and the ability to get things done. In my case this tendency was intensified by the length of time I had been in the job, which meant that so many people came to me for advice. I appreciated that this would be difficult for Graham Doggart, who was newly appointed, while I had been so long in the job.'

Rous was in no doubt that Doggart was eager to see him leave and install a man who would be more compliant. As early as the time that Rous was first considering the nomination for the Presidency of FIFA he wrote, 'Graham Doggart had detailed discussions with me, encouraging me to accept ... and it was apparent that he had someone in mind as a replacement for me.' It was clear to him that the person Doggart had in mind would not be his own choice, Walter Winterbottom.

Graham Doggart was a wealthy and influential man. He kept a permanent suite at the Dorchester Hotel for his London visits. Only the year before he had been elected as Chairman of the FA by the 80 Council members. He had their backing. He was a Cambridge man, a cricket blue and a member of the full committee of the MCC; he had also played soccer as an amateur for Cambridge University, the Corinthians and England. He was a leading figure in an FA Oxbridge axis which included the likes of Professor Harold Thompson, an Oxford soccer blue and the founder of Pegasus.

Although Denis Follows was not an Oxbridge man himself – he was educated at the universities of London and Nottingham – he too represented the amateur sporting establishment. He was elected as an FA councillor in his position as the Chairman of the Universities Athletic Union. As the Hon. FA Treasurer he would have had close personal contact with Doggart.

But backing Denis Follows in preference to Walter was bound to be a controversial matter and one that would attract media scrutiny. The tide has closed over the sands of history leaving no evidence of Doggart's involvement but it is possible that in Thompson he found a willing ally, a man with a grudge against Rous, a combative man who would fire the bullets for him and take the can for it if it went wrong.

The press campaign caused much bitterness within the FA and Walter was accused by the Thompson/Follows camp of having been behind it. That was of course untrue and was immediately rebutted by Graham Doggart in a personal hand written letter to Walter the next day:

20 February 1962
My Dear Walter,
I felt I must write to you at once to say how distressed I was, that anyone should for a moment entertain the thought that you might have inspired certain comment recently in the newspapers. I know that such a thing for you to do would be utterly impossible, and completely alien to your nature.

I can think of no one in football who commands universal esteem and respect more than you do, not only for your contribution to the game, but for your high ideals and character.

I do hope you won't be too disappointed at yesterday's Council decision. The sad thing to me was that either you or Denis had to lose in the ballot! So far as I am concerned, although I feel I hardly need to tell you – my regard for you personally, as well as for your outstanding ability has never been higher than it is today – just spoken to you on the phone! – I am confident that your influence and standing with the FA, and throughout the whole world, will go on increasing.
Yours ever,
Graham

The letter is ambiguous with regard to Doggart's own position. He liked and respected Walter and would certainly have wanted him to remain as Director of Coaching. It could be interpreted that he washed his hands of the affair and remained on the sidelines or the letter could have assuaged a feeling of guilt.

If Doggart's 'Brutus' was led by Thompson's 'Cassius', there is no doubt that Thompson – a ruthless and ambitious man who became Vice Chairman of the FA in 1967 and Chairman from 1976-1981 – had the political skill to orchestrate the downfall of Walter's aspiration to be the FA Secretary.

Walter took his defeat on the chin. He did not discuss it with anyone, at the time or later. It was another of his setbacks in life that had to be overcome. When Graham Doggart unexpectedly died in the following year he wrote a letter of commiseration to his widow. She replied, 'I was most touched by your kind and understanding letter,' and revealed the close personal relationship that she and her husband had with Walter. It showed his care for others and that he had put the whole matter behind him. There was no looking back.

From the time of the election of the new FA Secretary in February 1962 until he left the Football Association in December 1962, he worked harder than ever. He prepared a 40-page memorandum for Sir Stanley with detailed proposals for the management of 1966 World Cup in England. One FA councillor was moved to write a complimentary letter to Sir Stanley Rous: 'The index alone proves what a comprehensive, precise, and forward looking document this is, and in point of fact it would really enable the Football Association to go into action and stage the World Cup almost any time,' 'I was particularly impressed with the four pages "Statistics and Analysis" under Finance, which is a matter of such great importance. Everything seems to have been clearly set out including the committees required, schedule of dates, grounds and their requirements, travel and accommodation. The detail is remarkable even down to the six suggestions of the form souvenir gifts might take and the note about the possible clash of dates with the Wimbledon tennis.'

The election of the new FA Secretary had been just three months before the England team left for South America. Now Walter was concentrating on the England team's preparation for the World Cup

Finals in Chile. He had spent four years building a team capable of winning. When he went to Chile only he knew that whatever the outcome, he would resign from the FA on his return. After his disappointment at not being elected he was even more determined to achieve that most elusive of goals – to bring back the Jules Rimet trophy. The last two years had given him every reason to believe that he could.

CHAPTER 17

THE FINAL
CURTAIN

1962

O n Thursday 17 May, ten days after their 3-1 win against Switzerland at Wembley, the 22-man England squad left for South America. Like many of the players Jimmy Armfield believed they would do well: 'I set off believing we had a genuine chance of winning the World Cup... by 1962 Walter had put together a side that was, if anything, stronger [than the 1958 team before the Munich disaster].'

Walter himself was confident but realistic. Speaking to Clive Toye of the *Daily Express* he said, 'If we strike it happy – by that I mean hitting our best form at the right time – England can go all the way to the semi-finals. After that in the semi-final and final it's a question of who you are drawn against, injuries, and which team has the most tiring programme. But we are quite capable of reaching the final if we start well and are full of confidence.'

The 17 hour BOAC flight to Lima, Peru was tiring. 'It was a journey that never seemed to end,' recalled Armfield, 'a journey to the end of the earth, which it virtually was – there isn't much between Southern Chile and Antarctica.' The team played a warm up match against Peru in Lima. Beforehand the press were critical saying this match carried the risk of injury or a morale sapping defeat. Walter thought it was a valuable final test against South American opposition. England dominated the game and won 4-0 with a Jimmy Greaves hat-trick, giving them a morale boosting start to their campaign.

Moving on to Santiago, Chile the next day, the England squad had a 90 minute drive inland before reaching Rancagua, the small town where they would meet Hungary, Argentina and Bulgaria in their qualifying group games. Compared to the other three venues Rancagua was out in the sticks, isolated and 2,500 feet high in the Andes Mountains. It was something of a shock for the players. Jimmy Armfield described the Rancagua stadium as a 'decent Conference ground' by today's standards. The teams training camp was at Coya, the headquarters of the American mining firm, the Braden Copper Company – a one hour train ride on a single track railway from Rancagua. The company village, which was used as a rest and recreation centre for their executives, was put at the disposal of the England party. The team stayed in chalet bungalows with twin bedded rooms. The facilities included a nine hole golf course, bowling alley, cinema, swimming pool, tennis courts and of course a training pitch. The meals were served in a large dining room and the British style cooking was supervised by a grey haired kindly English woman, Bertha Lewis, who looked after her charges like a mother.

From the outset there was controversy about the location. It was secluded, private, peaceful and away from prying eyes; but some players found it isolated and lonely. It had fresh clean air but not the buzz of a big city. Jimmy Armfield thought the accommodation was 'pretty primitive, like student accommodation really... but the bottom line was we were there to represent England in the World Cup and for that privilege we were prepared to put up with a few hardships.' Bobby Charlton concurred that the 'facilities at the camp were not luxurious but were more than adequate.' One England player on the day of his arrival was reported to have said 'I feel so fed up I could cry.' Bobby Charlton did not hear that remark, but he did recall one player, who didn't play in the tournament, saying, 'don't score today lads, let's go home at the first opportunity.' Not entirely serious perhaps but it reflected a poor attitude amongst some players.

The press – who were critical of the choice of the luxury hotel England had used in the bustling centre of Gothenburg in 1958 – were on this occasion supportive. Brian Glanville commented that the setting appeared idyllic and that England had got the retreat that everybody wanted. Donald Saunders found it a pleasing contrast to the dust and noise of Santiago where some less fortunate teams were billeted: 'This time it was generally conceded that England had the best camp.'

For the first game against Hungary Walter kept the same team that had beaten Peru en route to Chile. With Bobby Robson injured and Peter Swann taken ill, Walter kept Bobby Moore in to replace Robson in midfield and Maurice Norman to replace Swan and partner Flowers in defence. Springett was in goal and Armfield and Wilson were the full backs. Moore and Haynes were in midfield and Douglas, Greaves, Hitchens and Charlton were the forwards. The team had trained hard for ten days, looked tremendously fit, and the wet chilly conditions suited them and yet inexplicably they played without inspiration and were beaten 2-1. Donald Saunders believed that the problem was that Haynes had been ineffective because Baroti, the Hungarian coach, had brought in the energetic Rakosis with the task of acting as a personal guard to Haynes which effectively prevented him from supplying the England forwards. The defence was strong with Armfield (soon to be voted the tournaments best right back) and Wilson outstanding. Springett made one costly mistake, misjudging a shot from 25 yards to give Hungary the lead. England drew level a quarter of an hour after the interval when the reliable Flowers converted a penalty. Jimmy Armfield remembered, 'It was wet and the surface was slippery. We were the better side for most of the match but with the score at 1-1 with a few minutes left, Ron [Flowers] slipped on the greasy surface to let in Florian Albert who scored the winner.' It was the worst possible start and the mood on the train back to the camp was sombre.

The next match against Argentina, who had beaten Bulgaria 1-0 in their first game, was crucial. 'I did not envy Winterbottom the job of persuading a beaten team that they were equal to the task' wrote Saunders; 'I do not know how he achieved it but I am happy to record that he was successful.' The only change to the team was at centre forward, where Walter preferred Peacock to Hitchens, perhaps on the grounds that he was taller and stronger and more likely to withstand the battering expected from Navarro, the Argentinian centre half. Donald Saunders was one of the press party that had strongly attacked the inclusion of Peacock in the squad, but confessed that the Middlesborough centre forward justified his presence and made him and his colleagues eat their words. In the 60th minute he soared above the Argentine defence to head a centre from Bobby Charlton under the bar. Almost everyone was convinced that the ball had crossed the line before Navarro pushed it out with his hand, but the Russian referee, Latychev, awarded a penalty. The dependable Flowers stepped up to score again. England looked a different team to the one beaten 48 hours earlier by Hungary, with Haynes once more a commanding presence in midfield. The whole team was on song with only Greaves looking unhappy and unable to escape his marker. Armfield's cross crashed the ball against the cross bar and Charlton made it number two with a first time right foot shot. Roma, the goal keeper, could only parry a hard shot from Douglas and Greaves was there to put it in the net. Argentina scored a late goal to make it 3-1 when England appeared to tire but it could not dampen the heady atmosphere in the England dressing room after the game.

In the final game England only had to draw with Bulgaria to qualify for the quarter finals. Some of the press thought that the selectors should rest key players before a likely semi-final place but Walter was unwilling to take the chance. The match ended goalless: Greaves missed a couple of sitters and then England played safe with a nine-man defence, disappointing the crowd with a distinctly un-entertaining game-plan. 'I had six cups of coffee during that match,' recalled Frank Wilson of the *Daily Mirror*, 'but that still didn't keep me awake.' Charlton thought it was the worst game he had ever played in – that it was not what football was about – and had a loud and angry dispute with his captain, Haynes, who was happy to be celebrating the draw that took to them through to the quarter finals.

Afterwards Saunders thought that resting five key players against Bulgaria would have left the team fresher for the quarter final against Brazil – but as Walter often remarked, the press can never be proved wrong as their team never has to take the field.

Chile's 2-0 win over Russia was probably the most dramatic event of the 1962 World Cup, releasing unprecedented national fervor, but England's quarter-final game against Brazil produced some of the best football seen, helping to redeem the tournament from the violence and negativity that had prevailed in many of the qualifying matches. 'It was a match that delighted all true soccer lovers,' declared Donald Saunders. 'Here was the fast, open, attacking game that the World Cup was meant to promote.'

There was just one change to the team, Hitchens replacing Peacock at number nine. Walter told the press that Peacock had been troubled by a slight muscle strain. Greaves thought that Winterbottom felt that Hitchen's experience of playing in Italy would be better suited against Brazil.

The England players went into the game confidently. 'We went down to the coastal resort of Vina del Mar in good enough heart,' recalled Bobby Charlton. 'The post Bulgaria recriminations had spent themselves without lasting problems and with Pelé gone [injured in the last match] we felt there was some reason for optimism.' But 'cometh the moment cometh the man' and the brilliance of Pelé was outshone by Garrincha. Brian Glanville eloquently captured the essence of the man the Brazilians called the 'little bird': 'To the panther swerve and acceleration, the deadly goal line cross, which one had seen in Sweden, Garrincha had now added a thumping shot in either foot and remarkable power in the air.'

An early goal for either side might ensure a semi final place and England nearly got it but Greaves rushed a cross from Charlton and volleyed over the bar. Shortly afterwards Hitchens and Douglas both missed good chances which, if they had gone in, might have made history. But it was Brazil that took the lead after 31 minutes: Garrincha, who was five foot seven inches tall, out-jumped the tall centre back Maurice Norman to head in a corner from Zagallo. It was no fluke by Garrincha or aberration by Norman – 'the little bird' did the same against Chile in the semi final.

Some thought England would crack but they fought back and were rewarded with an equaliser that rocked the Brazilians back on their heels. Haynes placed a free kick into the goalmouth, Greaves headed it against the post and Hitchens drove the rebound past the stranded Gylmar.

At half time the English reporters eagerly discussed the possibility of an English victory; even neutrals in the press box agreed that it was by no means out of the question. But Walter's hopes of leading his team to World Cup victory were dashed by two moments of genius from Garrincha. In the first he bent a 25 yard free kick though the wall with such power that Springett could only push it to Vava who nodded it home. The second was perhaps the most memorable goal of the tournament: his shot, again from 25 yards, seemed to be wide of the post but then it dipped and swung under the bar, leaving poor Springett helpless. Brazil went on to win the game 3-1.

It was a day when one world class player shone and another didn't. 'Jimmy Greaves gave another unhappy display,' commented

Glanville, 'especially in the second half when he seemed curiously shy of physical contact.' Walter was philosophical: he knew that such moments were beyond his control and that World Cups are won by teams with four or five world class players of whom at least one will produce a moment of genius on the day as Garrincha had for Brazil.

After the match Walter broke with FA rules and arranged for one or two players to talk to the press. Jimmy Armfield told them it was the most disappointing moment of his career (despite the fact he had been voted the best right back in the world). 'I firmly believe that if we had beaten Brazil we would have gone on to win the tournament,' he lamented to an eager journalist. His sentiments were borne out when Brazil brushed aside Chile (4-2) in the semi final and beat Czechoslovakia in the final (3-1). It was the end of Walter's fourth attempt to win the World Cup but this time there was no disgrace or recriminations.

But it was still a bitter pill for Walter and the players to swallow. The success of the outstanding 1960/61 season had, not unreasonably, built up expectations, only for them to be dashed in the ramshackle Rancagua stadium in a remote corner of Chile. Walter was left to reflect on the changes that upset the balance and confidence of his team.

Of the 11 regulars in the all conquering 1960/61 team only three had changed in Chile one year later, but they were key players: Bobby Robson who combined so well with Haynes in midfield, Peter Swan a rock in the centre of defence who had a telepathic understanding with Springett, and Bobby Smith who had such a productive partnership with Jimmy Greaves – one that Greaves was unable to replicate with Hitchens or Peacock. Fate had again played its hand against Walter as it had in 1958 when the Munich Air Disaster robbed him of three key players. The replacements who played in Chile, Maurice Norman, Bobby Moore and Alan Peacock did well, but they were coming into key positions in an established team and earning their first international caps in a World Cup. It was hardly ideal.

There can also be no doubt that loss of Greaves and Hitchens to Italy for most of the 1961/62 season had caused endless disruption to the team as Walter sought in vain for forwards of international calibre. Gerry Hitchens, a talented and established player who had played in 1961/62 season as a replacement for Smith, continued to disappoint. Jimmy Greaves and Johnny Haynes were world class players who inexplicably failed to achieve greatness in Chile. There had been some moaning about the training camp at Coya and this may have contributed to the morale of some players, particularly those not playing in the team. Jimmy Adamson, Walter's assistant manager was appalled at the level of homesickness experienced by a few players, particularly by those who knew they didn't have much chance of getting into the action. 'One thing for the future,' he said, 'was much more consideration for the overall mood of the squad.'

Whatever the reasons, the failure to win in Chile was difficult for the players to take because they believed they were good enough to win the tournament. 'In 1961 I firmly believed that England had a team that was good enough to go on and win the World Cup' said Greaves. 'I would go as far as to say that the England team of 1961 was actually better than the side that won the World Cup in 1966. To lose the services of three key players when we were on the point of leaving for South America ripped the spine out of that fine England team.'

Bobby Charlton believed that England had come closer to glory than many believed possible. 'In his last days in the job, Winterbottom, a symbol of the old amateur world in many eyes, had almost turned himself into a national hero. On top of that despite the vagaries of the system he had managed to form the nucleus of a side that I believed would be extremely serious runners in the 1966 World Cup.' 'But,' Charlton continued, 'I could see that a new and stronger form of leadership was required. Part of Walter would always be locked in the theoretical – it was part of him and his passion for the game. He was "donnish" in the best sense, kind and never given to heavy handed treatment of players or shows of bombast or ego, but it was clear that the days of the teacher would have to give way to those of the pro.'

Walter had chosen Jimmy Adamson as his assistant manager in Chile, the role in which he had used Billy Nicholson in Sweden. Jimmy had been a miner in the same village that Bobby Charlton came from, Ashington in County Durham. As a wing half in the Burnley side that won the League in 1960 he was voted England's Footballer of the Year in 1962, captaining the Burnley team that lost out in the Cup Final to a brilliant Tottenham. He was also an FA coach who had worked with Walter at Lillesall. In Chile Walter entrusted him with the important role of reminding players of their basic strengths and the need to carry them on the field, which he did with great authority.

Bobby Charlton was impressed by Adamson and his plain common sense advice. 'What you can never forget,' Adamson told Bobby, 'and if you do you let down both yourself and your team, is that generally speaking, if you are an influential player and you play badly, if you don't give it all you have, everybody else will follow suit and play badly.'

Adamson was Walters's preferred choice to take his place as England manager and Bobby Charlton was in no doubt that he would have been an excellent choice: 'He would surely have brought valuable insights and strength to the challenge presented by the departure of Walter Winterbottom. Unlike Walter, and this for the record is something that does not have to be couched in diplomatic terms, he would have been quite specific about his requirements of individual players and his requests would have been made in the specific language of professionals.'

Bobby Charlton's remarks were, of course, written with the benefit of hindsight. No one then had any inkling that Walter would shock the football world with his resignation two months after the 1962 World Cup; neither did anyone know that Jimmy Adamson would turn-down the offer of replacing Walter and that Alf Ramsey would be England's new manager before the end of the year. Only Walter knew that the defeat by Brazil was his last chance of leading England to World Cup victory. It made his disappointment even greater.

CHAPTER 18

A MILLION REGRETS

1962

On 1 August 1962, just six weeks after returning from Chile, Walter submitted his letter of resignation to the FA. The news hit the media like a bombshell. In the public's mind the England football manager had the highest profile job after the Prime Minister, and it was a big story because it was a job he had held for 16 years. BBC Radio announcements had been made in every news bulletin throughout the day. His press release stated that he was joining the Central Council of Physical Recreation (CCPR) as General Secretary on 1 January 1963 but would be working at the FA until the end of December in order to maintain continuity in the handover of his responsibilities.

He had timed the press release to coincide with leaving to go on holiday with his family and they left by train from Paddington for a cottage in Devon. It was the family's regular summer retreat: a haven where he had always found peace and quiet. But this time it proved impossible to avoid the press who quickly discovered his whereabouts and camped out on the sand dunes overlooking the cottage in Bantham.

Faced with such a massive media intrusion into his private space he confronted the journalists and photographers who were lying in wait and made a proposal to them: he would cooperate with interviews and photographs now if they would then leave and let him continue his family holiday in peace. They agreed and his resignation story dominated the next day's papers. The press treated him kindly and without exception regretted Walter's resignation and were generous in their praise.

Desmond Hackett in the *Daily Express* led with the back page story: 'WINTERBOTTOM WALK OUT HAS FA IN TIZZY'. After reporting Walter's career record he went on to say 'behind these bare facts lies the story of a man who had one failing in football – he could not bring himself to become a ruthless disciplinarian. He protected his players against criticism. He was in my opinion too faithful to internationals who were not always loyal to him.' The article quoted Graham Doggart and Denis Follows who both wanted to make it quite clear that the move had been entirely of Walter's seeking and that it had completely surprised them.

In a Q and A interview with the *Daily Express*, Walter remained somewhat guarded:

Q: Did the failure to get the FA Secretary job influence your decision?
WW: Whatever position I was in I would have been tempted to take this job. It is simply coincidence that it came up so soon after the appointment of the Secretary of the FA.
Q: Have you any regrets at leaving the FA?
WW: Yes. I am sorry we have not won the World Cup.
Q: Has there been opposition to your methods?
WW: No. There is always criticism but you must expect that.
Q: Will you be relieved to step out of the spotlight?
WW: I do not like leaving the job before it is completed... the trouble was that my job was invariably judged on what the England team did, yet it covered a much wider field.

Roy Peskett of the *Daily Mail* led with the headline: 'WINTERBOTTOM QUITS FA – NO MORE SACK THREATS'. The reason for this headline can be found in a comment Walter makes deep in the article which reveals some bitterness at the hands of the public and the media: 'I have a million regrets at leaving the FA but a least I will be going to a job in which people don't want me thrown out if the team lose one match.' The article went on to consider the task of finding his successor and speculated on who that might be.

Brian James of the *Daily Mail* reviewed Winterbottom's England record and concluded, 'Played 137 lost 28 ... is that failure?'

L.N. Bailey provided readers of the *Daily Telegraph* with a factual account of the circumstances surrounding the resignation and concluded that 'although Winterbottom hid his feelings behind a brave smile there is little doubt that he was a frustrated man.' Bailey squashed any idea that Winterbottom's departure had anything to do with England's failure to get past the quarter final stage in Chile. Like every other newspaper the *Daily Telegraph* speculated on a successor, naming Jimmy Adamson, Ron Greenwood the manager of West Ham, Bill Nicholson the Spurs manager, and Alf Ramsey, who had led Ipswich Town to their triumph as champions in their first season in Division One. 'No doubt the FA will receive plenty of applications for the post but as Mr Winterbottom was also Director of Coaching as well as team manager it will not be easy to find a man with the necessary qualifications.'

Little was known about the CCPR or why Walter had decided to join this organisation. The decision of the FA Council to elect Follows as FA Secretary was a snub which Walter felt deeply. He had reached a point in his career where he felt that he had given all that he had and he was ready for a new challenge. If could not continue to reform English football as the Secretary of the Football Association then it would have to be elsewhere. It is unthinkable that he would not have discussed his future confidentially with his mentor, Sir Stanley Rous, a man who had the highest regard for Walter.

Sir Stanley was influential and well connected in the wider world of sport. One of the organisations with which he was connected and which was close to his heart was the CCPR, where he had been Chairman of the Executive Committee since 1945. Although the CCPR did not have a high public profile in Britain, it was the only organisation that represented the overall interests of sport and recreation. All sporting governing bodies were affiliated to the CCPR. It was influential in assisting sporting bodies to achieve their aims – as Director of Coaching Walter had been closely involved with the CCPR in seeking their assistance in helping the county FA's to run coaching courses – and it was an independent and influential body that spoke for sport with one voice to the outside world and government.

The founder of this organisation and its long serving General Secretary was Phyllis Colson. The work of the CCPR is covered later but in the words of HRH the Duke of Edinburgh, 'the CCPR transformed the concept of recreation in Britain.' In the 37 years since Miss Colson had founded the CCPR it had grown from a fledgling body with donations of £300 to a national organisation with a full time staff of 400 and an annual budget of £1,250,000.

But in April 1962, quite unexpectedly, Miss Colson announced her retirement to the dismayed officers of the organisation, telling them that she would continue in her position until no later than 31 March 1963. Attempts were made to get her to change her mind, but to no avail. In his book, *Service to Sport,* Justin Evans, who was her deputy, contemplated the reasons. She was well below retirement age and although she had always suffered from pain and physical disability through chronic diabetes and rheumatoid arthritis her condition had not noticeably deteriorated. Nor in his opinion had there been any decline in her clarity of thought, powers of organisation and strength of will. Like many who knew her well he speculated as to why she suddenly resigned: 'No one knows for certain, but some who know her best feel that, apart from the continuing strains of work itself and some personal dissensions which worried her a lot, she was far sighted enough to see that the future of the CCPR, which she had built up, would be bound up with certain tendencies in the world of sport which were inimical to some of the ideals to which she had devoted her life.'

Soon after Miss Colson resigned Sir Stanley wrote a personal note to Walter in April, with a draft of the advertisement for the CCPR job, advising him that it would probably appear in June when he was with the England team in Chile and that he should warn Ann to look out for it and send a pre-prepared letter requesting more information and an application form. On 14 May 1962, the month after Miss Colson's resignation announcement, and a month before he left for Chile with the England team, Walter wrote to Sir Percy Lord asking permission to use his name as a referee for the position. He stressed the need for his plans to be kept strictly confidential as it was imperative that the media should have no inkling of his intentions; he was not going to let his chances be unintentionally sabotaged again. His application was submitted on his return from the World Cup on 14 June, along with 150 other candidates and he resigned from the Football Association on 1 August. It can only be speculation as to whether Miss Colson was persuaded to step down by Sir Stanley Rous in the long term interest of the organisation or whether she had some other reason.

When the media frenzy surounding his resignation subsided Walter was at last able to relax. For 12 years Bantham had been an oasis of calm away from football and his high pressure job. The village, accessible only by a single track Devon lane, benefited from being part of the Evans Estate, owned by the Cow and Gate heiress and it had remained mostly unchanged by development. The hamlet was simply a street which led down to the sea; a row of small thatched cottages on one side, unpretentious houses on the other, a 16th century pub, the Sloop Inn, and a general store with a post office. For the most part the inhabitants were farm hands and fisherman. A few wealthy families owned houses, including the 'Clarkes' Shoes' family and Frank Adams, an entrepreneur with land, property and businesses in the Reading area. Walter had met Frank when he was at the Air Ministry and they had become friends. They saw more of each other when Walter moved to the FA because Frank was an FA councillor and the owner of Wycombe Wanderers Football Club. Because they were such good friends Frank invited Walter to use his holiday home, 'The Whiddens' – the top floor apartment of his house overlooking the South Hams and the River Avon estuary. This was the sanctuary that Walter escaped to with his family each year.

For Walter and the children it was paradise. Days were spent on the beach with Janet, Brenda and Alan building elaborately sculptured sand castles in the shapes of boats and aeroplanes. At low tide they would walk across the vast expanse of sand exposed by the tide to Burgh Island to enjoy locally caught fish for lunch. Sometimes they took a small boat up the Avon estuary with a picnic or hiked along the cliff tops in the bracing sea air. In the early evenings Walter would organise a cricket match on the beach. It usually began with just the Winterbottoms, but soon other families joined in and it became a fun but keenly contested daily event. Later in the evening, without the distractions of television, the family enjoyed reading and games; card games like racing demons, scrabble, draughts, dominoes and monopoly.

On his return to 22 Lancaster Gate three weeks later there was still much to be done in the four months remaining before he left. He produced his final annual report on the FA Coaching Scheme reflecting progress made and yet highlighting how much remained to be done. England was still a long way behind other European countries who were leading the way in developing modern coaching methods.

That year he had planned, organised and supervised 16 national courses for 1200 students including professional players, referees, schoolmasters, schoolboys, administrators, coaches and trainers. But now Walter was also at the forefront of international developments in education and was busy planning and directing courses and conferences in conjunction with FIFA and UEFA.

International conferences with other Associations promoted the exchange of information and co-operation. Reporting on a UEFA coaches' conference he attended in Germany, he said that it was evident from lectures and discussions that coaches in European countries insisted on ball practice to a far greater degree than their English counterparts. Training schemes were described that required talented young players to have at least two to three hours of ball practice four times a week. The observations of British coaches at the conference echoed his own conclusions from what he had seen in Chile: all players needed to strive to improve basic skills performed at match tempo. There was absolutely no substitute for dedicated practice for long hours. Only in this way would young players be able to improve ball control, pass accurately under pressure, adapt play from defense to attack, shoot accurately and be willing to take scoring chances. It was sadly a fact that in England too many youngsters just wanted to play a match and were unwilling to dedicate themselves to practice. It was a characteristic that set them apart from young players on the continent.

The annual summer course for referee instructors that Walter ran at Lilleshall considered material for an advanced syllabus, but teaching for referees was now also being developed through international cooperation. In July 1961 Walter attended a FIFA conference of international referees in Italy. It revealed wide differences of opinion in relation to refereeing control and underlined the need for uniformity of interpretation of the laws of the game. Similar differences existed amongst English referees and he organised a conference for League referees at Birmingham University under the auspices of the FA and the Football League.

International coaches were now sharing knowledge at the highest level with the aim of improving overall standards. At the conclusion of the World Cup in Chile the newly formed World Federation Conference of Football Coaches and Team Managers met to discuss the important technical problems in the development of the game.

The number of courses for coaches in Europe was growing and there were exchange visits by coaches. Sepp Herberger, the West German team manager, was guest lecturer at Lilleshall and Walter was invited to lecture and demonstrate on modern aspects of fitness training at a West German course at Grunberg and the East German course in Berlin.

There was also progress on the development of schools football. The FA and the English Schools Football Association (ESFA) ran three one-day conferences for schoolmasters in London, Birmingham and Bolton. Over 100 schoolmasters at each venue saw a demonstration of coaching techniques by Walter supported by four national coaches and in the afternoon had discussions with League managers. The conference was a well received and Walter expressed his hope that it would become a regular event.

Five and six-a-side games were growing in importance, something that Walter encouraged for both skills training and competition. He provided guidance on the rules and organisation of small sided games in a widely distributed FA pamphlet and wrote an article on the topic in the *FA Book for Boys.* '

Although the World Cup in Chile had only just ended and he would be leaving at the end of 1962 Walter's thoughts were now focused on the 1966 World Cup in England. On his return from Chile in June he wrote a report which recommended to the FA Technical Committee that they should arrange regional meetings with club managers to discuss ways that the selection, training and performance of the England team could be improved in preparation for 1966. The power of League clubs in the structure of English football was an inescapable reality and their cooperation was essential. Four meetings were held with League managers during

September in Manchester, York, London and Birmingham, attended by the most senior members of the FA – Joe Mears, the Chairman of the Technical Committee, Graham Doggart, Chairman of the FA, and Denis Follows, Secretary of the FA. Walter was present in his capacity as the England Team Manager. 32 club managers were present including Matt Busby (Manchester United), Jimmy Milne (Preston North End), Harry Potts (Burnley), Bill Shankly (Liverpool), Alan Brown (Sunderland), Vic Buckingham (Sheffield Wednesday), Don Revie (Leeds United), Ted Bates (Southampton), Johnny Carey (Leyton Orient), Tommy Docherty (Chelsea), Ron Greenwood (West Ham), George Smith (Portsmouth), Billy Wright (Arsenal), Stan Cullis (Wolverhampton Wanderers), Joe Mercer (Aston Villa) and Gill Merrick (Birmingham).

The meetings made a breakthrough. They established a new understanding between the national manager and club managers which provided the foundations for England's World Cup success four years later. From the outset the discussions were frank and open, with all managers giving their assurances that they would do all they could to help England. At last Walter felt that his efforts at getting the support of club managers were paying dividends. The main topics they discussed were the selection of the team, the release of players for practice sessions and the international fixture list. Time was also made available for an open forum.

On the subject of team selection there was universal agreement that this should be the sole responsibility of the England team manager and that club managers were in a better position to provide the England manager with advice than a selection committee. A system of greater coordination was agreed: the England manager would brief a panel of experienced managers on his plans and they would report the progress of existing and potential international players. Regular regional managers meetings with the England manager were agreed at which players form and performance could be discussed.

Interestingly the experienced managers expressed the view that the system of selection was not the most important factor in determining England's success – generally, it was thought that the best available teams had been fielded. [By this time the press had concluded that Walter was pretty well getting his own way on team selection.] In their opinion more important factors were: the selection of players from so many different clubs and the limited opportunity of practicing and playing together; the time of year when the tournament was played; and the work of clubs in developing players to reach higher standards of ability for England selection. It was music to Walter's ears. At last the message that he had been preaching for 16 years was being understood by club managers and accepted by the most senior officials of the Football Association. It didn't mean that the problems of the England team manager would go way, far from it, but now there was a healthy dialogue, a common objective, and the incentive of supporting England's bid to win the World Cup as host country in four years time.

The lack of opportunity for the England team to train and practice together was not as easy to resolve. Managers were sympathetic but the fixture list of club games and international matches was already crowded and unless the pressure could be eased by the FA and the Football League the problem would remain. One idea put forward was the suggestion of playing all internationals in mid-week. Another was playing some internationals at the beginning of the season and then having up to a four week 'international season' after the league fixtures had been completed. Although such ideas might have been more idealistic than realistic at least regular managers meetings would ensure more cooperation in arranging international team get-togethers.

Walter also wanted more access to promising young players and suggested that they should be brought together more frequently for training sessions at selected club grounds. These sessions did not have to coincide with international matches and he wanted managers to join their players if possible. Clubs agreed and promised to release young players for training and match practice in preparation for the UEFA International Youth tournament (Under-18) and for the tournament itself during the Easter 1963 period (England won the tournament with a team including the likes of Tommy Smith (Liverpool), Ron Harris (Chelsea), David Pleat (Nottingham Forest), John Sissons (West Ham) and David Sadler (Manchester United)).

Walter explained that the presence of journalists at international practice sessions was unhelpful because it encouraged players to put on a special performance and it made it more difficult for him to draw attention to faults of team work. The tradition of clubs allowing a paying audience to watch when the England team played practice matches was also discouraged by Walter.

He asked that when matches had no special importance that players on the fringe of selection should be tried and the practice of playing fully established players to attract spectators at less important international matches should be discontinued.

The timing of the World Cup Tournament at the end of a long tiring season was seen as being to England's detriment and managers proposed that if possible it should be played in early August, adjusting the start of the League season if necessary. This idea appears to have been well received by FIFA because the 1966 World Cup Tournament was played between 11-30 July and the League fixtures were completed on 16 April.

Senior FA officials, meanwhile, had the question of Walter's successor on their minds. The need for a replacement was an urgent priority. On 8 August, the consultative committee (empowered to act with the powers of the full council in intervals between meetings) met to consider the matter. It did not take long for the members to decide that Walter's job should be split into two and that the FA should seek both a Director of Coaching and an England Team Manager. Graham Doggart, the FA Chairman said, 'doubtless if the two roles had been filled by anyone other than Mr. Winterbottom the split would have been made much sooner, but as Mr. Winterbottom had grown up with both, it would have been a difficult decision for either him or some other body to take as to which post he should have filled and which he should have given up. Whichever way the decision went it would have been taken by some to indicate that there was dissatisfaction at the way in which he carried out his duties in the post which was relinquished.' Two selection committees consisting of senior FA officials were duly convened and began advertising the two positions. It was a sensible decision taken at the right time. Looking back, Sir Trevor Brooking, the FA's Director of Football Development, commented 'it was incredible that one man could have managed both jobs.'

The position of Director of Coaching received 19 applications and a short list of four was interviewed by the selection committee on 8 October. They had no hesitation in offering the job to Allen Wade, a 36-year-old lecturer in physical education at Loughborough College. He accepted it the following day and took up his duties at the beginning of January. 'His strong qualifications,' said Graham Doggart, 'both in the theory and practice of the game, as well as his wide knowledge of physical education in its broadest sense will ensure that the coaching structure of the FA, so soundly built up by Mr. Winterbottom, will be further strengthened and developed by Mr. Wade.'

The job of England team manager received 59 applications but the committee decided that none of the candidates were suitable. It was then offered to Jimmy Adamson, the captain of Burnley, who had been Walter's first choice. He had no managerial experience but Walter maintained that there was no real link between the skills needed to run a successful club and those needed to run a national side. 'I felt we needed a good coach and we went for Jimmy Adamson – who'd been my assistant with England – so we could maintain some continuity,' Walter recalled. In the event Adamson turned the job down because he and his wife did not wish to uproot their family and move to London.

The selection committee then asked Graham Doggart to seek the permission of the Chairman of Ipswich Town to approach Alf Ramsey. Doggart went to Ipswich on 17 October and met with Ramsey for two hours. He was impressed with Ramsey's attitude to the challenge. But Dave Bowler, Ramsey's biographer, said he had reservations: the 46-year-old coach was very loyal to Ipswich Town with whom he had had such outstanding success. Life in Ipswich was good and he was generally liked there; he'd also grown used to managing a club of Ipswich's size and the distinct lack of press intrusion that came with it. But he was ambitious and he was patriotic; the *Times* newspaper went so far as to suggest that he took the job from a sense of duty. He was certainly not moving for money: Bowler said that his new salary was reportedly £4,500 a year, about the same as he was earning at Ipswich.

Alf's next meeting with Doggart was in London on 24 October and this time Walter joined them for lunch. It was after this that Ramsey accepted the offer and his appointment was announced on 25 October, although it was agreed that he would not begin at the FA until Ipswich had completed their League fixtures in May 1963.

At the FA Council meeting on 3 December, Graham Doggart summarised the proceedings for members and told them, 'I would also like to pay tribute to the invaluable assistance I received from Mr. Winterbottom in the final stages of the negotiation.' Walter played an important part in securing Alf Ramsey's agreement and was able to reassure him that although managing the national team was quite different from managing a club side, and not without its fundamental problems, he could now expect more cooperation from club managers and the sole responsibility for the selection of the team.

It has been generally assumed by the press and football writers that Ramsey laid down terms that included having the sole responsibility for team selection but it is likely that Walter himself can be given credit for the end of the era of the selection committee. In his biography of Alf Ramsey, *Winning Isn't Everything*, Bowler quoted from an interview he had with Walter: 'Denis Follows was in charge of the process and I said to him that one man who could do the job would be Alf. The one thing I insisted on was that the new man shouldn't have to put up with the selection committee.' Walter may have been criticised for not challenging the selection system during his own reign but he should get the credit for changing it for Alf Ramsey.

Walter's 139th and final game as manager of the England team was against Wales in a British Championship match at Wembley on Wednesday, November 21, 1962. England won 4-0 in a one-sided game in which they reduced Wales to a hard running, hard tackling hopelessness, but did little to rouse the crowd. A 2:15pm kick off, a bleak, icy November afternoon, a stadium scarred by stark scaffolding, piles of girders and pyramids of bricks for the new roof, live coverage on television; all conspired to keep the attendance to 27,500 – the lowest ever for an England home game. Harold Shepherdson, 'the man with the magic sponge,' who was at Walter's side for the last time, described it as 'a sad, almost sombre afternoon. The giant crane on the half finished roof seemed to sum it all up as it dipped in farewell salute to one of the nicest men football has ever known.'

In the national press the game itself was overshadowed by tributes to Walter. The *Times* headline was 'END OF ENGLISH FOOTBALL EPOCH':

Only in the future, when things find there right perspective, will anyone be able to measure Winterbottom's efforts for the Football Association and England. With the League pulling in an opposite direction to the national body throughout – or in most of – his 16 years of office, and with the unwilling cooperation of the clubs in the release of players for team preparation, he can still hold his head high ... win, lose or draw today Winterbottom can withdraw from the scene satisfied within himself.

When Walter walked out of the Wembley dressing room for the last time he took with him a complete set of crystal glasses – a gift which had been subscribed to by most of the players who had represented England during Walter's 16-year reign. Jimmy Armfield telephoned Ann to find out what the most appropriate gift would be and made the presentation in the dressing room after the game, the players still in their mud stained shorts and shirts, the steaming dressing room littered with the familiar after match debris of bandages, cotton wool and empty tea cups. 'It was in the dressing room that the players took their private farewell of the man of whom they were so very fond,' recalled Harold Shepherdson. It was a touching moment. Later, meeting the press, Walter contained his emotions: 'The presentation was a complete surprise. It was very nice of the lads. It makes you regret all the more leaving the game you love.' Speaking to John Bromley of the *Daily Mirror* he quipped, 'They must have known that I was going to get drunk tonight!'

When asked for his thoughts Sir Stanley Rous was fulsome in his praise, 'Walter was the best signing the FA ever made: not simply because of his managership, but because of the other wonderful things he did for football. I felt for a long time that the FA revolved around Walter and his schemes.'

Interviewed by Brian James of the *Daily Mail*, Walter urged supporters to get behind the England team: 'Yesterday, driving down the Empire Way, through the few going to the game, Jimmy Greaves turned to me and said "Look at this – nobody cares. When we come down here to play Scotland next spring this road will be packed with a sea of tartan." He's right and it's a terrible thing. England asks a lot of her players, asks that they look like world beaters in every match. But how often are the people behind their team? Only when we go into a match nobody thinks we can win do they cheer... I'm leaving the scene. Even so this is vital to me – this support for 1966 which we need now! I'd like to leave behind for Alf Ramsey and the players a national team that has the nation behind it. With support, even now we could whack the world.'

'WINTERBOTTOM'S LAST WORDS' was the headline in the *Daily Mirror* in which Ken Jones described Walter's blue print for our soccer future. In the article Walter passionately stated the case for coaching; that our future as a power in world football hinged around coaching; that coaches needed to go on looking for the factors that mean success in soccer. 'It is useless to say that we will attempt to improve a player if we treat the whole thing in a shallow manner,' said Walter. 'The coach must get down and work, work and work at his subject.'

Walter went on to criticise the constraints of the League system: 'Part of our failure in international football hinges on the demands that are made on our players in League football. The feeling is for quick tackling defenders and an open all action game. This serves to make our forwards want to part with the ball quickly. In international football we are faced by retreating defences that demand players to carry the ball hard and fast at the opposition. We are still seeking players who are prepared to run into a position simply to open up a gap for someone else. All too often players are only prepared to run if they think they will get the ball.'

Perhaps Walter's departure was best summed-up by Roy Ullyett of the *Daily Express*, the doyen of sports cartoonists, in the way that satirical cartoonists do so well. He depicted Walter's head within the twin towers of Wembley and four cartoon characters representing the fans, the players, the selectors and the press, each with a speech bubble over their heads: The fans: 'Nice chap but he wouldn't listen to us.' The players: 'Honestly Walter we were trying every match.' The selectors: 'Unfortunately he always had us to guide him.' The press: 'Bouquets or brickbats, he always had our respect.'

Even at his last match he was still innovating. After training at White City the players were driven to a London clinic for the most exhaustive medical check-up they had ever had, which included probing work rate, oxygen consumption and pulse recovery rate. From this a dossier was created for each player and results were then added before and after each international. This policy was carried through the youth, Under-23 and amateur teams. The idea was copied from the best continental and South American teams. It was continued and enhanced in subsequent years and was supplemented early in Alf Ramsey's reign by the appointment of a team doctor, Dr Alan Bass, who accompanied the England party at all times.

To this day Walter Winterbottom has the unique distinction of being England's first, youngest and longest serving England team manager. In all matches in which he was in charge, England played 139, won 78, drew 33, and lost 28; goals for 383, against 196. At home England only lost six matches in 16 years. England won the British championship in 13 out of his 16 seasons (seven times outright and six times sharing top place). In the World Cup Tournament England qualified on all four occasions, reaching the quarter finals twice, playing 28 matches, winning 15, drawing 7 and losing 6; goals for 75 against 35 (these figures include World Cup qualifying matches).

His most important legacy to football was the development of the national coaching scheme. He may not have originated the idea, or run the first coaching course – that came from Sir Stanley Rous, but he took the seed of the idea and nurtured it to a point where it was a model to sporting organisations throughout the world. The basic text books used at courses were the product of his ideas. Walter touched the lives of so many famous coaches who were not just trained, but inspired by him. Many were grateful for the help he gave them in securing their jobs. Two of his staunchest disciples reached the highest rung in English football – both Ron Greenwood and Bobby Robson became the England team manager.

In January 1963 Walter was the subject of a BBC Radio series called 'People Today,' hosted by Rex Alston, which looked back on

Walter's life and time with the FA. Perhaps one of the most interesting questions Walter was asked was which of his two jobs at the FA he preferred. His reply was revealing:

'That's a very good one. Well, my interest would obviously be in my old post of education – that of teaching – that of looking into this broader field, Director of Coaching. It has more scope to it. But the challenge is really in the other job, and whilst I've been able to get on well in developing the coaching scheme – because it's been something where you can get positive results, you can see these results, you can see the progress you're making, the fulfilment of being England team manager must be reaching the pinnacle – that of winning the World Cup – this I haven't done, and I think the challenge would draw me back into this, although it's a world where you can work extremely hard and unless you have the throw up of talent at the right moment, and it all fits the right occasion – you can fail. This is true of football generally – of all sport generally.'

FA council members bade their farewells to Walter and Sir Stanley Rous on 3 December 1962 at a luncheon given by the FA at the Great Western Hotel, Paddington. In recognition of his distinguished 28 years of service, Sir Stanley was presented with an inscribed silver salver, a cheque for £1,000 and a personal gift of a desk and chair subscribed to by the members. Walter also received an inscribed silver salver. It was a great sadness to him when his house was burgled some years later and it was stolen. It was a senseless theft because, being inscribed, it had no retail value and was probably melted down.

Walter also received a cheque for £5,000 'in view of the esteem in which he was held and in full and final settlement of royalties.' He had received no royalties for the coaching books he had written. He did not seek them now and the amount due was negotiated by his accountants. It was a just recognition of his personal contribution to the development of coaching. He used the money to treat himself to something he had always wanted. At the age of 49 he bought his first car: a Ford Zephyr Six Mk. III. At a price of just under a £1,000 it still left him enough to pay-off the mortgage on his Stanmore home.

He would have treasured more highly the words of the FA Chairman, Graham Doggart: 'It can be said without fear of contradiction that no official has ever served the FA with greater loyalty, devotion and single mindedness than Mr. Winterbottom. He will take with him the good wishes not only of the FA but also every lover of the game.'

CHAPTER 19

WINTERBOTTOM'S NEW WORLD

1963 – 1972

All the world's a stage
And all the men and women merely players
They have their exits and their entrances
And one man in his life plays many parts

William Shakespeare

'WINTERBOTTOM'S NEW WORLD' was the headline on the back page of *the Daily Express* on December 14, 1962. Photographs showed Walter inspecting the site of the CCPR's new National Sports Centre at Crystal Palace, a groundbreaking facility costing £2.2 million which was due to open a year later. It would provide London with its first Olympic size swimming pool, a diving pool, an all-weather athletics track, a covered sprint training track, all-weather outdoor soccer pitches and an indoor sports arena which could be adapted for tennis or basketball as well as accommodation for visiting athletes. It was a wonderful step forward in providing world class training and competition facilities for international athletes but Britain lagged a long way behind the rest of Europe.

'What a great pity that this is the first of its kind and not at least the tenth,' Walter lamented.

When Walter arrived at his new office on 1 January he was greeted, not by a red carpet but white. London was in the grip of a bitter winter and he trudged through the snow in his Wellington boots to report for work at the Bedford Square office of the CCPR. He had been recognised in the New Year's Honours list with the award of an O.B.E. for 'Services to Football' but he was in little doubt about the size of the new challenge that lay ahead in the wider field of sport.

The most important work of the CCPR in the early post war years was the help that their technical staff – a department of 40 to 50 people – was able to give national governing bodies in adopting and developing organised coaching schemes. There were high profile national events such as the Festival of Youth and Sport at the Empire pool, Wembley in 1948 and the Festival of Football at the Empress Hall in 1949 in which Walter gave a demonstration of coaching methods. More ambitious plans included the opening of National Recreation Centres, including Lilleshall (which had been used extensively by Walter as the home of football coaching) and Crystal Palace but by far the most significant event in the history of the CCPR came about in an unexpected and modest way because of Walter's friend Dave Munrow.

Dave Munrow and Walter had been lecturers together at Carnegie College and developed a strong friendship. Munrow was an academic in the field of sport. He had a BSc before obtaining his Diploma from Carnegie and becoming Director of Physical Education at Birmingham University. There he introduced the first British degree course in physical education in 1947. It was no easy task building a new university department in post war Britain – there was an element of suspicion and prejudice about the worthiness of physical education as a course of undergraduate study. It was similar to the resistance Walter faced when he was introducing football coaching around the same time.

In 1957 when Munrow published a pamphlet titled *Britain in the World of Sport*, he could have had no idea of the long term impact it was to have. It drew attention to the handicaps suffered by sports bodies and amateur sportsmen and women in trying to prepare for any form of international competition and gave a searching analysis of many of the factors affecting sport in Great Britain. Walter was at the FA preparing for the 1958 World Cup when the pamphlet was written but it is inconceivable that Munrow would not have spoken to him for advice on aspects affecting football.

A.L. Colbeck, who was an experienced member of the CCPR's technical staff, was moved by the argument put forward in Munrow's pamphlet and proposed a resolution at the CCPR's annual conference calling for the Council to respond to the challenge raised by the paper. When the Executive Committee met there was general agreement that the whole subject of the development of physical recreation should be referred to a small impartial body, qualified to hear evidence and reach conclusions, which could investigate and make recommendations about the many current problems affecting sport. In the summer of 1957 the CCPR announced the appointment of the Wolfenden Committee on Sport.

The formal terms of reference given to the committee were very broad: 'To examine the factors affecting the development of games, sports and outdoor activities in the United Kingdom and to make recommendations to the Central Council of Physical Recreation as to any practical measures which should be taken by statutory or voluntary bodies in order that these activities may play their full part in promoting the general welfare of the community.'

Sir John Wolfenden, the chairman of the committee, was the Vice Chancellor of Reading University and exceptionally well qualified in the field of education and social services. He had been the headmaster of two public schools and had worked on several government committees (and was probably best known to the public as the chairman of the committee that recommended the decriminalisation of homosexuality). The committee was a distinguished group whose members provided a wide range of experience in education, government, business and sport. The first meeting was held at the CCPR offices in Bedford Square in January 1958. Their final report, 'Sport and the Community', was presented to the CCPR in September 1960.

The Wolfenden Committee received written and oral evidence from almost 200 organisations and individuals from the world of sport. Walter was well aware of the work of Wolfenden: Dave Munrow was a member of the Committee, and as the Director of Coaching at the Football Association Walter was one of those consulted. The report was published after two years of comprehensive enquiry. It contained over 50 recommendations on aspects of sports development, but one key recommendation stood out: Wolfenden decided unanimously that there was no hope of sport getting the 'new deal' that was required unless a new body, independent of the Ministry of Education, was set up, which would receive finance from the government and disperse it in the most appropriate directions. They proposed the establishment of a Sports Development Council.

The report received widespread attention in the media. It was covered by 63 newspapers and periodicals – even *The Economist* devoted two pages to it. For the most part editorial comment and analysis was positive and even enthusiastic, although inevitably there were cartoons based on humorous confusion between the Wolfenden reports on sport and homosexuality. The 10,000 copies that were printed quickly sold out and a reprint of 5,000 copies soon followed. This was a topic which had captured the public interest.

The CCPR immediately circulated the report to all relevant organisations, government ministers and Members of Parliament. They were divided on issue of a Sports Development Council. Governing bodies overwhelmingly supported it but within the CCPR Executive Committee there was a difference of opinion. From his office at the Football Association Walter had watched these developments with interest and discussed them with Dave Munrow. There was already a wind of change in favour of sport blowing through Westminster. In the run up to the general election of 1959 the Conservative Party had produced a report titled 'The Challenge of Leisure' and the Labour Party followed suit with a document entitled 'Leisure for Living'.

But things moved slowly. The Wolfenden report was first debated in the House of Lords in February 1961 and then in the House of Commons in April, but no conclusions were reached. Meanwhile the case for a Sports Council was given further support in 1962 by Denis Molyneux, a brilliant young lecturer and colleague of Munrow at Birmingham University. He published an important pamphlet titled *Central Government Aid to Sport and Physical Recreation in Countries of Western Europe.*

This was the moment that Walter stepped onto the wider stage of sport where, in the next 16 years, he would emerge as a new kind of public figure. One who had worked as a teacher, a professional footballer, a football administrator and as England team manager. He was part of the new meritocracy who was to have a profound effect on Britain in the second half of the 20th century. The struggle to establish a Sports Council and get the new deal that Wolfenden envisaged was just beginning. It became a long fought battle and Walter was in the thick of it.

When Walter announced to the world that he was leaving football to join the CCPR, the media, the public and many in football were surprised. But it was not the leap into the unknown that they imagined. He was returning to his roots – the development of physical education – and he knew many of the staff and council members (including Dave Munrow, Clinton Sayer, Peter McIntosh and Harry Littlewood) from his time at Carnegie College. He knew others from coaching courses he had run in conjunction with the CCPR when he was at the FA. And of course he was reunited with his mentor, Sir Stanley Rous, the chairman. Walter soon showed that he had no intention of conceiving the post of General Secretary of the CCPR as Phyllis Colson had and he introduced many changes in attitudes, relationships and ways of working. Walter shared with Phyllis Colson the capacity for unremitting hard work but his unrivalled contacts in the world of international and professional sport, and experience in the men's side of physical education, brought a new impetus to the organisation.

Phyllis Colson's autocratic style of management was replaced by Walter's more collegiate approach. It had always been her practice to arrive in the office before the staff, opening all the mail and redirecting it, with instructions, as she thought appropriate. On taking over Walter immediately changed this procedure, receiving only mail that was personally addressed to him and giving more responsibility to managers.

At the Football Association Walter had been used to dealing with the politics of the amateur establishment and the power of professional League clubs. Now his politics began with a capital 'P'. Sport had become a political football. From the discussions he had with Dave Munrow he was convinced that implementation of the Wolfenden report and introduction of a Sports Council was the way forward. It was a view not shared by Phyllis Colson, and it remained to be seen which political party would be most likely to commit to Wolfenden. The first three months in which Phyllis Colson was handing over to Walter were difficult: Dave Munrow and Peter McIntosh were two members of the CCPR who had strenuously pursued the Wolfenden recommendation that a Sports Council should be created and Walter encouraged them. But they were opposed by Phyllis Colson who persuaded Stanley Rous, the chairman, and Arthur Gem, his deputy, to line up in opposition to Wolfenden.

In only his second month at the CCPR Walter and Phyllis Colson met with Lord Hailsham to discuss the Wolfenden recommendations, a meeting that was also attended by representatives of the British

Olympic Association and the National Playing Fields Association. Hailsham had been appointed as the Conservative Government's Minister for Science 'with special responsibility for sport,' and a discussion took place on issues arising from the possible formation of a Sports Council. Subsequently Walter and Phyllis Colson sent separate memoranda to Hailsham with their own and divergent views. There were debates in both the House of Commons and the House of Lords. Lord Hailsham, who had renounced his peerage and was now Quintin Hogg, continued to resist the idea.

Meanwhile Walter set about the task of meeting as many of the governing bodies as possible. He attended annual dinners and as the guest of honour took the opportunity to encourage and praise their efforts. He was a natural and entertaining after dinner speaker, always able to strike a balance between humour and the serious issues that affected the organisation. Weekends were spent not at football matches, but attending national championships in a diverse range of sports.

An important part of the CCPR's work was the provision of courses to introduce novices to a new sport: from climbing to pot holing, from gliding to sub-aqua (scuba diving), from archery to badminton; here was something for everyone and Walter encouraged his own family to join in, and they took part in white-water canoeing at Plas y Brenin in Wales and sailing at the National Sailing Centre at Cowes.

Finally a change in policy for sport came about with a change of government. The Conservatives were defeated in a General Election in 1964, concluding a 13-year reign that had seen four prime ministers – Churchill, Eden, Macmillan and Douglas-Home. It marked the end of a long line of blue-blooded rulers from the aristocracy. Britain was never again to be ruled by the aristocracy but the next decade of socialism brought its own turbulent problems.

Harold Wilson, who won the election for Labour, represented a change in the social order. He came from a middle class background, was educated at grammar school and became a brilliant scholar at Oxford. Labour had been expected to win comfortably but a late Tory surge in the polls meant that they only won with a narrow majority of four seats. Denis Howell, who had been re-elected as the Labour MP for Small Heath, Birmingham, had been best known as the first MP to referee a professional football match. He was not one of the MPs nervously awaiting a phone call from Number 10 to find out whether they would be offered a position in the new government so he was pleasantly surprised when he telephoned George Brown to congratulate him on being appointed Deputy Prime Minister. Brown confided: 'Harold tells me that he wants you to be in the government.' Howell waited anxiously and finally a call came late on Sunday night saying that the Prime Minister wished to see him early the next morning. When they met, Harold Wilson said, 'I would like you to go to Education and look after schools and sport. You will be the first Minister for Sport, it will be very exciting.'

Howell's first brush with civil service mandarins could have come straight from the TV series *Yes Minister*. 'May I say minister,' said Sir John Lang, the Parliamentary Secretary who would be his principal advisor, 'I have read most of your speeches in opposition. I know that your party is committed to the idea of a Sports Council. It is not for me at our first meeting to advise you against the idea, but I would like the opportunity to present a paper setting out all the arguments against the proposal.'

Howell sought the advice of two friends who he asked to join him at his London flat. By a stroke of extraordinary good fortune for Walter, the men he turned to were Dave Munrow and Denis Molyneux, who Howell knew from their Birmingham connection. They had a long discussion about the type of Sports Council that Howell wanted to create. Both Munrow and Molyneux firmly believed that Denis Howell should chair the new body. 'From my own experience in dealing with the Ministry of Education at Birmingham University,' said Munrow, 'I can tell you that we will never get the Sports Council off the ground unless your ministerial authority is present.' Time was against them. The government had a small majority and a further election could not be far away. The goal must be to launch the Sports Council as soon as possible: to show that it was a successful organisation that was radically reshaping the sports scene, bringing new hope and encouragement. The arguments were convincing and Denis Howell quickly and enthusiastically adopted the suggestion that he should chair the new body.

They then moved on to discuss who should be the chief officer. Several possible names were considered but it was hardly surprising that Munrow and Molyneux should suggest Walter. His credentials were excellent, and he was the General Secretary of the CCPR to which every sport in the country was affiliated. No one else in the country had such influence they reasoned. Furthermore, if Walter wasn't chosen for the position, how was the new Sports Council going to relate to the CCPR and its staff? His position as the former England football manager was not a consideration but his reputation was a useful bonus. Howell considered that the arguments in favour of Walter were overwhelming.

They turned their attention to the membership of the Council and Denis Molyneux suggested that they should identify the Council's main areas of interest and develop a structure around these. He proposed four principal development areas: facilities and planning, coaching and development, international participation and lastly research. It was agreed that Walter would have to be consulted on all of these matters before any decisions were made. The three men left with a feeling of great excitement.

When Denis Howell met with Sir John Lang he told him, 'notwithstanding all the excellent arguments in your paper as to why we should not establish a Sports Council, I have in fact decided to do so.' Without a moment's hesitation Lang replied, 'Very good, minister, in that case allow me to advise you on how best to proceed.'

Denis Howell asked Walter and Sir Stanley Rous to meet him to discuss the matter. They listened carefully and then voiced a number of concerns, in particular an overlap between the staff of the two organisations and control of the National Recreation Centres. But Walter had another worry on his mind. What would happen if they wholeheartedly supported Howell's proposals, but Labour lost the next election, which could not be far away?

Howell then surprised them by saying, 'I would like Walter to be the chief officer of the Sports Council.' The proposal was unexpected and there was a long silence. Finally Walter replied: 'I am very flattered to be considered, but I need time to think about it. What I can say is that I would not wish to come on a permanent basis, and if I did come I would need to retain my links with the CCPR.'

This appeared to be a stumbling block until John Lang – who Quintin Hogg affectionately called 'the wiliest monkey in the Whitehall jungle' – raised his head which had been buried in his hands and suggested a secondment. It was a canny solution that met with everyone's approval.

On 3 February 1965 the Government announced in both Houses of Parliament that they had decided to establish a Sports Council with Denis Howell as the chairman, Walter as the Director, and members serving in a personal capacity. No doubt the government's narrow majority was an influencing factor in deciding to set up an 'advisory' Sports Council – rather than the executive body that had been promised. An executive body would have required a Royal Charter with a long time table for special legislation and time was of the essence.

There was an air of euphoria leading up to the announcement in the House and Denis Howell suggested to Harold Wilson that the occasion should be marked by a reception at 10 Downing Street. However this was delayed by the grave illness of Sir Winston Churchill, who had suffered a severe stroke on 15 January and lay in a coma, dying. As a gesture of respect for the great man, public announcements were few and far between until after his state funeral on 30 January, 1965.

And so the birth of the Sports Council was duly celebrated on 11 February 1965 with an invitation to meet the Prime Minister at 10 Downing Street. It was a happy occasion attended by the chairman, Denis Howell, the members of the council, Walter, his staff and a galaxy of sporting stars, including tennis player Virginia Wade, boxer Howard Winstone and swimmer Anita Lonsborough.

In the interim period Walter met regularly with his deputy director, Denis Molyneux to thrash out strategies and agree papers that they wanted to bring before the new Sports Council. It had taken six years of political machination and procrastination but its time had come. It was the dawn of a new era in British sport; they were ready to go. Denis Howell was an enthusiastic 'hands on' supporter of sport and set about his new role with gusto. His profile and his 'nose' for publicity put sport high on the political and public agenda. Walter liked him personally: they shared a love of sport and Walter felt that here was a man who could get things done. Howell, who had Harold Wilson's backing, generated the political drive. They were supported by Sir John Lang, now a retired civil servant and former Head of the Admiralty, for whom Walter had a high regard. Sir John was particularly valuable to Walter for his knowledge of government departments and experience in working constructively across complex areas of departmental responsibilities.

Howell's first task as Chairman of the Sports Council was to appoint the members. Howell, Lang, Walter and Denis Molyneux met informally to discuss its composition. The structure they agreed followed the lines that Molyneux had first suggested. The Council members brought a wide range of experience from the world of sport, leisure and local government. They were appointed as individuals and not representatives of any other interest, acting part time within a committee structure. The full Council met six times a year and its four main committees also met six times a year to discuss, and approve or reject the recommendations put before them by Walter and his executive team.

In the House of Commons the introduction of the Sports Council and Walter's appointment was welcomed by both sides: Quintin Hogg for the Conservative opposition and Phillip Noel Baker for Labour. Not everyone was as easily impressed. At a meeting requested by HRH Prince Phillip (who was President of the CCPR and prominently associated with the National Playing Fields Association), Howell was somewhat taken aback when the Duke of Edinburgh said 'this Sports Council you have appointed: there isn't one of them who knows his arse from his elbow.' Howell, a working class Labour MP later reflected, 'If this was to be the level at which our discussions were to be conducted I would be very much at home!'

Prince Phillip's remark was not aimed at Walter. They enjoyed a working relationship, initially through football, and later the CCPR and the Duke's other connections with sport. Walter got on well with him but he did have to grit his teeth when he was introduced by Prince Phillip as 'He's football: you know those players who go around kissing each other.'

Walter frequently had contact with members of the royal family who were involved in some way in the world of sport and with the Queen herself, and they were often guests at the Queen's garden parties. He was invited to a small private lunch with the Queen in 1962, his last year at the FA, when the eight guests included the famous actress Dorothy Tutin, David Attenborough from the BBC and John Piper who had created the stained glass windows for the new Coventry Cathedral. Walter told Ann afterwards how pleasantly surprised he was at how natural the Queen had been and how much he had enjoyed the general conversation.

In the early days the only staff at the embryonic Sports Council offices in Richmond Terrace were Walter, his efficient and loyal secretary, Sheila Hughes (who had been with him at the Football Association and the CCPR), and Denis Molyneux, his deputy. There was a small team of civil servants and support was provided by the CCPR. Walter and Denis spent long hours together developing strategy and became good friends. Denis recalled that they played squash three times a week at Walter's club, the RAC in nearby Pall Mall, and that he lost on all but one occasion! The RAC Club, of which Walter was a lifelong member, had always been an oasis of calm in a turbulent world. He liked its solid establishment ambience, its marbled swimming pool and the squash courts where he played regularly with the club's Pakistani professional. It was a place where he could take a midday break for squash or a swim and a light snack lunch or entertain more formally in the club's splendid dining room.

A key part of the Sports Council strategy that Walter and Denis developed was the creation of regional sports councils – devolving the execution of policies to a local level – and establishing them was a priority. Councillors and planning officers from local authorities wanted a majority representation on these councils and initially this caused some concern amongst the sports bodies but Howell – a former local authority man himself – knew that the local authorities would be the great financial providers. The CCPR provided the secretariat and the regional sports councils were serviced by CCPR staff.

The results were a revelation, bringing about an astonishing change in the attitude of local authorities. One regional director commented: 'Previously regional staff had been directed to the tradesman's entrance. Now they entered by the front door, sometimes with the red carpet, and were directed to the office of the chief executive or mayor.'

A very significant development was a change in central government policy that had enabled regional and local government to spend more money on sport and recreation, and it was this, coupled with grant aid, which unlocked the potential for large capital sums to be made available for sport. This was the rocket fuel that was ignited by the regional sports councils.

The 1966 World Cup was the first international event that Walter worked on with Denis Howell. The minister had opportunely secured £500,000 from Harold Wilson to assist the Football Association in the preparations for hosting the competition. The overriding need was to bring the selected grounds up to the standard required by spectators and players, but it was also important to provide facilities for the world's media, officials and guests from abroad – international prestige did not rest solely on England's performance on the pitch! To assess these needs and decide how to award Government grants, Howell put together a high powered team: Sir Stanley Rous (President of FIFA), Alan Hardaker (Secretary of the Football League), Denis Follows (Secretary of the FA), Sir John Lang, his principal private secretary and Walter, whose experience as the England team manager in the previous four World Cups was invaluable. Their tour of the grounds attracted widespread TV, radio and press publicity, and helped to create much wider public interest in the competition, which up to that point had seemed rather remote to the British public. Well informed decisions were made on construction priorities and criteria set for the percentage of grant that could be applied to different types of work, which not only ensured that the venues were fit for the event, but as far as possible provide a legacy of long term improved facilities.

England's famous World Cup victory in 1966 was a great fillip to the country – one that Harold Wilson took full political advantage of – and although he said nothing to anyone Walter must have enjoyed much personal satisfaction. He had been involved in the planning of the event at the FA, in the provision of ground facilities with Denis Howell and of course many of the players, including the captain Bobby Moore, had been introduced to the England team when he was the manager. Jimmy Hill thought of Walter's contribution when he remembered the historic moment: 'I can still recall the emotion when the final whistle blew and the players turned to receive the acclaim of the crowd; standing alongside Joe Mercer, we had tears streaming down our cheeks. It wasn't only that England had won; I was thinking of all the faith and hard work that had gone into the development of coaching over the last few years. Walter Winterbottom was the original inspiration of this new era, although it was Alf Ramsey who was the hero of the multitude. Ron Greenwood, another fervent supporter of Winterbottom, produced three of the 11 heroes at West Ham. What a contribution that turned out to be towards England's success!'

In their book, *Sport in Britain*, Richard Holt and Tony Mason asked 'why then did he [Walter] ignore the England team on the eve of its greatest triumph? Was it awareness of the Celtic sensitivity... or did he simply think the World Cup had little to do with the lives of ordinary men and women?' It was a strange question. On the day of that dramatic final he was in fact alongside the BBC TV commentator Kenneth Wolstenholme giving his expert half time summary on the tactics of the two teams. His wife, Ann, dismissed any suggestions that he might have had regrets about resigning as the England team manger three years earlier, that it might have been him and not Alf Ramsey enjoying this moment of glory. 'It did not enter his head', she said. 'There was no jealousy. That would have been sour grapes. He was not that kind of man. He was as pleased and proud as any Englishman.'

But she did recall that he was involved in an embarrassing moment at the banquet for the England team at the Royal Garden Hotel, Kensington: 'A man on our table, I can't recall who it was, was rather drunk and saying "it's all very well Alf Ramsey getting the credit but it was Walter's team." Walter was acutely embarrassed and asked him to desist, but the man continued and threatened that he would stand up and repeat what he had been saying.' Walter and Ann got up and left early to diffuse a potentially embarrassing situation.

Very few people would have known that Walter was also involved in the 1966 World Cup as the director of the FIFA Technical Study Group. It was an idea he suggested to Sir Stanley

Rous in 1965: that a group of experienced coaches should study the World Cup to collect factual data and opinion on preparation by the national coaches. They would study the matches and submit a report with recommendations to FIFA. Five coaches were invited to join the group; from Russia, Brazil, England (represented by Ron Greenwood) Switzerland and West Germany. When Dettar Cramer from West Germany was forced to withdraw because of duties with the German team, Walter was invited to take his place and direct the study.

The 1960s were a period of great social change. The decade may have been called the 'swinging sixties', and best-known for the Beatles, Carnaby Street, Mary Quant, the mini and youth culture, but perhaps more significantly, technology was impacting affluence, mobility and mass communication. 'It was inevitable,' said Walter, 'that our attitudes and habits in sport and physical recreation would change also.' He told the delegates at an international conference for coaches at Crystal Palace in 1966 that 'sport was part of our behaviour: the way we live ... and the two-day weekend and the longer annual holiday had greatly improved the opportunity for leisure activity.'

Television was coming of age and having an important impact on sport. It was estimated that some 400 million people in 29 countries watched the 1966 World Cup Final. For minor sports such as show jumping, skating, swimming, gymnastics and auto cycle cross country, television had been a boon, bringing new sources of revenue and introducing the sports to many new followers. Television had created a new marketing opportunity – sponsorship – and this provided much-needed additional revenue for sport, especially the minor sports.

Walter knew from his experience at the FA how critically important schools were in encouraging the development of sport in adult life. 'It is difficult to exaggerate the immense influence which school physical education and school sport exerts on the whole pattern of post school sporting activity,' he told delegates at the Crystal Palace conference. 'Physical education had a fundamental place in the school timetable and a vast amount of voluntary work was undertaken by teachers outside school hours.' (It was a bitter irony that as more money was provided for facilities and coaching, that sport in schools should experience a decline in the 1980s as the result of decisions by teachers unions to end voluntary help with sport by teachers).

The first Olympiad that Walter attended as Director of the Sports Council was in Mexico in 1968 (he had been to the 1952 Olympics in Helsinki as the manager of the Great Britain football team). Walter understood that athletes did not like meeting dignitaries shortly before their event when their minds were focused on competing. He suggested a schedule to Denis Howell that would allow them to learn about team preparations whilst still encouraging the athletes. His itinerary enabled them to make informal visits to the training camps a week before their event – covering all 26 sports in which GB athletes were competing. Walter knew the heads of all the governing bodies and informally introduced them to Denis Howell. Their interest was well received by athletes and officials alike and it was a routine that Denis appreciated and repeated in subsequent Olympics.

The report of Sports Council working party, 'Planning for Sport', published by the CCPR in 1968, showed a new approach to the challenge of assessing needs for community sports grounds, including swimming pools, sports halls (then a very new idea to local authorities) and other indoor facilities. But the bright future Walter planned was being threatened by a black economic storm cloud.

In the late 1960s Britain sank into a period of economic stagnation. There was never enough money for sport and it was frustrating that the Arts Council seemed less vulnerable to cuts. 'Why does the Arts Council always get more money than we do?' asked an inquisitive John Coghlan. Walter simply shrugged his shoulders enigmatically 'They've got friends in higher places' he said.

Faced with years of economic difficulty and high inflation Walter introduced creative strategies that stretched budgets further. The most successful were 'dual use' and 'joint planning.' The concept of 'dual use' was simple and based on plain common sense: School sports facilities were not being used in the evenings, weekends or in school holidays. 'Why,' argued Walter 'could they not be used by the wider community in these down times, and the schools receive grants if they made their sports facilities available to other users?'

'Joint planning' was an important pioneering concept Walter encouraged, particularly in relation to schools. An education authority developing a new or an enlarged secondary school would include physical education spaces: a gymnasium, a small swimming pool, a dance studio or outdoor playing facilities. If the local authority or municipality could be persuaded, a capital contribution could enlarge the gymnasium to a sports hall, the pool to a full length swimming facility and with other comparatively small additions, such as squash courts or a weight training area, the complex could become a local sports centre serving the school by day and the broader community in evenings, the weekend and school holidays. Regional sports council staff, armed with a growing body of technical experience and research, were the prime movers in bringing together the education authorities and local councils.

But the CCPR was becoming uncertain about its future. The regional staff had fallen under the control of the Sports Council. They were concerned about their weakening autonomy and Justin Evans, the acting General Secretary, was due to retire at the end of 1967. After much discussion a solution was agreed in which Walter would return to his position as General Secretary of the CCPR but would also continue to be the Director of the Sports Council. Walter now had two jobs again, as he had done at the Football Association. It improved the coordination of the two organisations but it was not a solution that made everyone happy.

The matter was raised in the House of Lords on 17 February 1968.

'Mr Winterbottom would be wearing two hats,' said Lord Aberdare a member of the CCPR's executive committee. Lord Aberdare continued, 'No doubt as Director of the Sports Council, he [Winterbottom] had been asked to brief the Government spokesman in the debate. But what would have been his position if he [Lord Aberdare] had asked Mr Winterbottom, as General Secretary of the CCPR to brief him?' The debate contained many expressions of appreciation of the work of both the Sports Council and the CCPR, but also continued to reflect MP's widespread disappointment that the Sports Council was an advisory body and had not been given executive status.

The workload on CCPR staff had increased substantially as a result of demands from the Sports Council, and Walter was sensitive to the pressure on national and regional staff. 'Walter seemed to have a wonderful way of motivating people,' said Denis Molyneux. 'He was always respectful of the expertise of individual staff members and encouraging and supportive of their expertise.' He added: 'Above all else, Walter was a brilliant communicator. I watched him work over a number of years and in a variety of situations – with a group of players on the sports field, a conference of administrators, or a group of hard bitten politicians or chief executives. He had a great ability to establish an early rapport with a group – often with a couple of jokes against himself – before getting over the message of the day succinctly and effectively.'

In 1971 Harold Wilson asked Denis Howell to go to Moscow as the minister representing the British Government for the celebration of the 50th anniversary of the Russian Revolution. The event was to be a spectacular Spartakiada (a traditional Russian festival of sport). The Russians had invited sports leaders from around the world and the Prime Minister agreed that Walter should go with Denis. Harold Wilson had one piece of advice for them based on personal experience: 'They will try to get you drunk, toasts every few minutes, and each time you will be expected to empty your glass. Make sure that when you sit down at the table you ask for a bottle of water and whenever you can fill your vodka glass with water.'

Howell was frequently grateful for Walter's widespread international contacts. On the evening that they flew into Moscow they were met by the Soviet Vice President of FIFA – an old friend of Walter's – who entertained them. Walter, having been to Moscow with the England team, was wary of Russian hospitality. Howell was less experienced and despite Wilson's warnings, felt unwell after a dinner at a Gorky Street restaurant. Walter knew the answer. He knocked on Howell's door in the morning and insisted that he should get up and go to the Moscow baths with Soviet officials who would guarantee a cure.

After the children left home Walter and Ann no longer went to Bantham for their annual holiday. In fact Walter never went on holiday again. He used his annual leave from the Sports Council to coach football, responding to the requests that he had been unable to accept when he was at the FA. He was invited to Turkey, Israel, Egypt, Greece and Mexico by their Football Associations and returned many times, even on occasions running referees courses. He was not paid a fee but all his expenses were met and he was able to take Ann with him and find time to relax.

Coaching football was a pleasant diversion from the ongoing political conflicts in the period from 1965-1972. The Sports Council was still an advisory body, not a fully fledged independent body like the Arts Council as Walter wanted, and the role and status of the CCPR was a thorny problem that worried him. It was his dream to have one umbrella organisation for sport, that was independent of government, but there were many obstacles in the way.

In an initiative to show the way forward Walter wrote a confidential memorandum titled 'The Sports Council and its Future' which was circulated to members of the Sports Council and the CCPR Executive Board. It was a constructive and far-sighted document, and although it fairly reflected the interests of all parties, it was clear that Walter wanted to merge the CCPR with an independent Executive Sports Council. There were many at the CCPR who remained unconvinced and favoured the retention of existing advisory status with certain modifications.

It did not help Walter's cause when, in March 1970, Denis Howell convened a two-day conference of members of the Sports Council, the Sports Councils for Wales and Scotland and Regional Sports Councils. He made it quite clear that in his opinion the Sports Council should remain an advisory body and that the CCPR should continue to carry out its existing functions as an independent organisation.

This was a period in which Walter was walking on eggshells. He was determined to bring change but he had great respect for the experience and loyalty of the CCPR staff and wanted to ensure that they were fairly treated if the CCPR was merged with the Sports Council. But as an advisory body, the Sports Council was directly under the control of government and he was in no doubt that had to change. The Sports Council's relationship with government only worked because Walter had an excellent relationship with Denis Howell, a minister who was committed to sport. There was no guarantee, indeed it was unlikely, that this would continue under any shade of government.

Once again change came with a new government. In June 1970 the Labour Government was defeated and Ted Heath became the Conservative Prime Minister. The shadow Minister for Sport, Charles Morrison, had set up a study group to consider government's responsibilities for sport and recreation and consulted Walter. Their report recommended an executive Sports Council, established by statute and independent of government.

By now Sir Stanley Rous, although regretting the likely disappearance of the CCPR, had concluded – no doubt persuaded by Walter – that amalgamation was a natural solution. Finally in June

1971, Eldon Griffiths, the new Conservative Minister for sport announced his decision 'To enhance the status of the Sports Council, to give it executive powers and widen its responsibilities and seek a Royal Charter similar to that for the Arts Council. The new chairman of the independent body would be Dr Roger Bannister. Scotland and Wales would have their own Sports Councils.

In July 1971 the CCPR accepted the minister's invitation to go into voluntary liquidation, but asked that the interests of the staff should be fully safeguarded and that several members of the CCPR Executive should serve as members of the Sports Council. Finally, after years of navigating rock strewn political waters, Walter was rewarded with an amicable and mutually acceptable solution. No one had done more to bring about this watershed in sporting history than he had. A new age in the chronicle of British sport had begun under the leadership of Walter and his new chairman Dr. Roger Bannister. Walter's efforts were rewarded in the 1972 New Year's Honours list with a CBE for services to sport.

But it was not the last throw of the dice. The capitulation of the CCPR Executive was controversial. 'It was inconceivable to me that the CCPR, as the democratic assembly of sport in this country, entirely voluntary in character, would surrender their position, but they did!' said Denis Howell. An indignant Howell set out to oppose the granting of a Royal Charter, and informed Willie Whitelaw, the minister responsible for Royal Charters, that if it was the CCPR's wish, Her Majesty's Opposition would oppose it in the House. He then informed Sir Stanley Rous, who said that if that was how he felt he should meet with the CCPR Executive and put his point of view. When he arrived he found that Sir Stanley Rous was not present, which seemed unusual. His deputy, Arthur Gem, chaired the meeting. Howell set out his arguments, sat back in his chair, took a long draw on his cigar and waited for questions. To his astonishment there were none. He looked to Walter – still in his dual role as the CCPR General Secretary and Director of the Sports Council – but he remained stony faced and silent. Arthur Gem then thanked Howell for coming and wished him a happy Christmas. Howell was dumbfounded and his opposition to the government's plans collapsed. There were important legal issues affecting the amalgamation, but these were resolved and the acquisition and merger of the CCPR, its staff and its assets, formally took place on 17 April 1972.

Then, in an extraordinary turn of events, HRH Prince Philip, who was President of the CCPR, asked Denis Howell to come to Buckingham Palace. He told him that he had no intention of being the president of a moribund organisation and proposed that the CCPR should be reborn with a new role and asked if Howell would like to be the new chairman. Howell accepted and Peter Lawson, the acting General Secretary, who had been tasked with running down the CCPR prior to joining the Sports Council, was appointed as the new General Secretary. It was a move that took everyone by surprise. 'When it became clear that I had become chairman in order to rescue the CCPR from oblivion the shock to many people was considerable', said Howell. 'One astonished member of the Sports Council staff choked, "Good God, you are going to restart the CCPR!"'

Walter himself was bitterly opposed to the formation of a 'new' CCPR in 1973, and did much to curtail its power and influence; but it remained a thorn in his side for many years to come.

CHAPTER 20

SPORT FOR ALL

1972 – 1978

Sport has the power to change the world, the power to inspire, the power to unite people in a way that little else can.

Nelson Mandela

Walter had worked for 16 years at the Football Association to gain acceptance for coaching at all levels. He spent his next 16 years persuading government of the importance of sport and the need for it to be given a higher priority in the nation's affairs.

The 'Sport for All' campaign was launched to raise the profile of sport, not just with the public and governing bodies but within national and local government. The idea for the campaign came from the Council of Europe, a cultural organisation representing the governments of 15 democratic European nations. Norway had pioneered the concept of sport in the community and it was picked up by the committee chaired by Walter that met to share ideas for the development of sport in Europe.

Walter presented the idea to the Sports Council and the 'Sport for All' campaign, planned and researched under his direction, was launched in the early autumn of 1972. A manifesto was produced setting out its aims and demands for more facilities to meet the anticipated increased growth in participation. A huge print run of 500,000 copies was circulated. Promotional merchandise – including car stickers, posters, button badges, and banners – were widely distributed, while a banner hung underneath the scoreboard at Wembley Stadium proclaimed 'Sport for All.'

The problem with the 'Sport for All' concept was that it was so all-embracing. The Sports Council wanted to make participation in sport more available to the general public but they also wanted to improve international performances. These were objectives at the opposite ends of the spectrum, but in the middle there was a need to provide for specific target groups: housewives, children leaving school, the elderly, the disabled, ethnic minorities. To embrace all social classes where, with the exception of football, sports clubs had traditionally been the preserve of the middle classes, was a Herculean task.

Walter initially focused on local authorities and voluntary clubs. Honorary club officers and officials had been a long standing tradition of amateur sport in Britain, but professional, well-trained full time staff was essential if sport was to develop and be run in a more business-like fashion. Here Walter's experience at the Football Association, the country's oldest and wealthiest governing body, was directly relevant. He saw the need for each sport to have a professional headquarters organisation – sound administration was essential, after all – and more sports should have their own national coach who could develop a coaching network. The Sports Council provided funding and expertise to the voluntary organisations which were the life blood of sport. Sir Roger Bannister believed that this was possibly Walter's most important legacy to sport: 'He raised the standards of governing bodies and gave them new impetus to bringing in professional coaches and wherever possible tried to see that governing bodies [there were 82 of them] had a sound and reliable administration.'

Recognising the need for a comprehensive guide to the planning and design of sport and recreational projects, the Sports Council's Technical Unit for Sport (TUS) was formed with a team of architects, engineers and quantity surveyors. They were briefed to come up with technically sound but innovative and low-cost solutions for sports facilities. Examples of their designs ranged from church conversions to joint provision modern sports halls, from the conversion of disused railway stations to large modern leisure centres, from air-supported structures to timber-roofed swimming pools. The work of the TUS was supplemented by the publication of an ever-increasing range of technical bulletins and pamphlets.

The structure of the Sports Council meant that Walter, the full time chief executive, had to work closely with the part time, but influential, chairman – a relationship that was key to his success at the Sports Council. Denis Howell was Walter's first chairman. Denis was a professional politician who knew the 'ins' and 'outs' of government at national and local level: he knew where the power resided. Perhaps more importantly he had a deep and lasting love of sport at all levels: when asked once by Harold Wilson what his political ambitions were he made it clear that he was content to serve as Minister for Sport and did not seek political advancement. It must have come as a surprise to the Prime Minister. Howell stayed with the sport portfolio and was Walter's minister for 10 of the 14 years he served as Director of the Sports Council. They had a close professional relationship, were good friends and their wives shared this friendship.

Sir Roger Bannister, his next chairman, was in every way different from Denis Howell. He was of course, a sporting legend – the first man to break the four minute mile. In his professional life he was a consultant neurologist of considerable eminence. First appointed to the Sports Council as chairman of the research and statistics committee, where he was supported by Denis Molyneux, he had a considerable intellect and was responsible for research into the connection between fitness and health and later did important research into the problems of drugs in sport.

Sir Roger became the Chairman of the new executive Sports Council in 1972. He was not particularly knowledgeable about sport, other than varsity athletics, but his popular high media profile was a great asset to the Sports Council. Where he lacked experience he turned to Walter. 'We had a very happy relationship,' Bannister recalled. 'He was very much more experienced than I was, having spent his whole life with governing bodies.' Bannister wasn't a political man and was perhaps rather naïve regarding Whitehall, but he was happy to be advised by Walter. 'He had a view of his own about how things should be done' said Bannister. 'He was a leader who directed the organisation and the staff very effectively.' Coghlan thought Walter had a good working relationship with Bannister 'but there was some tension at times. Walter could be a little abrupt and demanding even with his chairman.'

Ann recalled a time when Walter was summoned with Roger Bannister to see Margaret Thatcher who was then Secretary of State for Education and Science. Their intention was to draw her attention to the long term damage caused by her policy of selling-off school playing fields. In the manner for which she was renowned she berated them on a range of issues including football hooliganism. Untypically angry after being unable to speak for 20 minutes, Walter said 'I can see madam, that we are wasting your valuable time.' He stood up and left the room. Everyone was shocked; in the ante room outside an aide rushed up to him and apologised saying that Mrs Thatcher had not been properly briefed on the meeting.

Ministers dealt with Walter. Bannister did not like to argue the point with the Whitehall mandarins; it was something he left to Walter. 'They were terrified of him' said Coghlan. With the exception of Denis Howell, Walter found ministers to be well intentioned but with no real understanding of the business of sport.

Whitehall feared Walter, resenting his power, authority and

expertise. Even worse, he wasn't 'one of them' and couldn't be controlled. A behind-the-scenes effort by civil servants was made to scupper his appointment as Director in 1972, but thankfully for sport it was snuffed out. Walter wasn't even aware of the internal infighting, or if he was, he never made mention of it.

Denis Howell had been the shadow minister for sport since the Conservatives came to power in 1970 and spent his time in opposition as chairman of the 'new' CCPR. It was frustrating for Walter to suffer their constant niggling. It was the only time that Walter and Denis Howell did not see eye to eye. But in the General Election of 1974 Labour returned to power and Howell resumed his post as Minister for Sport. But now things were different. Previously he had been the minister and the Chairman of the Sports Council and a very active 'hands on' chairman at that. Now Bannister was the chairman of a body that was no longer part of a government department, and was protected by Royal Charter. 'Bannister' complained Howell, 'had developed a new style of leadership.'

When Howell asked him what he thought the role of the minister should be, Bannister replied: 'To fight the Treasury for as much money as possible and make this available to the Sports Council to distribute as they determine.' Howell responded, 'You know from previous experience that is not the way I operate.'

The matter came to a head soon afterwards and Bannister tendered his resignation on a point of principle. His successor was Sir Robin Brook, who was already a member of the Sports Council and had been a long standing treasurer of the CCPR. Howell reluctantly had to accept that he was no longer the chairman, but Walter and Sir John Lang worked out a compromise whereby he could attend meetings whenever he wished. It wasn't a situation that Howell liked, but because of the personalities involved he reluctantly admitted that 'it worked reasonably well for the next five years.'

Sir Robin Brook was a man Walter got on with: a man who gave him the support that he needed to get things done. He was a man who did not suffer fools gladly. On one occasion Brook and Winterbottom were summoned to a meeting with Eldon Griffiths, at Marsham Street and were kept waiting in a reception room. After ten minutes an aide announced that the minister had been delayed by half an hour. Sir Robin stood up and said 'Please inform the minister that we have had to go to another meeting.' Vice-Chairman, John Disley, thought Brook was a 'brilliant chairman.'

Coghlan described Walter as an *'éminence grise.'* Like Cardinal Richelieu's grey coated secretary, Walter was the power behind the scenes, always at the heart of things, dealing with ministers, senior civil service mandarins, the chairman, members of the Sports Council and his own senior staff, but he was rarely in the foreground. At Council meetings he spoke in a way that was assured. He was in control and usually got acceptance for his point of view because Council members respected him. Coghlan described Walter as authoritarian in his book *Sport and British Politics*, but later corrected this, saying that he did not mean that he was dictatorial but that he was always in command.

As Walter's Deputy Director, John Coghlan was in a better position than most to observe him at work: 'I learned from his handling of Whitehall. He saw the good in people and encouraged them and he reaped where he sowed. He was a man of vision, authority, dedication and single-mindedness but one who treated his staff with gentleness, kindness and understanding.'

Walter was also not afraid to delegate responsibility and praise staff when it was deserved. His approval for work well done was brief but sincere. Coghlan recalled an occasion when they went to Whitehall to make a case for add on payments for unsocial hours worked by regional staff. Coghlan, who had been the regional director for the West Midlands area, understood that staff in the field frequently had to work in the evenings, so when it came to the presentation Walter asked him to explain the working environment. It went well and the extra payments were awarded. 'Afterwards,'

Coghlan remembered, 'Walter said, "you did well there John." It was nice to have a pat on the back. He was very thoughtful in that way.'

Walter had his own way of handling people, always judging whether a matter was important and avoiding unnecessary conflicts. Coghlan remembered a memo circulated by a senior member of staff which was, in Coghlan's opinion, rude and critical. 'What are you going to do about it?' he asked. 'Nothing' replied Walter. 'I've known him since we were at Carnegie. It's the way he is. Just ignore it.'

Bill Slater, the ex-England footballer, who was chairman of the Sports Development Committee, saw Walter as quite a dominant figure who could be tough: 'A member of the Sports Council spoke very rudely to me in a committee meeting which I was chairing. Later I had a phone call from that person who said "Walter is very, very, angry and I am required to telephone and apologise to you."'

As Vice Chairman, John Disley was also able to observe the way Walter worked and in particular noticed how he handled confrontation: 'He wasn't a pragmatist. He was logical and rational and his decisions came from a background in physical education. He knew when to walk away from someone before they said no. He would say "let's talk about this again" and avoid a show down. It makes for a good administrator.'

In 1976 the Labour government set up a Royal Commission on gambling and asked the Commission to enquire how money raised from gambling could be used for good causes, including sport. John Disley was appointed as one of the commissioners. Hopes were raised when its findings recommended a national lottery with sport as a major beneficiary. But nothing was done. Labour talked about the recommendations and the Conservative Party ignored them. Meanwhile in Western Europe sport continued to thrive on the proceeds of national lotteries and football pools, which supplemented resources made available from central and local government. It was an idea, like so many with which Walter was associated, ahead of its time. Belatedly, under John Major's government a national lottery was launched in 1994 with the proceeds going to good causes. Today, Sport England (formerly known as the English Sports Council) and UK Sport (the organisation responsible for elite performance) receive a total annual funding of £355 million of which £193 million comes from the National Lottery.

With money tight, one of Walter's concerns was how our top athletes could compete at the highest level. He knew that the Soviet system excelled because of heavy state subsidies for full-time athletes, who were often given a nominal state job with a salary that gave them all the time they needed for training and competition. In North America the college sports scholarship scheme was able to nurture the best talent without the athletes having any constraints of time or money. In West Germany a different model had evolved: the Deutscher Sportbund (DSB) – the German Sports Federation, established in 1950 – had worked with the German Olympic Committee to set up the Deutsche Sporthilfe to raise funds to assist sportsmen and women preparing for high-level competition.

For some months Walter had been seized with the idea of emulating the West Germans, and creating a mechanism for injecting finance into elite performance. He met Lord Rupert Neville, the chairman of the British Olympic Association, privately and asked whether the BOA would care to develop this idea in Britain. Together they concluded that it would be politically insensitive to do this with a Sports Council grant when many other social programmes remained unfulfilled. But they could both see that because elite level performance had a high sponsorship profile there was an exciting opportunity to tap new sources of funding.

So on a warm afternoon in the late spring of 1975 Walter called John Coghlan into his office. 'John,' he said, 'I want you to go over to Frankfurt and see how the Deutsche Sporthilfe scheme works in West Germany and then start something similar here.'

It was how Walter managed. He surrounded himself with bright people, told them what he wanted and expected them to get on with it. Coghlan went to Germany and received the maximum cooperation from the Chairman and Director of Deutsche Sporthilfe. Walter decided to set up the Sports Aid Foundation (SAF), closely based on the West German model and Coghlan was given the responsibility for developing the necessary structures. The SAF was launched in autumn 1975 in time to assist potential medal winners in the forthcoming 1976 summer Olympic Games in Montreal. Denis Howell – who had influence and contacts – helped to recruit governors who were successful businessmen with connections in the city, in commerce, industry and show business.

Sport was now being seen as having a wider role in society – adding a new dimension to community life, bridging gaps between ethnic groups and cultures and ameliorating social problems like juvenile crime. In its annual report, the Sports Council chastised the government for not understanding this: 'If we were not so laggardly in providing the right kind of facilities in our cities the outbreaks of violence and vandalism that are not only terrorising citizens here but giving Britain a bad reputation abroad, might not occur.'

It was becoming clear that whilst the development of facilities in Britain was making good progress it was often missing the inner cities. With little money available, what there was had to be used as effectively as possible. Walter understood that good leadership was as important as facilities – he had seen for himself how boys responded to football training on a piece of wasteland in Scotland Road, Liverpool, when he was a student teacher – and he developed a number of experimental leadership schemes in deprived areas. Courses for teachers and leaders were run, and a programme of coaching sessions for football, boxing, weightlifting, athletics, cricket and table tennis was introduced. Some 120 projects were assisted including the provision of 58 hard surfaced kick-about areas. These were rudimentary beginnings but regrettably the lessons were not learned by the government.

Walter believed that if sport was to play a much larger role in society it could only be achieved by large scale government funding. But in accepting government money there was a price to pay. Whitehall held the purse strings and the mandarins wanted control over how it was spent. The adage, 'he who pays the piper calls the tune' was never more apposite. It was a Faustian pact. Only the government had the power, the influence and the finance to change the place of sport in society. But with the money came – despite the protection of a Royal Charter – a gradual erosion of independence. 'It grew like Topsy,' said John Disley. 'Once you got on the roller coaster you couldn't get off. The government was where the money was and sport had to follow the money.'

The Sports Council became more involved in international collaboration, and as Chairman of the Committee for the Development of Sport (CDS), Walter increasingly involved himself in Council of Europe affairs. The 'Sport for All' concept was adopted by Canada and the USA, and later the United Nations used the campaign through UNECSO to spread the gospel of sport in the community to all developing nations. 'His mind and heart was on getting this done' said Coghlan; 'he was highly thought of throughout Europe.'

Soon after Denis Howell returned to office in 1974, Walter went to see him to explain the work he was doing in Europe and the progress that was being made. A particular concern was the politicisation of sport and sports administration in Eastern Europe. Walter encouraged Denis Howell to become involved and add his support to the idea that sports ministers should meet together just as foreign ministers and colleagues from other specialist interests did within the EEC. At this time the Council of Europe had emerged as a major and more widely based organisation – certainly as far as sport was concerned – than the EEC. On the flight to Strasbourg for his first meeting with 23 ministers for sport from Western Europe, Denis Howell was looking over his speech.

'Do you mind if I read it Denis?' asked Walter.

When he finished reading it he queried, 'This isn't you talking is it?'

'No,' Howell replied. 'As a minister my speeches are written by civil servants.'

'Tear it up,' Walter urged, 'You're a natural speaker. It will be far more effective if you say what you want and deliver it off the cuff.'

The speech was well-received and Howell was asked to chair subsequent meetings of European Sports Ministers. Walter had the confidence and that happy knack of being able to make suggestions that would motivate others from any walk or station in life (he once sat next to Princess Diana – who was the guest of honour at a luncheon at Wembley before an England game – and suggested to her: 'Years ago the guest of honour used to go on the pitch and kick the ball off before the start of the game.' She clapped her hands together and with that slightly coy but charming smile she had said, 'oh, I would like to do that!').

On reaching the Civil Service mandatory retirement age of 65 Walter left the Sports Council. He was knighted for his services to sport in the New Year's Honours List in 1978. Looking back on his 14 years at the helm, Walter would have had good reason to enjoy a sense of satisfaction. He had spearheaded a revolution in the provision of sport but it is much more likely that he would have been thinking about how much remained to be done.

There can be no question that financial support (grant aid) from the Sports Council in the 1970s led to immense growth in the provision of sports and leisure facilities by voluntary organisations and sports clubs. Local authorities, backed by encouragement and technical support from the Sports Council, moved mountains: in 1971 there had been 12 sports centres, but 499 had been added by 1981. All-weather sports pitches, many fitted with floodlights and running tracks, were also part of this extensive building programme.

To the 440 swimming pools that existed in 1971, a further 524 were added by 1981. These were facilities that were available to all ages and social groups at low admission prices.

The CCPR took the view in 1985 that 'Sport for All' is not as yet a total reality, but for the very many it has touched it has clearly evoked in them responses and the quality of their lives has been enriched by such contact and experience.'

'Walter was a great leader with a mission,' said John Coghlan. 'He had dreamed the dream and it had brought great success. Today the Sports Council, now renamed UK Sport, is a vibrant organisation with great power, financed by law through the National Lottery. He was the pioneer who brought it all together.'

There was some speculation at the time of his retirement that Walter may have wanted to stay on and take the part time role of Chairman when Sir Robin Brook retired. It seems unlikely. Ann had never heard him mention that possibility. For her part she found him pale and exhausted by a lifetime of service and in the latter years, political battles. When she attended his official farewell party she told the guests: 'You've had the best of him. Now I can take home what's left of him.'

As he left the party Walter's last words to John Coghlan were, 'you will take care of Sheila, won't you.' Sheila Hughes had been his loyal secretary since he had been at the Football Association. He had seen her promoted to an executive position as Secretary to the Sports Council, but worried that she might be vulnerable without his protection. He was right to be concerned: the new chairman, Dickie Jeeps, wanted to sack her. Coghlan made it quite clear that would be unwise, because she was too valuable to senior staff and the Council. Such was her contribution that Coghlan thought she should have been honoured, but with Jeeps there she never was.

Denis Howell was generous in his tribute to Walter:

Walter is the sort of man that you automatically expect to be a permanent fixture. Of all the men I know the description 'he has a safe pair of hands' fits him the best. When, in 1964, I invited him to become the first Director of the Sports Council there was still lingering, if muted hostilities in some quarters, but I never had any doubts that I had taken the right decision. We had differences of opinion from time to time... but we always kept our friendship in good repair and it was a delight to find his great service to sport acknowledged by the award of a knighthood, so richly deserved. I may add that throughout all his public service Walter enjoyed the wonderful support of his wife Ann and British sport has much cause to be grateful for that too.

CHAPTER 21

THE FINAL
YEARS

1978 – 2002

A nn surveyed the avalanche of paper on the dining room table and sighed. 'I thought you were retired now? How am I expected to clean and dust with papers that "may not be disturbed" everywhere?' Walter was working on his technical report on the 1978 World Cup for FIFA.

He felt guilty that he had neglected Ann: guilty about a life with months away from home each year: at coaching courses, on England tours, matches at weekends, trips to the Olympics and World Championships and working late in his study. He had resolved to spend his retirement with Ann and ignore the requests that kept coming along. He had not aspired to a knighthood but he privately appreciated the recognition of his service to sport and was proud to share it with his wife. She was now Lady Winterbottom: she valued the honour and it made him feel less guilty when he did accept assignments in his retirement.

Walter was prudent. Conscious that he was ten years older than Ann, and that his pension would die with him, he arranged his financial affairs so that she would be provided for. They moved from their large family house in Stanmore to a small house on an estate in Cranleigh. Cranleigh – a large village in the leafy countryside in the shadow of the Surrey hills – was a happy choice for his retirement years. It was there that Walter and Ann made a new life for the next 24 years which gave him pleasure and contentment. They were living close to their eldest daughter, Janet, and their four grandchildren who went to school in Cranleigh. The grandchildren were often unannounced guests, often seeking Walter's help with homework. On one occasion Julia, their youngest grandchild arrived on the doorstep one mid-morning and announced that she had run away from school. After giving her a drink and listening to her story, Walter quietly walked her back to the school, where to his concern he discovered that she had not even been missed.

It wasn't difficult for him to accept the invitation from FIFA to go to Argentina for the 1978 World Cup as the Director of the Technical Study. After the first technical report he wrote for FIFA in 1966 he was asked to continue in this role in Mexico (1970) and West Germany (1974). It was a pleasure to be involved again at the highest level of football in his retirement. Although commissioned by FIFA under Sir Stanley Rous and subsequently Dr. João Havelange, Walter's reports – which summarised the observations of an international panel of coaches – were independent and uncompromising in their recommendations. They provided a wealth of information that was of incalculable value to FIFA, future host countries, national football associations and national coaches.

One of the most controversial issues was the structure of both the preliminary and the final competition: everyone had a view on it, especially the media and now, with mass television coverage, the general public. All the national coaches wanted to see a fair competition between the 16 best teams in the world. Europe and South America wanted greater representation. FIFA however wanted to encourage the development of football in the emerging countries in Africa, Asia and North America. Spectators wanted exciting matches without inconsequential games against weak teams or in leagues where the result had no bearing on the outcome. National coaches did not want to see the number of games or the duration of the tournament extended. Walter carefully put forward all sides of the argument with the study group's own recommendations.

His reports contained detailed observations of match play, characteristics of team performances and statistics. Different approaches by team managers to technique, fitness, and training were of special interest to Walter. In Mexico he paid particular attention to team headquarters and the growing importance of issues such as sports medicine, psychological and physiological problems, and the integration of players from different social backgrounds.

Match control was always a contentious issue in the World Cup. Wide differences could be seen in a referee's interpretation of the laws, not just between countries in northern and southern Europe, but more significantly between Europe and South America. Red and yellow cards were introduced in Mexico in 1970, but in Argentina in 1978 Walter noted that some referees did not caution players or show the yellow card even for serious fouls. He made comprehensive recommendations on how higher standards of refereeing should be achieved.

Walter hated the defensive football that dominated the 1970s: even the national coaches who were its perpetrators regretted it. The trouble was that the high stakes of winning and losing and the success of the Italian *catenaccio* system, encouraged the defensive football which was so unattractive to spectators. Coaches set up their teams to avoid losing a match in the group stage at any cost. It was a subject that Walter gave much thought to. The problem was that coaches believed that it was easier to get good results by playing defensively. There were some who argued that only a change in the laws of the game could change this negative obsession with defensive techniques. Walter did not agree. The study group argued, and national coaches agreed, that the remedy lay in the hands of coaches and players. Walter believed that until bold attacking play could be seen to succeed, then the defensive game, with its screens of seven to eight players in front of the goalkeeper and only two or three attackers, would predominate.

Ubiquitous defensive tactics prevailed but where others despaired Walter saw hope. In West Germany in 1974 he reported, 'those who put their faith in a return to attacking football in the future will be encouraged to learn that the two teams who consistently produced high returns in the number of penetrative attacks were the two finalists – West Germany and the Netherlands.' He had kept an analysis of penetrative attacks using a simple technique he had developed; he ignored all play which took place in midfield, concentrating on play when an attack was made into a 25 metre zone from the goal line at either end. An attack was only recorded if it appeared to be a threat to goal – for example a long pass from downfield which was immediately cleared was not recorded. A corner was.

With growing worldwide television coverage the pressure to win at all costs increased the pressure on fair play. Fair play had always been a cornerstone of Walter's values in life and in the game itself. 'Football is a game to be enjoyed,' he wrote. 'Unfair methods of play provoke antagonism and destroy the genuine competitive spirit of sport. They spoil the game for those who participate and those who watch. Much of the game's future rests with coaches everywhere. They are the educators; they can instill the desire in young players to behave correctly – to play with strength and skill, shunning any cheating or foul act.'

Walter went to Spain as a member of the FIFA Technical Study group for the last time in 1982 and Heinz Marotske was one of the coaches on the panel. 'Walter was a wonderful man' he said. 'There are three things that you need to know about Walter. He was a gentleman. That was proved many times. He was English and that could have made it difficult for him because Germany, Switzerland, Austria and Netherlands all had much more advanced coaching systems than England, but it was not a problem for him because he was so knowledgeable. And the third thing is that he knew how to write reports that got to the heart of the matter.'

Walter continued to be consulted by FIFA on coaching matters as a member of the FIFA Honorary Panel for Coaching Courses until he was 81.

Inevitably as a celebrity, however unassuming, in a small community Walter was frequently asked to take part in local affairs and was always willing to present prizes, give talks about football or serve as the president of local sports clubs. He was invited to join the Cranleigh branch of Probus. For many senior business and professional leaders retirement can come as a serious shock to the system, sometimes even leading to depression and ill health. Probus is an international organisation which helps them to make the adjustment, providing an opportunity for members to meet like-minded individuals for fellowship. Meetings are informal, limited in numbers and usually take place over a luncheon with a guest speaker. Walter was an enthusiastic supporter throughout his retirement, serving his term as chairman during which he formed a second Cranleigh group to cater for its growing popularity.

But despite his resolution to spend all his time with Ann it was inconceivable that a man like Walter would not be tempted to take up projects that challenged or interested him. Denis Howell, who had appointed Walter as his personal advisor, asked him to go to Australia and New Zealand in 1979. His primary role was to use his experience at the Sports Council to advise these countries on the role of government in developing sport in the community. At the same time, as a member of the FIFA honorary coaching panel, he was invited to coach football, and it was this that grabbed the newspaper headlines as he undertook an arduous six week whistle-stop tour throughout the subcontinent. As the ex-England manager he attracted huge interest wherever he went. He was doing what he loved best, with his track suit on, coaching players at all levels and inspiring audiences with his passion for coaching. The national newspaper, *The Australian,* hailed him as 'Soccer's Visionary.'

Dennis Howell also asked him to advise the Government on how British interests overseas could be promoted through sport and suggest ways in which British manufacturers of sports equipment could compete with foreign firms. It was the kind of challenge he relished.

Walter was shocked to find that a mere £17,000 was allocated by the British Government to sports programmes overseas. In contrast France spent FF10.6m and in addition paid the salaries of 400 overseas teachers of physical education. Germany was spending DM 11.2m. It was clear to him that European industrial nations had embarked upon a new kind of colonialism: spreading their economic power and political influence. They did it for political and ideological reasons and benefited from business growth and export trade. And they used their influence very successfully. Britain, meanwhile, was simply left behind. What the government failed to understand was that developing countries saw sport as a way of gaining major influence on the world stage: a way for an emerging country to be seen and heard. Cultural links favoured by the British Council just did not cut it. The blindingly simple issue was eloquently summed up by one distinguished Kenyan visitor to the Sports Council who pleaded: 'Send us please more sports administrators and coaches and less oboists.'

By the time Walter presented his report, Margaret Thatcher had swept to power in the 1979 election and Denis Howell had been replaced by the new Conservative Minister for sport, Hector Munro. The report was clear, concise and made specific recommendations. The response, however, was discouraging; in some cases the issue was misunderstood, perhaps deliberately, and then the whole matter was dropped, never to be seriously raised again by the government. Walter was disappointed and frustrated. It resurrected – as it had in 1953 when the Hungarians came to Wembley – the spectre of a nation that was arrogant, resting on former glories and unwilling to accept that other countries may have found a better way to do things.

Even with these duties Walter still had plenty of time to try new sports. He taught himself to play golf, reached a respectable handicap and coached his grandson Peter. He bought golf coaching books and studied the game. He practiced shots over and over again. Although he belonged to the local golf and country club and had a regular foursome, he gained as much pleasure from practicing on his own on the nine-hole course at Cranleigh School. If an approach shot failed to reach the green he would drop balls until he got the shot right. Bowls was another game that Walter discovered late in life. The league matches stirred his competitive instincts and he enjoyed the companionship that came from playing in a team again. And there was still time to indulge his love of cricket: he was not to be disturbed whilst watching every ball of an England test match on television.

In 1979, the year after he retired, he was made an Honorary Vice President of the Football Association. It was a fitting reward for his outstanding contribution to English football and his loyalty to the Football Association. Sir Walter was in illustrious company with the Duke of Marlborough, the Earl of Derby, Air Vice-Marshal Hall, Admiral Sir Terence Lewin, Lt-Gen Sir James Wilson, Sir Andrew Stephen, Sir Stanley Rous, Sir Cyril Hawker, Lord Netherthorpe, the Earl of Harewood and Sir Denis Follows. It was an honour that meant a great deal to him.

The principle benefit of being an Honorary Vice president of the FA was being invited to every FA match at Wembley as a VIP guest. Football and the three lions of England were carved into Walter's heart and he attended every England game and every FA Cup Final for the next 22 years, sometimes taking an awestruck grandchild with him. These were occasions he really looked forward to. At the luncheon prior to an afternoon match or the dinner after evening kick-offs he would circulate the room. Walter knew almost everyone it seemed and they greeted him enthusiastically. Neither did he hesitate to introduce himself to those he didn't know. He was treated with much warmth and great respect by FA officers, in particular Bert Millichip who was the Chairman from 1981-1996; Ted Croker who was the Secretary from 1973-1989 and Graham Kelly who followed him from 1989-1998. Although Walter had been out of football for many years he kept up to date with players, teams and tactics. Everyone wanted to know what he thought about the match and because his views were based on his statistical observations and the record of penetrative attacks that he noted on the back of the team sheet, they listened with interest. His passion for football and loyalty to the England team did not diminish with age. When England lost or performed poorly he felt the pain as much he did when he was the manager. But he was never critical of England or club managers, always seeing the positives and empathising with their problems. 'He used to write me fantastic letters of support when I was the England manager,' Bobby Robson recalled.

Walter enjoyed the opportunity to mix with the interesting people who came to Wembley, whether they were the Prime Minister or the Archbishop of Canterbury, the Chairman of the FA, an FA councillor, a member of the staff or a former England player; and they were always interested to talk to him. He would speak frankly and honestly on any subject but was always discreet. When asked by a director of Newcastle United about the performance of his team, Walter would say, 'you have got a good new manager. He will know better than me.'

Walter always cared about the coaches he knew and respected. Terry Venables would often see him at England matches: 'He would always come across the room to speak to me, ask me for an update and how things were going – others would just raise a hand to acknowledge you. He was always very interesting to talk to; he was an innovator of the top quality. He put the marker down for the FA and others to follow.'

Even in later years when he had a good idea he did not hesitate to pursue it. Like many others, he was often frustrated by players who failed to retreat the full ten yards at free kicks. Watching the 1995 Cup Final between Everton and Manchester United, with bright sun shining on a perfectly cut green pitch with ten yard stripes, the idea suddenly occurred to him: 'Why don't referees use the stripes as a guide to enforcing the ten yard distance?' He wrote to Ken Ridden, the Director of Refereeing at the Football Association who agreed with his suggestion that clubs should standardise the width of stripes and promised to take the matter up with the FA Technical Committee and representatives of the Premier League and the Football League.

Walter remained willing to help football whenever he could. In 1982 his name was suggested at a press conference held by League Secretary Graham Kelly which announced the formation of a committee to make proposals for the restructuring of the Football League. No Chairman was announced, but Kelly said they were looking for 'someone who is independent and can take an impartial view.' Brian Scovell, writing in the *Daily Mail* suggested that 'Winterbottom, who retains the respect of the football community, meets those requirements.' In an interview Scovell asked Walter if he was willing to be considered and he replied:

Whoever takes the post will find it a difficult job. I'm ready to do my bit if asked because I would do anything I can to help the game. Restructuring the League has been talked about many times but there have not been many changes because the ninety two clubs have always looked at it from their own point of view... but there's more to it than reducing the First Division. The malaise goes deeper than that. There are so many other reasons why football is less appealing these days, including the change in sporting habits and the rise in popularity of other sports. The hooligan element has had a serious effect on attendances. It's an accumulative thing. Once people start grumbling that tends to influence other people and it spreads.

Scovell went on to say that as a former FA man Walter might find that the League would prefer someone more independent but it was unlikely that they would find anyone of his unique background. He was not invited to serve.

In the 1980s Walter was in the public arena again when he became involved in the controversial issue of artificial playing surfaces. In the 1950s, frustrated by the condition of pitches during the depths of winter, he had encouraged the development of all-weather playing surfaces for training and taken a keen interest in how manufacturers were making technical developments. He had always believed that synthetic grass had the potential to provide an all-weather playing surface for competitive matches which would overcome the impossibility of playing good football on grass pitches that were frequently bare, bumpy, frozen or muddy. So in 1984 when the Football Association asked him to be chairman of an Advisory Group to look into the use of artificial grass surfaces in League Football he willingly accepted the challenge.

The reason for the investigation stemmed from a request the Football League received from Queen's Park Rangers (then in the Second Division) to play their fixtures on artificial turf. (By a strange and prophetic coincidence, ten years earlier when Terry Venables was a player with Queens Park Rangers, he had written a futuristic novel titled *They Used to Play on Grass*.) Jim Gregory, the entrepreneurial chairman of QPR, concerned that a major property asset, the stadium, was underutilized, saw the commercial possibilities: minimal maintenance costs but above all a revenue generator with multiple use by other local football teams, other sports such as hockey, American football and even pop concerts. This was something outside the scope of the League rules but after much discussion and consultation the League approved the QPR request and over the following four years 12 more clubs from lower leagues received permission to play on artificial turf.

Although most clubs had serious reservations this was clearly something that the FA had to take seriously. Aware of the emotional resistance he faced Walter knew that only a factual and scientific response could dissolve the myths surrounding what the cynics called 'plastic pitches' and with the help of the Sports Council, technical tests were carried out which were designed to measure every aspect of ball and player interaction with the surface. It was the first comparison study ever done. 11 grass pitches in various divisions of the League were examined scientifically and compared with synthetic pitches then in existence. 'We laid down measurements by which artificial surfaces would have to compare with the best of the new sand structured type grass pitches' said Walter. 'The performance of some of the grass pitches was quite hopeless.'

'The Winterbottom Report,' which was published in 1985, established criteria by which future requests to the Football League Management Committee were judged. The required standard was presented to synthetic pitch manufacturers at a conference at Lilleshall and it was on this information that future development was based. The Winterbottom Report was the only major scientific research on the subject in the world and attracted widespread international interest.

It should have paved the way for the future but three years later resistance to all-weather artificial pitches continued unabated. Clive White, writing in the *Daily Telegraph* commented: 'With the sort of ill-timing, not to mention lack of forethought which England's national game sometimes delights in, criticism of all-weather artificial pitches reached boiling point this week just as the popular grass surfaces yielded to sub-zero temperatures.' He was referring to the remarks of Liverpool manager Kenny Dalglish after Liverpool played Luton at Kenilworth Road. Reiterating the view of his Everton counterpart, Howard Kendal, Dalglish declared that 'they should all be ripped up. They're ideal for training on, that's all.' 24 hours later, reported White, the Football League management committee announced they would be supporting West Ham's proposal to suspend further introduction of these pitches for three years.

Not for the first time in his life Walter found himself frustrated by the football establishment's unwillingness to have an open mind to new ideas. When he came back from the 1950 World Cup in Brazil with Stanley Rous they tried to introduce the idea of floodlit football matches. It was met with similar suspicion and mistrust. 'Everyone opposed it,' said Walter; 'yet initially we only suggested it for training purposes. It was a further two years before the football authorities permitted them, and then only in certain matches where both clubs were in agreement.'

Despite stubborn resistance to artificial pitches he remained optimistic. 'As time goes on these pitches will improve. We're getting to the stage where they will be able to produce a pitch that can improve upon the performance of a good grass surface. But the development needs a little time. I could understand them slowing down the introduction of artificial pitches, but I think closing the door like this is quite ridiculous.' He refuted the idea that teams with these pitches had an advantage. 'This hasn't proved to be so. In fact they've played just the same away and got better results. Anyway most clubs now practice on these pitches more than they play matches on grass.'

In the light of ongoing controversy the Football League appointed a Commission of Enquiry into Playing Surfaces with David Dein (then Vice-Chairman of Arsenal) appointed as Chairman. Walter, now the leading authority on artificial surfaces, was invited to be one of the members.

The Commission's enquiry was comprehensive and wide ranging, covering all aspects of the playing characteristics of both natural and synthetic grass and how natural grass surfaces could be improved.

The Winterbottom Report was used as a technical yardstick. Extensive interviews were undertaken with club administrators, players, managers and referees; consumer research took into account the views of the paying public. Its work included consultations with the leading manufacturers of synthetic pitches, research into injuries on both types of pitches and study of the commercial benefits of synthetic football pitches.

After 16 meetings and two years of investigation, the Commission's report was inconclusive and subjective. Although synthetic pitches compared well with grass in all aspects except the speed of ball roll – which was faster – the majority opinion favoured the tradition of natural grass. Their recommendation was to ban all artificial surfaces in the First Division and Second Division (with the exception of Luton Town, Oldham Athletic and Preston North End). In the face of such stubborn resistance the experiment failed and in 1994 Preston North End became the last club to abandon their synthetic pitch.

Walter remained phlegmatic: 'Traditionally those people who played on grass, and love to play on it, will continue to do so. But the new generation won't mind which they play on. It was the same with tennis and hockey. In the long run it will come. I just hope it isn't delayed too much by prejudice.'

The debate continues and technology has helped manufacturers to make significant improvements. In 2001 FIFA launched its 'Quality Concept for Football Turf' which 'mirrors the quality of natural grass pitches required to play the game at a very high level.' In 2008 the European Championship qualifying match between Russia and England was played on an artificial pitch in the Luzhniki stadium in Moscow. On 18 November 2011, BBC Sport's correspondent Paul Fletcher wrote 'artificial pitches could make a shock comeback if some Football League Clubs get their way.' In his article Fletcher explained how much better artificial pitches are today and that top clubs in Italy, France, Netherlands, Switzerland and Russia are using them. The latest of these pitches is called the third generation, more commonly known as '3G'. There are now plans for a fourth generation. They are considered by many to be better than grass for most of the English season.

The international tide of acceptance for artificial turf has turned but England lags behind. Football League rules require a vote in favour by 50 per cent of clubs. There is support amongst some lower tier clubs but even optimists think it could take ten years before artificial pitches are accepted. Walter, if he was still alive, would no doubt have smiled wryly and shrugged his shoulders. His wish that 'it isn't delayed too long by prejudice' now seems a forlorn hope, but it is ever more likely that his vision that football will be played on artificial turf which is as good as, or better than natural grass, will eventually be realised.

The Commission of Enquiry into Playing Surfaces was not the first public enquiry Walter had served. In 1971 he had the unenviable task of heading the government enquiry in to the Ibrox disaster when 66 people were crushed to death attempting to exit the stadium by the fatal stairway 13. The enquiry discounted the initial version of events which suggested that fans who were leaving tried to get back in when Colin Stein scored an equaliser for Rangers in the last seconds. The enquiry believed that the crush was caused simply by the downward force of so many supporters attempting to leave at the same time. The momentum of the crowd meant that once people started to fall there was no way of holding the mass of bodies back and crash barriers buckled. His report made extensive recommendations and ground safety remained a subject on which he felt strongly. He was an early advocate of all-seater stadia and was often consulted on the subject.

In the 1970s and 80s a malaise gripped soccer: defensive play, violence on the field, soccer hooliganism, falling attendances and corruption were on-going concerns for the football authorities. The *Daily Mail* ran a series on soccer's problems – 'Soccer in Our Time.'

Brian Scovell headlined his article: 'WINTERBOTTOM IS THE MAN TO STOP THIS CORRUPTION'. Scovell went on to reveal the generally held view amongst managers that professional football had become corrupt. The reporter instanced bribes to the parents of schoolchildren, 'tapping up' players at other clubs who then mysteriously lose form, illegal hand outs, illegal bonuses and even it was suggested bribes to opposition players to influence a result.

Scovell continued: 'The game needs someone to revolutionise the thinking of the people in it, merge the two controlling bodies and start planning for the future generations of footballers. I can think of only one man who has integrity and credentials to carry through this enormous mandate – former England team manager Walter Winterbottom.'

The further the years rolled by from the halcyon days of post-war football, the greater was the interest in the period. Nostalgia for the era of the golden greats such as Mathews, Finney, Lofthouse, Wright, Edwards and Byrne grew, and Walter was regularly asked for interviews by biographers, journalists and TV and radio producers. He was mildly amused that anyone was interested after so long, but was always pleased to help, provided that he was sure that he would not be asked to make any comments about the FA or subsequent England managers. In 1993 he participated in a BBC 2 TV series on the *History of British Football* and two years later in a BBC Radio 5 series on famous players. In 1999, just three years before he died, he was the subject of an in depth interview with Jimmy Hill in a series for Sky Sports called *The Last Word*.

In his later life Walter thought more about religion. Ann had always been a regular churchgoer and now they went to church together. They discussed the fact that he had never been confirmed and she encouraged him to think about it. The turning point was meeting a new vicar, the Reverend Nigel Nicholson. He and Walter had stimulating intellectual discussions and soon Walter did sign on for confirmation classes. It was an enlightening experience which he shared with his family without being overzealous. The evening class for adults covered all ages and the discussions were lively with Walter challenging any aspects that did not make sense to him (the Reverend Nicholson later said that confirmation classes were never the same after Walter left!). At the age of 78 he was confirmed and an extraordinary thing happened. When it was Walter's turn to come forward for the laying on of hands by the bishop, Ann, who was in the front row next to Walter heard muffled movement behind her. As she turned around she saw the whole congregation in the packed church rise to their feet unbidden in a spontaneous and silent expression of their love for the man. It was a meaningful and moving moment.

The church and its community became an important part of Walter's life and he valued the fellowship that it brought. Encouraged by his friend Nigel Nicholson he and Ann renewed their marriage vows in a touching service and celebration of their marriage on the occasion of their 50th wedding anniversary.

Throughout his life Walter was always generous in helping his family. As a young man playing for Manchester United he had bought a house for his parents. Following their deaths he kept in close touch with his relatives in Oldham by phone and by letter (he was a diligent letter writer) and was touched when his brother in law, Jack Dakin, (who had married his sister Fanny), wrote with family news and told him that his Robin Reliant (a three wheeler van) had packed-up, but he was saving up for a second hand one he had seen that was in immaculate condition. With no further ado Walter sent him the money and was 'tickled-pink' when Jack sent him photos of the new van.

Sir Stanley Rous died in July 1986 at the age of 91. His death marked the end of an era in football. Amongst his last words were 'I do hope football never becomes anything other than a game.' He was honoured with a memorial service in Westminster Abbey where friends and representatives from football and the wider world of sport came to pay tribute to this great man. Walter read the first lesson. As he sat in his pew he must have reflected on the enormous impact that Sir Stanley had on his life and perhaps his good fortune in meeting him for the first time at Carnegie College forty seven years earlier. When asked what she thought Walter's relationship was with Sir Stanley, Rose-Marie Brietenstein, his long standing personal assistant, thought carefully and then replied: 'I don't think it was as if they were close friends. Their relationship was a professional one, but they had enormous personal respect for each other.' They shared the same values and had an unshakable mutual trust, as was evidenced by Stanley's choice of Walter as the executor of his will.

Walter had his share of setbacks in life but nothing could have prepared him for the sudden death of his son, Alan. He and Ann were staying at their daughter Janet's house. It had been a glorious summer's day and all the windows and doors were open to catch the faint evening breeze. He was watching television when the phone rang. It was Alan's wife, Amanda with the most terrible news: Alan was dead. He was only 39. It seemed incomprehensible. They had been on holiday together in Formentera in the Balearics. Amanda had returned early and had just received a phone call to say that Alan had been on a boating trip and suffered an aneurism. By the time he could be taken to hospital he was dead. On hearing the news Walter was silent for a long time. He did not talk about it then, later or ever again. He did not even discuss it with Ann. It was a profound and terrible shock but in his silence there was a sense that this was something that one had to bear with fortitude and dignity. Perhaps it was also something common to his generation – the need to suppress emotions, the British stiff upper lip – but it was also part of his own character; he was a warm loving person but always in control of his feelings.

As Walter's 80th birthday approached he was asked what he felt about a big party to celebrate his life. He was not against the idea and Jimmy Hill, who was a long-time friend and admirer, offered to organise it. Jimmy knew all the old England players and he had also been a member of the Sports Council, so was ideally qualified. He suggested that the party should be held at the Savoy Hotel where the general manager was a Fulham supporter. (Jimmy had been both a player and chairman at Fulham FC). He offered Jimmy very favourable terms and helpfully provided sponsors for the champagne and wine on the understanding, naturally, that he would be invited to sit on the same table as Johnny Haynes.

It was an evening that brought Walter much pleasure and everyone an unbridled night of nostalgia. The list of 80 guests – from football, the CCPR and the Sports Council – included Tom Finney, Nat Lofthouse, Johnny Haynes, Jimmy Armfield, Bobby Charlton, Don Howe, Bill Slater, Sir Roger Banister, Denis Howell, Bert Millichip, Bill Nicholson, Bertie Mee and Walter's secretary of 34 years, Sheila Hughes. Despite his age and the emotion of the occasion Walter spoke with the warmth, sincerity and humour that his friends remembered. Instead of formal speeches in reply they were offered an open mike to pay their tributes, with a fair share of good natured leg-pulling:

John Disley (past Vice-Chairman of the Sports Council): 'Walter used to send me out all over the country to dinners and openings and give me my speech. Where's my speech tonight Walter?'

Bobby Charlton: 'The trouble was Walter we couldn't understand your half time talks.'

Jimmy Armfield [on getting his first cap against Brazil in front of 160,000 in the Maracana Stadium]: 'Walter, you picked me for my first cap at left back. You said, "They've got Julinho on the right wing. He's very quick but I am sure you can hold him." My first touch in international football was to pick the ball out of the net after 90 seconds!'

In his final years Walter's health began to fail. The first sign came at the Manchester United v Crystal Palace Cup Final. During the official luncheon he collapsed at the table. He was immediately rushed to the Wembley emergency medical centre. Nothing untoward was discovered and he was well enough to go home after a few hours (he was disappointed when he heard he had missed a 3-3 thriller!). There were repeats of this symptom and upsettingly for him it happened three more times at Wembley over the next few years, suggesting that it might have been brought on by excitement or stress. He was deeply upset and embarrassed by these public incidents which finally led to him declining future invitations to matches.

He had become very averse to stress. Just over two years before he died he was watching the 1999 UEFA Champions League Final between Manchester United and Bayern Munich on television. At half time, with United losing 1-0, he went to bed, saying that watching the game was too stressful. When United scored twice in the final three minutes of extra time the shouts of others rang through the house. It distressed him. How sad it seemed that the man who had led his England team out in front of hostile crowds of 100,000 in stadiums around the world, should now find it too stressful to watch the club he probably cared most about winning the Champions League.

There were warning signs about his health in the last two years. It was a difficult, painful and unpleasant time. His doctor had suggested a hospital examination but he never went. Five months before he died he sent an e-mail to his six grandchildren. Perhaps it was prescient but above all the missive epitomised his optimism and enthusiasm for life:

I realise that I am fast approaching the venerable age of 90 years and as I get older I am given to moments of happy reflection and contemplation of the past present and future. Like Louis Armstrong, the American singer with the husky voice, 'I see skies are blue and raindrops too, and I say to myself what a wonderful world.'

I recall things about my early life in Oldham, such as marching through the streets playing my drum in the Boy Scouts band and, then learning how to dance in the studio of my ex-schoolboy chum and helping to organise the visit of a thousand Oldham schoolchildren to London, and I say to myself 'What a Wonderful World.'

Then the wartime years and the great joy of meeting Ann, and dancing and dining with her in posh London restaurants despite the flying bombs: and now the unfolding futures of grandchildren and great-grandchildren. Yes, it's a wonderful world!

So do keep in touch Peter, Nicola, Stephen, Julia, Rebecca and Charlotte.

As always,

Grandpa

Walter was taken to the Royal Surrey County Hospital on 8 February 2002 for an operation. When he was opened up a cancer of the colon was discovered that was so far advanced that it was inoperable. He died on Saturday evening, 16 February 2002. Ann, Janet, Brenda and his grandchildren took turns to keep a 24 hour vigil by his bed. His granddaughter, Charlotte, was there at the moment he died.

A thanksgiving service for his life was held on 1 March 2002 at St Nicolas Church, Cranleigh. St Nicolas, a large church, was rarely full, but on this occasion it was packed: on one side family and friends and on the other a distinguished gathering from the world of football and sport. Amongst the readings and addresses his granddaughter, Julia, read the words from Louis Armstrong's song, 'It's a Wonderful World'.

He will be best remembered by the nation as the first England team manager. He could be proud of his record over 16 years: played 139, won 78, drew 33, lost 28: goals for 383, against 196 – a win percentage of 56 per cent. Comparisons with other England managers would be invidious or misleading but to put it into context Alf Ramsey – who is considered by many to be the most successful of the 14 England managers that followed, and of course won the World Cup – managed 113 games and had a win percentage of 61%.

Walter built three great England teams: the golden era of Hardwick, Matthews, Finney, Carter and Mannion, which from 1946 to 1948 enjoyed a run of 18 unbeaten games with 16 wins; then, prior to the Munich air disaster in 1957, with Wright, Edwards, Byrne and Taylor, his team won 13 and lost only one of 18 matches. Then in the glorious season of 1960/61, with Greaves, Charlton, Robson, Haynes and Armfield, England won seven out of nine games, losing only one, and the team amazingly racked up 45 goals (an average of 5 per game!) with only 14 goals against. History will not show what part luck, timing and disaster played, only that England failed to advance past the quarter-finals in four World Cups.

Inevitably, as every England manager who followed discovered, he was the scapegoat when England lost. As he said himself with an ironic smile, he would be remembered more for the loss of England's home record to Hungary in 1953 and the humiliating defeat by the USA in the World Cup in 1950, than the glorious victories he most enjoyed: 10-0 away to Portugal in 1947, 4-0 away to Italy in 1948, 4-2 at home to Brazil in1956 and 9-3 at home to Scotland in 1961.

Perhaps Jimmy Armfield summed it up astutely: 'He had a difficult time, did Walter. An amateur and antediluvian Football Association never gave him the final responsibility for selecting his team. In the early years he had to deal with players from the golden age who thought they had nothing to learn from coaching. Initially club managers from the 'old school' were resistant to his ideas and the changes he was trying to bring about. He was criticised by some football writers for being tactically inept and unable to communicate with players in their own language. It was true that he was an intellectual, and that this gave him the capacity to think deeply about the game and the changes that he needed to make, but it was an unfair criticism. In fact Bill Slater dismissed it: 'He was a qualified teacher and he expressed himself well. If some did not want to listen to what he had to say that was their problem. There were players who would not respond to coaching from anyone. I played with

Stanley Matthews when I was at Blackpool. He had his own routine. It never crossed his mind that coaching could help him and he could not see that coaching could help other members of the team to get the best of his own undisputed skills.' But football writers like Brian Glanville and David Miller frequently made the criticism which was raised in the anonymous obituary in the *Daily Telegraph*: 'Winterbottom's problems were compounded by his failure to communicate with his players. Although he shared their background, his pedagogic manner and long winded tutorials on opponents, led them to complain that it was like being at the Oxford Union.'

Incensed by the obituary, Jimmy Hill wrote a letter to the *Daily Telegraph* in response:

Sir,

Walter Winterbottom, charming man that he was, would already have forgiven the compiler of your somewhat misleading obituary of February 19. To suggest that Walter could not communicate, let alone inspire professional players, is nonsense. If there were those that could not understand his theories, they were in a measly minority. If some superstars initially made fun of his educated approach they soon came to appreciate what he had to offer.

If there was a criticism that even his devoted supporters might concede it was perhaps that he was too nice. Billy Wright, such an admirer of his manager thought 'he was not afraid to criticise either, but there were times when he could have been more emphatic with erring players. I felt that if he had been blunter he would have lent far greater weight to his points and that the players concerned would have felt their responsibilities more.'

It was a point echoed a decade later by Jimmy Armfield: 'Walter was phlegmatic. On occasions it's good to deal with it. I remember we were playing against Scotland, Alf was the manager. The ball came to me on the edge of the box and I turned and kicked it into

Baxter's legs and he ran through, crossed the ball and they scored. Alf Ramsey came up to me after the match and I said 'I'm sorry, it was my fault, I should have booted it away.'

He said 'you won't do that again will you?'

'No' I said.

'No, you won't,' he replied.

'What he meant' explained Armfield 'was if you do that again you will be out. Now Walter would never have said that, but Alf did.'

Armfield thought perhaps Walter was too loyal to his players. It echoed the criticism previously made by Desmond Hackett of the *Daily Express* when Walter resigned from the FA: that he could not bring himself to become a ruthless disciplinarian and protected his players against criticism.

Walter's legacy to English football, however, is not as manager of the national team, but as the founder of the national coaching structure. He made no secret of his belief that his job as FA Director of Coaching was the more important of the two roles. He coached the coaches. His courses at Lilleshall inspired a new generation of coaches to preach his gospel and laid the foundations for England's success in 1966. It was his influence on men like Buckingham, Brown, Allison, Nicholson, Hill, Sexton, Greenwood, Robson and Howe that may be seen as his greatest contribution to dragging English football out of its complacent isolation. His technical knowledge was profound and it was disseminated from international players to schoolboys, at coaching courses, in his ground-breaking book, *Soccer Coaching* and through publications and films.

There was universal praise in the obituaries for Walter's work as FA Director of Coaching, but they neglected to credit his part in the foundation and early years of the Sports Council. It was here that he made a difference to the lives of people everywhere, elite athletes, men and women, boys and girls, of every age, from every social class. There can hardly be a town or city in the England that now has a swimming pool or multi-purpose sports centre that was not directly or indirectly a result of Walter's inspiring leadership and passion to increase the importance of sport in society. Sports governing bodies are now more professionally run and able to provide grass root and elite coaching facilities that were in no small part due to his drive and organisational ability.

After he died, there were tributes from sports writers, players, coaches and managers who remembered him affectionately as much for the person he was as for his professional career. He was kind, sincere and deeply loyal to his players and his staff. His enthusiasm and encouragement touched everyone with whom he dealt. 'I've never met a more cultured man,' said Jimmy Greaves. 'He was a true gentleman, kind and intelligent. I was only 19 when I made my first appearance for him and he looked after me like I was his own son.'

Beneath the easy manner that made him at home in any company was a man with a deep knowledge of the game, a man of vision with sharp intelligence and unimpeachable integrity. Unconcerned with his own achievements, he was not only devoid of ego but always seemingly concerned with higher and more pressing affairs.

There were many who wondered how English football might have developed if he had not been so shamefully passed over for the job as Secretary of the FA – a job for which even his most severe critics thought that he was admirably suited.

Jimmy Hill wrote in the *Daily Telegraph*: 'The real sadness for English football is that the councillors of the FA failed to do justice to Walter's enormous contribution. In electing Denis Follows, instead of Walter, as Sir Stanley's successor, they virtually eliminated England's best football brain for years from continuing to serve English football.'

Graham Kelly, who spoke from his experience as Secretary of the Football League from 1978 to 1989 and Chief Executive of the Football Association from 1989 to 1998 wrote in *The Independent*: 'How was the Football Association so perverse as to let

Winterbottom drift out of football' and went on to say 'the wealth of Winterbottom's legacy is impossible to calculate.'

Jeff Powell of the *Daily Mail* seems to have got to the heart of the man: 'He took football not by storm but by self-effacing charm, unflagging courtesy and a willingness to impart all his wisdom with a generosity of spirit which sought no reward other than to see the seeds he planted flourish. Had he been in his scholarly pomp today he could have made a fortune lecturing on the subject he loved, except that he would never have asked for a penny.

He was the father of modern English football.'

CHAPTER 22

EULOGY

At Walter's thanksgiving service in St Nicolas Church, Cranleigh, on 1 March 2002, Sir Bobby Robson, gave a personal and touching eulogy:

You know, you never know how to begin at such a warm, sincere, memorable and obviously sad occasion as this, except I must say I am deeply flattered and privileged to have been asked by the Winterbottom family to make this tribute to Walter. I say Walter, because many times after his knighthood I tried to call him 'Sir Walter' when I met him frequently on the circuit, and each time he would say to me, 'Bobby, it was Walter in our times together and it's Walter now.' Such was the man.

There is no doubt that I owe to him my entire international career, both as a player and as a manager. To Walter there is no doubt he was my mentor. He was my father figure in football and I wouldn't be in the position I am today without his encouragement, his guidance, and his inspiration. I learned, like most of you I think, of his death on the same Sunday evening as Newcastle United played Manchester City in the FA Cup in front of an estimated audience of about 10 million people – and 52,000 screaming Geordies as well – and what's more, two former England managers were up against each other that night. How ironic: myself and Kevin Keegan. The terribly sad news was actually given to me while I was making a television report after the match; and the news simply blunted my whole evening's excitement and thrill at our victory, and I have to say, the result was forgotten.

I drove home in complete daze, hardly remembering the three sets of traffic lights and the three villages that I have to go through to get home every day. All I could see really, through the windscreen, was Walter's face, and my mind went back to think about the marvellous, wonderful, career he had: 16 years at the helm of English football. I had eight. Walter doubled that. And he had the most successful record of any England manager, and the players he managed were just great players: Matthews, Tom Finney and Tommy Lawton, Wilf Mannion and Raich Carter, Nat Lofthouse, Alf Ramsey, Billy Wright, Len Shackleton and Jackie Milburn – two players from Newcastle who were my heroes when I was a kid. And later on, in another decade when I played, there was Johnny Haynes, Bobby Charlton, Duncan Edwards, Jimmy Greaves and many others. They were England's finest players and in today's market they would be priceless. And Walter, he had them all. I then got around to thinking about my first game under Walter in 1957, and in those days you learned through the press – no press conference – you picked up the evening paper and there was your name if you were in the team. And I remember it, I thought wow – I can see it now in the stop press in the evening paper in West Bromwich where I was playing – it said 'Robson, right half,' and I couldn't believe it. I thought 'the coach knows his stuff' [pause for laughter], and I was thrilled. I couldn't wait for the match and I remember going to talk to him just the day before the match was to be played at Wembley – a full house against the French – and I remember saying to Walter, 'Walter, tell me what's it going to be like? What do I face?'

He looked at me and said, 'well, it's not going to be easy. In fact it's going to be extremely difficult.' He said, 'you've got to be realistic and think that you're going to be playing against the very best that the French have got.'

As I got whiter he said, 'but remember, you're playing with the very best that England have got, and your own contribution is vital. But never mind that... if you get a bit nervous or a tired give the ball to Tom Finney. He will keep it for ten minutes until you recover [pause for laughter], and I did many times [pause for laughter], and I remember the day of the match and his pre-match team talk. He said 'We must get off to a good start. We must take the initiative. If we can get a goal in the first minute that will unsettle the French.' I thought, easy! [laughter]. So he said, 'Bobby, what I want you to do is pass the ball to Tommy Taylor. Tommy Taylor will pass it back to Billy Wright, and Billy Wright will play a square ball to Jimmy Armfield.' And he said, 'As that is progressing, you and Tommy Taylor get up front. Jimmy Armfield will then play the ball down the line to Tom Finney, Tom will control the ball and beat his opponent. He'll hit the byline and pull it back and Bobby, you will score [laughter].

He said 'Any questions?' [laughter]

I said 'Yes, just one Walter.'

'What is it?'

I said, 'Which side of the goalkeeper do you want me to put the ball, [laughter] right or left?' He was silent for a few moments. I thought, my word, I've stumped the coach. I won't be in next time. He said 'Bobby, get two and put one on either side.' [laughter] And I did! I scored twice on my debut and I thought – I'm in for the next match.

And I'll never forget my first cap because I played with some Manchester United players: Duncan Edwards, Roger Byrne, Tommy

Taylor – and it was the last international match that those players played because they were all dreadfully killed in that plane disaster, if you remember. We were working towards the 1958 World Cup in Sweden and if you imagine the blow that was to English football, and particularly to Walter, who was building a fine team, and it was a very sad occasion: that was their last game, so it will always be with me.

And then later on – I'm still looking through the windscreen wipers. I am still on my way home and still thinking about him – my mind went back to perhaps one of Walter's greatest days: one of our greatest days in English football. Well, maybe the second greatest day, because the greatest day was obviously the day that England won the World Cup in 1966, just a little bit later. It was when we beat Scotland 9-3 in a wonderful match. The Scots had Denis Law and Dave Mackay on the pitch in those days, and others – I think we beat 11 – and I scored the first goal after nine minutes. And after the match my wife came to me, and she said, 'I'm terribly sorry, I have to tell you something' – she never went to Wembley, it was very rare – 'I got caught in a traffic jam and I missed the goal.' I said oh, oh, right, okay. And the next time we met I said to Walter, 'Walter, you'll never believe this. You remember the goal I scored when we beat Scotland at Wembley 9-3, and I scored the first goal?' He said, 'Yes' 'I said 'Well my wife got caught in a traffic jam. She missed the goal.' Walter looked at me and he said 'Bobby, don't tell your wife I said this, but the most important thing', he said, 'is that you didn't!' [laughter]. So you can see, Walter had a fine sense of humour. He liked his players to be happy. He liked the players to play jokes with each other. He was quite chuffed about it.

But he had such an array of other qualities. He had a calm, delightful, unassuming charm. He was extremely kind. He was very sincere and he was extremely, extremely, loyal to his players. He was a man of high intellect and he was the most perfect gentleman. I always considered – I tried to consider myself – to be a student of the game. If I was, Walter was my tutor. He was a visionary. He had a vast knowledge of the world game, and he could impart that knowledge better than any person I have ever known in football. He was extremely eloquent in his delivery and easily understood; indeed I could listen to him for hours on football and I would never get bored, such was the quality of his words. And he was always interesting. I actually admired him greatly for that. Walter knew football inside-out and as Director of Coaching for the Football Association, as well as the England Team Manager, he conducted summer coaching courses of an extremely high quality and standard, ensuring, of course, that we kept abreast of the modern game, particularly after Hungary came to Wembley in 1953 and showed us there was another way of playing, another style of football. Walter saw that, adapted it, and modernised our own game.

It was during my days with England, as a player, Walter came to me and to Don Howe who was a colleague of mine – a very good player, a fine player, still working at the Arsenal Football Club now – and he said to us two, 'what are you two going to do when you finish playing?' Well we didn't know, we didn't really think window cleaning was an option! So he said 'I want you to come to Lilleshall, you two, and I want you to get the qualifications. I want you to get your diplomas in coaching and I want you to stay in the game. The game has to be taken on. The game has to be kept going forward. We need young players who are finishing their careers to come into football. Well, I went [to Lilleshall], and that's certainly the reason I went into management, and I have an awful lot to thank him for in that respect. He left England as you may remember, or as I'm telling you, in 1962. Alf Ramsey took charge in 1962 and 20 years later – and I can hardly believe this – exactly 20 years later, I was appointed manager of England. And I appointed Don Howe as my assistant. And I would never believe on that particular day 20 years prior, that I would, or could, follow Walter to the England managership, and I didn't ever think I could get anywhere near his vast quality.

During my time with the England team Walter stayed in touch with me and that was something I really appreciated. He used to write me such wonderful letters, supportive letters, letters of help and encouragement, passages of great encouragement, particularly when results hadn't gone our way – he knew I didn't need it when we'd won anyway – 'Don't panic' he would say, 'Stay calm. You're doing fine. The next game and the next result is the next most important step. Don't read the press too much. Stay your own man. Pick your own players; don't pick theirs. The country is right behind you and so am I.' What a man. What a great man! He also taught me two great qualities which I think you have to have in football – some have it, some don't; some try, some don't – sportsmanship in defeat and humility in victory. And Walter had those two qualities in abundance – in abundance! And I try to maintain those elements all through my professional life.

Ladies and gentlemen, Sir Walter Winterbottom was a lovely man. He was a special man. He was respected the world over for his insight, innovative style and absolutely unbridled enthusiasm for the game. He gave so much to football and this marvellous national game of ours. Walter is such a sad loss to us all, and he will be missed by many, and together with Ann, I am on that list.

Thank you.

EPILOGUE

Throughout his 16 years as the FA's Director of Coaching, Walter campaigned on recurring themes. The need for more coaches, higher standards of coaching, coaches who could teach, who could inspire, men who were leaders. He was looking for men who were willing to learn, who would take an active part in a coaching session but not show off their skills in demonstrations, who would strive to achieve higher standards and understand the sports sciences; he wanted coaching to be treated as a respected profession and for coaches to have a rewarding career path. They came to take their badges at his residential coaching courses at Lilleshall and generations of coaches followed.

In players he wanted above all, better ball skills – the ability to be able to control the ball at match tempo and in match situations before a pass was made. It was, he insisted, something that should be taught at an early age. He passionately believed that practice with the ball was fundamental and that coaching showed players how to practice. Young players in Europe were getting up to two to three hours of ball practice four times a week. In England they were getting nothing like that and he advocated dedicated practice for long hours. For practice to be effective he stressed that there had to be better facilities to enable boys to overcome the English winter weather. Floodlights, all-weather surfaces and indoor gymnasiums were desperately needed.

For years he ridiculed the mantra of endless laps round the pitch to achieve fitness: best summed-up by his comment from an earlier chapter: 'A billiards player does not practice by walking round the table.' Fitness, he argued, could be better achieved by well-designed circuit training routines using a ball.

Much of his effort was aimed at schoolchildren and he inspired and encouraged hundreds of schoolmasters to become qualified coaches. He believed that professional clubs should widen their horizons, expanding membership to all youngsters with outstanding potential, providing a range of age groups that could develop under the club's professional coaching umbrella. At that time Ajax and other clubs in Holland and Spain were already showing how this should be done.

A persistent concern was 'the gap' – the period between boys leaving school at 15 and adulthood. Many young players were lost to the game simply because they were not catered for. He urged clubs at all levels, professional and amateur, to establish youth teams and competitive leagues.

When Allen Wade succeeded Walter as Director of Coaching, he said, 'there are two stages through which worthwhile ideas must pass before they are accepted. In the first stage they are ignored, in the second ridiculed. Coaching has passed through these stages and is now accepted as a necessary process in the education and development of more skilful players at all levels.' It summed up the pioneer work that Walter did.

50 years have passed since Walter left the Football Association. Much has changed but much remains unchanged. John Peacock, the

FA's Head of Coaching still echoes Walter's words: 'We must produce good teachers of the game who will educate and inspire players.'

Coaching has been through many phases, reviews and blueprints, often thwarted by the same structural and political obstacles Walter faced. In 2007 John Peacock said in a report, 'in comparison with our European counterparts we do not place the same degree of importance on the status of coaching in this country.' To dramatically illustrate that statement and get some sense of perspective about how far England still lags behind European counterparts, one only has to look at the number of qualified coaches. Germany has 34,970 Pro 'A' and 'B' level coaches, Spain has 23,905 and England a mere 2,769.

But now under the leadership of Sir Trevor Brooking, the FA's Director of Football Development, a new philosophy has emerged which is encapsulated in the FA's 'Future Game' document published in 2010. Its objective is for England to develop home-grown players who match up to the foreign talent being recruited into the English game. To do that technical ability has to be instilled into players from a very young age. Age-specific coaches will take players along a pathway, beginning with mini soccer in the 5-11 age group, through 9 v 9 and then 11 v 11 in the 12-16 age group, with the emphasis on boys having the confidence and ability to play out from the back and pass through midfield. When they reach the 17-21 age group they should have all the technical skills and the emphasis will switch to competition and winning. It's a long-term plan.

The 'whole game' coaching and playing philosophy expressed in the Future Game is now being crystallised in a tangible expression with the building of the FA's 'University of Football' at St Georges Park, Burton on Trent – a world-class coaching facility developed with the support of all the elements within the game which opened in autumn 2012. Fundamentally it is a place where coaches will be taught how – as well as what – to coach, teach, inspire and influence. It has comprehensive resources for the education and training, not just of coaches, but referees and all those engaged in every aspect of football management. Its world-class facilities include state of the art medical and sports science services. In the words of David Bernstein, the FA chairman, 'it will be the focal point of an unprecedented coaching education revolution that will reach from grass roots football participation in every corner of England right up to the pinnacle of all our England teams.'

St George's Park is certainly something Walter would have most wholeheartedly approved of. Its objectives and philosophy capture much of his own vision for the future. 'He might say it has come 30 years later than he would have wished' said Sir Trevor Brooking, 'but I hope he would have said that it has exceeded anything that he dreamed of.'

ACKNOWLEDGEMENTS

A biography like this could not have been written without a great deal of help from many people. I am particularly indebted to those who gave me encouragement, technical advice and read the manuscript: Ken Goldman, the editor of *Soccer Coaching* the magazine of the London Football Coaches Association; Brian Scovell, football journalist and author of *The England Managers*; and Alastair Paterson.

Jimmy Armfield, Tommy Banks and Bill Slater were ex England players who were able to give me firsthand accounts. Terry Venables and John Cartwright gave me coaching insights.

I am most grateful to Sir Trevor Brooking at the Football Association for providing the foreword and advice, his able PA Emma Kernan-Staines, and David Barber, who was an ongoing source of knowledge.

Rose-Marie Breitenstein was a patient source of information about Sir Stanley Rous and his relationship with Walter. Heinz Marotzke and Walter Gagg helped to explain Walter's relationship with FIFA.

Much information exists about any man who has such a high profile as the England team manager. Very little is generally known about Walter's role with the CCPR and the Sports Council. I was therefore especially lucky to be able to reach Denis Molyneux, John Disley, John Coghlan and Sir Roger Bannister who were able to shed much light on the pivotal part Walter played in the development of British sport in the 1960s and 1970s. Nick Rowe and Melina Greensmith at Sport England (previously the Sports Council) and Kate Lawrence at the Sport and Recreation Alliance (formerly the CCPR) kindly gave me access to archived records.

David Miller gave me a view from the media of the day and I am grateful to Jeff Powell of the *Daily Mail* for the inspiration of the title. Neil Carter and Tony Mason from De Montfort University were able to guide me towards existing academic research.

Andy Ellis at the Writers Bureau provided much needed encouragement, help and support in the writing process. My literary agent, Kirsty Mclachlan had a steadfast belief in the book and I am forever grateful to her for ensuring that it was published. I am of course especially indebted to Allie Collins and her team at John Blake Publishing who ensured that Walter's story will reach a wide audience and take its place in sporting history, and her copy editor Joel Simons who helped me see the book as a reader and significantly improve it.

Finally I must add my appreciation of support from family members – Lady Ann Winterbottom who gave her approval and was a constant source of family information, Brenda Coles, who gave me all Walter's speeches with her analysis, and my wife Janet, who for three years lived with an examination of everything her father had ever done and who has provided endless support as my in-house editor.

To all of you I give my heartfelt thanks.

BIBLIOGRAPHY

Armfield, Jimmy. *Right Back to the Beginning*, (Headline 2004)

Bowler, Dave. *Winning isn't Everything – The biography of Sir Alf Ramsey*, (Victor Gollancz 1998)

Brown, Alan. *Team Coach*, (Merlin 1993)

Butler, Bryon. *The Official History of the Football Association*, (Queen Ann Press 1991)

Charlton, Bobby. *My England Years*, (Headline 2008)

Coglhan, John. *Sport and British Politics*, (Falmer Press 1990)

Delany, Terence. *A Century of Soccer*, (Sportsman's Book Club 1965)

Edworthy, Niall. *The Second Most Important Job in the Country*, (Virgin 1999)

Evans, Justin H. *Service to Sport, CCPR 1935-1972*, (Pelham Books 1974)

Ferrier, Bob. *Soccer Partnership*, (Heinemann 1960)

Finney, Tom. *Tom Finney*, (Headline 2003)

Glanville, Brian. *England Managers*, (Headline 2007)

Glanville, Brian. *Soccer Nemesis*, (Secker and Warburg 1955)

Glanville, Brian. *The Sunday Times History of the World Cup*, (Times Newspapers 1973)

Glanville, Brian/Jerry Weinstein. *World Cup*, (Robert Hale 1958)

Greaves, Jimmy. *Greavsie*, (Sphere 2003)

Greenwood, Ron/Bryon Butler. *Sincerely Yours*, (Willow Books 1984)

Haoul, Mark/Tony Williamson. *Forever England*, (Tempus 2000)

Hardwick, George/John Wilson. *Gentleman George*, (Juniper 1998)

Hayes, Dean. *England! England!* (Sutton Publishing 2004)

Haynes, Johnny. *Football Today*, (Arthur Barker 1961)

Hill, Jeffrey. *Sport, Leisure and Culture in Twentieth Century Britain*, (Paulgrave 2002)

Hill, Jimmy. *The Jimmy Hill Story*, (Hodder and Stoughton 1998)

Holt, Richard/Tony Mason. *Sport in Britain*, (Blackwell 2000)

Howell, Denis. *Made in Birmingham*, (Queen Ann Press 1990)

Liversedge, Stan, *This England Job*, (Soccer Book Publishing 1996)

McKinstrey. Leo. *Sir Alf*, (Harper Sport, 2006)

Miller, David. *Stanley Matthews*, (Pavilion 1989)

Mourant, Andrew/Jack Rollin. *Essential History of England*, (Headline 2002)

Puskas, Ferenc. *Captain of Hungary*, (Cassell 1955)

Rous, Sir Stanley. *Football Worlds*, (Faber and Faber 1978)

Saunders, Donald. *World Cup 1962*, (Heinemann 1962)

Scovell, Brian. *The England Managers*, (Tempus, 2006)

Shaoul, Mark /Tony Williamson. *Forever England*, (Tempus 2000)

Shepherdson, Harold/Roy Peskett. *The Magic Sponge*, (Pelham 1968)

Taylor, Matthew. *The Association Game*, (Pearson Education 2008)

Taylor, Rogan /Andrew Ward. *Kicking and Screaming. An Oral History of Football in England* (Rogan Books 1995)

Varley, Nick. *Golden Boy – a biography of Wilf Mannion*, (Aurum 1997)

Wade, Allen. *FA Guide to Training and Coaching*, (Heinemann 1967)

Wilson, Jonathan. *The Anatomy of England*, (Orion Books 2010)

Winterbottom, Walter. *Modern Soccer*, (Educational Productions 1958)

Winterbottom, Walter. *Soccer Coaching*, (Naldrett 1952)

Winterbottom, Walter. *Training for Soccer*, (Heinemann 1960)

Wright, Billy/Bryon Butler. *One Hundred Caps and All That*, (Robert Hale, 1961)

OTHER SOURCES

My Story (Walter Winterbottom's unpublished memoir written for his grandchildren)

The FA Book for Boys, 1948-1962

The FA Year Book, 1948-1962

FA News

FA library – Minutes of FA Council Meetings, 1946-1962

Manchester United FC

Soccer Coach – London Football Coaches Association Magazine

British Library Newspapers

englandfootballonline

statto.com

aboutmanutd.com

APPENDIX 1

GAMES PLAYED FOR MANCHESTER UNITED

28/11/36	Div.1	Leeds United (a)	1-2
5/12/36	Div.1	Birmingham City (h)	1-2
12/12/36	Div.1	Middlesbrough (a)	2-3
19/12/36	Div.1	West Bromwich Albion (h)	2-2
25/12/36	Div.1	Bolton Wanderers (h)	1-0
26/12/36	Div.1	Wolverhampton Wanderers (a)	1-3
28/12/36	Div.1	Bolton Wanderers (a)	4-0
1/1/37	Div.1	Sunderland (h)	2-1
2/1/37	Div.1	Derby County (h)	2-2
9/1/37	Div.1	Manchester City (a)	0-1
16/1/37	FA Cup	Reading (h)	1-0
23/1/37	Div.1	Sheffield Wednesday (a)	0-1
30/1/37	FA Cup	Arsenal (a)	0-5
3/2/37	Div.1	Preston North End (h)	1-1
6/2/37	Div.1	Arsenal (a)	1-1
13/2/37	Div.1	Brentford (h)	1-3

20/2/37	Div.1	Portsmouth (h)	0-1
27/2/37	Div.1	Chelsea (a)	2-4
6/3/37	Div.1	Stoke City (h)	2-1
13/3/37	Div.1	Charlton Athletic (a)	0-3
20/3/37	Div.1	Grimsby Town (h)	1-1
26/3/37	Div.1	Everton (h)	2-1
27/3/37	Div.1	Liverpool (a)	0-2

SEASON 1937/38

11/9/37	Div.2	Barnsley (h)	4-1
13/9/37	Div.2	Bury (a)	2-1
18/9/37	Div.2	Stockport County (a)	0-1
25/9/37	Div.2	Southampton (h)	1-2

CAREER RECORD AT MANCHESTER UNITED

1936-37	21 Football League, 2 FA Cup, 9 Central League, 1 Lancashire Cup
1937-38	4 Football League, 17 Central League, 2 Lancashire Cup (1 goal), 1 Manchester Cup
1938-39	25 Central League

APPENDIX 2:
GAMES AS ENGLAND MANAGER

WALTER WINTERBOTTOM'S CAREER RECORD AS ENGLAND TEAM MANAGER

Venue	P	W	D	L	F	A	GD	FTS	CS	FAv	AAv	Pts%	W/L
Home	58	40	12	6	194	82	+112	1	15	3.354	1.414	79.3	+34
Away	68	36	16	16	172	93	+79	11	16	2.529	1.368	64.7	+20
Neutral	13	2	5	6	17	21	-4	5	3	1.308	1.615	34.6	-4
Total	139	78	33	28	383	196	+187	17	34	2.755	1.410	68.0	+50

Definitions

P = played, W = won, D = drew, L = lost, F = goals for, A = goals against, GD = goal difference, FTS = failed to score, CS = clean sheet, FAv = goals for average, AAv = goals against av, Pts% = percent of maximum points using 2 for a win and one for a draw. W/L = Win/lose difference.

Full international caps shown in brackets. Wartime international caps not included. Captain is shown in bold.

1946

Home International Championship
Sep 28   Windsor Park, Belfast   N.IRELAND   W 7-2   Carter H,
Mannion 3, Finney, Lawton, Langton   57,111
Swift (1), Scott (1), **Hardwick** (1), Wright W (1), Franklin (1),
Cockburn (1), Finney (1), Carter H (7), Lawton (9), Mannion (1),
Langton (2)

Friendly
Sep 30   Dalymount Park, Dublin   R. of IRELAND   W 1-0
Finney   32,000
Swift (2), Scott (2), **Hardwick** (2), Wright W (2), Franklin (2),
Cockburn (2), Finney (2), Carter H (8), Lawton (10), Mannion (2),
Langton (2)

Home International Championship
Nov 13   Maine Road, Manchester   WALES   W 3-0   Mannion
2, Lawton   59,121
Swift (3), Scott (3), **Hardwick** (3), Wright W (3), Franklin (3),
Cockburn (3), Finney (3), Carter H (9), Lawton (11), Mannion (3),
Langton (3)

Friendly
Nov 27   Leeds Road, Huddersfield HOLLAND   W 8-2   Lawton
4, Carter H 2, Mannion, Finney   32,435
Swift (4), Scott (4), **Hardwick** (4), Wright W (4), Franklin (4),
Johnston (1), Finney (4), Carter H (10), Lawton (12), Mannion (4),
Langton (4)

1947

Home International Championship
Apr 12   Wembley, London   SCOTLAND   D 1-1   Carter H
98,200
Swift (5), Scott (5), **Hardwick** (5), Wright W (5), Franklin (5), Johnston (2), Matthews (18), Carter H (11), Lawton (13), Mannion (5), Mullen (1)

Friendlies
May   3   Highbury,   London   FRANCE   W   3-0   Finney, Mannion, Carter H   54,389
Swift (6), Scott (6), **Hardwick** (6), Wright W (6), Franklin (6), Lowe (1), Finney (5), Carter H (12), Lawton (14), Mannion (6), Langton (5)

May 18   Zurich   SWITZRLAND   L 0-1   –   34,000
Swift (7), Scott (7), **Hardwick** (7), Wright W (7), Franklin (7), Lowe (2), Matthews (19), Carter H (13), Lawton (15), Mannion (7), Langton (6)

May 25   Lisbon   PORTUGAL   W 10-0   Lawton 4, Mortensen 4, Finney, Matthews   65,000
Swift (8), Scott (8), **Hardwick** (8), Wright W (8), Franklin (8), Lowe (3), Matthews (20), Mortensen (1), Lawton (16), Mannion (8), Finney (6)

Sep 21   Brussels   BELGIUM   W   5-2   Lawton 2, Mortensen, Finney 2   54,326
Swift (9), Scott (9), **Hardwick** (9), Ward (1), Franklin (9), Wright W (9), Matthews (21), Mortensen (2), Lawton (17), Mannion (9), Finney (7)

Home International Championship
Oct 18 Ninian Park, Cardiff WALES W 3-0 Finney,
Mortensen, Lawton 55,000
Swift (10), Scott (10), **Hardwick** (10), Taylor P (1), Franklin (10),
Wright W (10), Matthews (22), Mortensen (3), Lawton (18),
Mannion (10), Finney (8)

Nov 5 Goodison Park, Liverpool N.IRELAND D 2-2
Mannion, Lawton 67,980
Swift (11) Scott (11), **Hardwick** (11), Taylor P (2), Franklin (11),
Wright W (11), Matthews (23), Mortensen (4), Lawton (19),
Mannion (11), Finney (9)

Friendly
Nov 19 Highbury, London SWEDEN W 4-2 Mortensen 3,
Lawton (pen) 44,282
Swift (12), Scott (12), **Hardwick** (12), Taylor P (3), Franklin (12),
Wright W (12), Finney (10), Mortensen (5), Lawton (20), Mannion
(12), Langton (7)

1948

Home International Championship
Apr 10 Hampden Park Glasgow SCOTLAND W 2-0 Finney,
Mortensen 135,376
Swift (13), Scott (13), **Hardwick** (13), Wright W (13), Franklin (13),
Cockburn (4), Matthews (24), Mortensen (6), Lawton (21), Pearson
(1), Finney (11)

Friendlies
May 16 Turin ITALY W 4-0 Mortensen, Lawton, Finney 2
58,000
Swift (14), Scott (14), Howe (1), Wright W (14), Franklin (14),

Cockburn (5), Matthews (25), Mortensen (7), Lawton (22), Mannion (13), Finney (12)

Sep 26   Copenhagen   DENMARK   0-0   –   41,000
Swift (15), Scott (15), Aston (1), Wright W (15), Franklin (15), Cockburn (6), Matthews (26), Hagan (1), Lawton (23), Shackleton (1) Langton (8)

Home International Championship
Oct 9   Windsor Park, Belfast   N.IRELAND   W 6-2   Matthews, Mortensen 3, Milburn, Pearson   53,629
Swift (16), Scott (16), Howe (2), **Wright W** (16), Franklin (16), Cockburn (7), Matthews (27), Mortensen (8), Milburn (1), Pearson (2), Finney (13)

Nov 10   Villa Park, Birmingham   WALES   W 1-0   Finney   –   67,770
Swift (17), Scott (17), Aston (2), Ward (2), Franklin (17), **Wright W** (17), Matthews (28), Mortensen (9), Milburn (2), Shackleton (2), Finney (14)

Friendly
Dec 2   Highbury, London   SWITZERLAND   W 6-0   Haines 2, Hancocks 2, Rowley, Milburn   48,000
Ditchburn (1), Ramsey (1), Aston (3), **Wright W** (18), Franklin (18), Cockburn (8), Matthews (29), Rowley (1), Milburn (3), Haines (1), Hancocks (1)

1949

Home International Championship
Apr 9   Wembley, London   SCOTLAND   L 1-3   Milburn   98,188
Swift (18), Aston (4), Howe (3), **Wright W** (19), Franklin (19),

Cockburn (9), Matthews (30), Mortensen (10), Milburn (4), Pearson (3), Finney (15)

Friendlies
May 13   Stockholm   SWEDEN   L 1-3   Finney   37,500
Ditchburn (2), Shimwell (1), Aston (5), **Wright W** (20), Franklin (20), Cockburn (10), Finney (16), Mortensen (11), Bentley (1), Rowley J (2), Langton (9)

May 18   Oslo   NORWAY   W 4-1   Mullen, Finney, Morris (own goal)   36,000
Swift (19), Ellerington (1), Aston (6), **Wright W** (21), Franklin (21), Dickinson (1), Finney (17), Morris (1), Mortensen (12), Mannion (14), Mullen (2)

May 22   Paris   FRANCE   W 3-1   Morris 2, Wright W   61,308
Williams (1), Ellerington (2), Aston (7), **Wright W** (22), Franklin (22), Dickinson (2), Finney (18), Morris (2), Rowley J (3), Mannion (15), Mullen (3)

Sep 21 Goodison Park, Liverpool R. of IRELAND L 0-2 –   51,487
Williams (2), Mozley (1), Aston (8), **Wright W** (23), Franklin (23), Dickinson (3), Harris P (1), Morris (3), Pye (1), Mannion (16), Finney (19)

Home International Championship
Oct 15   Ninian Park, Cardiff   WALES   W 4-1   Mortensen, Milburn 3   61,079
Williams (3), Mozley (2), Aston (9), **Wright W** (24), Franklin (24), Dickinson (4), Finney (20), Mortensen (13), Milburn (5), Shackleton (3), Hancocks (2)

Nov 16   Maine Road, Manchester   N. IRELAND   W 9-2
Rowley J 4, Froggatt J, Pearson 2, Mortensen 2   69,762

Streten (1), Mozley (3), Aston (10), Watson (1), Franklin (25), **Wright W** (25), Finney (21) Mortensen (14), Rowley J (4), Pearson (4), Froggatt J (1)

Friendly
Nov 30   White Hart Lane, London   ITALY   W 2-0   Rowley J, Wright W   71,797
Williams (4), Ramsey (2), Aston (11), Watson (2), Franklin (26), **Wright W** (26), Finney (22), Mortensen (15), Rowley J (5), Pearson (5), Froggatt J (2)

1950

Home International Championship/World Cup Qualifiers
Apr 15   Hampden Park, Glasgow   SCOTLAND   W   1-0   Bentley   133,300
Williams (5), Ramsey (3), Aston (12), **Wright W** (27), Franklin (27), Dickinson (5), Finney (23), Mannion (17), Mortensen (16), Bentley (2), Langton (10)

Friendlies
May 14   Lisbon   PORTUGAL   W 5-3   Finney 4 (2 pens), Mortensen   65,000
Williams (6), Ramsey (4), Aston (13), **Wright W** (28), Jones WH (1), Dickinson (6), Milburn (6), Mortensen (17), Bentley (3), Mannion (18), Finney (24)

May 18   Brussels   BELGUIM   W   4-1   Mullen, Mortensen, Mannion, Bentley   55,854
Williams (7), Ramsey (5), Aston (14), **Wright W** (29), Jones WH (2), Dickinson (7), Milburn (7), (Mullen) (4), Mortensen (18), Bentley (4), Mannion (19), Finney (25)

The World Cup Finals 1950 (Brazil)
Group Stage – Pool 2
Jun 25   Rio   CHILE   W 2-0   Mortensen, Mannion   29,703
Williams (8), Ramsey (6), Aston (15), **Wright W** (30), Hughes L (1), Dickinson (8), Finney (26), Mannion (20), Bentley (5), Mortensen (19), Mullen (5)

Jun 29   Belo Horizonte   USA   L 0-1   –   10,151
Williams (9), Ramsey (7), Aston (16), **Wright W** (31), Hughes L (2), Dickinson (9), Finney (27), Mannion (21), Bentley (6), Mortensen (20), Mullen (6)

July 2   Rio   SPAIN   L 0-1   –   74,462
Williams (10), Ramsey (8), Eckersley (1), **Wright W** (32), Hughes L (3), Dickinson (10) Matthews (31), Mortensen (21), Milburn (8), Bailey E (1), Finney (28)

Home International Championship
Oct 7   Windsor Park, Belfast   N.IRELAND   W 4-1   Baily E 2, Lee J, Wright W   50,000
Williams (11), Ramsey (9), Aston (17), **Wright W** (33), Chilton (1), Dickinson (11), Matthews (32), Mannion (22), Baily E (2), Lee J (1), Langton (11)

Nov 15   Roker Park, Sunderland   WALES   W 4-2   Baily E 2, Mannion, Milburn   59,137
Williams (12), **Ramsey** (10), Smith L (1), Watson (3), Compton L (1), Dickinson (12), Finney (29), Mannion (23), Milburn (9), Baily E (3), Medley (1)

Friendly
Nov 22   Highbury, London   YUGOSLAVIA   D 2-2   Lofthouse 2   61,454

Williams (13), **Ramsey** (11), Eckersley (2), Watson (4), Compton L (2), Dickinson (13), Hancocks (3), Mannion (24), Lofthouse (1), Baily E (4), Medley (2)

1951

Home International Championship
Apr 14 Wembley, London SCOTLAND L 2-3 Hassall, Finney 98,000
Williams (14), Ramsey (12), Eckersley (3), Johnston (3), Froggatt J (3), **Wright W** (34), Matthews (33), Mannion (25), Mortensen (22), Hassall (1), Finney (30)

Friendlies
May 9 Wembley, London ARGENTINA W 2-1 Mortensen, Milburn 60,000
Williams (15), Ramsey (13), Eckersley (4), **Wright W** (35), Taylor J (1), Cockburn (11), Finney (31), Mortensen (23), Milburn (10), Hassall (2), Metcalfe (1)

May 19 Goodison Park, Liverpool PORTUGAL W 5-2 Nicholson, Milburn 2, Finney, Hassall
52,686 Williams (16), **Ramsey** (14), Eckersley (5), Nicholson (1), Taylor J (2), Cockburn (12), Finney (32), Pearson (6), Milburn (11), Hassall (3), Metcalfe (2)

Oct 3 Highbury, London FRANCE D 2-2 Medley (own goal) 57,603
Williams (17), Ramsey (15), Willis (1), **Wright W** (36), Chilton (2), Cockburn (13), Finney (33), Mannion (26), Milburn (12), Hassall (4), Medley (3)

Home International Championship
Oct 20   Ninian Park, Cardiff   WALES   D 1-1   Baily E   60,000
Williams (18), Ramsey (16), Smith L (2), Wright W (37), Barrass (1), Dickinson (14), Finney (34), Thompson T (1), Lofthouse (2), Baily E (5), Medley (4)

Nov 14   Villa Park, Birmingham   N.IRELAND   W 2-0 Lofthouse 2 57,889
Merrick (1), Ramsey (17), Smith L (3), Wright W (38), Barrass (2), Dickinson (15), Finney (35), Sewell (1), Lofthouse (3), Phillips (1), Medley (5)

Friendly
Nov 28   Wembley, London   AUSTRIA   D 2-2   Ramsey (pen), Lofthouse   100,000
Merrick (2), Ramsey (18), Eckersley (6), **Wright W** (39), Froggatt J (4), Dickinson (16), Milton (1), Broadis (1), Lofthouse (4), Baily E (6), Medley (6)

1952

Home International Championship
Apr 5   Hampden Park, Glasgow   SCOTLAND   W 2-1   Pearson 2 133,991
Merrick (3), Ramsey (19), Garrett (1), **Wright W** (40), Froggatt J (5), Dickinson (17), Finney (36), Broadis (2), Lofthouse (5), Pearson (7), Rowley J (6)

Friendlies
May 18   Florence   ITALY   D 1-1   Broadis   93,000
Merrick (4), Ramsey (20), Garrett (2), **Wright W** (41), Froggatt J (6), Dickinson (18), Finney (37), Broadis (3), Lofthouse (6), Pearson (8), Elliot (1)

May 25   Vienna   AUSTRIA   W 3-2   Lofthouse 2, Sewell   65,000
Merrick (5), Ramsey (21), Eckersley (7), **Wright W** (42), Froggatt J
(7), Dickinson (19), Finney (38), Sewell (2), Lofthouse (7), Baily E
(7), Elliot (2)

May 28   Zurich   SWITZERLAND   W 3-0   Sewell, Lofthouse 2
33,000
Merrick (6), Ramsey (22), Eckersley (8), Wright W (43), Froggatt J
(8), Dickinson (20), Allen R (1), Sewell (3), Lofthouse (8), Baily E (8),
Finney (39)

Home International Championship
Oct 4   Windsor Park, Belfast   N.IRELAND   D 2-2   Lofthouse,
Elliot   58,000
Merrick (7), Ramsey (23), Eckersley (9), Wright W (44), Froggatt J
(9), Dickinson (21), Finney (40), Sewell (4), Lofthouse (9), Baily E
(9), Elliot (3)

Nov 12   Wembley, London   WALES   W 5-2   Finney, Lofthouse
2, Froggatt J, Bentley   94,094
Merrick (8), Ramsey (24), Smith L (4), Wright W (45), Froggatt J
(10), Dickinson (22), Finney (41), Froggatt R (1), Lofthouse (10),
Bentley (7), Elliot (4)

Friendly
Nov 26   Wembley, London   BELGUIM   W 5-0   Elliot 2,
Lofthouse 2, Froggatt R   68,333
Merrick (9), Ramsey (25), Smith L (5), Wright W (46), Froggatt J
(11), Dickinson (23), Finney (42), Bentley (8), Lofthouse (11),
Froggatt R (2), Elliot (5)

1953

Home International Championship
Apr 18 Wembley, London SCOTLAND D 2-2 Broadis 2
97,000
Merrick (10), Ramsey (26), Smith L (6), **Wright W** (47), Barrass (3),
Dickinson (24), Finney (43), Broadis (4), Lofthouse (12), Froggatt R
(3), Froggatt J (12)

Friendlies
May 17 Buenos Aires ARGENTINA D 0-0 (abandoned after
23 mins, waterlogged pitch) 80,000
Merrick (11), Ramsey (27), Eckersley (10), **Wright W** (48), Johnston
(4), Dickinson (25), Finney (44), Broadis (5), Lofthouse (13), Taylor
T (1), Berry (1)

May 24 Santiago CHILE W 2-1 Taylor T, Lofthouse 56,398
Merrick (12), Ramsey (28), Eckersley (11), **Wright W** (49), Johnston
(5), Dickinson (26), Finney (45), Broadis (6), Lofthouse (14), Taylor
T (2), Berry (2)
May 31 Montevideo URUGUAY L 1-2 Taylor T 66,072
Merrick (13), Ramsey (29), Eckersley (12), **Wright W** (50), Johnston
(6), Dickinson (27), Finney (46), Broadis (7), Lofthouse (15), Taylor
T (3), Berry (3)

Jun 8 New York USA W 6-3 Broadis, Finney 2, Lofthouse 2,
Froggatt R 7,271
Ditchburn (3), Ramsey (30), Eckersley (13), **Wright W** (51), Johnston
(7), Dickinson (28), Finney (47), Broadis (8), Lofthouse (16),
Froggatt R (4), Froggatt J (13)

Home International Championship/World Cup Qualifier
Oct 10 Ninian Park, Cardiff WALES W 4-1 Wilshaw 2,
Lofthouse 2 61,000

Merrick (14), Garrett (3), Eckersley (14), **Wright W** (52), Johnston (8), Dickinson (29), Finney (48), Quixall (1), Lofthouse (17), Wilshaw (1), Mullen (7)

Friendly
Oct 21   Wembley, London   REST OF EUROPE   D 4-4   Mullen 2, Mortensen, Ramsey (pen)   96,000
Merrick (15), Ramsey (31), Eckersley (15), **Wright W** (53), Ufton (1), Dickinson (30), Matthews (34), Mortensen (24), Lofthouse (18), Quixall (2), Mullen (8)

Home International Championship/World Cup Qualifier
Nov 11   Goodison Park, Liverpool   N.IRELAND   W   3-1   Hassall 2, Lofthouse   70,000
Merrick (16), Rickaby (1), Eckersley (16), **Wright W** (54), Johnston (9), Dickinson (31), Matthews (35), Quixall (3), Lofthouse (19), Hassall (5), Mullen (9)

Friendly
Nov 25   Wembley, London   HUNGARY   L   3-6   Sewell, Mortensen, Ramsey (pen)100,000
Merrick (17), Ramsey (32), Eckersley (17), **Wright W** (55), Johnston (10), Dickinson (32), Matthews (36), Taylor E (1), Mortensen (25), Sewell (5), Robb (1)

1954

Home International Championship/World Cup Qualifier
Apr 3   Hampden Park, Glasgow   SCOTLAND   W 4-2   Broadis, Nicholls, Allen, Mullen   134,544
Merrick (18), Staniforth (1), Byrne R (1), **Wright W** (56), Clarke H (1), Dickinson (33), Finney (49), Broadis (9), Allen R (2), Nicholls (1), Mullen (10)

Friendlies

May 16   Belgrade   YUGOSLAVIA   L 0-1   –   60,000
Merrick (19), Staniforth (2), Byrne R (2), **Wright W** (57), Owen (1), Dickinson (34), Finney (50), Broadis (10), Allen R (3), Nicholls (2), Mullen (11)

May 23   Budapest   HUNGARY   L 1-7   Broadis   92,000
Merrick (20), Staniforth (3), Byrne R (3), **Wright W** (58), Owen (2), Dickinson (35), Harris P (2), Sewell (6), Jezzard (1), Broadis (11), Finney (51)

The World Cup Finals 1954 (Switzerland)
Group Stage – Pool 4

Jun 17   Basle   BELGIUM   D 4-4   Broadis 2, Lofthouse 2   14,000
Merrick (21), Staniforth (4), Byrne R (4), **Wright W** (59), Owen (3), Dickinson (36), Matthews (37), Broadis (12), Lofthouse (20), Taylor T (4), Finney (52)
Jun 20   Berne   SWITZERLAND   W 2-0   Wilshaw, Mullen   30,000
Merrick (22), Staniforth (5), Byrne R (5), McGarry (1), **Wright W** (60), Dickinson (37), Finney (53), Broadis (13), Taylor T (5), Wilshaw (2), Mullen (12)

Quarter Final

Jun 26   Basle   URUGUAY   L 2-4   Lofthouse, Finney   35,000
Merrick (23), Staniforth (6), Byrne R (6), McGarry (2), **Wright W** (61), Dickinson (38), Matthews (38), Broadis (14), Lofthouse (21), Wilshaw (3), Finney (54)

Home International Championship

Oct 2   Windsor Park, Belfast   N.IRELAND   W 2-0   Haynes, Revie   59,000
Wood (1), Foulkes (1), Byrne R (7), Wheeler (1), **Wright W** (62),

Barlow (1), Matthews (39), Revie (1), Lofthouse (22), Haynes (1), Pilkington (1)

Nov 10   Wembley, London   WALES   W 3-2   Bentley 3   89,789
Wood (20), Staniforth (7), Byrne R (8), Phillips (2), **Wright W** (63), Slater (1), Matthews (40), Bentley (9), Allen R (4), Shackleton (4), Blunstone (1)

Friendly
Dec 1   Wembley, London   W.GERMANY   W 3-1   Bentley, Allen R, Shackleton   100,000
Williams (19), Staniforth (8), Byrne R (9), Phillips (3), **Wright W** (64), Slater (2), Matthews (41), Bentley (10), Allen R (5), Shackleton (5), Finney (55)

1955

Home International Championship
Apr 2   Wembley, London   SCOTLAND   W 7-2   Wilshaw 4, Lofthouse 2, Revie   96,847
Williams (20), Meadows (1), Byrne R (10), Armstrong (1), **Wright W** (65), Edwards (1), Matthews (42), Revie (2), Lofthouse (23), Wilshaw (4), Blunstone (2)

Friendlies
May 15   Paris   FRANCE   L 0-1   –   54,696
Williams (21), Sillett P (1), Byrne R (11), Flowers (1), **Wright W** (66), Edwards (2), Matthews (43), Revie (3), Lofthouse (24), Wilshaw (5), Blunstone (3)

May 18   Madrid   SPAIN   D 1-1   Bentley   125,000
Williams (22), Sillett P (2), Byrne R (12), Dickinson (39), **Wright W** (67), Edwards (3), Matthews (44), Bentley (11), Lofthouse (25), Quixall (4), Wilshaw (6)

May 22 Oporto PORTUGAL L 1-3 Bentley 52,000
Williams (23), Sillett P (3), Byrne R (13), Dickinson (40), **Wright W** (68), Edwards (4), Matthews (45), Bentley (12), Lofthouse (26), Quixall (5), Wilshaw (7), Blunstone (4)

Oct 2 Copenhagen DENMARK W 5-1 Revie 2 (1 pen), Lofthouse 2, Bradford 53,000
Baynham (1), Hall (1), Byrne R (14), McGarry (3), **Wright W** (69), Dickinson (41), Milburn (13), Revie (4), Lofthouse (27), Bradford (1), Finney (56)

Home International Championship
Oct 22 Ninian Park, Cardiff WALES L 1-2 own goal 60,000
Williams (24), Hall (2), Byrne R (15), McGarry (4), **Wright W** (70), Dickinson (42), Matthews (46), Revie (5), Lofthouse (28), Wilshaw (8), Finney (57)

Nov 2 Wembley, London N.IRELAND W 3-0 Wilshaw 2, Finney 60,000
Baynham (2), Hall (3), Byrne R (16), Clayton (1), **Wright W** (71), Dickinson (43), Finney (58), Haynes (2), Jezzard (2), Wilshaw (9), Perry (1)

Friendly
Nov 30 Wembley, London SPAIN W 4-1 Atyeo, Perry 2, Finney 95,550
Baynham (3), Hall (4), Byrne R (17), Clayton (2), **Wright W** (72), Dickinson (44), Finney (59), Atyeo (1), Lofthouse (29), Haynes (3), Perry (2)

1956

Home International Championship

Apr 14   Hampden Park, Glasgow   SCOTLAND   D 1-1   Haynes
132,817
Matthews R (1), Hall (5), Byrne R (18), Dickinson (45), **Wright W** (73), Edwards (5), Finney (60), Taylor T (6), Lofthouse (30), Haynes (4), Perry (3)

Friendlies

May 9   Wembley, London   BRAZIL   W 4-2   Taylor T 2
Grainger 2   97,000
Matthews R (2), Hall (6), Byrne R (19), Clayton (3), **Wright W** (74), Edwards (6), Matthews S (47), Atyeo (2), Taylor T (7), Haynes (5), Grainger (2)

May 16   Stockholm   SWEDEN   D 0-0   –   35,000
Matthews R (3), Hall (7), Byrne R (20), Clayton (4), **Wright W** (75), Edwards (7), Berry (4), Atyeo (3), Taylor T (8), Haynes (6), Grainger (2)

May 20   Helsinki   FINLAND   W 5-1   Wilshaw, Haynes, Astall, Lofthouse 2   20,177
Wood (3), Hall (8), Byrne R (21), Clayton (5), **Wright W** (76), Edwards (8), Astall (1), Haynes (7), Taylor T (9), (Lofthouse 31), Wilshaw (10), Grainger (3)

May 26   Berlin   W.GERMANY   W 3-1   Edwards, Grainger, Haynes   90,000
Matthews R (4), Hall (9), Byrne R (22), Clayton (6), **Wright W** (77), Edwards (9), Astall (2), Haynes (8), Taylor T (10), Wilshaw (11), Grainger (4)

Home International Championship

Oct 6 Windsor Park, Belfast   N.IRELAND   D 1-1   Matthew S 58,420

Matthew R (5), Hall (10), Byrne R (23), Clayton (7), **Wright W** (78), Edwards (10), Matthews S (48), Revie (6), Taylor T (11), Wilshaw (12), Grainger (5)

Nov 14 Wembley, London   WALES   W 3-1   Haynes, Brooks, Finney   93,796

Ditchburn (4), Hall (11), Byrne R (24),Clayton (8), **Wright W** (79), Dickinson (46), Matthews S (49), Brooks (11), Finney (61), Haynes (9), Grainger (6)

Friendly

Nov 28 Wembley, London   YUGOSLAVIA   W 3-0   Brooks, Taylor T 2   75,000

Ditchburn (5), Hall (12), Byrne R (25), Clayton (9), **Wright W** (80), Dickinson (47), Matthews S (50), Brooks (2), Finney (62), Haynes (10), (Taylor T 12), Blunstone (5)

World Cup Qualifier

Dec 5 Molineux, Wolverhampton   DENMARK   W 5-2   Taylor T 3, Edwards 2   54,083

Ditchburn (6), Hall (13), Byrne R (26), Clayton (10), **Wright W** (81), Dickinson (48), Matthews S (51), Brooks (3), Taylor T (13), Edwards (11), Finney (63)

1957

Home International Championship

Apr 6 Wembley, London   SCOTLAND   W 2-1   Kevan, Edwards   97,520

Hodgkinson (1), Hall (14), Byrne R (27), Clayton (11), **Wright W**

(82), Edwards (12), Matthews S (52), Thompson T (2), Finney (64), Kevan (1), Grainger (7)

World Cup Qualifiers
May 8   Wembley, London   R. of IRELAND   W 5-1   Taylor T 3, Atyeo 2   52,000
Hodgkinson (2), Hall (15), Byrne R (28), Clayton (12), **Wright W** (83), Edwards (13), Matthew S (53), Atyeo (4), Taylor T (14), Haynes (11), Finney (65)

May 15   Copenhagen   DENMARK   W 4-1   Haynes, Taylor T, Atyeo   35,000
Hodgkinson (3), Hall (16), Byrne R (29), Clayton (13), **Wright W** (84), Edwards (14), Matthews S (54), Atyeo (5), Taylor T (15), Haynes (12), Finney (66)

May 19   Dalymount Park, Dublin   R. of IRELAND   D 1-1   Atyeo   47,000
Hodgkinson (4), Hall (17), Byrne R (30), Clayton (14), **Wright W** (85), Edwards (15), Finney (67), Atyeo (6), Taylor T (16), Haynes (13), Pegg (1)

Home International Championship
Oct 19   Ninian Park, Cardiff   WALES   W 4-0   Haynes 2, Finney, own goal   58,000
Hopkinson (1), Howe D (1), Byrne R (31), Clayton (15), **Wright W** (86), Edwards (16), Douglas (1), Kevan (2), Taylor T (17), Haynes (14), Finney (68)

Nov 6   Wembley, London   N. IRELAND   L 2-3   A'Court , Edwards   40,000
Hopkinson (2), Howe D (2), Byrne R (32), Clayton (16), **Wright W** (87), Edwards (17), Douglas (2), Kevan (3), Taylor T (18), Haynes (15), A'Court (1)

Friendly

Nov 27 Wembley, London FRANCE W 4-0 Taylor T 2,
Robson R 2   64,349
Hopkinson (3), Howe D (3), Byrne R (33), Clayton (17), **Wright W**
(88), Edwards (18), Douglas (3), Robson R (1), Taylor T (19),
Haynes (16), Finney (69)

1958

Home International Championship

Apr 19 Hampden Park, Glasgow SCOTLAND W 4-0
Douglas, Kevan 2, Charlton R   127,874
Hopkinson (4), Howe D (4), Langley (1), Clayton (18), **Wright W**
(89), Slater (3), Douglas (4), Charlton R (1), Kevan (4), Haynes (17),
Finney (70)

Friendlies

May 7 Wembley, London PORTUGAL W 2-1 Charlton R 2
72,000
Hopkinson (5), Howe D (5), Langley (2), Clayton (19), **Wright W**
(90), Slater (4), Douglas (5), Charlton R (2), Kevan (5), Haynes (18),
Finney (71)

May 11 Belgrade YUGOSLAVIA L 0-5 – 55,000
Hopkinson (6), Howe D (6), Langley (3), Clayton (20), **Wright W**
(91), Slater (5), Douglas (6), Charlton R (3), Kevan (6), Haynes (19),
Finney (72)

May 18 Moscow USSR D 1-1 Kevan 102,000
McDonald (1), Howe D (7), Banks T (1), Clamp (1), Wright W
(92), Slater (6), Douglas (7), Robson R (2), Kevan (7), Haynes
(20), Finney (73)

The World Cup Finals 1958 (Sweden)
Group Stage – Pool 2
Jun 8   Gothenburg   USSR   D 2-2   Kevan, Finney (pen)   49,348
McDonald (2), Howe D (8), Banks T (2), Clamp (2), **Wright W** (93),
Slater (7), Douglas (8), Robson R (3), Kevan (8), Haynes (21),
Finney (71)

Jun 11   Gothenburg   BRAZIL   D 0-0   –   40,895
McDonald (3), Howe D (9), Banks T (3), Clamp (3), **Wright W** (94),
Slater (8), Douglas (9), Robson R (4), Kevan (9), Haynes (22),
A'Court (2)

Jun 15   Boras   AUSTRIA   D 2-2   Haynes, Kevan   16,800
McDonald (4), Howe D (10), Banks T (4), Clamp (4), **Wright W**
(95), Slater (9), Douglas (10), Robson R (5), Kevan (10), Haynes
(23), A'Court (3)

Play-Off
Jun 17   Gothernburg   USSR   L 0-1   –   23,182
McDonald (5), Howe D (11), Banks T (5), Clayton (21), **Wright W**
(96), Slater (10), Brabrook (1), Broadbent (1), Kevan (11), Haynes
(24), A'Court (4)

Home International Championship
Oct 4   Windsor Park, Belfast   N.IRELAND   D 3-3   Charlton R
2, Finney   58,000
McDonald (6), Howe D (12), Banks T (6), Clayton (22), **Wright W**
(97), McGuinness (1), Brabrook (2), Broadbent (2), Charlton R (4),
Haynes (25), Finney (75)

Friendly
Oct 22   Wembley, London   USSR   W 5-0   Haynes 3, Charlton R
(pen), Lofthouse   100,000

McDonald (7), Howe D (13), Shaw G (1), Clayton (23), **Wright W** (98), Slater (11), Douglas (11), Charlton R (5), Lofthouse (32), Haynes (26), Finney (76)

Home International Championship
Nov 26   Villa Park, Birmingham   WALES   D 2-2   Broadbent 2
41,581
McDonald (8), Howe D (14), Shaw G (2), Clayton (24), **Wright W** (99), Flowers (2), Clapton (1), Broadbent (3), Lofthouse (33), Charlton R (6), A'Court (5)

1959

Home International Championship
Apr 11   Wembley, London   SCOTLAND   W 1-0   Charlton R
98,329
Hopkinson (7), Howe D (15), Shaw G (3), Clayton (25), **Wright W** (100), Flowers (3), Douglas (12), Broadbent (4), Charlton R (7), Haynes (27), Holden (1)

Friendlies
May 6   Wembley, London   ITALY   D 2-2   Charlton R, Bradley
92,000
Hopkinson (8), Howe D (16), Shaw G (4), Clayton (26), **Wright W** (101), Flowers (4), Bradley (1), Broadbent (5), Charlton R (8), Haynes (28), Holden (2)

May 13   Rio   BRAZIL   L 0-2   –   160,000
Hopkinson (9), Howe D (17), Armfield (1), Clayton (27), **Wright W** (102), Flowers (5), Deeley (1), Broadbent (6), Charlton R (9), Haynes (29), Holden (3)

May 17   Lima   PERU   L 1-4   Greaves   50,306
Hopkinson (10), Howe D (18), Armfield (2), Clayton (28), **Wright W**

(103), Flowers (6), Deeley (2), Greaves (1), Charlton R (10), Haynes (30), Holden (4)

May 24   Mexico City   MEXICO   L 1-2   Kevan   83,000
Hopkinson (11), Howe D (19), Armfield (3), Clayton (29), **Wright W** (104), McGuinness (2), Flowers (7), Holden (5), Bradley (2), Greaves (2), Kevan (12), Haynes (31), Charlton R (11)

May 28   Los Angeles   USA   W 8-1   Charlton R 3 (1 pen), Flowers 2, Bradley, Kevan, Haynes   14,000
Hopkinson (12), Howe D (20), Armfield (4), Clayton (30), **Wright W** (105), Flowers (8), Bradley (3), Greaves (3), Kevan (13), Haynes (32), Charlton R (12)

Home International Championship
Oct 17   Ninian Park,   Cardiff   WALES   D 1-1   Greaves   62,000
Hopkinson (13), Howe D (21), Allen A (1), **Clayton** (31), Smith T (1), Flowers (9), Connelly (1), Greaves (4), Clough (1), Charlton R (13), Holliday (1)

Friendly
Oct 28   Wembley,   London   SWEDEN   L   2-3   Connelly, Charlton R   80,000
Hopkinson (14), Howe D (22), Allen A (2), **Clayton** (32), Smith T (2), Flowers (10), Connelly (2), Greaves (5), Clough (2), Charlton R (14), Holliday (2)

Home International Championship
Nov 18   Wembley, London   N.IRELAND   W 2-1   Baker, Parry 60,000
Springett R (1), Howe D (23), Allen A (3), **Clayton** (33), Brown (1), Flowers (11), Connelly (3), Haynes (33), Baker (1), Parry (1), Holliday (3)

1960

Home International Championship

Apr 9 Hampden Park, Glasgow SCOTLAND D 1-1 Charlton R (pen) 129,193

Springett R (2), Armfield (5), Wilson (1), **Clayton** (34), Slater (12), Flowers (12), Connelly (4), Broadbent (7), Baker (2), Parry (2), Charlton R (15)

Friendlies

May 11 Wembley, London YUGOSLAVIA D 3-3 Douglas, Greaves, Haynes 60,000

Springett R (3), Armfield (6), Wilson (2), **Clayton** (35), Swan (1), Flowers (13), Douglas (13), Haynes (34), Baker (3), Greaves (6), Charlton R (16)

May 15 Madrid SPAIN L 0-3 – 77,000

Springett R (4), Armfield (7), Wilson (3), Robson R (6), Swan (2), Flowers (14), Brabrook (3), **Haynes** (35), Baker (4), Greaves (7), Charlton R (17)

May 22 Budapest HUNGARY L 0-2 – 90,000

Springett R (5), Armfield (8), Wilson (4), Robson R (7), Swan (3), Flowers (15), Douglas (14), **Haynes** (36), Baker (5), Viollet (10), Charlton R (18)

Home International Championship

Oct 8 Windsor Park, Belfast N.IRELAND W 5-2 Smith R, Greaves 2, Charlton R, Douglas 60,000

Springett R (6), Armfield (9), McNeil (1), Robson R (8), Swan (4), Flowers (16), Douglas (15), Greaves (8), Smith R (1), **Haynes** (37), Charlton R (19)

World Cup Qualifier

Oct 19 Luxembourg LUXEMBOURG W 9-0 Greaves 3, Charlton R 3, Smith R 2, Haynes 5,500

Springett R (7), Armfield (10), McNeil (2), Robson R (9), Swan (5), Flowers (17), Douglas (16), Greaves (9), Smith R (2), **Haynes** (38), Charlton R (20)

Friendly

Oct 26 Wembley, London SPAIN W 4-2 Greaves, Douglas, Smith R 2 80,000

Springett R (8), Armfield (11), McNeil (3), Robson R (10), Swan (6), Flowers (18), Douglas (17), Greaves (10), Smith R (3), **Haynes** (39), Charlton R (21)

Home International Championship

Nov 23 Wembley, London WALES W 5-1 Greaves 2, Charlton R, Smith R, Haynes 65,000

Hodgkinson (5), Armfield (12), McNeil (4), Robson R (11), Swan (7), Flowers (19), Douglas (18), Greaves (11), Smith R (4), **Haynes** (40), Charlton R (22)

1961

Home International Championship

Apr 15 Wembley, London SCOTLAND W 9-3 Robson R, Greaves 3, Douglas, Smith R 2, Haynes 2 97,350

Springett R (9), Armfield (13), McNeil (5), Robson R (12), Swan (8), Flowers (20), Douglas (19), Greaves (12), Smith R (5), **Haynes** (41), Charlton R (23)

Friendly

May 10 Wembley, London MEXICO W 8-0 Hitchens, Charlton R 3, Robson R, Douglas 2, Flowers (pen) 77,000

Springett R (10), Armfield (14), McNeil (6), Robson R (13), Swan (9), Flowers (21), Douglas (20), Kevan (14), Hitchens (1), **Haynes** (42), Charlton R (24)

World Cup Qualifier
May 21   Lisbon   PORTUGAL   D 1-1   Flowers   65,000
Springett R (11), Armfield (15), McNeil (7), Robson R (14), Swan (10), Flowers (22), Douglas (21), Greaves (13), Smith R (6), **Haynes** (43), Charlton R (25)

Friendlies
May 24   Rome   ITALY   W 3-2   Hitchens 2, Greaves   90,000
Springett R (12), Armfield (16), McNeil (8), Robson R (15), Swan (11), Flowers (23), Douglas (22), Greaves (14), Hitchens (2), **Haynes** (44), Charlton R (26)

May 27   Vienna   AUSTRIA   L 1-3   Greaves   90,000
Springett R (13), Armfield (17), Angus (1), Miller (1), Swan (12), Flowers (24), Douglas (23), Greaves (15), Hitchens (3), **Haynes** (45), Charlton R (27)

World Cup Qualifier
Sep 28   Highbury, London   LUXEMBOURG   W 4-1   Pointer, Viollet, Charlton R 2   33,409
Springett R (14), **Armfield** (18), McNeil (9), Robson R (16), Swan (13), Flowers (25), Douglas (24), Fantham (1), Pointer (1), Viollet (2), Charlton R (28)

Home International Championship
Oct 14   Ninian Park, Cardiff   WALES   D 1-1   Douglas   61,566
Springett R (15), Armfield (19), Wilson (5), Robson R (17), Swan (14), Flowers (26), Connelly (5), Douglas (25), Pointer (2), **Haynes** (46), Charlton R (29)

World Cup Qualifier
Oct 25 Wembley, London PORTUGAL W 2-0 Connelly, Pointer 100,000
Springett R (16), Armfield (20), Wilson (6), Robson R (18), Swan (15), Flowers (27), Connelly (6), Douglas (26), Pointer (3), **Haynes** (47), Charlton R (30)

Home International Championship
Nov 22 Wembley, London N.IRELAND D 1-1 Charlton R 30,000
Springett R (17), Armfield (21), Wilson (7), Robson R (19), Swan (16), Flowers (28), Douglas (27), Byrne J (1), Crawford (1), **Haynes** (48), Charlton R (31)

1962

Friendly
Apr 4 Wembley, London AUSTRIA W 3-1 Crawford, Flowers (pen), Hunt 50,000
Springett R (18), Armfield (22), Wilson (8), Anderson (1), Swan (17), Flowers (29), Connelly (7), Hunt (1), Crawford (2), Haynes (49), Charlton R (32)

Home International Championship
Apr 14 Hampden Park, Glasgow SCOTLAND L 0-2 – 132,441
Springett R (19), Armfield (23), Wilson (9), Anderson (2), Swan (18), Flowers (30), Douglas (28), Greaves (16), Smith R (7), **Haynes** (50), Charlton R (33)

Friendlies
May 9 Wembley, London SWITZERLAND W 3-1 Flowers, Hitchens, Connelly 35,000

Springett R (20), Armfield (24), Wilson (10), Robson R (20), Swan (19), Flowers (31), Connelly (8), Greaves (17), Hitchens (4), **Haynes** (51), Charlton R (34)

May 20 Lima PERU W 4-0 Flowers (pen), Greaves 3 32,565
Springett R (21), Armfield (25), Wilson (11), Moore (1), Norman (1), Flowers (32), Douglas (29), Greaves (18), Hitchens (5), **Haynes** (52), Charlton R (35)

World Cup Finals 1962 (Chile)
Group Stage – Group 4
May 31 Rancagua HUNGARY L 1-2 Flowers (pen) 7,938
Springett R (22), Armfield (26), Wilson (12), Moore (2), Norman (2), Flowers (33), Douglas (30), Greaves (19), Hitchens (6), **Haynes** (53), Charlton R (36)

Jun 2 Rancagua ARGENTINA W 3-1 Flowers (pen), Charlton R, Greaves 9,794
Springett R (23), Armfield (27), Wilson (13), Moore (3), Norman (3), Flowers (34), Douglas (31), Greaves (20), Peacock (1), **Haynes** (54), Charlton R (37)

Jun 7 Rancagua BULGARIA D 0-0 – 5,700
Springett R (24), Armfield (28), Wilson (14), Moore (4), Norman (4), Flowers (35), Douglas (32), Greaves (21), Peacock (2), **Haynes** (55), Charlton R (38)

Quarter Final
Jun 10 Vina del Mar BRAZIL L 1-3 Hitchens 17,736
Springett R (25), Armfield (29), Wilson (15), Moore (5), Norman (5), Flowers (36), Douglas (33), Greaves (22), Hitchens (7), **Haynes** (56), Charlton R (39)

European Nations Cup Qualifier

Oct 3   Hillsborough, Sheffield   FRANCE   D 1-1   Flowers (pen)
35,380

Springett R (26), **Armfield** (30), Wilson (16), Moore (6), Norman (6), Flowers (37), Hellawell (1), Crowe (1), Charnley (1), Greaves (23), Hinton A (1)

Home International Championship

Oct 20   Windsor Park, Belfast   N.IRELAND   W 3-1   Greaves, O'Grady 2   55,000

Springett R (27), **Armfield** (31), Wilson (17), Moore (7), Labone (1), Flowers (38), Hellawell (2), Hill F (1), Peacock (4), Greaves (24), O'Grady (1)

Nov 21   Wembley, London   WALES   W 4-0   Connelly, Peacock 2, Greaves   27,500

Springett R (28), **Armfield** (32), Shaw G (5), Moore (8), Labone (2), Flowers (39), Connelly (9), Hill F (2), Peacock (3), Greaves (25), Tambling (1)

APPENDIX 3:
HONOURS

YEAR HONOUR

1963 OBE for Services to Football
1972 CBE for Services to Sport
1977 British Sports Writers Trophy for outstanding achievement outside competition
1977 Knighthood for Services to Sport
1978 Honorary Vice President of The Football Association
1995 Honorary Fellow of the British Sports Administration
1999 Sports Coach UK (formerly the Dyson Award and Coaching Hall of Fame)
2002 Inducted to The Football Association Hall of Fame.
2008 London Football Coaches Association inaugurate the annual 'Sir Walter Winterbottom Coach of the Year' award4-2-4 system 236, 237, 245

INDEX